CHARLES IVES

Charles Ives, Yale Graduation, 1898
The Charles Ives Papers, Music Library, Yale University

CHARLES IVES

A Bio-Bibliography

Geoffrey Block

Foreword by J. Peter Burkholder

Bio-Bibliographies in Music, Number 14
Donald L. Hixon, Series Adviser

Greenwood Press
New York • Westport, Connecticut • London

7/10/89   # 18258068

ML
134
.I9
B6
1988

Library of Congress Cataloging-in-Publication Data

Block, Geoffrey Holden.
    Charles Ives, a bio-bibliography / Geoffrey Block ; with a
foreword by J. Peter Burkholder.
       p.   cm. — (Bio-bibliographies in music, ISSN 0742-6968 ; no.
14)
    Includes indexes.
    ISBN 0-313-25404-4 (lib. bdg. : alk. paper)
    1. Ives, Charles, 1874-1954—Bibliography. 2. Ives, Charles,
1874-1954—Discography. 3. Music—Bio-bibliography. I. Title.
II. Series.
ML134.I9B6   1988
016.78'092'4—dc19   88-21316

British Library Cataloguing in Publication Data is available.

Copyright © 1988 by Geoffrey Block

Library of Congress Catalog Card Number: 88-21316
ISBN: 0-313-25404-4
ISSN: 0742-6968

First published in 1988

Greenwood Press, Inc.
88 Post Road West, Westport, Connecticut 06881

Printed in the United States of America

The paper used in this book complies with the
Permanent Paper Standard issued by the National
Information Standards Organization (Z39.48-1984).

10 9 8 7 6 5 4 3 2 1

To Jacqueline
for her Ivesian
balance of *substance* and *manner*
and
To Jessamyn Halil
In honor of her premiere, April 10, 1988

Contents

Foreword
J. Peter Burkholder

A book like this offers students of Charles Ives's music two great gifts. The more obvious is the work it saves us by gathering into one volume material that has been widely scattered and hard to find. It has been difficult to locate information on early performances of Ives's music, including reviews; there is now one place to look. Many items in the bibliography are neither listed in standard indexes nor cited in earlier studies, and many others are in relatively inaccessible journals or archives; now it is easier to discover not only what exists but what is said.

The less obvious gift of such a book is that it provides an opportunity for taking stock. The annotations on several hundred books, essays, and reviews on Ives's music offer a history of the critical reception of Ives's music, charting a course from obscurity to crusade to fad to its present secure place in the repertoire. We can follow debates about what Ives's music means, how we should listen to it, how it might be analyzed, and whether it is the work of a master or of an incompetent. We can sense the rise of what Frank R. Rossiter called "the Ives Legend" and see the demythologizing of Ives in recent scholarship since Rossiter's landmark biography (**B215**). And when we know what has been done, we have a better sense of what still needs to be accomplished.

Some of the most urgent tasks are still the most basic. The series of critical editions sponsored by The Charles Ives Society is far from complete. Major works remain unpublished in any form, have fallen out of print, or are available only in corrupt versions. Performing parts for most of Ives's orchestral and chamber works are old, often full of errors, and sometimes hard to obtain. Even players who love Ives's music choose not to perform it because of these problems. Wider appreciation of Ives's music will come as more performers play it more often, and that depends squarely on making the music itself available and usable in good editions.

There are often two or more versions of a work, sometimes separated by decades. The vexed questions of which version to publish and how to reconcile variants recently became more vexed in 1985 when John Kirkpatrick, at the dinner celebrating his 80th birthday, suggested that in many cases Ives's later revisions obscured the logic or destroyed the poetry of a work. According to Kirkpatrick, some of these changes were made in anger, others in a spirit of "competitive athletics," staying ahead of the musical vanguard by changing consonances into dissonances, as Elliott Carter had observed Ives doing to *Three Places in New England* in 1929 (**B668**). It may be the role of the editor to defend the integrity of a piece Ives wrote in his thirties from the incongruous alterations made by a much older Ives. The earlier version is generally clearer and more euphonious, but the later is often more familiar. Which is to be preferred? How are we to judge? The new edition of *The Unanswered Question* (**W28:1** and **B573**) presents both early and later versions; we may hope that it becomes a model for others and that early versions of many more works become available in print and on recordings. Facsimile editions of some of Ives's autograph scores with relevant sketches would also be welcome.

Along with the critical editions of the music itself, a critical and annotated edition of Ives's letters, diaries, and uncollected memoranda would be of great use to Ives scholars. A full-scale study of Ives's work and writings in insurance would balance our picture of his work in the two worlds of music and business. Another very helpful source would be an updated version of Kirkpatrick's magnificent "Temporary Mimeographed Catalogue of the Music Manuscripts" (**B7**), incorporating the many changes and corrections that have accumulated in the last three decades, including parallel listings of the microfilm frame numbers and the original negative numbers (now standard ways to refer to the manuscripts). Under the auspices of The Charles Ives Society, Paul C. Echols is at work on a catalogue raisonné for Ives (**B6**), oriented towards the works themselves rather than towards the manuscripts, as is Kirkpatrick's.

Another basic task is to correct the dating of Ives's compositions. For the most part, the dates currently used rely on Ives's own testimony in his work lists, in his diaries and letters, and in dates, memos, and datable addresses marked on his music manuscripts. John Kirkpatrick has corroborated many of Ives's dates, but has also proven that many are wrong and that some of the dates and addresses on the manuscripts were added years later (**B7** and **B8**). Now there are new reasons to doubt Ives's veracity. In a new study, Maynard Solomon argues that Ives, seeking to assert his priority in discovering new musical techniques, redated many of his pieces years too early and credited many of his own ideas and innovations to his father George (**B314**). Solomon's challenge calls into question virtually all of Ives's testimony about his own development, making even more urgent the task of verifying the date of each stage of each composition. Solomon's psychoanalytical approach is in part a continuation of and in part a response to the work of Stuart Feder, whose application of psychoanalytical method to the relationship between Ives and his father has opened up a potentially fruitful line of inquiry.

According to Solomon, one of the principal reasons Ives redated his manuscripts and portrayed his father as the most important influence on his own music was to obscure the strong influences he had felt from contemporary European composers. Indeed, the picture of Ives as an American original, fostered by Ives himself and elaborated by the Cowells (**B354**) and others, is now being challenged, as the direct influences from European composers on Ives's music become better established and the veracity of his own account is called into question. John Jeffrey Gibbens's 1985 thesis (**B360**) is a model influence study, showing how Ives may have come to know Debussy's music, why Ives might have been interested in it, and how Ives's music apparently changed as a result. There is still much to be done in discovering what music Ives heard and studied and tracing the influence on his music of such modern composers as Mahler and Stravinsky, as well as the slightly older Wagner, Franck, Brahms, Tchaikovsky, and Dvorak. Similarly, there is more work to do in showing what Ives learned from the American classical and vernacular music he knew, building on the studies of Neely Bruce (**B247**), Jonathan Elkus (**B579**), Judith Tick (**B185**), and others. As the music of the nineteenth-century United States becomes better known itself, from performing traditions of hymns, marches, and rags to the classical music of the New England School, new links to Ives's music will be discovered. And as his experience and knowledge of contemporary European music becomes better documented, Ives may come to be seen as an American Mahler or Bartók, synthesizing the vernacular music of his region with the mainstream classical tradition, rather than as an isolated Yankee tinkerer.

There is more to learn about the aesthetic, religious, and philosophical influences on Ives. Elsewhere, I have called into question the presumption that Emerson and Thoreau exercised an overwhelming influence on Ives's philosophy (**B296**), but they clearly played a vital role; what was it? Where did Ives learn his idealism, and why and when did he begin to apply it to music? What theologies did he encounter throughout his life, and how did he reconcile their differences? Mark Sumner Harvey's 1983 dissertation (**B288**) begins to answer this last question. How does Ives compare with his American contemporaries in other fields, from the arts to politics? What does his music mean, and what is the relation between music and program? Aesthetic questions have been addressed most often from an interpretative or critical point of view, as if the answers are self-evident in the music or essays before us, but they are not. In both music and prose, Ives wrote in a language that we cannot presume to know until we learn it, and our opinions about what he means to say will be on firmer ground if we can discover more biographical and sociocultural confirmation for them.

Critical understanding of Ives's music also depends upon figuring out how the music works. Robert P. Morgan's articles on spatial form in

Ives (**B256**) and on what Ives has in common with Varèse (**B406**) have opened up new approaches that remain to be explored. Younger scholars today are working on the pitch structure of Ives's music from at least two directions: interpreting it within the framework of tonality, including using analytical methods based on Heinrich Schenker's approach; and interpreting it as atonal, using the approach of Allen Forte (**B251**) and other set theorists. A consensus may emerge from this that Ives is at times tonal, at other times atonal, and that the coherence of his larger compositions derives from his ability to move freely from one to the other at will, often satisfying the requirements of both.

As Ives's procedures are compared to those of other European and American composers of his and earlier eras, we may see them with new clarity. One of the key insights into Ives's music is Lawrence Starr's explanation in two 1977 articles of Ives's stylistic heterogeneity as a form-building element (**B700** and **B808**). Once one conceives of heterogeneity as a musical method rather than as evidence of incompetence or aesthetic confusion, parallels suggest themselves easily, from the quickly changing figuration of Mozart to the sudden juxtapositions of Stravinsky. It seems entirely possible that a coherent theory of Ives's music can be synthesized, building on Starr's insight and drawing upon analytical approaches, including those of Schenker and Forte, that have worked for the music of Ives's teachers and contemporaries.

Finally, the study of Ives's sketches holds great promise, in disentangling variant versions, in confirming or confuting analytical insights, and in showing the relation of the structure of Ives's music to his compositional process. Work on sketches has already begun, most notably in Sondra Rae Clark's study of variants in the *"Concord" Sonata* (**B690** and **B694**) and of course in the preparation of editions. The greatest rewards may come from treating Ives's entire output as a giant sketchbook, each new piece relying on techniques discovered or musical ideas worked out in any number of earlier pieces, studies, or sketches. Once the manuscripts themselves are dated securely, it may be possible through a synthesis of analysis, sketch study, and influence studies to write a definitive account of Ives's development as a composer.

These are only some of the areas that are attracting attention, and work in these and all the others will be greatly facilitated by this book. We may all be grateful to Geoffrey Block, both for gathering together the information assembled here and for the wealth of new research this book is certain to inspire.

Preface

Charles Ives: A Bio-Bibliography, like other volumes in the Greenwood Bio-Bibliography Series, consists of four principal parts: **Biography**; **Works and Performances**; **Discography**; and **Bibliography**. The following remarks will hopefully orient readers to the occasionally idiosyncratic *modus operandi* of the present volume and thereby enhance its usefulness.

In his **Foreword** J. Peter Burkholder explores the current state of Ives research and ideology and proposes ways in which this Bio-Bibliography might aid the next generation of Ives scholarship. Professor Burkholder (University of Indiana), author of *Charles Ives: The Ideas Behind the Music* (New Haven and London: Yale University Press, 1985) **(B296)** and its forthcoming companion volume, *The Evolution of Charles Ives's Music*, has had a major impact on how we understand and think about Ives and is rapidly gaining distinction as one of the leading musicologists of his generation.

In the **Biography** I have chosen to present a relatively brief review of the principal known "facts" and to address several controversies that have thus far eluded consensus, for example, the unanswered and perhaps unanswerable question of why Ives was unable to complete any new works during the last thirty years of his life.

Series advisor Donald L. Hixon in his **Preface** to Greenwood's inaugural Bio-Bibliography, *Thea Musgrave: A Bio-Bibliography* (1984) describes the procedure used in the **Works and Performances** section: "Following each title is a listing of premiere and other selected performances, with references to commentaries from performance reviews cited in the **Bibliography**. Each work is preceded by the mnemonic **"W"** (**W1**, **W2**, etc.) and each performance of that work is identified by successive lowercase letters (**W1a**, **W1b**, **W1c**, etc.)." Whenever possible, citations for each of 285 Ives works include the following information: 1) title; 2) date of composition; 3) instrumentation; 4) publisher; 5) duration; and 6) other, e.g., derivations from [der. from] and developments into [dev. into] other Ives works, and poets of song texts. Information on *Premieres and Other Selected Performances* includes dates, cities, names of halls, a description of the occasion, performing groups, conductors, and soloists.

The **Works** correspond for the most part to John Kirkpatrick's *Catalogue* **(B7)**, in which Ives's compositions are arranged according to five genres: *Orchestral and Band, Chamber Music, Keyboard, Choral and Partsongs*, and *Songs*, and further distinguished within each genre by type (e.g., Symphonies, or Music for Chamber or Theater Orchestra). The list also reflects several changes in genre attribution offered by Kirkpatrick and Paul Echols in *The New Grove Dictionary of American Music* (**B8**), and with few exceptions draws from the latter list for its determination of Ives works, including those currently thought lost or incomplete. Unfortunately, the information and organization contained in Echols's forthcoming *catalogue raisonné* of Ives's works, was received too late to be incorporated.

In contrast to other discographies in this series, the present **Discography**, also organized according to genre, lists only those recordings that are current and readily available, i.e., those listed in the Summer 1987 *Schwann*. For more comprehensive compilations readers are referred to the discographies by Richard Warren (**B17**) (for recordings issued prior to December 31, 1971) and Carol J. Oja (**B16**) (for recordings issued between 1972 and 1979). Again quoting Hixon: "Each recorded work is preceded by the mnemonic **"D"** (**D1**, **D2**, **D3**, etc.). Reference is made to commentaries on the recordings cited in the **Bibliography**."

The 817 annotated entrées in the **Bibliography** comprise the main course of this Bio-Bibliography. Although the number of bibliographical items is large, it should be emphasized that a sizable number of sources have been omitted. I have tried to include all available books and dissertations on Ives, the majority of master's theses, and a sample of senior theses. I have excluded a somewhat higher proportion of foreign-language articles and reviews and a large number of general Ives appreciation articles. For the most part I have devoted more attention to and excluded fewer articles that have appeared since Ives's centennial in 1974, reviews of premieres, studies of genres and single works, and articles relating to Ives and his contemporaries. I have also found it necessary to omit annotated references for all but a handful of the excellent introductory prefaces and critical notes that accompany the Ives Society critical editions. With the exception of a few forthcoming books and articles, I did not include entries for works published after December 31, 1987.

In determining which reviews in books, journals, and newspapers were historically or critically significant I have relied in part on the length of the source but more often on my own judgment. If I have offended anyone through oversight or deliberate exclusion, I plead temporary insanity and hope that I have not omitted too many essential or favorite items. For most references I have tried to convey the contents and the perspective of its author, often through direct quotation, and, when appropriate, to offer additional commentary on the quality or usefulness of a given source.

In arranging and placing sources, genres or specific Ives compositions are given priority. Thus, composer Elliott Carter's review of *"Concord" Sonata* will be found under **Works: Keyboard** and Aaron

Copland's survey of Ives's songs will be located under **Works: Songs** and not **Ives and His Contemporaries**. To alleviate possible uncertainties in locating a number of ambiguous entries, additional cross-references will appear within the **Bibliography**. If an entry includes a discussion of more than one work in the same genre, it will be listed under a **General** section for that genre. With a few silent exceptions, entries which contain references to more than one genre will be placed chronologically with the **Biographical and Aesthetic Articles, General Stylistic Studies, Reviews, and Critical Evaluations (1889-1987)**. In the **Works** sections the entries are arranged chronologically within each sub-heading; in the **Biographical and Aesthetic Articles, etc**. the entries are arranged alphabetically by author for each listed year.

   The purpose of the **Appendixes** is to present in a conveniently centralized format useful information that is distributed throughout the text. Two **Indexes** conclude the volume: an index of all authors, co-authors, and panelists who contributed to the **Bibliography** and a complete index of names (personal, corporate, and geographical) and titles.

Acknowledgments

Without the generous sponsorship of the University of Puget Sound it would have been impossible to complete this project in two years. A Lantz Junior Fellowship (Spring Term 1986) gave me the much-needed time to locate and then read countless sources and to complete more than half of the annotations. Supplementary funding gave me the opportunity to purchase a considerable number of sources unavailable through inter-library loan.

The Puget Sound library staff headed by Desmond Taylor provided gracious, generous, and swift assistance, and contributed to my enjoyment of the hunting-gathering process. Lorraine Ricigliano in the beginning and later Christine Fisher worked indefatigably to help me obtain library materials at Puget Sound and other libraries. Mary Beth Baker assisted me with information for Appendix 5, Theodore Taranovski translated the Russian and Serbo-Croatian sources, and Michel Rocchi translated several of the Italian articles. Thanks also to the Music Department office staff for their good-natured largess. I am figuratively, and perhaps should be literally as well, in debt to Joan Soderland, our Academic Microcomputer Coordinator, for devoting countless hours in order to transfer the book from disc to the printed page so beautifully. Ms. Soderland waged a never-ending battle to UNDO, or at least partially DELETE, my semi-functional computer illiteracy without ever pressing QUIT, and I thank her for that.

I am grateful to the library staffs of the University of Washington, Pacific Lutheran University, The Jewish National & University Library, the music libraries at Juilliard and Eastman, and to Victor Cardell and Helen Bartlett of Yale University for providing special services. Yale University also readily granted permission to use Ives's graduation photograph (Yale '98), housed in its Ives Collection, as the frontispiece. Ives scholars, professors in other specialties, and friends helped me locate or sent me their own forthcoming work and other difficult-to-obtain sources. In alphabetical order they include: Arthur Berger, John Boswell, Leslie Britton, William Brooks, J. Peter Burkholder, Betty E. Chmaj, Michael Daugherty, Stuart Feder, H. Wiley Hitchcock, Wayne Shirley, Maynard Soloman, Lawrence Starr, Keith Ward, and John Wiley.

John Kirkpatrick's *Catalogue* (**B7**) and his list of works in *The New Grove Dictionary of American Music* (**B8**), Frank Rossiter's biography (**B215**), and Philip Newman's dissertation (**B790**) were invaluable sources when it came to preparing the **Works and Performances**. Paul Echols, who assisted Mr. Kirkpatrick in *"Amerigrove,"* helped fill-in some additional gaps, and James Sinclair kept me well apprised of the status of forthcoming editions sponsored by The Charles Ives Society. In preparing the **Discography** CRI, Varèse/Sarabande, Laurel, Crystal, and Spectrum record companies, Pennsylvania State University, and especially Richard Warren's discography (**B17**) provided me with many details missing from the *Schwann Catalogue*.

The work of Kirkpatrick, the Cowells, and Rossiter created a solid foundation of Ives biography, and future students of Ives will always be grateful for what they have accomplished. Although prudence inhibits me from attempting to name them here, my gratitude to another several dozen scholars, composers, performers, editors, and critics who have written thoughtfully, provocatively, and often eloquently on Ives, will be readily apparent from the exuberant entries they inspire. I would like to extend my deepest gratitude, however, to Peter Burkholder for honoring this book with its **Foreword**, for his advice and encouragement, and for providing a new dimension to Ives studies that has contributed greatly to my own understanding and ability to evaluate the vast Ives literature.

Special thanks to Don Hixon, advisor to the Greenwood Bio-Bibliography series, and Greenwood editor, Marilyn Brownstein, for their flexibility and understanding, and to Scott Pierson for his meticulous proofreading.

Also to Andrew Buchman, who never tired of supplying me with missing sources, and to Denise Cooney, both of whom joyously shared my enthusiasm for Ives and this project.

Finally, in contrast to Harmony Ives, who would not let her husband share "what she had done," I am relieved to report that my wife, Jacqueline, has given me permission to acknowledge my appreciation to her for possessing the stamina, and the love, to read an annotated bibliography as if it were a novel (a distinction that she may long retain), and in the process locating an impressive number of previously undetected errors.

CHARLES IVES

Biography

The remarkable career of Charles Ives (October 20, 1874-May 19, 1954) has been retold in literally hundreds of biographical profiles published since Henry Bellamann's review of *"Concord" Sonata* first appeared in *The Double Dealer* (**B661**). Bellamann wrote in 1921 that *"Concord" Sonata* displayed "a broad, strong and original style with no recognizable derivations from Debussy, Strauss or Strawinsky [*sic*]." Although the degree to which Ives was independent of his contemporaries has been challenged in recent studies, even his detractors acknowledge that this eccentric loner from Danbury, Connecticut anticipated by several decades a startling number of twentieth-century musical practices (e.g., atonality, polytonality, polyrhytms, serialism, quarter tones, tone clusters, polychords, and aleatory music). More significantly, by his extensive use of American musical resources such as marches, hymns, popular songs, and ragtime, Ives became the first major American composer to abandon the "courtly muses of Europe" and thus establish an authentic American voice.

Not surprisingly, considering his nearly total artistic isolation, composing on evenings, weekends, and holidays during his peak creative years (1898-1916) and the difficulties his music presented for performers as well as listeners, public performances and recognition came late to Ives. Nevertheless, by 1939 the influential critic, Lawrence Gilman, had assessed *"Concord" Sonata* as "the greatest music by an American" (**B670**), election to the National Institute of Arts and Letters followed in 1946, and in 1947 Ives's *Third Symphony* was awarded the Pulitzer Prize. For many years since Bellamann's article, Charles Ives has been widely regarded as America's greatest composer, or as Leonard Bernstein has said, "our Washington, Lincoln and Jefferson of music" (Columbia KS 6155). Although the Ives legend would continue to grow, Ives already stood as a powerful symbol of the American artist, several decades before his death in 1954 at the age of seventy-nine.

Biographers are in virtually unanimous agreement that Ives's first and major lifelong influence was his father, George Edward Ives (1845-1894), a versatile performer and band leader, who while still in his teens (1860-1862) studied Bach, harmony, and counterpoint under a skilled German immigrant, Carl Foeppl, before forming and leading the First Connecticut Heavy Artillery Band for the duration of the Civil War (1862-1865). Readers even superficially acquainted with Ives's life are familiar with the tale of George Ives asking his son "to sing a tune like *The Swanee River* in Eb, but play the accompaniment in C....This was to stretch our ears and strengthen our musical minds" (*Memos*, p. 115 [**B378**]). According to Ives's *Memos*, dictated in 1932, George himself possessed an extraordinary experimental musical mind and had anticipated several of the avant-garde techniques (e.g., polytonality, microtones, and spatial music), attributed to his son. Ives summarizes his father's careful musical nurturing in the following glowing terms:

> Besides starting my music lessons when I was five years old, and keeping me at music until he died, with the best teaching that a boy could have, Father knew (and filled me up with) Bach and the best of the classical music, and the study of harmony and counterpoint etc., and musical history. Above all this, he kept my interest and encouraged open-mindedness in all matters that needed it in any way (*Memos*, pp. 114-115).

Under his father's guidance Charles began to compose at the age of twelve. By the time he entered Yale, he had produced a considerable number of compositions, including the still frequently performed *Variations on America* for organ (1892), marches, songs, and some radically avant-garde psalm settings, for example the bitonal *Psalm 67* (ca. 1894). At thirteen Ives became a professional organist, "the youngest in the state." He was also an accomplished pianist and drummer and an excellent althlete in baseball and football.

At Yale (1894-1898) Ives began his studies with the composer and theorist, Horatio Parker, newly appointed Professor of Music. Although Parker ("a composer and widely known") could not measure up to Ives's father, ("not a composer and little known...but by far the greater man") (*Memos*, p. 115), Ives's assessment of Parker was not as one-sidedly negative as is often reported: "I had and have great respect and admiration for Parker and most of his music." (*Memos*, p. 49). George Ives had fostered his son's experimental nature and appreciation of the vernacular as well as the cultivated traditions, but as J. Peter Burkholder writes, "Ives needed the rigorous training in counterpoint and longer musical forms that Parker gave him and was aided further in adopting the classical tradition by Parker's idealism and total devotion to that tradition" (**B296**, p. 66).

Also at Yale Ives wrote his *First Symphony* (1895-98) and a number of songs under Parker, but for the most part he reserved his serious efforts at composition for the Center Church, where he was employed as organist throughout his four years in New Haven. Among the compositions performed there under choirmaster John Griggs, the person who helped Ives "to help fill up that awful vacuum" following the death of his father in November 1894 (*Memos*, p. 258), were the *First String Quartet* (1896) and numerous organ and choral works, many of which were lost or incorporated into other compositions. Ives's popularity as well as the social contacts he acquired from New Haven's Hopkins Grammar School, which he attended for three terms in order to prepare scholastically for Yale (1893-94), contributed to his election into various select societies, for which Ives wrote a considerable number of shows and songs in the vernacular tradition. Two such songs were published in the *Yale Courant* in 1896, and *The Bells of Yale* appeared in the Yale Glee Club publication, *Yale Melodies*, in 1903. Three other compositions were commercially published while Ives was at Yale, all in 1896: *William Will* (a campaign song for McKinley), *For You and Me!* (a male barbershop glee), and the *Intercollegiate March* for band.

Upon his graduation from Yale, Ives joined the actuarial department of the Mutual Insurance Company in New York City as a clerk with the starting salary of five dollars per week. One year later he met Julian Myrick at Mutual's agency, Charles H. Raymond & Co., thus launching a long and mutually advantageous association and partnership. On New Year's Day 1907 the two men established their own agency under Washington Life, Ives and Co., and when Washington sold out to Pittsburgh Life, they returned to Mutual Life on New Year's Day 1909 with their own agency, Ives and Myrick. Within a few years Ives and Myrick would become the most prosperous life insurance agency in New York, and the year before Ives retired from the business in 1930 (upon further deterioration of his already precarious health), their agency had become the nation's largest, grossing $49 million (Rossiter, pp. 112-113 [**B215**]). One of the secrets of their phenomenal success was the manner in which they divided their responsibilities: Myrick worked directly with their clientele and Ives trained their agents. As part of his role in the partnership Ives wrote a series of innovative and practical treatises and manuals on insurance psychology and the philosophy of estate planning, e.g., *The Amount to Carry* (1920) in *Essays and other Writings* (**B660**) and *Broadway* (1922) in *Memos* (**B378**) [*see also*: **Appendix 3**]. In addition to his scientific approach to selling policies, Ives in these writings expressed his sincere (and occasionally Transcendental) belief that life insurance performed an altruistic service for humanity.

Shortly after leaving Yale, Ives established his career-long pattern of composing on evenings and Saturdays. Despite his strenuous life in business, Ives managed to complete a conservative oratorio in the Parker mold, *The Celestial Country*, the *Second Symphony*, the *Pre-First Violin*

Sonata, and numerous smaller works within the next four years. In
1902 Ives, who had considered a career as an organist and had occupied
continuous positions as organist at various churches in Danbury (1889-
1893), New Haven (1893-1898), and the Bloomfield Presbyterian Church
(1898-1900), resigned from his final organ post at the prestigious Central
Presbyterian Church in New York, a post he had held since 1900. The
resignation, which perhaps not coincidently occurred several days after
the premiere performance and modest, albeit positive reviews of *The
Celestial Country* in the New York press (**B753-754**), marked Ives's final
retreat from a professional musical life. Ives thus embarked on a
composing career that was unprecedented in its isolation. His Sundays
now freed for composition, Ives embarked on a formidable number of
major works, many of which he worked on simultaneously for the next
few years, including the *First Piano Sonata* (main work 1902-1909
although partially sketched in 1901), the *First Violin Sonata* (1902-1908),
the *Third Symphony* (1904), *Thanksgiving* (1904), and the *Trio for Violin,
Cello, and Piano* (1904-1911).

For the ten years after leaving Yale, Ives lived at three residences in
New York, each affectionately named Poverty Flat, with friends he met at
his alma mater. One of these friends, David Twichell, also from Ives's
class of '98, introduced Ives to his sister Harmony (1876-1969) in 1896.
Another meeting in 1905 led to an extended courtship and a marriage in
June 1908 as well as an exodus from Poverty Flat. Harmony Twichell
was the daughter of Reverend Joseph Twichell, a prominent civic as well
as spiritual leader and Mark Twain's friend and pastor in Hartford since
1896. In 1900 Harmony became a registered nurse, and for the next two
years she worked as a nurse in the Chicago slums and later in a series of
private and public nursing positions, including a month at the Henry
Street Settlement in New York in 1905 soon after Ives's courtship had
begun.

According to Kirkpatrick, the love between Charles and Harmony
inspired "a new self-confidence, exploding a whole world of far-out
music" (**B8**, p. 505). Included among these experimental works are
Hallowe'en, Over the Pavements, In the Cage, The Unanswered Question,
and *Central Park in the Dark.* In 1906 Ives suffered a mild heart attack,
the first of many occasions when Harmony's training as a nurse would
prove indispensable to her husband, who would remain in poor health
throughout most of their otherwise blissful marriage. Childless as a
result of a hysterectomy in 1909, the Ives's adopted Edith Osborne
(1914-1956), the infant daughter of a family they sponsored in 1915 as
part of the Fresh Air Fund. In 1912 they had purchased a home in West
Redding, Connecticut overlooking Danbury; late in 1914 they began a
long-standing pattern of spending winters in New York (on 164 E. 74th

St. after November 1926), interrupted only for a six-week vacation in London (Summer 1924) and an extended European sojourn to England, Scotland, Germany, and Italy (May 1932-July 1933).

Burkholder credits Harmony as largely responsible for guiding Ives into perhaps his most significant new musical direction after 1908, "the representation of life experiences and of literature in music, a conscious celebration of America and American music, and high spiritual and moral aims for music" (**B296**, p. 95) and within the next eight years Ives completed an ambitious series of works based on a variety of historical, literary, and philosophical themes including New England Transcendentalism. After completing his *First Piano Sonata* and *First Violin Sonata* (begun in 1901 and 1902 respectively) shortly after his marriage, Ives embarked on the work upon which his reputation largely rests: three violin sonatas, three of the four "Holidays," the first two orchestral sets, and the *Robert Browning Overture*. This considerable creative activity culminated with two of his most highly regarded and certainly most often discussed compositions: the *Second Piano Sonata "Concord, Mass., 1840-1860"* (1910-1915) and the *Fourth Symphony* (1909-1916).

After 1916 Ives was unable to finish any large works. He did manage a thorough revision, probably a recomposition of *Psalm 90*, according to Harmony, "the only work that he was satisfied with" (**B8**, p. 508), and between 1919-1921 he composed a large collection of nearly forty swan songs, including twenty-six songs in 1921 alone. A *Universe Symphony* begun in 1911 remained a torso when he ceased working on it in 1928 and by 1926 with the song, *Sunrise*, Ives had completed his final newly-composed work. Not long thereafter as Harmony Ives related to Henry Cowell, "he came downstairs one day with tears in his eyes and said he couldn't seem to compose any more--nothing went well, nothing sounded right" (*Memos*, p. 279).

Why Ives stopped composing as early as he did remains a controversial and unresolved issue. Burkholder (**B296**, pp. 113-114) surveys a wide range of theories: Harmony Ives ("broken health and creative exhaustion") (Rossiter [**B215**], p. 156; John Kirkpatrick (Ives "double life" of insurance man and parttime composer) (**B7**, p. 419 and **B8**, p. 508); Colleen Davidson (the disillusionment brought about by World War I) (**B345**, pp. 175-176); Frank R. Rossiter (the overwhelmingly negative critical reaction to *"Concord" Sonata* and *114 Songs*, which Ives had published at his own expense and sent free of charge to a representative sample of musicians in 1921 and 1922) (**B215**, pp. 186-187), Stuart Feder (the completion of a long mourning process for his father who had died at the age of forty-nine, Ives's age in 1923) (**B475**); and David Wooldridge (an unsubtantiated hypothesis that Ives abandoned composition in 1916 to play the stock market) (**B192**, pp. 182-183 and 187). Burkholder also offers his own view: "It may be that the exalted ideals and purposes for music that Ives outlined in the *Essays* became impossible for him to live up to, once he had made them explicit in writing" (**B296**, p. 114). Although he acknowledges partial validity to several of the theories he cites, Burkholder dismisses the explanation most frequently espoused, Ives's frail health, by pointing out that even in 1917 or 1918 before the October heart attack, Ives had virtually ended his composing career.

Although no Ives score appeared in print between *The Bells of Yale* in 1903 and the publication at his own expense of *"Concord" Sonata* (1921) and *114 Songs* (1922), a number of semi-public performances of Ives took place between *The Celestial Country* premiere in 1902 (**W89a**) and Ives's musical retirement in the early 1920s. Like the cantata, these performances ended in disappointment and led nowhere. Frank A. Fichtl, conductor of the Hyperion Theater in New Haven, read through the first and second *Ragtime Dances* (**W21a**), New York Symphony conductor Walter Damrosch stumbled through the second movement of the *First Symphony* in 1910 (**W1b**), and a German concertmaster, Franz Milcke, suffered a portion of the first page of Ives's *First Violin Sonata*, at the composers's Redding home, probably in 1914 (**W59b**). Yet another unfortunate performance occurred when *In Flanders Fields* was sung at a luncheon for the managers of Ives's parent insurance company (**W180a**). A modestly successful performance finally transpired several months later when David Talmadge, who had read through all or most of Ives's violin sonatas with Ives in 1914 and 1915, played the *Third Violin Sonata* at the Carnegie Chamber Music Hall (**W62a**).

Rossiter perhaps rightly considers Ives's decision to send copies of *"Concord" Sonata* and *114 Songs*, "the most important event in the history of his public recognition" (**B215**, pp. 179-180). Among the recipients of the sonata was Henry Bellamann, who in 1921 and 1922 organized lecture-recitals in Columbia, South Carolina and Atlanta (**W65e-f**), wrote the substantial and positive review of the work in *The Double Dealer* cited earlier, and in 1933 contributed a broad profile on Ives in *The Musical Quarterly* (**B326-327**). But despite the considerable psychological benefits of such a positive response to Ives, Bellamann lacked the musical contacts to do much more.

Ironically, the first professional musician so positioned to assist Ives was the French pianist and founder of the Franco-American Musical Society (the Pro Musica after 1925), E. Robert Schmitz. Schmitz had not received a copy of either the sonata or the songs, but had apparently discovered Ives (the composer) while seeking insurance with Ives and Myrick in 1923. This chance meeting led to the performances under the sponsorship of the Pro Musica selected from Ives's more avant-garde works, the *Chorale* from the *Three Quarter-Tone Pieces* at Chickering Hall and the *Chorale* and *Allegro* the following week at Aeolian Hall (1925) **(W84a)**. Undoubtedly the most significant Ives performance in the 1920s took place on January 29, 1927, again sponsored by the Pro Musica, when Eugene Goossens conducted the first two movements of the *Fourth Symphony* at Town Hall **(W7a)**. Two years later, the avant-garde composer, Henry Cowell, with indispensable financial help from Ives, published the second movement of this work in his newly-established *New Music Quarterly*.

Cowell, the first composer who understood what Ives was trying to accomplish, was able to secure additional performances in the United States and Europe, and again with Ives's help, publications. Cowell also introduced Ives to the conductor, Nicholas Slonimsky, who in 1931 led the Boston Chamber Orchestra in the premiere of *Three Places in New England*, conducted additional performances of this work in Havana and Paris, and presented the premiere of *Washington's Birthday* with the New Music Society Orchestra, the first recorded Ives composition in 1934 **(D16)**. In 1932 Aaron Copland, a much less radical composer than Cowell, generated a performance of seven Ives songs, including *Charlie Rutlage*, at the highly regarded and widely reviewed festival at Yaddo in Saratoga Springs, New York **(W133a** and **B775-776)**, and in 1939, Kirkpatrick, after more than ten years of labor, performed *"Concord" Sonata* at the Town Hall concert **(W65a)** and elicited the glowing praise of *New York Herald Tribune* critic Lawrence Gilman **(B670)**.

In the 1940s Ives gained additional friends and supporters whose passionate and tireless efforts gradually brought Ives's music to the attention of the American musical public through performances and editions of his unusually problematic manuscripts. Lou Harrison's decision to perform Ives's *Third Symphony* before a Carnegie Chamber Music Hall audience in 1946 **(W3a)** gave this work the exposure needed for it to receive the fifth Pulitzer Prize in music one year later. In 1949 Harrison brought the *First Piano Sonata* into a performable state and persuaded his friend, William Masselos, to premiere the work **(W64a)**. The charismatic Leonard Bernstein premiered the *Second Symphony* with the New York Philharmonic in 1951 as a guest conductor and would continue to champion Ives's music throughout his subsequent tenure as musical director.

By 1955, one year after Ives's death, the biography by Henry Cowell and his wife Sidney appeared and asserted unreservedly that Ives ranked along with Stravinsky, Schoenberg, and Bartók as one of the four major composers of the century **(B354)**. The same year Harmony Ives gave all of her husband's music manuscripts to Yale University. In 1960

Kirkpatrick had completed his "Temporary Mimeographed Catalogue," an elaborate and comprehensive account of every available scrap (**B7**) and in 1972 the indefatigable Ives performer and scholar had meticulously edited and copiously appendixed Ives's *Memos* (**B378**).

The most recent major Ives performance took place in 1965, when the phenomenally difficult *Fourth Symphony* finally received its first complete performance, a highly publicized event in a Carnegie Hall concert with Leopold Stokowski (and two assistants) conducting his American Symphony Orchestra (**W7d**). Ives's centennial year in 1974 brought about more premieres and repeated performances, significant publications such as Rossiter's biography (**B215**) and Perlis's oral history (**B318**), countless appreciations in dozens of magazines and journals, and certainly not least, the four-day Charles Ives Centennial Festival-Conference in New York and New Haven, "the first international congress ever to be dedicated to an American composer" (**B251**, p. x).

By the late 1980s scholarly attention to Ives's life and work clearly has entered a new phase. In addition to Burkholder's enlightening biographical and stylistic studies (**B296-297** and **B462**), The Charles Ives Society was issuing an impressive number of critical performing editions and a thoroughly revised catalogue (**B6**), and dissertations on Ives had proliferated to fifty-four [*see* **Appendix 5**]. As this volume goes to press, Maynard Solomon's provocative essay, "Charles Ives: Some Questions of Veracity," the first article on Ives to appear in the *Journal of the American Musicological Society* (**B314**), had provoked an immediate and front-page acquiescence from Donal Henahan in the Arts & Leisure section of *The New York Times*, "Did Ives Fiddle With the Truth?" (February 21, 1988, section 2, pages 1 & 25).

But it was too soon to know whether or not future biographers would view Will Crutchfield's earlier *New York Times* response to withdrawn performances and "second-hand opinions and witticisms" of Ives's music, "Why Our Greatest Composer Needs Serious Attention" (**B309**), as the warning of a Cassandra.

Works and Performances

ORCHESTRAL AND BAND [W1-40]
See: **B410-583**

ORCHESTRAL [W1-37]
SYMPHONIES [W1-9]
See: **B410-540**

W1   *FIRST SYMPHONY* (1895-1898) [Peer, 1971; ed. Frank Samorotto, Peer, commissioned in 1988] 37 min. 2-2 (E.hn)-2-2 (cbsn ad lib.), 4-2-3-1, timp, str *See*: **B435-438**
1. Allegro (1895) [derived from **W200:1**]
2. Adagio molto
3. Scherzo: Vivace
4. Allegro molto (1897-1898)

Premiere

W1a 1953 (April 26): Washington, DC; National Gallery of Art; National Gallery Orchestra; Richard Bales, conductor (American Music Festival) *See*: **B435**

Other selected performances

W1b 1910 (March 19): New York; New York Symphony; Walter Damrosch, conductor [Informal reading of last three movements]

W1c 1965 (November): Chicago; Chicago Symphony Orchestra; Orchestra Hall; Morton Gould, conductor

W2   *SECOND SYMPHONY* (1900-1902) [Southern, 1951; ed. Jonathan Elkus, Peer, commissioned in 1988] 39 min.
pic-2-2-2-2-cbsn 4-2-3-1-timp-snd-bd-str *See*: **B439-462**
1. Andante moderato (1900-1901) [der. from lost organ sonata and lost *Down East Overture*]
2. Allegro (1900-1901) [der. from lost overture *In These United States*]
3. Adagio cantabile (1902) [der. from lost organ prelude, 1896; rejected version of **W1:2**]
4. Lento maestoso (?1901) [der. from lost *Town, Gown, and State Overture*, 1896]

5. Allegro molto vivace (1902) [der. from lost overture *The American Woods*, 1889]

Premiere

W2a 1951 (February 22): New York; Carnegie Hall; New York Philharmonic; Leonard Bernstein, conductor *See:* **B439-444** and **B446**

W3 *THIRD SYMPHONY ("THE CAMP MEETING")* (1904) [ed. Lou Harrison, Arrow, 1947; ed. Lou Harrison, assisted by Henry Cowell, AMP, 1964; ed. Kenneth Singleton, AMP, 1988] 23 min. 1-1-1-1, 2-0-1-0, bells (ad lib.), str
See: **B463-468**
1. Andante "Old Folks Gatherin'" [der. from lost organ prelude, 1901]
2. Allegro "Children's Day" [der. from lost organ prelude, 1901]
3. Largo "Communion" [der. from lost organ communion, 1901; dev. into **W178**]

Premiere

W3a 1946 (April 5): New York; Carnegie Chamber Music Hall; New York Little Symphony Orchestra; Lou Harrison, conductor *See:* **B463-465**

W4 *A SYMPHONY: "NEW ENGLAND HOLIDAYS"* (1904-1913) 40 min.
See: **B469-478**
1. *Washington's Birthday* (1909) [AMP, 1974; ed. James B. Sinclair, AMP, 1988] 9 1/2 min. fl (pic), hn, perc, Jew's harp (opt) [or 2 cl], str, bells or pf (opt.), extra hn or tbn (opt.) *See:* **B413** and **B469-470**
2. *Decoration Day* (1912) [ed. James B. Sinclair, Peer, 1988] [der. from **W61**] 9 min. 3 (pic)-3 (E.hn)-3-2, 4-2-3-1, timp, perc, str, ossia for Eb cl. *See:* **B471**, **B473**, and **B475**
3. *The Fourth of July* (1911-1913) [AMP, 1974; ed. Wayne Shirley, AMP, 1988] [der. from **W22**] 6 min. 4-2-4-4, 4-3-3-1, timp, perc, xyl, bells, pf, str *See:* **B415**, **B472**, and **B476-478**
4. *Thanksgiving and/or Forefathers' Day* (1904) [ed. Jonathan Elkus, Peer, 1988] [dev. from lost organ prelude and postlude, 1897] 15 1/2 min. 3 (pic)-2-2-2 (cbsn), 4-3-3-1, timp, perc, bells, mixed chorus (ad lib.) cel, pf, str

Premieres

W4a 1920 (Spring): New York; Carnegie Hall; National Symphony Orchestra; Paul Eisler, conductor [Reading of *Decoration Day*]

W4b 1931 (September 3): San Francisco; New Music Society Orchestra; Nicholas Slonimsky, conductor [*Washington's Birthday*]

W4c 1931 (December 27): Havana; Havana Philharmonic; Amadeo Roldan; conductor [*Decoration Day*]

W4d 1932 (February 21): Paris; Paris Symphony Orchestra; Nicholas Slonimsky, conductor [*The Fourth of July*]

W4e 1954 (April 9): Minneapolis; Northrop Memorial Auditorium; Minneapolis Symphony Orchestra; Antal Dorati, conductor [World Premiere of *Thanksgiving* and the complete four-movement cycle]

Other selected performances

W4f 1914 (November) and 1915 (Spring): New York; Globe Theater [two run-throughs of *Washington's Birthday*]

W4g 1918 or 1919: New York: Ives's residence at 120 East 22nd St.; Members of the New York Symphony Orchestra; organized by Reber Johnson, Assistant Concertmaster [run-through of *Washington's Birthday*]

W4h 1961 (March 1): New York; Hunter College; Manhattan School Orchestra; Jonel Perlea, conductor [New York premiere of *Decoration Day*] *See*: **B471**

W4i 1966 (August 24): London; New Philharmonica; Frederik Prausnitz, conductor [Promenade Concerts, British premiere of *The Fourth of July*] *See*: **W7e** and **B415**

W4j 1967 (September 29): London; London Symphony Orchestra; Aaron Copland, conductor [*Decoration Day*] *See*: **B415** and **B472**

W5 *FIRST ORCHESTRAL SET (A NEW ENGLAND SYMPHONY; THREE PLACES IN NEW ENGLAND)* (1908-?1914 and 1929) [Birchard, 1935; ed. James B. Sinclair, Presser, forthcoming (Ives's small orchestra version of 1929); ed. James B. Sinclair, Mercury, 1976 (full orchestra version); original version of "The Saint-Gaudens," Presser, under consideration] 19 min.
small orchestra version: 1-1 (E.hn)-1-1,
2-2-1, per, pn, str (7-2-2-1)
full orchestra version: 2 (pic); 2 (E.hn)-2-2 (cbsn), 4-2-3-1, timp, snd, bd, cym, gong (sm tam-tam),

pn, cel, org, 2 hp, str   *See*: **B479-493**
1. The Saint-Gaudens in Boston Common (1911-1912)
2. Putam's Camp, Redding, Connecticut (1912) [der. from **W22** and **W23**]
3. The Housatonic at Stockbridge [dev. into **W146**]

Premieres

W5a 1931 (January 10): New York; Town Hall; Boston Chamber Orchestra; Nicholas Slonimsky, conductor [Chamber Version]

W5b 1931 (June 6): Paris; Maison Gaveau (Salle des Concerts); Members of the Concerts Walther Straram; Nicholas Slonimsky, conductor (Sponsored by the Pan American Association of Composers) [Chamber Version]   *See*: **B479-485**

W5c 1974 (February 9): New Haven; Woolsey Hall; Yale Symphony Orchestra, John Mauceri, conductor [Full Orchestra Version]

W6   *SECOND ORCHESTRAL SET* [Original title: *Elegy to Stephen Foster*] (1909-1915) [ed. James B. Sinclair, Peer, forthcoming 1989] 16 min.
3-0-3-2, 1-4-4-1, perc, cel/bells, hp, org, zither,
pf(2), str   *See*: **B416** and **B494-496**
1. An Elegy to our Forefathers (1909)
2. The Rockstrewn Hills Join in the People's Outdoor Meeting (1909) [der. from **W21**]
3. From Hanover Square North, at the End of a Tragic Day, the Voice of the People Again Arose (1915)

Premiere

W6a 1967 (February 18): Chicago; Orchestra Hall; Chicago Symphony Orchestra; Morton Gould, conductor   *See*: **B494**

Selected performances

W6b 1969 (May 7): New York; Carnegie Hall; Buffalo Philharmonic; Lukas Foss, conductor [New York premiere]   *See*: **B495**

W6c 1970: Berlin Philharmonic; Lukas Foss, conductor   *See*: **B496**

W7   *FOURTH SYMPHONY* (1910-1916) [*New Music* 2, no. 2 (1929) (second movement); ed. Theodore A. Seder, Romulus Franceschini, and Nicholas Falcone, AMP, 1965 (complete); ed.

William Brooks (first movement), James B. Sinclair (second movement), Kenneth Singleton (third movement), Wayne Shirley (fourth movement), AMP, in progress] 30 min.
4 (2 pic)-2-3 (al sax in Eb, ten sax in Bb, bar sax in Eb)-3, 4-6-4-1, timp, perc, solo pf, pf (4-hands), cel, org, hp (2), str, mixed chorus (ad lib.) *See*: **B497-538**
1. Prelude: Maestoso (1910-1911) (Text: "Watchman, tell us of the night," by John Bowring) [der. from **W59:3**]
2. Allegretto (1911-1916) [der. from **W23** and **W65:2**; dev. into **W82**]
3. Andante moderato (1909-1911) [der. from **W41:1**]
4. Largo, SATB ad lib (1911-1916) [der. from lost *Memorial Slow March*, organ 1901]

Premieres

W7a 1927 (January 29): New York; Town Hall; New York Philharmonic; Eugene Goossens, conductor (Meeting of the Pro-Musica Society) [First and Second Movments] *See*: **B498-499**

W7b 1939 (January 20 and February 24): New York; Town Hall; John Kirkpatrick, piano [arr. of Third Movement] *See*: **W133c**, **B34**, and **B36**

W7c 1942 (April 13): New York; Columbia Concert Orchestra; Bernard Herrmann, conductor (WABC radio broadcast) [Third Movement]

W7d 1965 (April 26): New York; Carnegie Hall; American Symphony Orchestra; Leopold Stokowski, conductor [complete] *See*: **B503**, **B506-508**, **B510**, **B512-518**

Other selected performances

W7e 1966 (April 24 and September 13): London; BBC Symphony Orchestra; Gunther Schuller, conducting *See*: **W4h**, **B415**, and **B520** [British premiere]

W7f 1976: The Hague; The Concertgebouw; Hague Residentie Orchestra; Cristobal Halffter, conductor [Holland Festival American Bicentennial] *See*: **B532**

W8 *THIRD ORCHESTRAL SET*, small orchestra (1919-1926) Three unfinished movements [dev. into **W55** and **W151**]
1. Hymn tune movement
2. Comedy of Danbury reminscence
3. Hymn-tune movement

Premiere

W8a 1978 (March 16): Fullerton, CA; California State University at Fullerton; Keith Clark, conductor

W9 *UNIVERSE SYMPHONY* [unfinished and incomplete] (1911-1918) [Facsimile/Transcription and Diplomatic Facsimile Edition of Fragments, Peer, forthcoming] *See*: **B539-540**
1. Section A "Past: Formation of the waters and mountains"
2. Section B "Present: Earth, evolution in nature and humanity"
3. Section C "Future: Heaven, the rise of all to the Spiritual"

OTHER MUSIC FOR SYMPHONY ORCHESTRA [W10-16]
See: **B541-546**

W10 *Postlude in F* (1895) [ed. Kenneth Singleton, AMP, in press]

W11 *Overture in g* [incomplete, ?unfinished] (?1895)

W12 *Yale-Princeton Football Game* (?1898) [arr. and ed. Gunther Schuller, AMP] 3 min.
4 (pic)-3 (E.hn)-3 (bar sax)-4,
4-4-3-1, timp, perc, pf, str

Premiere

W12a 1970 (November 24): New York; Carnegie Hall; American Symphony Orchestra; Gunther Schuller, conductor

W13 *The General Slocum* [unfinished] (1904) [arr. and ed. Gunther Schuller, AMP] 3 min. 4 (pic)-3 (E.hn)-3 (bar sax)-4, 4-4-3-1, timp, perc, pf, str.

Premiere

W13a 1970 (November 24): New York; Carnegie Hall; American Symphony Orchestra; Gunther Schuller, conductor

W14 *Emerson Overture/Concerto*, piano and orchestra (1907) [unfinished and incomplete; dev. into **W65:1**; **W78:2 & 9**, and **W80**]

W15 *Robert Browning Overture* (1908-1912) [ed. Henry Cowell and Lou Harrison, Peer, 1959; ed. Jonathan Elkus, Peer, forthcoming] [dev. into **W161**] 19 min.

3 (pic)-3 (E.hn)-2-3 (cbsn), 4-2-3-1, timp, perc, str
See: **B416** and **B541-546**

Premiere

W15a 1956 (October 14): New York; Carnegie Hall; Symphony of the Air; Leopold Stokowski, conducting *See*: **B541**

Other selected performance

W15b 1966 (December 19): New York; Carnegie Hall; American Symphony Orchestra; Leopold Stokowski, conducting *See*: **B544**

W16 *Matthew Arnold Overture* (1912) [incomplete; dev. into **W236**]

MUSIC FOR CHAMBER OR THEATRE ORCHESTRA [W17-37]
See: B548-577

W17 *Holiday Quickstep* (1887) [ed. James B. Sinclair, Merion, 1975] [dev. into lost band arrangement] piccolo, 2 cornets, 2 violins, piano *See*: **B559-560**

Premiere

W17a 1888 (January 16): Danbury; Taylor's Opera House; George Ives's Theater Orchestra; George Ives, conductor *See*: **B559**

Other selected performance

W17b 1974 (March 3): New Haven; Sprague Hall, Yale University; Yale Theater Orchestra; James B. Sinclair, conductor. *See also*: **W18-20**, **W22-23**, **W29**, and **W39**.

W18 *March No. 2, with A Song of a Gambolier* (1892) [ed. Kenneth Singleton, Peer, 1977]
[der. from **W68**; dev. into **W185**]
fl-cl-cor-trb-tub-per-str (2 viol I, 2 viol II). *See*: **W17b**

W19 *March No. 3, with My Old Kentucky Home* (1892) [ed. Kenneth Singleton, Presser, 1975] [der. from lost piano version]
fl-cl-cor-trb-tub-per-str (2 viol I, 2 viol II). *See*: **W17b**

W20 *Fugue in 4 keys, on The Shining Shore*, for trumpet, flute, and strings (1897) [ed. John Kirkpatrick, Merion, 1975]. See: **W17b** and **B562**

W21   *Ragtime Dances Nos. 1-4*, small orchestra [incomplete] (1902-1904) [ed. James B. Sinclair, Peer, in press] [dev. into **W4:4**; der. from and dev. into **W22** and **W75**; dev. into **W6:2**, **W27:2**, and **W64:2a/b & 4b**]

Premieres

W21a 1904 (May 21): New Haven; Hyperion Theater; Frank A. Fichtl, conductor [*Ragtime Dances Nos. 1 and 2*]

W21b 1976 (February 26): New Haven; Sprague Hall, Yale University; The Chamber Orchestra of New England; Kenneth Singleton, conductor [*Ragtime Dance No. 3*]

W21c 1984 (March 17): New York; Symphony Space; New England Ensemble [New York premiere of *Ragtime Dances Nos. 1-4*] *See*: **B290** and **B295**

W22   *Overture and March "1776,"* small orchestra (1903) [ed. James B. Sinclair, Merion, 1976] [dev. into **W4:3** and **W5:2**] 3 min.
2 flutes (piccolos), oboe, Bb clarinet, 2 Bb cornets, trombone, piano, bells (ad lib.), drums (snare, bass, cymbals), strings *See*: **W17b** and **B562**

W23   *Country Band March*, small orchestra (1903) [ed. James B. Sinclair, Merion, 1976] [dev. into **W5:2**, **W7:2**, **W65:2**, and **W82**] 4 min.
flute (piccolo, Bb clarinet, Eb alto saxophone, Bb cornet, 2 trombones (I and II), strings (without violas), piano, drums (snare, bass, cymbals)
See: **W17b** and **B563-564**

W24   *Autumn Landscapes from Pine Mountains*, small orchestra [lost] (1904)

W25   *Over the Pavements*, small orchestra (1906-1913) [Peer, 1954; ed. Kenneth Singleton, Peer, under consideration] [dev. into **W50**] 5 min.
piccolo, clarinet, bassoon (or saxophone), trumpet, trombones (I,II, III), cymbal, drum, piano

W26   The Pond, small orchestra (1906) [ed. Jacques-Louis Monod, Boelke-Bomart, 1973] [dev. into **W143**] 1 min. *See*: **B557-558**

W27   *Set for Theatre or Chamber Orchestra* (1906-1911) [*New Music Quarterly* 5, no. 2 (January 1932; reprint ed. Edwin F. Kalmus;

ed. Kenneth Singleton, Presser, commissioned in 1988] 7 1/2 min.
oboe/flute, clarinet, English horn, timpani, bells, strings *See*:
B566-567
1. *In the Cage* (1906) [der. from and dev. into **W195**]
2. *In the Inn* (1906-1911) [der. from **W21** and **W64:2b**]
3. *In the Night* (1906) [der. from **W44** and lost hymn-anthem, 1902]

Premiere

W27a 1932 (February 16): New York; New School for Social Research; Pan American Chamber Orchestra; Adolph Weiss, conductor (Pan American Association of Composers) *See*: **B566**

Other selected performances

W27b 1932 (February 21): Paris; Salle Pleyel; Orchestre Symphonique de Paris; Nicholas Slonimsky, conductor [*In the Cage* and *In the Night*]

W27c 1932 (March 5): Berlin; Beethovensaal; Berlin Philharmonic Orchestra; Nicholas Slonimsky; conductor [*In the Cage* and *In the Night*]

W27d 1932 (April 2): Budapest; Hungarian Symphony Orchestra; Nicholas Slonimsky, conductor (Hungarian Section of the International Society for Contemporary Music) [*In the Cage* and *In the Night*]

W27e 1971 (November 27): London; London Sinfonietta *See*: **B567**

W28 1. *The Unanswered Question* (1906) [Peer-Southern, 1953; ed. Paul Echols and Noel Zahler, Peer-Southern, 1986] 5 1/2 min.
flute I, II, III (or oboe), IV (or clarinet), trumpet (or English Horn, or oboe or clarinet), string qt or orch *See*: **B547, B568-573**
2. *Central Park in the Dark* (1906) [ed. Jacques-Louis Monod (notes by John Kirkpatrick), Boelke-Bomart, 1973] 7 1/2 min.
piccolo, flute, oboe, Bb (Eb clarinet), bassoon, C trumpet, trombone, percussion, 1 or 2 pianos, strings *See*: **B568**

Premiere

W28a 1946 (May 11): New York; McMillan Theatre; Juilliard Graduate School; Edgar Schenckman, on stage conductor; assistant, Theodore Bloomfield *See*: **B568**

Other selected performance

W28b 1953 (February 22): New York; Museum of Modern Art; Leopold Stokowski [*The Unanswered Question*]

W29 *Cartoons (Take-offs)*, small orchestra (c. 1898-1916) [incomplete **W50**] *See*: **W17b**
7 *Mike Donlin-Johnny Evers* (1907) [incomplete]
8 *Willy Keller at the Bat* (1907) [incomplete]

W30 *Set No. 1*, small orchestra (1907-1911) [ed. David Porter, AMP/Peer/Presser, under review] 9 min.
    1. *The See'r* (1908) [der. from lost *Beecher Overture*, ?1904; dev. into **W84:2** and **W160**]
    2. *A Lecture* (1907-1908) [dev. into **W190**]
    3. *The Ruined River* (1911) [dev. into **W91** and **W137**]
    4. *Like a Sick Eagle* (1909) [dev. into **W157**]
    5. *Calcium Light Night* (1911)
    6. *When the moon, or Allegretto sombreoso* (1907-1908) [Peer, 1958] [dev. into **W149**]
    6 1/2. **[W12]** [added later in a list]

W31 *The Gong on the Hook and Ladder (Firemen's Parade on Main Street)*, small orchestra (?1911) [Peer, 1960; ed. James B. Sinclair, Peer, 1979; ed. James B. Sinclair, Peer, in preparation (Allegro moderato: chamber version)] 3 min.
flute, Bb clarinet, bassoon, Bb trumpets (I,II), drums, triangle, timpani, (gong ad lib.), piano, strings *See*: **B547**

Premiere

W31a 1967 (January 22); New York; Philharmonic Hall; New York Philharmonic; Leonard Bernstein, conductor

W32 *Set No. 2*, small orchestra (?1912) [AMP/Peer/Presser, under consideration]
    1. *Largo "The Indians"* (1912) [dev. into **W145**] 2 min.
    2. *"Gyp the Blood" or Hearst!? Which is Worst?!* (1912) [unfinished] [realization by Kenneth Singleton, Peer, 1978] 1 min. orchestration unspecified by Ives; Singleton realization for flute, Bb clarinet, bassoon, C trumpet, strings
    3. *Andante "The Last Reader"* (1911) [dev. into **W134**] 2 min.

W33 *The Rainbow (So May It Be!)*, small orchestra (1914) [Peer, 1959] [dev. into **W139**] 1 min.
flute, basset horn/English horn, piano, strings

W34 *Quarter-tone Chorale*, strings (1913-1914) [ed. Alan Stout, Peters, 1976] [lost; dev. into **W84:3**]

Selected performance

W34a 1975 (May): New York; Juilliard String Quartet [New York premiere] *See*: **B574**

W35 *Tone Roads et al*, small orchestra (1911-1919) *See*: **B575-576**
1. Fast "All Roads Lead to the Center," flute, clarinet, bassoon, strings (1911) [Peer, 1949; ed. Richard Swift and John Kirkpatrick, Peer, forthcoming] 3 min.
2. Slow (1911-1919) [lost]
3. Slow and fast "Rondo rapid transit," flute, clarinet, trumpet, trombone, chimes, piano, strings (1915) [Peer, 1952; ed. Richard Swift, Peer, forthcoming] 3 min.

W36 *Set No. 3*, small orchestra (?1902-1918) [AMP/Peer/Presser, under consideration]
1. *Adagio sostenuto At Sea* (?1902/?1912) [Peer, 1969] [dev. into **W135**] 1 1/2 min. string quartet, double bass (opt), piano
2. *Luck and Work* (1916) [der. from **W152**] 30 sec. 1-2-1-1, 2-1-1-0, perc, pf (2), hp, str
3. *Premonitions* (1918) [dev. into **W155**] 1 1/2 min. 1-2-1-1, 2-1-1-0, perc, pf (2), hp, st

Premiere

W36a 1962 (December 6): New York; Carnegie Recital Hall; Gunther Schuller, conductor

W37 *Chromâtimelôdtune*, small orchestra (?1919) [reconstructed and completed by Gunther Schuller, MJQ Music, 1963, 1967; realization by Kenneth Singleton, MJQ Music, 1963, 1967, 1977] [der. from **W57**] 6 min.
oboe, Bb clarinet, bassoon, Bb trumpet, F horn, trombone, tuba, snare drum, chimes, piano, 3 violins,
viola, cello, double bass *See*: **B577**

Premiere

W37a 1962 (December 6): New York; Carnegie Recital Hall; Gunther Schuller, conductor

MUSIC FOR BAND [W38-40]
See: B578-579

W38   *March "Intercollegiate," with Annie Lisle* (1892) [Pepper & Co., 1896; ed. Keith Brion, Joseph Boonin, 1973] [der. from **W70**] 4 min.
piccolo, (flute), (oboe), (bassoons), Eb clarinet, Bb clarinets, (Eb alto clarinet), (Bb bass clarinet), (Bb contrabass clarinet), (Eb alto saxophone), Bb tenor saxophone, (Eb baritone saxophone), Eb cornet, Bb cornets, F horns, trombones, baritone, basses, drums [instruments in parentheses added by Brion]

Premiere

W38a   1892 (October): Danbury; Danbury Fairground; Danbury Band

Other selected performance

W38b   1897 (March 4): Washington, D.C.; New Haven Band and Washington Marine Band (McKinley Inauguration)

W39   *March, F and C, with Omega Lambda Chi* (1896) [ed. and arr. by Keith Brion, AMP, 1974] [der. from **W69**] 3 min.   *See:* **W17b**

W40   *Runaway Horse on Main Street* (ca. 1905; incomplete) [dev. into **W141** and **W274**]

CHAMBER MUSIC [W41-63]
See: B584-632

STRING QUARTETS [W41-43]
See: B587-596

W41   *First String Quartet "From the Salvation Army"* (1896) [Peer, 1963; ed. John Kirkpatrick corrected edition in press, Peer (not an Ives Society Critical Edition)] 22 min.
1. Chorale [der. from lost organ fugue; dev. into **W7:3**]
2. Prelude [? der. from lost organ prelude]
3. Offertory [? der. from lost organ prelude/offertory]
4. Postlude [der. from lost organ postlude, 1896]

Premiere

W41a   1957 (April 24): New York; Museum of Modern Art; Kohon String Quartet   *See:* **B589-590**

W42 *Pre-Second String Quartet* (1904-1905) [unfinished, lost; dev. into **W55:1, W280,** and **W285**]

W43 *Second String Quartet* (1907-1913) (Peer, 1954; repr. 1970; new edition, Peer, under consideration] 26 min. *See:* **B107, B587-588,** and **B594-596**
   1. Discussions (1911-1913)
   2. Arguments (1907-1911)
   3. The Call of the Mountains (1911-1913)

Premiere

W43a 1946 (September 15): Saratoga Springs, NY; Walden String Quartet

MUSIC FOR VARIOUS COMBINATIONS [W44-57]
See: **B597-602**

W44 *Prelude,* trombone, 2 violins, organ (?1899) [ed. Bruce Nichols, entitled *Prelude on "Abide With Me,"* Presser, under review] [dev. into lost hymn-anthem, 1902 and **W27:3**]

W45 *From the Steeples and the Mountains,* trumpet, trombone, 4 sets of bells (1901-?1902) (Peer, 1965; ed. Kenneth Singleton, Peer, in press) 3 1/2 min.

W46 *Largo,* violin, clarinet, piano (?1902) (Southern, 1953) [der. from **W58:2a,** ? part of **W47**] 6 1/2 min. *See:* **B597**

W47 *Trio,* violin, clarinet, piano (1902-?1903) [lost; ? incomplete **W46**]

W48 *An Old Song Deranged,* clarinet/English horn, harp, string quartet (?1903) [ed. Kenneth Singleton, Peer, forthcoming] [der. from **W234**] 2 1/2 min.

W49 **Trio,** violin, cello, and piano (1904-1911) [Peer, 1955; ed. John Kirkpatrick, Peer, 1987] 25 min. *See:* **B598-600**
   1. Andante moderato
   2. TSIAJ [this scherzo is a joke] (Medley on the Campus Fence)
   3. Moderato con moto

Premiere

W49a 1948 (May 24): Berea, OH; Baldwin-Wallace College Faculty Trio

W50   *Take-off No. 3 "Rube trying to walk 2 to 3!!!,"* clarinet, bassoon, trumpet, piano (1906) [dev. into **W25** and **W172**; *see also* **W29**]

W51   *Hallowe'en*, string quartet, piano (1906) [Boelke-Bomart, 1949; ed. Richard Swift and John Kirkpatrick, Peer, forthcoming] 2 1/2 min. *See*: **B601**

Premiere

W51a 1934 (May 28): Stringart String Quartet

W52   *Largo Risoluto No. 1 "as to the Law of Diminishing Returns,"* string quartet, piano (1906) [Peer, 1961; ed. Philip Lambert, Peer, under consideration] 3 min.

Premiere

W52a 1965 (February 19): New York; Town Hall; Kohon String Quartet *See*: **W53a**, **W55a**, and **B602**

W53   *Largo Risoluto No. 3 "a shadow made--a silhouette,"* string quartet, piano (1906) [Peer, 1961; ed. Philip Lambert, Peer, under consideration] 2 min. [*Largo Risoluto No. 2* is lost]

W54   *All the Way Around and Back*, clarinet, bugle, violin, bells, piano (1906) [Peer, 1971] 2 min.

W55   *A Set of 3 Short Pieces* (1903-1914)
   1. Largo cantabile *Hymn*, string quartet, double bass (1904) [Peer, 1966] [der. from **W8**; dev. into **W151**] 2 1/2 min.
   2. Scherzo *Holding Your Own*, string quartet (1903-1914) [Peer, 1958] 1 1/2 min. *See*: **W52a**
   3. Adagio cantabile *The Innate*, string quartet, double bass, piano (1908) [Peer, 1967] [dev. into **W171**] 2 1/2 min.

W56   *In Re Con Moto Et Al*, string quartet, piano (1913) [Peer, 1968] 4 min.

W57   *Chromâtimelôdtune*, brass quartet, piano (?1919) [arr. Gerard Schwarz, MJQ Music, 1963, 1967, 1977] [dev. into **W37**] 6 1/2 min.

SONATAS FOR VIOLIN AND PIANO [W58-63]
See: B603-632

W58   *Pre-First Violin Sonata* (1899-?1903)
1. Allegretto moderato (1899-1901) [ed. Eugene Gratovich, AMP, under consideration] [dev. into **W60:2**]
2a. rejected Largo, G (1901) [dev. into **W46**; ed. Paul Zukofsky, Southern, 1967] 6 1/2 min.
2b. Largo, D (1902-?1903) [dev. into **W59:2**]
3a. rejected Scherzo (1902) [unfinished; dev. into **W60:2**]
3. Adagio--Allegro (1902) [dev. into **W60:1**]

W59   *First Violin Sonata* (1902-?1908) [Peer, 1953] 21 min. *See*: **B613-614**
1. Andante--Allegro (1902-?1906)
2. Largo cantabile (1908) [der. from **W58:2**]
3. Allegro (1906-?1908) [der. from lost sacred song *Watchman*; dev. into **W7:1**]

Premiere

W59a   1946 (March 31): New York; Joan Field (violin); Ray Lev (piano)

Other selected performances

W59b   1914 (October 4?): Redding, Ives's summer residence; Franz Milcke tries the first movement

W59c   1928: San Francisco; New Music Concert

W59d   1966 (January 24): New York; Carnegie Hall; Paul Zukofsky (violin); Gilbert Kalish (piano) [Violin Sonatas Nos. 1-4] *See*: **B620**

W59e   1968 (March 13): Esther Glazer (violin); Easley Blackwood (piano) [Violin Sonatas Nos. 1-4] *See*: **B622**

W60   *Second Violin Sonata* (1907-1910) [G. Schirmer, 1951] 14 min. *See*: **B609-610, B612, B619,** and **B629**
1. Autumn (1907) [der. from **W53**; dev. into **W177**]
2. In the Barn (1907) [der. from **W58:1** and **W58:3a**]
3. The Revival (1909-1910) [der. from **W63:3a**]

Premiere

W60a   1924 (March 18): New York; Aeolian Hall; Jerome Goldstein (violin); Rex Tillson (piano) *See*: **B603-605**

Other selected performances
See: **W59d** and **W59e**

W61   *Decoration Day* (1912) [ed. John Kirkpatrick, Peer, forthcoming] 7 min. [dev. into **W4:2**]

W62   *Third Violin Sonata* (1913-?1914) [ed. Sol Babitz and Ingolf Dahl, Merion, 1951] 26 min.   *See:* **B609** and **B611-612**
  1. Adagio [der. from lost organ prelude, 1901]
  2. Allegro [der. from lost ragtime piece, 1902-1903]
  3. Adagio cantabile [der. from lost organ prelude, 1901]

Premiere

W62a   1917 (April 22): New York; Carnegie Chamber Music Hall; David Talmadge (violin); Stuart Ross (piano)

Other selected performances
See also: **W59d** *and* **W59e**

W62b   1945 (March 16): Los Angeles; Sol Babitz (violin); Ingolf Dahl (piano) [Evenings on the Roof Series]   *See:* **B608**

W62c   1949 (April 25): New York; Museum of Modern Art; Joan Field (violin); Simon Sadoff (piano) [Sponsored by The International Society for Contemporary Music, United States Section]

W63   *Fourth Violin Sonata "Children's Day at the Camp Meeting"* (1906-?1916) [Arrow, 1942; repr. AMP] 10 min.   *See:* **B625**
  1. Allegro (1914-?1916) [der. from G. Ives's Fugue in Bb, 1862, and lost sonata for trumpet and organ, 1901]
  2. Largo (1906-?1916)
  3. Allegro (1914-?1916) [dev. from sketch, 1905; dev. into **W176**]
  3a. rejected Adagio--Faster (1906) [dev. into **W60:3**]

Premiere

W63a   1940 (January 14): New York; Museum of Modern Art; Eudice Shapiro (violin); Irene Jacobi (piano)   *See:* **B606**

Other selected performances
See also: **W59d** and **W59e**

W63b   1942 (February 25): New York; Carnegie Hall; Joseph Szigeti (violin); Andor Foldes (piano)   *See:* **B607**

KEYBOARD [W64-88]
See: B633-734

PIANO SONATAS [W64-65]
See: B646-710

W64   *First Piano Sonata* (1901-1909) [ed. Lou Harrison and William
Masselos, Peer, 1954; ed. Paul Echols, Lou Harrison, and William
Masselos, Peer, 1979; new edition, Peer, under consideration] 35
min. [der. from **W21**] *See*: **B646-659**
1. Adagio con moto (1901-1909)
2a. 1st verse and chorus (1902-?1908) [der. from **W21**]
2b. 2nd verse and chorus *In the Inn* (1902-?1908) [der. from
W21; dev. into **W27:2**]
3. Largo--Allegro (1902-1909)
4a. 3rd verse and chorus (?1909)
4b. 4th verse and chorus (1902-?1908) [der. from **W21**]
5. Andante maestoso (1905-1908) [der. from and dev. into
W77:4]

Premiere

W64a   1949 (February 17): New York; Y.M.H.A. Hall; William
Masselos *See*: **B647**

Other selected performances

W64b   1949 (March 27): New York; Carnegie Hall; William
Masselos *See*: **B646**

W64c   1952 (March 19): Cambridge, MA; Harvard University;
William Masselos [Concluding concert of Aaron Copland's
Charles Eliot Norton Lectures 1951-1952] *See*: **B346** and **B648**

W64d   1974 (October 17): New York; Hunter College Playhouse;
William Masselos [Opening concert of the Ives Centennial
Festival-Conference] *See*: **B226**

W65   *Second Piano Sonata "Concord, Mass., 1840-60"* (1910-1915)
[Redding, CT, by author; second edition prepared by Ives with the
assistance of George F. Roberts, Arrow, 1947; reprint AMP, n.d.;
ed. John Kirkpatrick, as played by Kirkpatrick, AMP, forthcoming]
44 min. *See*: **B660-698**
1. "Emerson" (1911-1912) [der. from **W14**; dev. into **W78:9**]
2. "Hawthorne" (1911) [der. from **W7:2**, **W23**, and **W81**]
3. "The Alcotts" (1912-1914) [der. from lost *Orchard House
Overture*]

4. "Thoreau" (1910-1915) [dev. into **W179**]

Premiere

W65a 1939 (January 20): New York; Town Hall; John Kirkpatrick
See: **B337, B668, B670-671,** and **B675-777**

Other selected performances

W65b 1912: Ives [Private performance for Max Smith--Ives writes
that he "played partly from the sketch [middle section of
"Thoreau"] and a few improvisations in a few places, as it was not
all written out fully completed (but it was practically as it is now,
though there are a few places I'll have to clean up)" [*See*: *Memos*,
p. 186]

W65c 1914 (Spring): New York; Ives ["Impromptu church
concert"; "Emerson" and parts of "Hawthorne"]

W65d 1921 (August 3): Clifton Furness [Lecture-recital that
included a performance of "The Alcotts"]

W65e 1921 (after September): Columbia, SC; Lenore Purcell
[Lecture by Henry Bellamann with excerpts performed by Purcell]

W65f 1922 (January 4): Atlanta; Atlanta Music Club; Lenore
Purcell [Lecture by Henry Bellamann with excerpts performed by
Purcell] *See*: **B666**

W65g 1928 (March 5): Paris; Sorbonne Station of the Radio
Institute of Paris; Katherine Heyman [Radio broadcast of
"Emerson"]

W65h 1928 (May 1): New York; New York Historical Society;
Oscar Ziegler ["The Alcotts"]

W65i 1928 (November 20): New York; Town Hall; Anton Rovinsky
["Hawthorne"]

W65j 1938 (June 21): Stamford, CT; John Kirkpatrick [Private
lecture-recital]

W65k 1938 (November): Cos Cob, CT; Old House (private home);
John Kirkpatrick [Private lecture-recital; first performance from
memory] *See*: **B663**

W65l 1939 (February 24): New York; Town Hall; John
Kirkpatrick [Concert also included two groups of songs] *See*:
W133c, B34, B36, and **B669**

W65m 1939 (May 14): Concord, MA; First Parish Church; John Kirkpatrick [Performance sponsored by Emerson's grandson]

W65n 1939 (May 17): New York; University Club; John Kirkpatrick [Dinner in Ives's honor sponsored by the Yale Class of 1898]

W65o 1939 (June): Los Angeles; Evenings on the Roof; Frances Mullen ["Emerson"]

W65p 1974 (October 17): New York; Hunter College Playhouse; John Kirkpatrick [Opening concert of the Ives Centennial Festival-Conference] *See:* **B226**

OTHER MUSIC FOR PIANO SOLO [W66-83]
See: **B711-724**

W66 1. *New Year's Dance* (1886) [incomplete; ed. by Laurence Wallach, **B156**, pp. 330-331]
2. *London Bridge Is Fallen Down* (1891?) [ed. Kenneth Singleton, Peer, forthcoming] [Polytonal and Burlesque Exercise No. 5 (Kirkpatrick 7C5)]

W67 *March No. 1, with The Year of Jubilee* (?1890) [*Marches Nos. 1-6*, ed. Kenneth Singleton, AMP/Peer/Presser, forthcoming] [dev. into lost band arrangement and lost orchestra arrangement]

W68 *March [No. 2], with The Son of a Gambolier* (?1892; *See:* **W67** for edition) [incomplete; dev. into **W18** and **W185**]

W69 *March No. 3, with Omega Lambda Chi* (?1892; *See:* **W67** for edition) [dev. into **W39**]

W70 *March No. 5, with Annie Lisle* (1892; *See:* **W67** for edition) [dev. into **W38**]

W71 *March No. 6, with Here's to Good Old Yale* (1892-?1897; *See:* **W67** for edition) [three versions; dev. into lost band/orchestra arrangement]

W72 *March, G and C, with See the Conquering Hero Comes* (? 1893) 2 1/2 min.

W73 *March "The Circus Band"* (?1894) [dev. into W187]

W74   *[Invention], D* (?1896) [ed. Geoffrey Block, Presser, under consideration] 1 min.

W75   *Ragtime Dances* (1902-1904) [der. from and dev. into **W21**; dev. into **W64:2a/2b/4b**]

W76   *Three-Page Sonata* (1905) [ed. Henry Cowell, Mercury, 1949; ed. John Kirkpatrick, Presser, 1975] 9 min. *See:* **B50**, **B330**, **B711**, and **B714-717**

Premiere

W76a   1949 (April 25): New York; Museum of Modern Art; William Masselos [Sponsored by The International Society for Contemporary Music, United States Section] *See:* **B330** and **B714**

W77   *[Set of Five Take-Offs]* (1906-January 1, 1907) [ed. John Kirkpatrick, Peer, forthcoming]
   1. *The Seen and Unseen* 3 min.
   2. *Rough and Ready et al and/or The Jumping Frog* 3 min.
   3. *Song Without (Good) Words (Melody in F and Fb)* 3 1/2 min.
   4. *Scene Episode* [der. from and dev. into **W64:5**] 3 min.
   5. *Bad Resolutions and Good One* (? Jan 1, 1907)

Premiere

W77a   1968 (March 23): New York; Town Hall; Alan Mandel *See:* **B113** and **B712**

W78   *Studies* (1907-?1908) [incomplete] *See:* **B711** and **B719**
   1. [? Allegro] [incomplete]
   2. Andante moderato--Allegro molto [ed. Alan Mandel, Presser, under consideration] [dev. into cadenza for **W14**] 2 1/2 min.
   3. [lost]
   4. [? Allegro moderato] [incomplete]
   5. Moderato [con] anima [ed. Alan Mandel, Presser, in press] 3 min.
   6. Andante [renumbered No. 14] [ed. Alan Mandel, Presser, under consideration] 4 min.
   7. Andante cantabile [renumbered No. 15] [ed. Alan Mandel, Presser, under consideration] 2 1/2 min.
   8. Trio: Allegro moderato--Presto [ed. Alan Mandel, Presser, under consideration] 1 1/2 min.
   9. *The Anti-Abolitionist Riots* (1908) [ed. Henry Cowell, Mercury, 1949; ed. Keith Ward, Presser, in progress] 4 min. [der. from

cadenza for **W14** and **W65:1**] *See*: **B50** and **B723**   10-18. [?
lost]

Unidentified ?3-movement piece:

- [Allegro moderato] [renumbered No. 15] [ed. Alan Mandel,
Presser, under consideration] 4 1/2 min.

- Andante cantabile [incomplete; renumbered No. 16]

No. 18? [renumbered No. 23?] [ed. Alan Mandel, Presser, under
   consideration] 5 min.

19. untitled, amorphous sketch

20. [March:] Slow allegro or Fast andante [ed. John Kirkpatrick,
   Presser, 1981] 7 min. *See*: **B713**

21. *Some Southpaw Pitching* (?1909) [ed. Henry Cowell, Mercury,
   1949; ed. John Kirkpatrick, Presser, 1975] 2 1/2 min. *See*:
   B50

22. Andante maestoso--Allegro vivace (?1909) [*New Music* 21, no.
   (October 1947): 8-9; ed. John Kirkpatrick, Presser, 1973] 2
   min. *See*: **B711-712**

23. Allegro [ed. John Kirkpatrick, Presser, forthcoming] 5 min.

Premieres

W78a   1950 (April 3): New York; Jerrold Cox [No. 9 and 21] *See*:
B718

W78b   1968 (March 23): New York; Town Hall; Alan Mandel [Nos.
2, 5-7, 15, 18, 20, and 23] *See*: **B113** and **B712**

W79   *Waltz-Rondo* (1911) [ed. John Kirkpatrick and Jerrold Cox, AMP,
1978] 7 1/2 min. *See*: **B711** and **B713**

W80   *Four Transcriptions from Emerson* (?1917-?1922) [ed. John
Kirkpatrick, AMP, in progress] [der. from **W14** and **W65:1**] 21 1/2
min.

1. Slowly (?1917) 4 min.
2. Moderato (?1922) 4 min.
3. Largo (?1922) 3 1/2 min.
4. Allegro agitato--Broadly (?1922) 4 min.

Premiere

W80a   1948 (March 12): New York; W. Aitken

W81   *Varied Air and Variations* (?1923) [ed. John Kirkpatrick and Garry
Clarke, Presser, 1971] 6 min. *See*: **B711**

W82   *The Celestial Railroad* (?1924-1925) [ed. Paul Reale, AMP, in progress] [dev. into **W7:2**, **W23**, and **W65:2**] 10 min. *See*: **B724**

W83   *Three Improvisations* (recorded ? May 11, 1938 by Ives) [trans. and ed. Gail and James Dapogny, AMP, 1984] 3 min.

PIANO DUETS [W84]
See: **B725-732**

W84   *Three Quarter-Tone Pieces*, 2 pianos (1923-1924) [ed. George Pappastavrou, Peters, 1968; ed. George Pappastavrou, commissioned in 1988] 11 min. *See*: **B725-732**
1. Largo 4 min.
2. Allegro [der. from **W30:1**] 3 min.
3. Chorale [der. from **W34**] 4 min.

Premieres

W84a 1925 (February 8): New York; Chickering Hall; Hans Barth and Sigmund Klein [lecture by E. Robert Schmitz] [no.3.]

W84b 1925 (February 14): New York; Aeolian Hall; Hans Barth and Sigmund Klein [Franco-American Musical Society] [Nos. 2 and 3] *See*: **B725-726**

ORGAN MUSIC [W85-88]
See: **B733-737**

[ed. William Osborne, Presser, new commissioned edition of Ives's *Works for Organ* in 1988]

W85   *Variations on Jerusalem the Golden* (?1888) [dev. into lost band arrangement]

Premiere

W85a 1974 (April 21): Minneapolis, MN; University of Minnesota; Kim Kasling *See*: **B735**

W86   *Variations on America* (?1891) [Music Press, 1949; repr. Mercury; orch. arr. by William Schuman, Merion, 1964] 8 min. *See*: **B583**

Premiere

W86a 1891 (July 4): Brewster, NY; Ives

W87   *[Canzonetta], F* (?1893)

W88   *Prelude on Adeste fideles* (?1897) [Music Press, 1949; repr. Mercury] 3 1/2 min.

CHORAL AND PARTSONGS [W89-131]
See: **B738-770**

CANTATA [W89]
See: B752-757

W89   *The Celestial Country*, two solo quartets and SATB, string quartet, trumpet, euphonium, timpani organ (1898-1899) [text, Henry Alford] [ed. John Kirkpatrick, Peer, 1973 (piano-vocal score); full score, forthcoming] [organ part lost] 37 min. *See:* **B752-757**
1. *Far o'er Yon Horizon*, prelude, trio and chorus
2. *Naught That Country Needeth* [*114* (no. 98), *14*, and *Sacred Songs*]
3. *Seek the Things before Us*
4. *Intermezzo*
5. *Glories on Glories*
6. *Forward, Flock of Jesus* [*114* (no. 99), *10*, and *Sacred Songs*]
7. *To the Eternal Father*, chorale and finale

Premiere

W89a   1902 (April 18): New York; Central Presbyterian Church; Annie Wilson (soprano); Emma Williams (contralto); E. Ellsworth Giles (tenor); George A. Fleming (baritone); The Kaltenborn String Quartet [Franz Kaltenborn (1st violin); William Rowell (2nd violin); Gustave Bach (viola); Louis Heine (cello)]; Ives (organ) *See:* **B752-753**

Other selected performances

W89b   1975: Frankfurt; Hessian Radio Orchestra [First European performance] *See:* **B756**

W89c   1979 (April 21): London; Queen Elizabeth Hall; Taverner Choir; Andrew Parrott, conductor *See:* **B757**

OTHER MUSIC FOR CHORUS AND ORCHESTRA [W90-101] *See:* B766-770

W90   *Three Harvest Home Chorales*, SATB, 4 trumpets, 3 trombones, timpani, organ (?1898-1901) [Mercury, 1949; repr. Mercury, n.d.; ed. Paul Echols, Presser, in progress] 7 1/2 min. *See:* **B766**

1. *Harvest Home* (text, George Burgess; ?1898) ["The harvest dawn is near"]
2. *Lord of the Harvest* (text, John Hampton Gurney; ?1901)
3. *Harvest Home* (text, Henry Alford; ?1901) ["Come, ye thankful people"]

Premiere

W90a 1948 (March 3): New York; Carnegie Hall; Collegiate Chorale; Robert Shaw, conductor

W91   *The New River*, unison chorus, orchestra (1911) [text, Ives: "Down the river"] [full score by Henry Cowell] [Peer, 1971] [der. from **W30:3**; *114 Songs* (no. 6) 1 1/2 min.

Premiere

W91a 1934 (April 15): New York; Town Hall; Nicholas Slonimsky, conductor [with December (**W93**)]

W92   *Lincoln, the Great Commoner*, unison chorus, orchestra (1912) [text, Edwin Markham: "And so he came"] [*New Music*, 1932; repr. Merion; repr. Kalmus; ed. and arr. for chorus and piano by James G. Smith, Fostco Music Press, 1976] [dev. into **W142**; *114 Songs* (no. 11)] 4 min.

Premiere

W92a 1960 (February 10): New York; Carnegie Hall; Orchestra of America; Richard Korn, conductor *See:* **B768**

W93   *December*, unison chorus, brass, winds (1912-1913) [text, Folgore da San Geminiano, tr. Dante Gabriel Rossetti] [ed. Nicholas Slonimsky, Peer, 1963] [dev. into **W168**; *114 Songs* (no. 37)] 1 min. [*See:* **W91a**]

Premiere

W93a 1934 (April 15): New York; Town Hall; Nicholas Slonimsky, conductor [with *The New River* (**W91a**)]

W94   *Two Slants (Christian and Pagan)* (?1911-1913) [*114 Songs* (no. 9a and b)
1. *Duty*, unison chorus, orchestra [text, Ralph Waldo Emerson: "So nigh is grandeur"]
2. *Vita*, unison chorus, organ [text, Manlius: "Nascentes morimur"]

W95 *Walt Whitman*, unison chorus, orchestra (1913) [text, Walt Whitman: "Who goes there?"] [dev. into **W162**; *114 Songs* (no. 31)] 1 min.

W96 *General William Booth Enters into Heaven*, unison chorus, orchestra (1914) [text, Vachel Lindsay: "Booth led boldly"] [orch. by John J. Becker in collaboration with Ives; ed. Kenneth Singleton, Presser, under consideration] [unfinished; dev. into **W278**] 6 min.

W97 *Sneak Thief*, unison chorus, trumpet, piano four-hands (1914) [text, Ives: "People of the world"]

Premiere

W97a 1974 (October 21): New Haven; Sprague Hall; Yale University; Yale Theater Orchestra and Chorus; James B. Sinclair, conductor; Jere Lantz, chorus director

W98 *Majority (The Masses)*, unison chorus, orchestra (1914-1915) [text, Ives] [dev. into **W132**; *114 Songs* (no. 1)] 4 1/2 min.

W99 1. *He Is There!*, unison chorus, orchestra (1917) [text, Ives: "Fifteen years ago today"] [dev. into **W181:1**; *114 Songs*, (no. 50)] 3 min.
2. *They are There!*, unison chorus, orchestra (1942) [text, Ives: "There's a time"] [ed. Lou Harrison, Peer, 1961] [dev. into **W181:2**] 3 min. *See*: **B770**

Premiere

W99a 1959 (October 19): Norwalk, VA; Westport High School Auditorium; Norwalk Symphony Society; Westport Madrigal Singers; Quinto Maganini, conductor. [Announcement in *The New York Times*, October 18, 1959, page 37]

W100 *An Election ("Nov. 2, 1920")*, unison chorus, orchestra (1920) [text, Ives: "It strikes me"] [dev. into **W153**; *114 Songs* (no. 22)] 4 min.

W101 *Johnny Poe*, TTBB, orchestra (1925) [text, Benjamin R. C. Low: "When fell the gloom"] [unfinished; realized and ed. John Kirkpatrick, Peer, 1978] 3 1/2 min.

Premiere

W101a 1974 (October 20): Miami; Gusman Philharmonic Hall; Frederick Fennell, conductor; Miami Philharmonic Orchestra; University of Miami Chamber Singers

W101b 1981 (January 12): New York; Carnegie Hall; Brooklyn Philharmonia Orchestra and Chorus and C. W. Post College Chorus [New York premiere] *See:* **B767**

SACRED CHORAL MUSIC [W102-124]
See: **B758-765** and **B769**

W102 *Psalm 42*, SATB, organ (?1887) [text: "As pants the hart"] [ed. Wendell Kumlien, **B743**, pp. 393-402]

Premiere

?W102a 1887: Danbury, CT; Methodist Church

W103 *I Think of Thee, My God*, SATB (?1889) [text, John Monsell] [ed. Dale Jergenson, **B743**, pp. 413-416] [dev. into **W253**]

Premiere

W103a 1889 (February 21): Brewster, NY

W104 *Benedictus in E*, SATB, organ (?1888-1890) [text: "Blessed be the Lord God of Israel"] [ed. John Kirkpatrick, AMP, forthcoming]

Premiere

? W104a 1888-1889: Danbury, CT; Baptist Church

W105 *Turn Ye, Turn Ye*, SATB, organ (?1889-1890) [text, Rev. Josiah Hopkins] [ed. John Kirkpatrick, Mercury, 1973] [organ part lost]

Premiere

? W105a 1889 (April 14) or 1890 (April 13): Danbury, CT; Baptist Church

W106 *Crossing the Bar*, SATB, organ (?1890) [text, Alfred Lord Tennyson: "Sunset and evening star"] [ed. John Kirkpatrick, AMP, 1974] [organ part lost]

Premiere

? W106a 1890 (May 24) and/or 1891 (May 25): Danbury, CT;
Baptist Church

Other selected performance

W106b 1974 (October 21): New Haven; Sprague Hall; Yale
University; Yale Theater Orchestra and Chorus; James B.
Sinclair, conductor; Jere Lantz, chorus director [Modern
premiere]

W107 *Communion Service*, SATB, organ (?1890-1891) [ed. Wendell
Kumlien, **B743**, pp. 417-427] [organ part lost]

Premiere

? W107a 1890 (November): Danbury, CT; St. James Episcopal
Church

W108 *Bread of the World*, unison female choir, organ (?1891) [text,
Heber] [unfinished]

W109 *Search Me O Lord*, SATB (?1891-1892) [text, Psalm 139] [ed.
Wendell Kumlien, **B743**, pp. 435-436 and Kenneth Sole, **B750**,
pp. 198-200]

W110 *I Come to Thee*, SATB, organ (?1892) [text, Charlotte Elliott: "God
of my life"] [ed. John Kirkpatrick, AMP, 1983]

Premiere

? W110a 1892 (December 11): Danbury, CT; Baptist Church

W111 *Easter Carol*, solo quartet, SATB, organ (1892-1901) [text: "Wake,
wake, earth"] [ed. John Kirkpatrick, AMP, 1973]

Premiere

W111a 1892 (April 17): Danbury, CT; Baptist Church

Other selected performances

W111b 1893 (October 8 or 15): New Haven; St. Thomas Church

W111c 1895 (April 14): New Haven; Center Church [Easter]

W111d 1902 (March 30): New York; Central Presbyterian Church
[Easter]

W112 *Lord God, Thy Sea Is Mighty*, SATB, organ (?1893 or 1894) [ed. John Kirkpatrick, AMP, 1983)] [organ part lost]

W113 *Psalm 150*, 4-part treble (or boys) and SATB, organ (optional) (?1894) [text: "Praise ye the Lord"] [ed. John Kirkpatrick and Gregg Smith, Merion, 1972] 2 min.

Premiere

? W113a 1896 or 1897 (June 14): New Haven; Center Church; John Griggs, director

W114 *Psalm 67*, SATB (divided) (?1894) [text, "God be merciful unto us"] [AMP, 1939] 2 1/2 min. *See:* **B760**

Premiere

W114a 1937 (May 6): New York; WPA's Theatre of Music; Madrigal Singers; Lehman Engel, director

Other selected performance

W114b 1937 (August 29): New York; Madrigal Singers; Lehman Engel, director [CBS National Radio Broadcast]

W115 *Psalm 54*, SAATBB (?1894) [text, "Save me, O God"] [ed. John Kirkpatrick and Gregg Smith, Merion, 1973] 3 min.

W116 *Psalm 24*, SATB (divided) (?1894) [text, "The earth is the Lord's"] [Mercury, 1955] 2 1/2 min. *See:* **B758**

?W116a 1897-1898: New Haven, Center Church; Newark, NJ, Newark Presbyterian; Bloomfield, NJ, Bloomfield Presbyterian

W117 *The Light That Is Felt*, bass solo, SATB, organ (?1895) [text, John Greenleaf Whittier] [ed. Dale Jergenson, **B734**, pp. 464-472] [dev. into **W197**; *114 Songs* (no. 66)] 1 min.

Premiere

W117a 1895 (June 4): New Haven; Center Church; John Griggs (bass)

W118 *All-forgiving, Look on Me*, SATB, ?organ (?1898) [text, *Salve mundi salutare*, tr. Ray Palmer] [ed. John Kirkpatrick, Peer, in press] [?organ part lost]

W119 *Psalm 100*, SA and SATB, bells, organ (optional) (1898-?1899) [text, "Make a joyful noise"] [ed. John Kirkpatrick and Gregg Smith, Merion, 1975] 2 min.

Premiere

? W119a 1897-1898: New Haven, Center Church; Newark, NJ: Newark Presbyterian; Bloomfield, NJ: Bloomfield Presbyterian

W120 *Psalm 14*, SATB (divided) (?1899) [text, "The fool hath said"] [ed. John Kirkpatrick, Presser, in progress] [organ part lost] 3 1/2 min.

W121 *Psalm 25*, SATB (divided) (1899-?1901) [text, "Unto thee O God"] [ed. John Kirkpatrick and Gregg Smith, Merion, 1979] 8 min.

Premiere

W121a 1967 (October 24): Washington, D.C.; Arts and Industries Building; Gregg Smith Singers; Gregg Smith, director

W122 *Psalm 135 (Anthem-Processional)*, SATB (divided), trumpet, trombone, timpani, organ (?1900) [text, "Praise ye the Lord"] [ed. John Kirkpatrick, Presser, 1980] 3 min.

W123 *Processional*, TTBB or SATB or 4 trombones, organ or 4 violins, and organ or string orchestra (1901) [text, Rev. John Ellerton: "Let there be light"] [Peer, 1967; ed. J. Peter Burkholder, Peer, in progress] 2 min. *See:* **B769**

W124 *Psalm 90*, SATB (divided), bells, organ (1894, rev. 1924) [text, "Lord, thou has been"] [ed. John Kirkpatrick and Gregg Smith, Merion, 1970] 11 min. *See:* **B762-765**

SECULAR PARTSONGS [W125-131]

W125 *This Year's at the Spring*, SATB (?1889) [text, Robert Browning]

W126 *Serenade*, SATB (?1891) [text, Henry Wadsworth Longfellow: "Stars of the summer night"] [ed. John Kirkpatrick, Peer, forthcoming]

W127 *The Boys in Blue* (?1895) [ed. Kenneth Singleton, Peer, in press]

Premiere

W127a 1974 (October 21): New Haven; Sprague Hall; Yale
University; Yale Theater Orchestra and Chorus; James B.
Sinclair, conductor; Jere Lantz, chorus director

W128 *For You and Me!*, TTBB (?1895/1896) [Geo. Molineux, 1896; ed.
Clifford G. Richter, Boonin, 1973]

W129 *A Song of Mory's*, TTBB (1896) [text, Charles Edmund Merrill, Jr.]
[*Yale Courant* 33 (February Fourth Week, 1897); ed. Kenneth
Singleton, Peer, in press]

W130 *The Bells of Yale, or Chapel Chimes*, baritone solo, TTBB,
cello/piano (1897-?1898) [text, Huntington Mason] [ed. Kenneth
Singleton, Peer, in press]

Premiere

W130a 1897-1898: New Haven and fourteen other American
cities, including Brooklyn and Colorado Springs; Yale Glee Club
[All programs; *See*: *Yale Daily News*, November 29, 1897 and
January 24, 1898, and **B65**, p. 27]

W130b 1899 (June 27): New Haven: Hyperion; Yale Glee and
Banjo Clubs (Thirty-Third Annual Spring Concert)

W131 *O Maiden Fair*, baritone solo, TTBB, piano (1898-?1898)

SONGS [W132-285]
See: **B771-817**

Private Song Compilations

Songbook A (3 songs; 1 song missing) [private compilation, 1898 or 1899]

Songbook B (8 songs; 1 song missing) [private compilation, 1898]

Songbook C (8 songs) [private compilation, 1903?]

2 Songs. [private compilation, 1917 or 1918]

3 Songs. [private compilation, ?1919]

114 Songs. Redding, CT. [private compilation, 1922; repr. by AMP/Peer/Press, n.d.] *See:* **B771-773, B776-777, B789, B796,** and **B803**

50 Songs. [actually 52 songs] [private compilation, reprinted from plates of *114 Songs*, 1923]

Published Song Collections

7 Songs. Cos Cob Press, 1932; repr., Arrow, 1939; AMP, 1947.

34 Songs. New Music 7, no. 1 (1933); repr., Merion, n.d.

4 Songs. Mercury, 1933; repr., 1950.

19 Songs. New Music 9, no. 1 (1935); repr., Merion, n.d.

10 Songs. Peer, 1953. *See:* **B782-784**

12 Songs. Peer, 1954. *See:* **B786**

14 Songs. Peer, 1955. *See:* **B786**

9 Songs. Peer, 1956.

13 Songs. Peer, 1958.

Sacred Songs (12 songs). Peer, 1961.

11 Songs and 2 Harmonizations. ed. John Kirkpatrick, AMP, 1968. *See:* **B791**

3 Songs. AMP, 1968.

40 Earlier Songs. ed. John Kirkpatrick, AMP/Peer/ Presser, forthcoming.

114 SONGS

W132 [1] *Majority* (1921) [text, Ives: "The masses have toiled"] [der. from **W98**; *19 Songs*] 5 1/2 min.

W133 [2] *Evening* (1921) [text, John Milton: "Now came still evening on"] [*50 Songs*; *7 Songs*; orchestral realization, ed. Kenneth Singleton, AMP, 1983] 2 min. *See:* **B810**

Other selected performances

W133a 1932 (May 1): Saratoga Springs, NY; Hubert Linscott (baritone); Aaron Copland (piano) (Yaddo Festival) [with *Charlie Rutlage* (**W141**); *The Indians* (**W145**); *Maple Leaves* (**W154**); *The See'r* (**W160**); *Serenity* (**W173**); and *Walking* (**W198**)] *See*: **B774-775**

W133b 1932 (December 8): Hamburg, Germany; Musikhall, Kleiner Saal; Mary Bell (soprano); Henry Cowell (piano) (Sponsored by the Pan American Association of Composers) [with *The New River* (**W137**) and *The Indians* (**W145**)]

W133c 1939 (February 24): New York; Town Hall; Mina Hager (mezzo-soprano); John Kirkpatrick (piano) [with *The Indians* (**W145**); *The Greatest Man* (**W150**); *Ann Street* (**W156**); *The See'r* (**W160**); *The Side Show* (**W163**); *The Things Our Fathers Loved* (**W174**); *At the River* (**W176**); *Down East* (**W186**); *Autumn* (**W191**); *Walking* (**W198**); *Berceuse* (**B224**); and *General William Booth Enters into Heaven* (**B278**) *See*: **W7b, W651, B34, B36**, and **B669**

W134 [3] *The Last Reader* (1921) [text, Oliver Wendell Holmes: "I sometimes sit beneath a tree"] [der. from **W32:3**; *50 Songs*; *34 Songs*] 2 min.

Other selected performance

W134a 1942 (November 2): New York; Town Hall; Doris Doe (mezzo-soprano); Hellmut Baerwald (piano) [with *From "The Swimmers"* (**W158**); *Rough Wind* (**W200**); *The Children's Hour* (**W205**)]

W135 [4] *At Sea* (1921) [text, Robert Underwood Johnson: "Some things are undivined except by love"] [dev. from **W36:1**; *50 Songs*; *34 Songs*] 1 1/2 min.

W136 [5] *Immortality* (1921) [text, Ives: "Who dares to say the spring is dead"] [*50 Songs*; *34 Songs*] 1 1/2 min.

W137 [6] *The New River* (1913) [text, Ives: "Down the river comes a noise"] [der. from **W30:3**; *50 Songs*; *34 Songs*] 1 1/2 min. *See*: **W133b**

W138 [7] *Disclosure* (1921) [text, Ives: "Thoughts which deeply rest at evening"] [*50 Songs*; *12 Songs*; *Sacred Songs*] 1 min.

W139 [8] *The Rainbow (So May It Be)* (1921) [text, William Wordsworth: "My heart leaps up"] [der. from **W33**; *34 Songs*] 1 min.

W140 [9] *Two Slants, or Christian and Pagan* (1921) [der. from **W33**; *50 Songs*; *34 Songs*; *4 Songs*]
a) *Duty* [text, Ralph Waldo Emerson: "So nigh is grandeur to our dust"] 30 sec.
b) *Vita* [text, Manlius: "Nascentes morimus finisque ab"] 30 sec.

W141 [10] *Charlie Rutlage* (1920/1921) [text, D. J. O'Malley: "Another good cow-puncher"] [der. from **W40** and **W274**; orchestral realization, ed. Kenneth Singleton, AMP, 1983; *50 Songs*; *7 Songs*] 2 1/2 min *See*: **W133a**

W142 [11] *Lincoln, the Great Commoner* (?1913) [text, Edwin Markham: "And so he came from the prairie cabin"] [der. from **W92**; Peer, 1952] 4 min.

W143 [12] *Remembrance* (1921) [text, Ives: "A sound of a distant horn"] [der. from **W26**; chamber realization, ed. Kenneth Singleton, Presser, 1977; *50 Songs*; *12 Songs*] 1 min.

W144 [13] *Resolution* (1921) [text, Ives: "Walking stronger under distant skies"] [*50 Songs*; *19 Songs*] 1 min.

W145 [14] *The Indians* (1921) [text, Charles Sprague: "Alas for them their day is o'er"] [der. from **W32**:1; *50 Songs*; *34 Songs*] 2 min. *See*: **W133a-c**

W146 [15] *The Housatonic at Stockbridge* (1921) [text, Robert Underwood Johnson: "Contented river"] [der. from **W5**:3; *12 Songs*] 3 1/2 min.

W147 [16] *Religion* (?1910) [text, Lizzie York Case: "There is no unbelief"] [der. from lost anthem, 1902; *50 Songs*; *12 Songs*; *Sacred Songs*] 1 1/2 min.

W148 [17] *Grantchester* (1920) [text, Rupert Brooke] [*50 Songs*; *9 Songs*] 2 min.

W149 [18] *Incantation* (1921) [text, Lord Byron (Manfred): "When the moon is on the wave"] [der. from **W30**:6; *34 Songs*] 2 1/2 min.

W150 [19] *The Greatest Man* (1921) [text, Anne Timoney Collins: "My teacher said"] [*50 Songs*; *34 Songs*; *3 Songs*; AMP, 1942] 1 1/2 min.

Other selected performance

W150a 1940 (March 24): New York; Town Hall; John Charles Thomas (baritone); (piano) [with *The White Gulls*] *See*: **W133c** and **B778**

W151 [20] *Hymn* (1921) [text, Gerhardt Tersteegen, tr. John Wesley: "Thou hidden love of God" [der. from **W55:1**; *50 Songs*; *34 Songs*] 2 1/2 min.

W152 [21] *Luck and Work* (?1913) [text, Robert Underwood Johnson: "While one will search"] [der. from **W36:2**; *34 Songs*; *4 Songs*] 30 sec.

W153 [22] *"Nov. 2, 1920"* (1921) [text, Ives: "It strikes me that"] [der. from **W100**; *19 Songs*] 4 min. *See*: **B780**

W154 [23] *Maple Leaves* (1920) [text, Thomas Bailey Aldrich: "October turned my maple's leaves to gold"] [*7 Songs*] 1 min. *See*: **W133a**

W155 [24] *Premonitions* (1921) [text, Robert Underwood Johnson: "There's a shadow on the grass"] [der. from **W36:3**; *19 Songs*] 1 1/2 min.

W156 [25] *Ann Street* (1921) [text, Maurice Morris: "Quaint name, Ann Street"] [*34 Songs*] 1 min. *See*: **W133c** and **B788**

W157 [26] *Like a Sick Eagle* (?1913) [text, John Keats: "The spirit is too weak"] [der. from **W30:4**; *50 Songs*; *34 Songs*] 3 min.

W158 [27] *From "The Swimmers"* (1915) [text, Louis Untermeyer: "He grew in those seasons [rev. 1921; *34 Songs*; orch. version by James B. Sinclair, Presser, forthcoming] 1 1/2 min. *See*: **W134a**

W159 [28] *On the Counter* (1920) [text, Ives: "Tunes we heard in 'ninety-two'"] [*14 Songs*] 1 min.

W160 [29] *The See'r* (?1913) [text, Ives: "An old man with a straw in his mouth"] [der. from **W30:1**; *7 Songs*] 1 min. *See*: **W133a** and **W133c**

W161 [30] *From "Paracelsus"* (1921) [text, Robert Browning: "For God is glorified in man"] [der. from **W15**; *50 Songs*; *19 Songs*] 3 1/2 min.

W162 [31] *Walt Whitman* (1921) [text, Walt Whitman: "Who goes there?"] [der. from **W95**; *50 Songs*; *34 Songs*] 1 min.

W163 [32] *The Side Show* (1921) [text, Ives, after Pat Rooney: "Is that Mister Riley"] [der. from lost sketch, 1896; *12 Songs*] 30 sec. *See*: **W133c**

W164 [33] *Cradle Song* (1919) [text, A. L. Ives (1846): "Hush thee, dear child"] [*50 Songs*; *19 Songs*] 2 min.

W165 [34] *La Fède* (1920) [text, Ludovico Ariosto] [*50 Songs*; *19 Songs*] 1 min.

W166 [35] *August* (1920) [text, Folgore da San Geminiano, tr. Dante Gabriel Rossetti: "For August"] [*12 Songs*] 2 min.

W167 [36] *September* (1920) [text, Folgore da San Geminiano, tr. Dante Gabriel Rossetti: "And in September"] [*34 Songs*] 1 min.

W168 [37] *December* (?1913) [text, Folgore da San Geminiano, tr. Dante Gabriel Rossetti: "Last for December"] [der. from **W93**; *34 Songs*] 1 min.

W169 [38] *The Collection* (1920) [text, George Kingsley: "Now help us Lord"] [? der. from lost early anthem; *13 Songs*; *Sacred Songs*] 2 1/2 min.

W170 [39] *Afterglow* (1919) [text, James Fenimore Cooper, Jr.: "At the quiet close of day"] [*3 Songs* (?1919); *34 Songs*] 2 min.

W171 [40] *The Innate* (1916) [text, Ives: "Voices live in every finite being"] [der. from **W55:3**; *3 Songs* (?1919); *19 Songs*] 2 1/2 min.

W172 [41] *"1, 2, 3"* (1921) [text, Ives: "Why doesn't one, two, three"] [der. from **W50**; *4 Songs*] 30 sec.

W173 [42] *Serenity* (1919) [text, John Greenleaf Whittier: "O Sabbath rest of Galilee"] [der. from lost earlier version; *7 Songs*; for voice or unison voices and piano, AMP, ca. 1942] 3 min. *See*: **B813**

Other selected performance

W173a 1940 (March 15): New York; Carnegie Chamber Music Hall; Mary Bell (mezzo-soprano); Julius Hijman (piano) [with **W174**] *See*: **W133a**

W174 [43] *The Things Our Fathers Loved* (1917) [text, Ives: "I think there must be a place in the soul"] [*2 Songs* (1917 or 1918); *14 Songs*] 1 1/2 min. *See*: **W133c**, **W173a**, and **B815-816**

W175 [44] *Watchman* (1913) [text, John Bowring] [der. from **W59:3**; *50 Songs*; *14 Songs*; *Sacred Songs*] 1 1/2 min.

W176 [45] *At the River* (?1916) [text, Robert Lowry: "Shall we gather"] [der. from **W63:3**; *34 Songs*] 1 1/2 min. *See*: **W133c**

W177 [46] *His Exaltation* (1913) [text, Robert Robinson: "For the grandeur"] [der. from **W60:1**; *9 Songs*; *Sacred Songs*] 2 min.

W178 [47] *The Camp Meeting* (1912) [text, Ives, after Charlotte Elliott] [der. from **W3:3**; *13 Songs*; *Sacred Songs*] 4 min.

W179 [48] *Thoreau* (1915) [text, Ives, after Henry David Thoreau: "He grew in those seasons"] [der. from **W65:4**; *34 Songs*] 2 1/2 min.

W180 [49] *In Flanders Fields* (1917) [text, John McCrae] [*14 Songs*] 2 min.

Premiere

W180a 1917 (on or about April 15): New York; Waldorf-Astoria; McCall Lanham (voice); William Lewis (piano) (Mutual manager's luncheon)

W181 1. [50] *He Is There!* (1917) [text, Ives: "Fifteen years ago today"] [dev. into **W99a**; *40 Earlier Songs*] 3 min.
2. *They Are There!* (1942) [text, Ives: "There's a time in every life"] [dev. into **W99b**; *9 Songs*] 3 min.

W182 [51] *Tom Sails Away* (1917) [text, Ives: "Scenes from my childhood"] [*2 Songs* (1917 or 1918); *19 Songs*] 3 min.

W183 [52] *Old Home Day* (?1913) [text, Ives, after Virgil: "Go, my songs!"] [with fife, violin, and flute obbligato; *50 Songs*; *13 Songs*] 4 1/2 min.

W184 [53] *In the Alley* (1896) [text, Ives: "On my way to work"] [*13 Songs*] 1 1/2 min.

W185 [54] *A Son of a Gambolier* (1895) [text, ? after the Irish] [der. from **W68**; *9 Songs*] 4 min.

W186 [55] *Down East* (1919) [text, Ives: "Songs! visions"] [? der. from lost *Down East Overture*; *13 Songs*; *Sacred Songs*] 3 min. *See:* **W133c**

W187 [56] *The Circus Band* (?1894) [text, Ives: "All summer long we boys"] [der. from **W73**; *50 Songs*; *10 Songs*; arr. for unison chorus and small orchestra by George F. Roberts, Peer, 1969] 2 min.

W188 [57] *Mists* (1910) [text, Harmony Twichell Ives: "Low lie the mists"] [*50 Songs*; *34 Songs*; orchestral realization, ed. Kenneth Singleton, Presser, 1976] 2 min.

W189 1. *Wie Melodien zieht es mir* (?1898) [text, Klaus Groth] [*40 Earlier Songs*] 1 min.
2. [58] *Evidence* (1910) [text, Ives: "There comes o'er the valley a shadow"] [*9 Songs*] 1 min.

W190 [59] *Tolerance* (?1909) [text, Rudyard Kipling: "How can I turn from any fire"] [der. from **W30:2**; *34 Songs*] 1 min.

W191 [60] *Autumn* (1907) [text, Harmony Twichell: "Earth rests"] [der. from lost song, ?1902; *9 Songs*] 2 min. *See:* **W133c**

W192 1. *Minnelied* (?1892) [text, Ludwig Hölty: "Holder klingt der Vogelsang] [?*Songbook B*; *40 Earlier Songs*] 1 min.
2. [61] *Nature's Way* (1908) [text, Ives: "When the distant evening bell"] [*50 Songs*; *14 Songs*] 1 min.

W193 1. [?*The Song of the Dead*] (?1898) [text, Rudyard Kipling: "Hear now the song of the dead"] [*40 Earlier Songs*] 2 min.
2. *The Ending Year* (1902) [text, "Frail autumn lights"] [*40 Earlier Songs*] 2 min.
3. [62] *The Waiting Soul* (1908) [text, William Cowper: "Breathe from the gentle south"] [*50 Songs*; *12 Songs*; *Sacred Songs*] [2 min.]

W194 1. *The Sea of Sleep* (1903) [text, "Good night, my care and my sorrow"] [*40 Earlier Songs*] 1 1/2 min.

2. [63] *Those Evening Bells* (1907) [text, Thomas Moore] [*14 Songs*] 1 1/2 min.

W195 [64] *The Cage* (1906) [text, Ives: "A leopard went"] [der. from and dev. into **W27:1**; *14 Songs*] 1 min. *See*: **B809**

W196 [65] *Spring Song* (1907) [text, Harmony Twichell: "Across the hill"] [der. from lost song; *Songbook B*; *50 Songs*; *12 Songs*] 1 1/2 min.

W197 [66] *The Light That Is Felt* (1903) [text, John Greenleaf Whittier] [der. from **W117**; Mercury, 1950] 1 min. *See*: **B780**

W198 [67] *Walking* (1900-?1902) [text, Ives: "A big October morning"] [der. from lost anthem, 1898; *50 Songs*; *7 Songs*] 2 min. *See*: **W133a** and **W133c**

W199 [68] *Ilmenau* (1901) [text, Johann Wolfgang von Goethe: "Über allen Gipfeln ist Ruh'"] [*50 Songs*; Peer, 1952] 1 min.

W200 1. *On Judges' Walk* (1893-?1898) [text, Arthur Symons: "That night on Judges' Walk"] [dev. into **W1:1**; *40 Earlier Songs*] 1 1/2 min.
2. [69] *Rough Wind* (1902) [text, Percy Bysshe Shelley] [*34 Songs*] 1 1/2 min. *See*: **W134a**

W201 1. *Her Eyes* (?1892) [text, "Her eyes are like unfathomable lakes"] [*40 Earlier Songs*] 1 min.
2. [70] *Mirage* (1902) [text, Christina Rossetti [*50 Songs*; *10 Songs*] 1 min.

W202 1. *Widmung* (?1897) [text, Wolfgang Müller: "O danke nicht für diese Lieder"] [*40 Earlier Songs*] 1 min.
2. [71] *There Is a Lane* (1902) [text, Ives] [*50 Songs*; *9 Songs*] 1 min.

W203 1. [72] *Tarrant Moss* (?1898) [text, Rudyard Kipling: "I closed and drew for my love's sake"] [*Songbook A*; *Songbook B*] 1 min. (6 stanzas)
2. *Slugging a Vampire* (1902) [text, Ives: "I closed and drew, but not a gun" [*19 Songs*] 30 sec.

W204 [73] *Harpalus* (1902) [text, Thomas Percy (Reliques): "Oh Harpalus! thus would he say"] [*34 Songs*] 1 min.

W205 [74] *The Children's Hour* (1901) [text, Henry Wadsworth Longfellow: "Between the dark and daylight"] [*50 Songs; 34 Songs*] 2 min. *See:* **W134a**

W206 1. *Frühlingslied* (1896) [text, Heinrich Heine: "Die blaue Frühlingsaugen"] [*40 Earlier Songs*] 1 1/2 min.
2. [75] *I Travelled among Unknown Men* (1901) [text, William Wordsworth] [*50 Songs; 10 Songs*] 1 1/2 min.

W207 [76] *Qu'il m'irait bien* (?1897) [text, ?after Moreau "Ducky" Delano] [*12 Songs*] 2 min.

W208 [77] *Élegie* (1901) [text, Louis Gallet: "O doux printemps d'autrefois"] [*50 Songs; 9 Songs*] 4 min.

W209 [78] *Chanson de Florian* (?1898) [text, Jean Pierre Claris de Florian: "Ah, s'il est dans votre village"] [Mercury, 1950] 2 min. *See:* **B780**

W210 1. *Rosamunde* (?1895) [text, Wilhelmine von Chézy: "Der Vollmond strahlt"] [*40 Earlier Songs*] 1 1/2 min.
2. [79] *Rosamunde* (1898) [text, Bélanger: "J'attends, hélas, dans la douleur"] [*14 Songs*] 1 1/2 min.

W211 [80] *Weil' auf mir* (?1901) [text, Nikolaus Lenau] [*14 Songs*] 2 min.

W212 1. [81] *The Old Mother* (1900) [text, Aasmund Olafsen Vinje, tr. Edmund Lobedanz: "Du alte Mutter"] [second setting; for first setting see **W258**; *13 Songs*] 2 min.
2. *My Dear Old Mother* (1900) [text, Aasmund Olafsen Vinje, tr. Frederick Corder] [*13 Songs*]

W213 [82] *Feldeinsamkeit* (1897) [text, Hermann Allmers: "Ich ruhe still"] [*50 Songs; 19 Songs*] 2 1/2 min.
[82] *In Summer Fields* (1897) [text, Henry Chapman: "Quite still I lie"] [*50 Songs; 19 Songs*] 2 1/2 min.

W214 1. [83] *Ich grolle nicht* (1898) [text, Heinrich Heine] [*34 Songs*] 2 1/2 min.
2. *I'll Not Complain* (1898) [text, John Sullivan Dwight] [*34 Songs*] 2 1/2 min.

W215 1. *Ein Ton* (?1895) [text, Peter Cornelius: "Mir klingt ein Ton"] [*40 Earlier Songs*] 1 min.

2. [84] *From Night of Frost in May* (1899) [text, George Meredith: "There was the lyre"] [*50 Songs; 19 Songs*] 1 min.

W216 [85] *Dreams* (1897) [text, tr. from Baroness Porteous: "When twilight comes"] [*9 Songs*] 3 1/2 min.

W217 [86] *Omens and Oracles* (1899) [text, "Phantoms of the future"] [*10 Songs*] 2 min.

W218 [87] *An Old Flame, or A Retrospect* (1896) [text, Ives: "When dreams enfold me"] [*Songbook C; 13 Songs*] 1 min.

W219 [88] *A Night Song* (1895) [text, Thomas Moore: "The young May moon"] [*13 Songs*, Peer, 1952] 1 min.

W220 1. *Hear my Prayer, O Lord* (?1888) [text, Nahum Tate and Nicholas Brady: "O have mercy, Lord, on me"] [*14 Songs*] 1 min.
2. *When the waves softly sigh* (?1892) [text, ?Ives] [*14 Songs*] 1 min.
3. [89] *A Song for Anything* [text, Ives: "Yale farewell! we must part"] [*14 Songs*] 1 min.

W221 [90] *The World's Highway* (1906) [text, Harmony Twichell: "For long I wandered happily"] [*13 Songs*] 2 min.

W222 [91] *Kären, or Little Kären* [?1895) [text, Parmo Karl Ploug, tr. Clara Kappey: "Do'st remember, child"] [*50 Songs; 12 Songs*] 1 min.

W223 1. *Marie* (1896) [text, Rudolf Gottschall: "Marie, am Fenster sitzest du"] [*40 Earlier Songs*] 2 min.
2. [92] *Marie* (1896) [text, tr. Elizabeth Rücker, with alterations by Ives: "Marie I see thee, fairest one"] [*50 Songs; 14 Songs*] 2 min.

W224 1. *Wiegenlied* (?1900) [text, Des Knaben Wunderhorn: "Guten Abend, gute Nacht"] [*Songbook C; 40 Earlier Songs*] 2 min.
2. [93] *Berceuse* (?1903) [text, Ives: "O'er the mountain towards the west"] [*50 Songs; 13 Songs*] 1 min. *See:* **W133c**

W225 1. *Grace* (?1899) [text, "Sweetheart, sweetheart"] [*40 Earlier Songs*] 2 min.
2. [94] *Where the Eagle* (1906) [text, Monica Peveril Turnbull] [Cos Cob, 1935; *13 Songs; Sacred Songs; 3 Songs*] 2 min.

W226 1. *Sehnsucht* (?1899) [text, Christian Winther, tr. Edmund Lobedanz: "Ich konnte heute nicht schlafen"] [*40 Earlier Songs*] 1 1/2 min.
2. *Rosenzweig* (?1899) [text, Karl Stieler: "Wohl manchen Rosenzweig"] [*40 Earlier Songs*] 2 min.
3. [95] *Allegro* (1900) [text, Ives: "By morning's brightest beams"] [*13 Songs*] 2 min.

W227 [96] *[Romanzo di Central Park]* (1900) [text, Leigh Hunt: "Grove, rove, night, delight"] [*14 Songs*] 2 min.

W228 1. *Die Lotosblume* (?1895) [text, Heinrich Heine] [revised ?1899; *Songbook C*; *50 Songs*; *34 Songs*] 2 min.
2. [97] *The South Wind* (1908) [text, Harmony Twichell: "When gently blows"] [*50 Songs*; *34 Songs*] 2 min.

W229 [98] *Naught That Country Needeth* (1898-1899) [text, Henry Alford] [from **W89:2**; *14 Songs*; *Sacred Songs*] 4 min.

W230 [99] *Forward into Light* (1898-1899) [text, Henry Alford] [from **W89:6**; *10 Songs*; *Sacred Songs*] 4 min.

W231 [100] *A Christmas Carol* (1894) [text, Ives: "Little star of Bethlehem"] [*50 Songs*; *19 Songs*] 2 min.

W232 [101] *My Native Land, or Un rêve* (?1895) [text, Heinrich Heine] [first setting, see **W271**; *12 Songs*] 1 min.

W233 [102] *Memories, A, Very Pleasant, B, Rather Sad* (1897) text, Ives: "We're sitting" *10 Songs* 2 1/2 min.

W234 [103] *The White Gulls* (?1921) [text, Russian, tr. Maurice Morris] [*50 Songs*; *34 Songs*] 2 1/2 min. *See*: **W150a**

W235 [104] *Two Little Flowers* (?1921) [text, Harmony Twichell Ives: "On sunny days"] [*50 Songs*; *19 Songs*; *3 Songs*] 1 min. *See*: **W133c**

W236 [105] *West London* (1921) [text, Matthew Arnold: "Crouch'd on the pavement"] [der. from **W16**; *50 Songs*; *34 Songs*] 3 1/2 min.

W237 [106] *From "Amphion"* (1896) [text, Alfred Lord Tennyson: "The mountain stirred its bushy crown"] [*50 Songs*; *10 Songs*] 1 min.

W238 1. *In My Beloved's Eyes* (?1895) [text, W. M. Chauvenet: "I looked into the midnight deep"] [*40 Earlier Songs*] 1 min.

2. [107] *A Night Thought* (?1903) [text, Thomas Moore: "How oft a cloud"] [*50 Songs; 34 Songs]* 1 min.

W239 [108] *Songs My Mother Taught Me* (1895) [text: Adolf Heyduk, tr. Natalia Macfarren] dev. into **W48**; *50 Songs; 14 Songs* 2 1/2 min.

W240 [109] *Waltz* (?1895) [text, Ives: "Round and round the old dance ground"] [*12 Songs]* 2 min.

W241 [110] *The World's Wanderers* (1895) [text, Percy Bysshe Shelley: "Tell me, star"] [*50 Songs; 10 Songs]* 2 min.

W242 1. *Canon* (1893) [text, "Not only in my lady's eyes"] [*40 Earlier Songs]* 2 min.
2. [111] *Canon* (?1894) [text, Thomas Moore: "Oh the days are gone"] [*19 Songs]* 1 1/2 min.

W243 [112] *To Edith* (1919) [text, Harmony Twichell Ives: "So like a flower"] [der. from lost song, 1892; *3 Songs* (?1919); *50 Songs; 10 Songs]* 1 1/2 min.

W244 [113] *When Stars Are in the Quiet Skies* (?1898) [text, Edward George Bulwer-Lytton] [*50 Songs; 34 Songs]* 2 min.

W245 [114] *Slow March* (?1887) [text, Lyman Brewster and other members of Ives's family] [revised 1921; *10 Songs]* 2 min.

Songs Not Included in 114 Songs

W246 *At Parting* (?1889) [text, Frederic Peterson: "The sweetest flow'r that blows"] [*34 Songs]* 1 min.

W247 *Abide with Me* (?1890) [text, Henry Francis Lyte] [accompaniment revised, ?1898-1899; *13 Songs; Sacred Songs]* 4 min.

Premiere

W247a 1890 (May 25): Danbury, CT: Baptist Church; William Oakley (voice)

W248 *Far From My Heav'nly Home* (?1890) [text, Henry Francis Lyte] [*11 Songs and 2 Harmonizations]* 4 min.

W249 *Rock of Ages* (?1891) [text, Augustus Montague Toplady: "Rock of ages, cleft for me"] [organ accompaniment; *11 Songs and 2 Harmonizations*] 2 1/2 min.

W250 *My Lou Jeninne* (?1891) [text, "Has she need of monarch's swaying wand"] [*40 Earlier Songs*] 2 min.

W251 *In Autumn* (?1892) [text, "The skies seemed true above thee"] [*Songbook C*; *40 Earlier Songs*] 1 min.

W252 *A Perfect Day* (?1892) [text, "Bland air and leagues of immemorial blue"] [*Songbook C*; *40 Earlier Songs*] 2 min.

W253 *Through Night and Day* (?1892) [text, John Monsell, adapted by Ives: "I dream of thee, my love"] [der. from **W103**; *Songbook C*; *40 Earlier Songs*] 2 1/2 min.

W254 *[Friendship]* (1892) [text, "All love that has not friendship"] [*40 Earlier Songs*] 3 min.

W255 *There Is a Certain Garden* (1893) [text?] [*11 Songs and 2 Harmonizations*] 2 min.

W256 *Song for Harvest Season* (1893) [text, Greville Phillimore: "Summer ended"] [organ accompaniment or trumpet, trombone, and tuba; *34 Songs*] 1 min.

W257 *Song* (?1893) [text, Hartley Coleridge: "She is not fair to outward view"] [*40 Earlier Songs*]

W258 *The Old Mother* (?1894) [text, Aasmund Olafsen Vinje, tr. Frederick Corder: "Oh dearest mother"] [first setting, see **W212**; *Songbook C*] 2 1/2 min.

W259 *The All-enduring* (1896) [text, "Man passes"] [der. from and dev. into lost TTBB version; *Songbook B*; *40 Earlier Songs*] 9 min.

W260 *William Will* (1896) [text, Susan Benedict Hill: "What we want is honest money"] [Willis Woodward & Co., 1896; *40 Earlier Songs*] 7 min.

W261 *A Scotch Lullaby* (1896) [text, Charles Edmund Merrill, Jr.: "Blaw! skirlin' win'"] [*Yale Courant* 33 (December Third Week, 1896): 125-127; *11 Songs and 2 Harmonizations*] 2 min.

W262 *God Bless and Keep Thee* (?1897) [text, "I know not if thy love be as a flower"] [*11 Songs and 2 Harmonizations*] 2 min.

W263 *Her Gown Was of Vermilion Silk* (1897) [*40 Earlier Songs*] 2 min.

W264 1. *No More* (1897) [text, William Winter: "They walked beside the summer sea"] [*11 Songs and 2 Harmonizations*] 3 1/2 min.
2. *Hymn of Trust* (?1898) [text, Oliver Wendell Holmes: "[O] Love divine"[[*40 Earlier Songs*] 3 1/2 min.

W265 *The Love Song of Har Dyal* (?1898) [text, Rudyard Kipling: "Alone upon the housetops"] [*Songbook A; Songbook B; 40 Earlier Songs*] 2 1/2 min.

W266 1. [? *The Song of the Dead*] (?1898) [text, Rudyard Kipling: "Hear now the song of the dead"] [? *Songbook A; 40 Earlier Songs*]
2. *The Ending Year* (1902) [text, "Frail autumn lights"] [*40 Earlier Songs*]

W267 *Because of You* (1898) [text, "What have you done for me, dear one"] [*40 Earlier Songs*] 2 min.

W268 *I Knew and Loved a Maid* (?1898) [*40 Earlier Songs*] 2 min.

W269 *Flag Song* (1898) [text, Henry Strong Durand: "Accept you these emblems"] [der. from a lost song; Peer, 1968] 2 min.

W270 *Because Thou Art* (?1899) [text, "My life has grown so dear to me"] [*40 Earlier Songs*] 2 min.

W271 *My Native Land* (?1901) [text, tr. of Heinrich Heine] [second setting; *See:* **W232**; *Songbook C; 40 Earlier Songs*] 2 min.

W272 *Pictures* (1906) [text, Monica Peveril Turnbull: "The ripe corn bends low"] [*Songbook B; 11 Songs and 2 Harmonizations*] 3 min.

W273 *Soliloquy or a Study in 7ths and Other Things* (1907) [text, Ives: "When a man is sitting before the fire"] [*34 Songs*] 1 min.

W274 *Runaway Horse on Main Street* (?1909) [text, Ives: "So long, Harris"] [incomplete; der. from **W40**; dev. into **W141**] 45 sec.

W275 *A Farewell to Land* (1909) [text, Lord Byron: "Adieu, adieu! my native shore"] [*19 Songs*] 2 min.

W276 *Requiem* (1911) [text, Robert Louis Stevenson: "Under the wide and starry sky"] [*19 Songs*] 3 min.

W277 *Vote for Names* (1912) [text, Ives] [unfinished; for voice or unison voices and three pianos, Peer, 1968; ed. Nachum Schoffman]. *See*: **B817**.

W278 *General William Booth Enters into Heaven* (1914) [text, Vachel Lindsay: "Booth led boldly with his big bass drum"] [der. from **W96**; *19 Songs*; ed. Kenneth Singleton, Presser, under consideration] 6 min. *See*: **W133c**

W279 *On the Antipodes* (1915-1923) [text, Ives: "Nature's relentless, nature is kind"] [*19 Songs*] 3 min. *See*: **B812**

W280 *Aeschylus and Sophocles* (1922) [text, Walter Savage Landor: "We also have our pest"] [der. from **W42**; *19 Songs*] 4 min.

W281 *The One Way* (?1923) [text, Ives: "Here are things you've heard before"] [*11 Songs and 2 Harmonizations*] 3 min.

W282 *Peaks* (?1923) [text, Henry Bellamann: "Quiet faces that look in faith"] [*11 Songs and 2 Harmonizations*] 1 1/2 min.

W283 *Yellow Leaves* (?1923) [text, Henry Bellamann: "Heart-shaped yellow leaves"] [*11 Songs and 2 Harmonizations*] 2 min.

W284 *A Sea Dirge* (1925) [text, William Shakespeare (*The Tempest*): "Full fathom five thy father lies"] [*11 Songs and 2 Harmonizations*] 2 1/2 min.

W285 *Sunrise* (1926) [text, Ives: "A light low in the east"] [with instrumental (violin) obbligato; der. from **W42**; ed. John Kirkpatrick, Peters, 1977] 4 min. *See*: **B814**

Abbreviations of Publishers

AMP	Associated Music Publishers, Inc.
Arrow	Arrow Music Press
Kalmus	Edwin F. Kalmus
Mercury	Mercury Music
Merion	Merion Music
MJQ	MJQ Music, Inc.
Peer	Peer International Corp.
Peters	C. F. Peters

Presser   Theodore Presser Company
Southern   Southern Music Publishing Company

Other Abbreviations

der. from = derived from
dev. into = developed into

Discography

This list includes only those commercially-produced discs listed in
Schwann 39, no. 3 (Summer 1987): C132-C133. For a comprehensive
and detailed listing of all Ives recordings issued before December 31,
1971 see Richard Warren, *Charles E. Ives: Discography* (**B17**). For a
listing of Ives recordings issued between 1972 and 1979 and available as
of June 1980 see Carol J. Oja, *American Music Recordings: A Discography
of 20th-Century U.S. Composers*, pp. 171-180 (**B16**).

See references (e.g., *See*: **B150**) identify recording reviews located in the
BIBLIOGRAPHY section.

ORCHESTRAL AND BAND

Central Park in the Dark (W28:2)

D1   Leonard Bernstein, conductor; New York Philharmonic (CBS MP-
38777; also avaliable on cassette tape) [with *Decoration Day*;
Third Symphony; *The Unanswered Question*] *See*: **B150**

D2   Seiji Ozawa, conductor; Michael Tilson Thomas, conductor;
Boston Symphony; Tanglewood Festival Chorus (Deutsche
Grammophon DG 410933-1 GC) [with *Fourth Symphony* (Ozawa);
Three Places in New England (Thomas)] *See*: **B414**, **B428**, and
B487

D3   William Strickland, conductor; Members of the Oslo Philharmonic
Orchestra (Composers Recordings Inc. CRI SD-163) [with
Hallowe'en; *The Pond*; *Washington's Birthday*] *See*: **B97** and
B413

Circus Band March (W187) (arr. Farberman)
See: D11 (Farberman)

Country Band March (W23)

D4   Marice Stith, conductor; Cornell University Wind Ensemble and
Symphonic Band; Cornell University (CUWE-17) [with *March
Omega Lambda Chi*; *Overture and March 1776*; *They Are There*]

Decoration Day (see also: Symphony "Holidays") **(W4:2)**
See: **D1** (Bernstein)

The Fourth of July (see also: Symphony "Holidays") **(W4:3)**

D5   William Strickland, conductor; Goteborg Symphony (Composers Recordings Inc. CRI-180) See: **B97**

Fourth Symphony **(W7)**
See: *Symphonies Nos. 1-4* (complete);
D13 (Stokowski) and **D2** (Ozawa)

D6   José Serebrier, conductor; London Philharmonic Orchestra; The John Alldis Choir (Chandos ABR-1118; digitally remastered) See: **B177**, **B423**, **B527**, **B529-530**, and **B537**

D7   Leopold Stokowski, conductor; David Katz and José Serebrier, associate conductors; American Symphony Orchestra; Members of the Schola Cantorum of New York, Hugh Ross, director (CBS MS-6775; simulated stereo) See: **B419**, **B423**, **B426**, **B504**, **B506**, **B509**, **B523**, and **B537**

March Inter-Collegiate **(W38)**

D8   Gunther Schuller, conductor; The Incredible Columbia All-Star Band (CBS M-33513; also available on cassette tape) [with *March Omega Lambda Chi*]

D9   Marice Stith, conductor; Cornell University Wind Ensemble (Cornell University 2)

March Omega Lambda Chi **(W70)**
See: **D4** (Stith) and **D8** (Schuller)

Orchestral Set No. 2 **(W6)**

D10   Michael Tilson Thomas, conductor; Concertgebouw Orchestra (digital [CBS IM-37823]; compact disc [MK-37823]; cassette tape [IMT-37823]) [with *Third Symphony*] See: **B433**

Over the Pavements **(W25)**

D11   Harold Farberman, conductor; The Boston Chamber Ensemble (Cambridge CRM-1804) See: **B92**, **B97**, and **B532**

[with Farberman (**ORCHESTRAL AND BAND**): *The Pond (Remembrance)*; *The Rainbow (So May It Be)*; *Set No. 2, no. 1 (Largo: The Indians)*; *Tone Roads Nos. 1 and 3*; with Farberman (*See*: **CHAMBER MUSIC**): *Hallowe'en*; *Largo Cantabile (Hymn)*; with Luise Vosgerchian (piano) (*See*: **KEYBOARD**): *Three-Page Sonata*; with Corinne Curry (soprano) and Luise Vosgerchian (piano) (*See: SONGS* [8]): *Ann Street*; *The Cage*; *A Farewell to Land*; *General William Booth Enters Into Heaven*; *Ich grolle nicht*; *"1,2,3"*, *"Nov. 2, 1920" (An Election)*; *Religion*]

Overture and March 1776 **(W22)**
See: **D4** (Stith)

The Pond (Remembrance) **(W26)**
See: **D3** (Strickland) and **D11** (Farberman)

The Rainbow (So May It Be) **(W33)**
See: **D11** (Farberman)

Robert Browning Overture **(W15)**

D12   Harold Farberman, conductor; Royal Philharmonic Orchestra (Vanguard 10013; cassette tape [C-10013]) [with *The Circus Band March*; *Set for Theatre or Chamber Orchestra*; *The Unanswered Question*] *See*: **B150**

D13   Leopold Stokowski, conductor; American Symphony Orchestra; (CBS MP-38890; also available on cassette tape) [with *Fourth Symphony*] *See*: **B150, B417**

D14   William Strickland, conductor; Polish National Radio Orchestra; (Composers Recordings, Inc., CRI S-196) *See*: **B116** and **B543**

Second Symphony **(W2)**
See: Symphonies (complete)

D15   Michael Tilson Thomas, conductor; Concertgebouw Orchestra (CBS IM-37300 [digital]; also available on cassette tape) *See*: **B434**

Set for Theatre or Chamber Orchestra **(W27)**
(In the Cage, In the Inn, In the Night)
See: **D12** (Farberman)

D16   ["In the Night"] Nicholas Slonimsky, conductor; The Pan American
Chamber Orchestra (Orion ORD-7150 [monaural only]) [with
"Barn Dance" from *Washington's Birthday*]

Set No. 2, no. 1 **(W30:1)**
Largo (The Indians)
See: **D11** (Farberman)

Set No. 3, no. 3 **(W36:1)**
Adagio Sostenuto (At Sea)
See: **D11** (Farberman)

Symphonies Nos. 1-4 (complete) **(W1-3 *and* W7)**
See also: Second, Third, and *Fourth Symphony*

D17   Eugene Ormandy, Philadelphia Orchestra (*First*); Leonard
Bernstein, New York Philharmonic (*Second* and *Third*) Leopold
Stokowski, American Symphony Orchestra (*Fourth*), conductors
(3-CBS D3S-783) *See:* **B117, B150, B452-455,** and **B457**

Symphony "Holidays" (complete) **(W4)**
*See also: Washington's Birthday, Decoration Day,
The Fourth of July,* and *Thanksgiving*

D18   Donald Johanos, conductor; Dallas Symphony Orchestra
(Turnabout 34146; cassette tape [CT-4146]) *See:* **B114, B150,**
and **B474**

D19   William Strickland, conductor; Imperial Philharmonic of Tokyo
(*Washington's Birthday*); Finnish Radio Symphony Orchestra
(*Decoration Day*); Goteborg Symphony Orchestra (*The Fourth of
July*); Iceland Symphony Orchestra (*Thanksgiving*); (Composers
Recordings Inc. CRI S-190 [simulated stereo]) *See:* **B103**

Thanksgiving (see also *Symphony "Holidays"*) **(W4:4)**

D20   William Strickland, conductor; Imperial Philharmonic of Tokyo
(Composers Recordings Inc. CRI SD-177) *See:* **B97**

They Are There **(W181:2)** *(arr.)*
See: **D4** (Stith)

Third Orchestral Set: Overture **(W8)**

D21 Keith Clark, conductor; Pacific Symphony; (Andante AD-72402; compact disc VCD-47211 [distributed by Varèse/Sarabande])

Third Symphony **(W3)**
See: Symphonies (complete); **D1** (Bernstein); **D10** (Thomas)

D22 Dennis Russell Davies, conductor; St. Paul Chamber Orchestra (Pro PAD-149 [digital]; compact disc [CDD-149]; both available on cassette tape) *See:* **B434**

D23 Neville Marriner, conductor; The Academy of St. Martin-in-the-Fields (Argo ZRG 845)

Three Places in New England **(W5)**
See: **D2** (Thomas)

D24 Dennis Russell Davies, conductor; St. Paul Chamber Orchestra (Pro PAD-140 [digital]) *See:* **B493**

D25 Walter Hendl, conductor; Vienna Symphony Orchestra (Desto 6403E) *See:* **B64** and **B103**

D26 Eugene Ormandy, conductor; Philadelphia Orchestra (CBS MS-6684) *See:* **B103**, **B150**, and **B419**

Tone Roads Nos. 1 and 3 **(W35)**
See: **D11** (Farberman)

The Unanswered Question **(W28:1)**
See: **D12** (Farberman); **D1** (Bernstein)

D27 Lukas Foss, conductor; Milwaukee Symphony (Pro PAD-102; compact disc [CDD-102])

Washington's Birthday **(W4:1)**
See: Symphony "Holidays"; **D3** (Strickland); **D16** (Slonimsky)
Variations on "America" (arr. William Schuman)
See also: **Keyboard**

D28 Eugene Ormandy, conductor; Philadelphia Orchestra (CBS MS-7289)

D29   Robert Whitney, conductor; Louisville Orchestra (Louisville First Lou. 651 [monaural only])

CHAMBER

Complete Chamber Music Vol. I

D30   Frank Glazer (piano); Millard Taylor (violin); John Celentano (violin); Francis Tursi (viola); Alan Harris (cello); Stanley Hasty (clarinet); Artur Balsam (piano) (3-Vox SVBX-564)

Sonatas for Violin and Piano, Nos. 1-4; Trio for Piano, Violin and Cello; Largo for Violin and Piano; Largo Risoluto Nos. 1 and 2; Hallowe'en; In Re Con Moto Et Al; Adagio Cantabile (The Innate); Three Quarter-Tone Pieces; Largo for Clarinet, Violin and Piano.

Chromâtimelôdtune **(W57)**

D31   American Brass Quintet (realization by Gerard Schwarz, with the assistance of Keith Brion); John Eckert (trumpet); Edward Birdwell (French horn); Gerard Schwarz (trumpet, cornet, and flugelhorn); Arnold Fromme (tenor trombone), Robert Biddlecome (bass trombone) [with drum and cymbal] [with Jan DeGaetani in *Song for Harvest Season*] (Nonesuch H-71222) *See:* **B552**

Decoration Day **(W61)**
See: **D44** *(Kirkpatrick)*

From the Steeples **(W45)**
[*See:* **D31** (American Brass Quintet)]

D32   Lukas Foss, conductor; Buffalo Philharmonic (Turnabout 34398) *See:* **B150**

Hallowe'en **(W51)**
See: **D3** (Strickland); **D11** (Farberman)

Largo for Violin, Clarinet, and Piano **(W46)**
See: **D30** (Hasty, Taylor, and Glazer)

D33   Compinsky Ensemble; Kalman Bloch (clarinet); Manuel Compinsky (violin); Sara Compinsky (piano) (Townhall 2-Town S-3 [distributed by Sheffield Lab])

D34 Roy D'Antonio (clarinet); Myron Sandler (violin); Delores Stevens (piano) (Laurel LR-103 [distributed by Consortium])

Largo for Violin and Piano
(arr. of *Largo for Violin, Clarinet, and Piano*)
See: Largo for Violin, Clarinet, and Piano;
D30 (Hasty, Taylor, and Glazer)

D35 Paul Zukofsky (violin); Gilbert Kalish (piano) (2-Nonesuch HB-73025) [with *Sonatas for Violin and Piano Nos. 1-4*] *See*: **B177**, **B623**, and **B631**

Pre-First Violin Sonata **(W58)**

D36 Eugene Gratovich (violin); George Flynn (piano) (Finnadar 90023-1)

Quartets **(W41** and **W43)**

D37 Concord Quartet (Nos. 1 and 2): Mark Sokol (violin); Andrew Jennings (violin); John Kochanowski (viola); Norman Fischer (cello) (Nonesuch H-71306)

D38 Juilliard Quartet (Nos. 1 and 2): Robert Mann (violin); Earl Carlyss (violin); Raphael Hillyer (viola); Claus Adam (cello) (CBS MP-39753 [also available on cassette tape]) *See*: **B114**, **B150**, and **B592-593**

D39 Walden Quartet (No. 2): Homer Schmitt (violin); Bernard Goodman (violin); Eugene Weigel (viola); Robert Swenson (cello) (Folkways 3369 [monaural only]) *See*: **B64**, **B114**, and **B592-593**

Scherzo for String Quartet **(W55:2)**

D40 Kohon String Quartet: Harold Kohon (violin); Raymond Kunicki (violin); Bernard Zaslav (viola); Aaron Shapinsky (cello) (3-Vox SVBX-5305)

Set No. 3, no. 1 **(W36:1)**
Adagio Sostenuto (At Sea)

D41 James Ostryniec (oboe); Paul Hoffman (piano); Alard Quartet: Joanne Zagst (violin); Donald Hopkins (violin); Raymond Page (viola); Leonard Feldman (cello) (Composers Recordings Inc. CRI SD-501)

Sonatas for Violin and Piano **(W59-63)**
See: **D30** (Taylor and Glazer);
D35 (Zukofsky and Kalish)

D42   Jaime Laredo (violin); Ann Schein (piano) (No. 4) (Desto DC-6439)

D43   Myron Sandler (violin); Lowndes Maury (piano) (No. 2) (Crystal S-631)

D44   Daniel Stepner (violin); John Kirkpatrick (piano) (Nos. 1-5) (Musicmasters MM 20056/7)   *See:* **B631-632**

D45   Joseph Szigeti (violin); Andor Foldes (piano) (No. 4) (Composers Recordings Inc. S-390E). *See also:* **SONGS**.

D46   Paul Zukofsky (violin); Gilbert Kalish (piano) (Nos. 1-4) (2-Folkways 3346-7 [monaural only])

Song for Harvest Season **(W256)**
See: **D31** Jan DeGaetani and the American Brass Quintet

KEYBOARD

Complete Works for Solo Piano

D47   Nina Deutsch (3-Vox SVBX 5482) *See:* **B643**
The Bells of Yale (arr. Deutsch); *Five Takeoffs* [*The Seen and Unseen*]; *First Piano Sonata; Four Emerson Transcriptions; Second Piano Sonata ("Concord" Sonata); Three-Page Sonata; Variations on "America"* (arr. Deutsch); *Waltz-Rondo.*

Complete Piano Music

D48   Alan Mandel (4-Desto DST 6458-6461) *See:* **B118, B150, B635-637,** and **B642**
Allegretto (Invention); Anthem-Processional; Baseball Take-Off; Celestial Railroad; First Piano Sonata; Five Takeoffs [*The Seen and Unseen, Rough and Ready, Song Without (Good) Words, Scene Episode, Bad Resolutions and Good One*]; *March in G and D; Storm and Distress; Second Piano Sonata ("Concord" Sonata); Studies Nos. 2, 5-8, 9* [*The Anti-Abolitionist Riots*]*, 15, 18* [23 in Kirkpatrick Catalogue (**B7**)]*, 20, 21* [*Some Southpaw Pitching*]*, and 22; Three-Page Sonata; Varied Air and Variations (6 Protests); Waltz-Rondo.*

Allegretto (Invention)
See: **D48** (Mandel)

Anthem-Processional
See: **D48** (Mandel)

Baseball Takeoff
See: **D48** (Mandel)

The Bells of Yale **(W130)** (arr. Deutsch)
See: **D47** (Deutsch)

The Celestial Railroad
See: **D48** (Mandel)

First Piano Sonata **(W64)**
See: **D47** (Deutsch); **D48** (Mandel)

D49 John Cobb (Spectrum SR-155)

D50 Herbert Henck (Wergo 60101; compact disc [60-10150])

D51 Noel Lee (Nonesuch H-71169) *See:* **B114**

D52 William Masselos (Odyssey 32160059 [monaural only]) *See:* **B114**

D53 James Sykes ["In the Inn"] (Folkways 3348 [monaural only]) [with *Study No. 9 (Anti-Abolitionist Riots)*; *Study No. 21 (Some Southpaw Pitching)*; *Study No. 22; The Varied Air with Protests*] *See:* **B103** and **B634**

Five Takeoffs **(W77)**
See: **D47** (Deutsch); **D48** (Mandel)

Four Emerson Transcriptions **(W80)**
See: **D47** (Deutsch)

March in G & D **(W71)**
See: **D47** (Deutsch); **D48** (Mandel)

Second Piano Sonata ("Concord" Sonata) **(W65)**
See: **D47** (Deutsch); **D48** (Mandel)

D54 Gilbert Kalish (piano); Samuel Baron (flute); John Graham (viola) (Nonesuch H-71337) *See:* **B698-699** and **B708**

D55   Yvar Mikhashoff (piano) (Spectrum 12)

D56   George Pappastravrou (piano); Bonnie Lichter (flute) (Composers Recordings Inc. CRI-150) *See:* **B680-683**

D57   Roger Shields (piano) ["The Alcotts"] (3-Vox SVBX-5303) [with *Study No. 9 (The Anti-Abolitionish Riots)*; *Study No. 21 (Some Southpaw Pitching)*]

Storm and Distress
See: **D48** (Mandel)

Studies Nos. 2, 5-8, 15, and 18 **(W77)**
[23 in Kirkpatrick *Catalogue* **(B7)**]
See: **D48** (Mandel)

Study No. 9 (The Anti-Abolitionist Riots) **(W77)**
See: **D48** (Mandel); **D53** (Sykes); **D57** (Shields)

D58   Herbert Henck (Wergo 60112) [with *Study No. 20*; *Study No. 21 (Some Southpaw Pitching)*; *Study No. 22*; *Three-page Sonata*; *Three Quarter-Tone Pieces for Two Pianos* (with Deborah Richards); *Varied Air and Variations*; *Waltz-Rondo*]

Study No. 20 **(W77)**
See: **D48** (Mandel); **D58** (Henck)

Study No. 21 (Some Southpaw Pitching) **(W77)**
See: **D48** (Mandel); **D53** (Sykes);
D57 (Shields); **D58** (Henck)

Study No. 22 **(W77)**
See: **D48** (Mandel); **D53** (Sykes); **D58** (Henck)

Three-Page Sonata **(W76)**
See: **D11** (Vosgerchian); **D47** (Deutsch);
D48 (Mandel); **D53** (Sykes); **D58** (Henck)

Three Quarter-Tone Pieces for Two Pianos **(W84)**
See: **D30** (Balsam and Glazer); **D58** (Henck and Richards)

Variations on America **(W86)** (arr. Deutsch)
See: **Orchestral and Band**; **D47** (Deutsch)

Varied Air and Variations **(W81)**
See: **D48** (Mandel); **D53** (Sykes); **D58** (Henck)

Waltz-Rondo **(W79)**
See: **D47** (Deutsch); **D48** (Mandel); **D58** (Henck)

CHORAL AND PARTSONGS

The Celestial Country **(W89)**

D59   Hazel Holt (soprano); Alfreda Hodgson (alto); John Elwes (tenor);
John Nobel (baritone); London Symphony Orchestra and Schütz
Choir, Harold Farberman, conductor (Composers Recordings Inc.
CRI SD-314)

A Christmas Carol (arrangement)
See: **SONGS**

D60   William Noll, director; Choral Guild of Atlanta (Press P-5002;
casette tape [P-5402])

Psalm 67 **(W114)**

D61   Lukas Foss, director; Milwaukee Symphony; Wisconsin
Conservatory Chorus (Pro PAD-168 [digital]); also available on
cassette tape)

SONGS
See: **D11** (Curry and Vosgerchian);
D31 (Jan DeGaetani and the American Brass Quintet;
D45 (Radiana Pazmor [soprano]; Genievieve Pitot [piano]; Mordecai
Bauman [baritone]; Albert Hirsch [piano]
D60 (Choral Guild of Atlanta)

D62   Roberta Alexander (soprano); Tan Crone (piano) (Etcetera ETC
1020 [digital]); compact disc [KTC-1020] [both available on
cassette tape]) [26 songs]

D63   Jan DeGaetani (mezzo-soprano); Gilbert Kalish (piano) (Nonesuch
H-71325 [simulated stereo]) [17 songs] [DeGaetani[1]] *See:* **B800-
801** and **B804**

D64   Jan DeGaetani (mezzo-soprano); Gilbert Kalish (piano) (Bridge
BDG 2002 [simulated stereo] [9 songs] [DeGaetani[2]]

D65 William Parker (baritone); Dalton Baldwin (piano) (New World Records 300) [9 songs]

D66 Ted Puffer (tenor); James Tenney and Philip Corner (pianos) (Folkways Records FM 3344 and FM 3345 [monaural only]) [33 songs] [Puffer[1] and Puffer[2]] *See:* **B108** and **B792**

D67 Carolyn Watkinson (mezzo-soprano); Tan Crone (piano) (Etcetera ETC 1007 [simulated stereo]; also available on cassette tape) [5 songs]

114 SONGS

1. *Majority* (DeGaetani[1]; Puffer[2])
2. *Evening* (Alexander; Bauman; Puffer[2])
5. *Immortality* (Alexander; Puffer[2])
10. *Charlie Rutlage* (Alexander; Bauman; Puffer[2])
13. *Resolution* (Bauman)
14. *The Indians* (DeGaetani[1]; Puffer[1])
15. *The Housatonic at Stockbridge* (Alexander; DeGaetani[1])
16. *Religion* (Curry)
17. *Grantchester* (Puffer[2]; Watkinson)
19. *The Greatest Man* (Alexander; Bauman)
22. *"Nov. 2, 1920"* (Curry; Puffer[2])
23. *Maple Leaves* (Alexander; Puffer[2])
25. *Ann Street* (Bauman; Curry; DeGaetani[1]; Puffer[2])
26. *Like a Sick Eagle* (Alexander; DeGaetani[1]; Puffer[1])
27. *From "The Swimmers"* (Puffer[1])
28. *On the Counter* (Alexander)
29. *The See'r* (Alexander; DeGaetani[2])
30.   *From "Paracelsus"* (DeGaetani[1]; Puffer[1])
31. *Walt Whitman* (Puffer[2])
32. *The Side Show* (Alexander; De Gaetani[2]; Puffer[2]; Watkinson)
39. *Afterglow* (De Gaetani[2]; Puffer[2])
40. *The Innate* (DeGaetani[1])
41. *"1,2,3"* (Alexander; Curry; Puffer[2])
42. *Serenity* (Alexander; DeGaetani[1], Puffer[2])
43. *The Things Our Fathers Loved* (DeGaetani[1])
44. *Watchman* (Parker)
45. *At the River* (DeGaetani[1]; Parker)
46. *His Exaltation* (Parker)
47. *The Camp-Meeting* (Parker)
48. *Thoreau* (DeGaetani[1])
51. *Tom Sails Away* (Alexander; DeGaetani[2]; Puffer[2])
55. *Down East* (Alexander; DeGaetani[2])

57. *Mists* (Puffer[1])
60. *Autumn* (Alexander)
64. *The Cage* (Alexander; DeGaetani[1]; Puffer[1]; Watkinson)
65. *Spring Song* (Alexander)
67. *Walking* (Puffer[1]; Watkinson)
72. *Tarrant Moss (Slugging a Vampire)* (Alexander)
74. *The Children's Hour* (Puffer[1])
76. *Qui'il m'irait bien* (Parker)
77. *Elégie* (Parker)
78. *Chanson de Florian* (Parker)
79. *Rosamunde* (Parker)
83. *Ich grolle nicht* (Curry)
85. *Dreams* (Alexander)
93. *Berceuse* (Alexander)
96. *Romanzo di Central Park* (Alexander)
100. *A Christmas Carol* (DeGaetani[1]; Puffer[1])
102. *Memories* (Alexander; DeGaetani[1])
103. *The White Gulls* (DeGaetani[2]; Puffer[2])
104. *Two Little Flowers* (Alexander; Bauman; DeGaetani[2]; Puffer[2])
105. *West London* (DeGaetani[2]; Puffer[1])
108. *Songs My Mother Taught Me* (Alexander; DeGaetani[2])
111. *Canon* (Puffer[1])
114. *Slow March* (Alexander)

Songs Not Published in 114 Songs

A Farewell to Land (Curry; DeGaetani[1]; Puffer[2])
General William Booth Enters into Heaven (Curry; Pazmor; Puffer[1])
In the Mornin' (DeGaetani[1])
On the Antipodes (Puffer[2])
Song For Harvest Season (DeGaetani, **D31**)
Requiem (Puffer[1])
Sunrise (Parker)

Bibliography

COLLECTIONS, CATALOGUES, BIBLIOGRAPHIES, AND DISCOGRAPHIES

Collections

B1   New Haven. Ives Collection. John Herrick Jackson Music Library. Yale University. P.O. Box 2104A. Yale Station. New Haven, CT 06520-7440.

Comprehensive collection of Ives's Manuscripts and Papers, including the complete extant sketch and autograph scores, and Ives's literary writings, correspondence, scrapbooks, diaries, photographs, programs, writings about Ives, and Ives's collection of music by others. Nearly all items have been microfilmed. *See:* **B7** and **B9**

B2   New York. Music Division. The New York Public Library at Lincoln Center. 111 Amsterdam Avenue at 65th Street. New York, New York 10023.

Uncatalogued microfilm of all music manuscripts in the Ives Collection at Yale University (**B1**) and a large collection of photostats. Among the catalogued items in the collection are the following:

Chamber Music. Pieces for various groups of instruments. 9 volumes. Mostly reproduced from manuscript copy; Vol. 8 and most of Vol. 6 from autograph; one composition from Vol. 4 and four in Vol. 7 from printed edition.
Vol. 1. *Tone Roads Nos. 1 and 3*; *Processional "Let There Be Light"*; *From the Steeples and the Mountains*; *Largo Risoluto No. 1*; *Like a Sick Eagle*; *Scherzo "All the Way Around and Back.*
Vol. 2. *Scherzo (Over the Pavements)*; *Hallowe'en*; *The Indians.*
Vol. 3. *Largo Risoluto No. 2*; *The Pond*; *An Etude* [strings and piano]; *Chorale. Allegro* [quarter-tone piano].
Vol. 4. *Largo Cantabile*; *Scherzo and Adagio Cantabile* [strings, cello solo, and piano]; *The Se'er*; *The Last Reader*; *The Circus Band*; *Largo* [violin, clarinet, and piano]; *Allegretto Sombreoso from "The Incantation"*; *Adagio Sostenuto*; *Luck and Work.*
Vol. 5. *The Unanswered Question*; *Central Park in the Dark.*

Vol. 6. *Trio* [violin, cello, and piano]; *String Quartet No. 2.*
Vol. 7. *Song for Harvest Season; Largo* [quarter-tone piano]; *On the Antipodes; December; Aeschylus and Sophocles; Tolerance; The New River;*
Vol. 8. *Take offs in former days, athletic, tragic, compustic et al* [orchestra]; *Calcium Light Night...*arr. by Henry Cowell.
Vol. 9. *String Quartet No. 1.*

Collection of Piano Sketches. 54 pages. Reproduced from holographs, with additional notes by Henry Cowell in pencil.

Compilation From Newspapers, Magazines, Books, and Program Notes 1888-1950 re Music of Charles Ives. Typescript, 4 unnumbered vols. n.p., n.d. [Contained in Ives Collection, Yale University Music Library Archival Collection, Mss. 14, Series VIII, Box 55, folders 1-4; duplicate copies in Series X, Boxes 64 and 65.]

B3   Washington, D.C. The Music Division of The Library of Congress. Washington, D.C. 20540.

A large collection of uncatalogued photostats of Ives's musical manuscripts from the Ives Collection at Yale University (**B1**). Among the catalogued items are the following:

Manuscript collection of instrumental music, partly autograph. n.p. 4 volumes. Vol. 1, composers holograph; Vols. 2-4, part composer holographs, part copyist's manuscripts.
Vol. 1. *Trio for Violin, Cello, and Piano; String Quartet No. 2.*
Vol. 2. *The Unanswered Question; Andante con moto (The Last Reader); Allegro Moderato (The Rainbow); Central Park in the Dark.*
Vol. 3. *Tone Roads No. 3; Adagio (The Indians); Scherzo (Over the Pavements); Tone Roads No. 1.*
Vol. 4. *Tone Roads No. 1 and 3; From the Steeples and the Mountains; Largo Risoluto No. 1; Like a Sick Eagle; Scherzo (All the Way Around and Back).*

Photocopies of holographs: *All-forgiving, Look on Me; Canzonetta for organ; Chromâtimelôdtune* (arr. Schuller); *Fugues for organ in C minor and Eb major; God of My Life; Invention in D for piano; London Bridge Is Fallen Down; Love Does not Die; March No. 1 in F for piano; O Maiden Fair; Orchestra Sets Nos. 2 and 3; Organ interludes for hymns; Postlude for Orchestra in F; String Quartet No. l; Pre-First Violin Sonata; Piano Studies, Nos. 2, 5-8, 20 and 23; Universe Symphony* (sketches).

Catalogues

B4   Brooks, William, and J. Peter Burkholder. "Books in Bigelow Ives' Library and Identified by Him as Belonging to Charles Ives or His Family." Computer printout. Compiled Spring 1982, revised March 1984. *See also:* "A Manuscript list of books in the Charles Ives family home in West Redding, Connecticut," edited by Vivian Perlis in 1979 [Yale University Music Library Archival Collection, Mss. 14, Series X, Box 70, folder 3]. *See:* **B1**.

The library of Bigelow Ives, Charles Ives's nephew, contained less than 100 books. In their inventory Brooks and Burkholder each tackled approximately four shelves and noted titles, publication dates, and inscriptions. The inventory yielded no "smoking guns." Not only was it difficult to discern whose library the books originally belonged, books on Transcendentalism and other subjects known to be of interest to the composer were conspicuously absent.

B5   De Lerma, Dominique-René. *Charles Ives, 1874-1954: A Bibliography of His Music.* Kent, Ohio: Kent State University Press, 1970.

De Lerma's bibliographic citations include uniform titles, cutter numbers, media, poets or literary sources, dates, Kirkpatrick catalogue numbers **(B7)**, alternate titles, durations, notes, contents, publications, recordings, and cross and "See Also" references. The bibliography consists of the following indexes: Publication Index; Medium Index; Chronological Index; Index of Arrangers, Poets, and Librettists; Phonorecord Index; and Performer Index.

B6   Echols, Paul. *[Charles Ives: A Catalogue of His Music.]* Yale University Press, forthcoming.

The recent Institute for Studies in American Music describes this volume as "a catalogue raisonné of Ives's work to supplement the invaluable but limited *Temporary Mimeographed Catalogue of the Music Manuscripts...*by John Kirkpatrick **(B7)**." *I.S.A.M. Newsletter* 8, no. 1 (November 1987): 3. Produced under the sponsorship of the Charles Ives Society, the volume will offer revisions in genre classification and chronology, musical incipits, and a definitive numbering and alphabetical system.

B7   Kirkpatrick, John. *A Temporary Mimeographed Catalogue of the Music Manuscripts and Related Materials of Charles Edward Ives*

1874-1954. New Haven: Library of the Yale School of Music, 1960 (114 copies); reprint, 1973. [According to Perlis **(B9)**, p. 1, "Additions and corrections to the *Catalogue* made by Kirkpatrick since its original printing in 1960 are to be found only in the Music Library and Ives Society copies."]

Kirkpatrick's meticulous compilation made between 1954 and 1960 of Ives's music manuscripts, which Mrs. Harmony Ives donated to the Yale School of Music in September 1955, remains among the most important contributions to Ives scholarship. Following a brief manuscript history Kirkpatrick offers detailed descriptions of the contents (including marginalia) of each sketch and autograph score, arranged in seven categories: Orchestral Music; Chamber Music; Keyboard Music; Music for the Stage; Choral Music; Solo Songs; and Exercises, Other Music Etc. The *Catalogue* also contains numerous indexes: Titles and Incipits; Standard Song-texts and Hymn-texts; Dedications; Music Paper; Negative Numbers in Numerical Order; Tunes Quoted; Ives's Addresses and/or Telephone Numbers; Copies by Other Hands; Publishers; Names, etc.

B8   ____. "Ives, Charles E(dward)." In *The New Grove Dictionary of Music and Musicians,* edited by Stanley Sadie, vol. 9, pp. 414-429. London: MacMillan, 1980; reprinted with updated bibliography and a partially revised work-list assisted by Paul C. Echols in *The New Grove Dictionary of American Music,* edited by H. Wiley Hitchcock and Stanley Sadie, vol. 2, pp. 503-520. London: MacMillan, 1985.

An authoritative biographical sketch of Ives followed by a comprehensive list of Ives's extant and completed works arranged, like the *Catalogue* **(B7)**, according to the following genres: Orchestral and Band; Chamber Music; Keyboard; Choral and Partsongs; and Songs.

B9   Perlis, Vivian, compiler. *Charles Ives Papers. Yale University Music Library Archival Collection Mss 14.* Unpublished (January 1983) but typescripts are available for purchase from the John Herrick Jackson Music Library, Yale University. New Haven, CT. *See:* **B1**.

Indispensable for anyone who needs to use the Ives Collection at Yale University. A brief outline of its contents follows:

Series I - Boxes 1-23 Music Manuscripts (pp. 1-3)
Series II - Boxes 24-26 Literary Writings (pp. 4-21)
Series III - Boxes 27-39 Correspondence (pp. 22-158)

Series IV - Boxes 40-44 Scrapbooks (pp. 159-160)
Series V - Box 45 Diaries (pp. 161-162)
Series VI - Boxes 46-49 Photographs (pp. 163-173)
Series VII - Boxes 50-53 Programs (pp. 174-175)
Series VIII Boxes 54-59 Writings About Ives (pp. 176-184)
Series IX - Boxes 60-61 Ives's Collection of Music by Others (pp. 185-195)
Series X - Boxes 62-70 Miscellaneous (pp. 196-198)

Bibliographies

B10 Gleason, Harold and Warren Becker. "Charles Ives." In *20th-Century American Composers*, pp. 105-128. Music Literature Outlines-Series IV. 2nd edition. Bloomington, IN: Frangipani Press, 1981.

The most comprehensive published unannotated bibliography. Contains numbered listings of 25 books, 36 dissertations, and 355 articles on Ives arranged alphabetically and bibliographic references keyed to a numbered list of Ives's works. Also included is an outlined summary of Ives's melody, harmony, counterpoint, rhythm, form, and orchestration with examples of works for each stylistic characteristic.

B11 Henck, Herbert. "Literatur zu Charles Ives." *Neuland* 1 (1980): 25-27, 46 & 52; 2 (1981-82): 208 & 268-269; 3 (1983-84): 243-246.

More current and nearly as comprehensive an unannotated bibliography as Gleason/Becker **(B10)**. The 299 numbered sources, including 17 books listed at the outset of Vol. 1 and 282 articles selected from books and journals, are particularly rich in German contributions. Sources in each volume are arranged alphabetically.

B12 Schultz, Gordon A. "A Selected Bibliography of Charles Ives' Insurance Writings." *Student Musicologists at Minnesota* 6 (1975-1976): 272-279.

An annotated guide to thirteen of Ives's writings on life insurance (1916-1929) [nine of which are located in the archives of the Mutual Life Insurance Co. of New York], followed by a list of thirteen "of the more noteworthy advertisements which the Ives & Myrick Agency ran between 1918 and 1929. [For a list of Ives's published and unpublished insurance writings see **Appendix 3**, "Ives's Writings."]

Discographies

B13   Cohn, Arthur. "Charles Ives." In *Recorded Classical Music: A Critical Guide to Compositions and Performances*, pp. 902-928. New York: Schirmer Books, 1981.

Extensive critical annotated discography of available Ives recordings arranged by genre. Cohn describes each work briefly and explains the criteria he uses to single out a particular recorded performance as his personal favorite.

B14   Hall, David. "Charles Ives: A Discography. Parts, I, II, and III." *HiFi/Stereo Review* 13, no. 4 (October 1964): 142+; 13, no. 5 (November 1964): 102+; 13, no. 6 (December 1964): 92+.

The first comprehensive Ives discography. Using Kirkpatrick's *Catalogue* **(B7)** as his source, Hall arranges this discography chronologically from 1889 to 1921. For each work Hall cites discontinued as well as available recordings and provides brief critical remarks about the works as well as the performances.

B15   Morgan, Robert P. "The Recordings of Charles Ives's Music." *High Fidelity* 24, no. 10 (October 1974): 70-76.

Morgan offers a thoughtful critical survey, arranged by genre, of the Ives recordings in print in 1974. In his introductory remarks he explains Ives's emergence as an important composer: "Our world view seems to be catching up with his music, so that he speaks to us today with a directness and meaningfulness rivaled by few other composers."

B16   Oja, Carol J., ed. "Charles Ives." In *American Music Recordings: A Discography of 20th-Century U.S. Composers*, pp. 171-180. Institute for Studies in American Music. Brooklyn College of the City University of New York, 1982.

Unannotated discography of recordings released (with two 1971 exceptions) between 1972 and 1979 and available as of June 1980. Oja intended her discography to supplement Warren's comprehensive discography that listed all Ives recordings issued prior to December 31, 1972 **(B17)**. For each work, arranged alphabetically, Oja gives a date, identifies the performers, notes the record label and catalogue number, the record speed, number of discs, the date of release, and notes whether or not it is currently in print.

B17   Warren, Richard. *Charles E. Ives: Discography*. New Haven:
Historical Sound Recordings. Yale University Library, 1972
[distributed by Greenwood Press, Westport, CT]; updated edition
in preparation.

Comprehensive and detailed listing of all Ives recordings issued
before December 31, 1971. Warren arranges the recordings
alphabetically and provides a generous amount of information for
each, including text openings, Kirkpatrick catalogue numbers
(B7), text sources, specific recording dates, and "matrix number
or numbers, if different from record or side-numbers." A
discography that breaks all records for thoroughness and
usefulness. *See*: **B16**.

BIOGRAPHICAL AND AESTHETIC ARTICLES, GENERAL STYLISTIC STUDIES, REVIEWS, AND CRITICAL EVALUATIONS (1889-1987)

1889

B18 "Danbury Fifty Years Ago." *Danbury Evening News*, February 10, 1889. "Reprint (with slight change) from *Danbury Evening News*, Saturday, February 9, 1889, page 3, column 2."

"Charles Ives, a young son of George E. Ives, is to take charge of the organ at the West Street Congregational Church and will enter upon his duties as organist tomorrow. Charlie has inherited a generous supply of his father's musical talent." Earliest entry in Ives's Compiled References (1888-1935).

B19 Announcement. *Danbury Evening News*, October 21, 1889, page 3. Erroneously dated 1888 in Ives's Compiled References.

"Charles Ives presided at the organ at the Baptist Church yesterday. He is the youngest organist in the State." The reference concludes with the following parenthetical remark: "From Uncle Lyman's scrap book pinned under a notice of 'Alerts Beat Fountain Boys - 9 - 10 - No Home Runs - No Broken Noses' - Uncle Lyman was more interested in the Alerts' shortstop than in the Baptist organist."

1890

B20 Bailey, James Montgomery. "Last Evening's Concert: The Greatest Artistic Success of the Season." *Danbury Evening News*, June 12, 1890, page 4; reprinted in **B215**, pp. 30-31.

Ives's performance of Rossini's *William Tell Overture* and *Home, Sweet Home* (both arranged by Dudley Buck), a Bach *Toccata*, Mendelssohn's *Sonata in F Minor*, and Lemmens' *March Pontificale*, elicited praise and prophecy: "Master Ives deserves and receives great praise for his patient perseverance in his study of the organ, and is to be congratulated on his marked ability as a master of the keys for one so young. We predict for him a brilliant future as an organist."

1930

B21   Myrick, Julian S. "What the Business Owes to Charles E. Ives." *Eastern Underwriter* (Life Insurance Salesmanship Edition), September 19, 1930, part 2, page 18 [facsimile in **B318**, page 41].

Myrick's tribute to his partner of twenty years appeared upon Ives's retirement from their Mutual Life Insurance agency. The previous year their agency had sold $49 million of insurance, more than any agency in the country.

1931

B22   Howard, John Tasker. *Our American Music: Three Hundred Years of It*, pp. 576-578. New York: Thomas Y. Crowell Co., 1931; reprinted in Appendix 11 of *Memos* (**B378**).

In this important early history of American music, Howard offers a sympathetic treatment of Ives's radical musical views "behind his music." That Ives's music seemed less comprehensible to Howard is evident in his assessment of the *Fourth Symphony*: "If anything were needed to show the machine age gone wrong, this should take several prizes." By the third edition in 1954, the above comment had been eliminated, and although Howard would let stand his description of Ives as "a fascinating enigma," he would retain his admiration for Ives's "reckless courage" and acknowledge Ives's experimental innovations. Howard bases much of his information on a letter that Ives wrote to him, dated June 30, 1930 [reprinted in Appendix 11 of *Memos* (**B378**)].

1932

B23   Rosenfeld, Paul. "Charles E. Ives." *The New Republic* 71 (20 July 1932): 262-264.

Rosenfeld considers this "little-known composer" [i.e., Ives] "doubly distinguished...with his occupation of the place of the pioneer atonalist," and "the even more enviable position as one of the few originally gifted composers of impressionistic or descriptive or imitative music borne by America."

B24   "New York Artists Reshape America Over the Week End." *New York Herald Tribune*, July 10, 1932, page 14.

Ives emerged as America's musical hero at a weekend retreat in Pennsylvania. His principal advocate was Bernard Herrmann, who "insisted that Charles Ives 'is the Walt Whitman of American music.'" Herrmann continued: "We know that Mr. Ives belongs among the immortals and some day all the rest of America will know it. America will know it when it can appreciate the meaning of a new American tone, of a new dissonance. His music is our music. It is not European."

1933

B25 Einstein, Alfred. "American Music in Berlin." *Christian Science Monitor*, March 6, 1933, page 4; extended excerpt reprinted in **B215**, p. 232.

"The radical group of composers is, in its lack of traditional values, very international and very American--Mr. *Charles Ives is* [being], *in my estimation, the most original and national*....The distressing part lies in the fact that Germany now means very little to modern musical America."

1934

B26 Johnson, Axel, ed. "Ives, Charles." *The Music Lover's Guide* (February 1934): 173.

Partisan bibliographical entry, in which Ives is viewed as "the most original and most characteristically 'American' composer the United States has yet produced." Johnson indicts the professional musical establishment for its failure to perform and record Ives's music, and prophesies that "the future generation is going to have sardonic contempt of us for ignoring Ives and his music so long."

B27 Slonimsky, Nicholas. "Composer Who Has Clung to His Own Way." *Boston Evening Transcript*, February 3, 1934, section 3, pages 4-5.

After introducing Ives's multi-faceted career (i.e., "business man, maker of Constitutional amendments, writer, musician"), Slonimsky argues that "it is probable that his [Ives's] business activity created a sense of potential reality in him that made him try unusual methods in musical composition." He finds that "the case of Ives is all the more interesting because his musical abstention has not prevented his recognition, as yet by enthusiasts and seekers for the individual and the new." Slonimsky considered Ives in a paragraph as early as his "Composers of New England" [*Modern Music* 7 (February-March

1930): 24-27], but this article is the first of many articles Slonimsky devoted entirely to Ives.

1935

B28   Finney, Theodore M. *A History of Music*, p. 645. New York: Harcourt, Brace and Company, 1935.

"Charles Ives (1874-) has quietly developed a style which depends somewhat on New England folk idioms. He has been consciously independent of other influences, and therefore has produced music of radically modern interest. Perhaps because of the modesty with which Ives has presented his work, Americans did not immediately discern that he has been, in the matter of willingness to experiment, an American counterpart of Stravinsky and Schoenberg." Ives enters a music history text with a favorable assessment approximately the same length as that of David Stanley Smith.

1936

B29   Rosenfeld, Paul. "Ives." In *Discoveries of a Music Critic*, pp. 315-324. New York: Harcourt, Brace & Co., 1936.

A conglomeration of Rosenfeld's previous writings on Ives (**B23** and **B775**). As he surveys a number of Ives's compositions and explores some of the composer's aesthetic, Rosenfeld notes Ives's nationalism and heterogeneity. He attributes Ives's lack of recognition to the fact that "during the the first quarter of this century the musically highly cultured individual was still extremely rare in the American ranks." Also significant is Rosenfeld's assertion, antedating Gilman's famous review (**B670**) by three years, that Ives's *"Concord"* Sonata "indeed remains the solidest piece of piano music composed by an American."

1937

B30   Furnas, T. Chalmers. "Charles E. Ives." In *The Hills of God*, pp. 22-25. Amesbury, MA: The Whittier Press, 1937.

A paean to the Connecticut hills provides the backdrop to this poetic eulogy. Although Furnas accepts the notion that Ives's music cannot be played on "machine-made instruments" but only by "the human heart," he nevertheless asserts that "Ives has produced real music, modern music which is creative, constructive, and capable of vast influence on future composers who study his ideas and ideals. And this is much more than can be said of a very great proportion of modern music, or what is offered and sold as music."

1939

B31   Fletcher, Lucille [subsequently Wallop]. "A Connecticut Yankee in Music." Unpublished article intended for *The New Yorker* (1939). *See:* Yale University, Ives Collection, Mss 14, Box 56, folder 3 **(B1)**.

Extended and important early profile on Ives's life and thought. Fletcher supplements the biographical information circulated by writers such as Bellamann **(B326-327)** and Rosenfeld **(B29)** with rich and often rare anecdotal material, thoughtful explanations and observations. She also quotes liberally from Ives's political writings and reviews of Ives's music. [Fletcher, who married Ives's early champion, Bernard Herrmann, explains in *Ives Remembered* **(B318)** why she withdrew this article from publication.]

B32   Lieberson, Goddard. "An American Innovator, Charles Ives." *Musical America* 59, no. 3 (10 February 1939): 22+.

At the outset of this unusually positive early assessment of Ives's style, one of the first to include musical illustrations, Lieberson notes Ives's anticipation of twentieth-century musical techniques, but considers it "ridiculous to think of Ives only as a chronological phenomenon, for his music manifests a style which is unmistakably new and individual." In the main body of his article Lieberson surveys three representative songs (*Resolution, Soliloquy,* and *Down East*) as well as *"Concord" Sonata.* Lieberson reserves his highest praise for the large orchestral pieces, in which "Ives brings into full play his astounding ability to fluctuate, combine, and invent rhythms." Later in 1939 Lieberson began a long career as Director (and eventually President) of Columbia Masterworks, a company that under Lieberson's stewardship became an ardent commercial champion of Ives's music.

B33   Mellers, Wilfrid. "Music in the Melting Pot: Charles Ives and the Music of the Americas." *Scrutiny* 7 (March 1939): 390-403.

According to Mellers, Ives "is, if not a great composer, very nearly a great--a singularly rich and ripe--personality." He offers "a few notes on some of Ives's most characteristic technical discoveries" in melody, harmony and polyphony, sonority, rhythm, and concludes that Ives's philosophy reveals "an extreme moral naiveté, a naiveté which is demonstrably present in the technique," e.g., Ives's literal text setting in his songs and his preoccupation with capturing "the aural effects of natural phenomena" in his instrumental works. Mellers concludes that despite his "undeniable talent," Ives failed to create "a single authentic composition." *See*: **B41** and **B99**

B34 Perkins, Francis D. "Kirkpatrick Plays Program of Ives' Work." *New York Herald Tribune*, February 25, 1939, page 9. *See:* **W651** and **W133c**.

Review of the February 24 Town Hall all-Ives recital, in which Kirkpatrick encored his "sensitive and admirable" performance of *"Concord" Sonata* given in the same hall on January 20 and premiered his piano arrangement of the fugue from the *Fourth Symphony*, and the mezzo-soprano, Mina Hagar, performed fourteen Ives songs with "expressiveness and sympathetic insight." Perkins describes the sonata as "a work which stands apart in instrumental American music, which impresses with its imagination and re-creation of atmosphere, but which calls for no little further acquaintance." Perkins also imparts the view that "the strong and characterisic feature of the songs as a whole was not so much the salience of their musical ideas, considered apart, as the remarkable and convincing faithfulness with which they realized the subject, atmosphere, local color and essential emotions of their texts."

B35 Rosenfeld, Paul. "Advent of American Music" and "Advance of American Music." *The Kenyon Review* 1 (Winter 1939): 46-53 and 1 (Spring) 185-193.

Rosenfeld duplicates some of his earlier ideas on Ives (**B23, B29,** and **B775**) as he places Ives in the context of American culture. He attributes Ives's sudden rescue from anonymity to the "propaganda and performances" of Cowell and Slonimsky until "there dawned upon the observant the fact that a promise had been beautifully fulfilled." Rosenfeld also explains the "extrinsic factors" responsible for the neglect of worthy American composers such as Ives.

B36 Thompson, Oscar. "Views on an All-Ives Concert." *The New York Sun*, February 25, 1939, page 28. *See:* **W7b, W651,** and **W133c**.

Review of the February 24 Town Hall recital with Kirkpatrick and Mina Hager. The program consisted of an "encore" performance of *"Concord" Sonata* [performed at Town Hall on January 20], Kirkpatrick's piano transcription of the *Fourth Symphony* fugue, and fourteen songs. Concerning *"Concord" Sonata* Thompson voices "substantial doubts as to whether the work possesses the basic stuff to make a strong and intelligible appeal direct to the ear." He also expresses his disappointment that he was unable to hear the fugue in its orchestral glory and his verdict that the songs "lack the emotional and musical substance of the songs of the master."

1941

B37   Howard, John Tasker with the assistance of Arthur Mendel. *Our Contemporary Composers: American Music in the Twentieth Century*, pp. 243-247. New York: Thomas Y. Crowell Co., 1941.

Similar, albeit slightly expanded, presentation of the Howard's biographical survey of Ives published in *Our American Music* **(B22)**. Again the emphasis is on Ives's originality and uniqueness rather than his craft.

1942

B38   "To Continue Ives & Myrick Name." *Eastern Underwriter*, January 23, 1942, page 3.

Despite inaccuracies concerning Ives's musical life, this article provides a reliable summary of Ives's insurance career. Of special interest are the quoted comments of Ives's recently retired partner and second vice-president, Julian Myrick. Mr. Myrick discusses the division of labor during their twenty years of partnership, the importance of Ives's pamphlet, *The Amount to Carry* **(B375)**, to their agency, and the origins behind Ives's dedication to Myrick of *The Fourth of July*.

1943

B39   Kaufman, Helen L. "Charles Ives." *The Story of One Hundred Great Composers*. New York: Grosset & Dunlap, 1943 [reference in Yale Collection Box 55, folder 3, page 79]; reprinted 1957 [p. 73].

Although Kaufman's appreciative entry is brief and superficial, Ives's inclusion as early as 1943 among the pantheon of one hundred great composers, is intrinsically noteworthy and merits inclusion here.

B40   Logan, Adeline Marie. "American National Music in the Compositions of Charles Ives. M.M. thesis, University of Washington, 1943. 77 pp.

Superceded by Henderson's comprehensive dissertation (**B125**), this study is nevertheless historically significant as one of the earliest theses on Ives. Logan states that her purpose is "to determine the extent to which Charles Ives had made use of American national material in his composition; and second, to show his originality in handling this material." She divides Ives's American national music into patriotic songs, folk-airs, country-dances, Western influences, Indian influences, jazz rhythms, and hymns, and although she most often does not clarify the original source, she does provide musical illustrations from a representative sampling of works. Among her conclusions Logan notes Ives's centering "his attention on the parts of a folk-song that have reference to a familiar text" and Ives's practice of accompanying a portion of a melody with harmony that was originally associated with another segment of melody.

B41   Mellers, Wilfrid. "American Music (An English Perspective)." *The Kenyon Review* 5, no. 3 (Summer 1943): 357-375.

In a broad prefatory article to his 1965 study of American music (**B101**), Mellers describes Ives (pages 365-366) as "the first really authentic American composer." He regards Ives's "eclectic, experimental, and chaotic" music as the "first great step in American music history--the emergence of the vernacular," but is unable to credit Ives with achieving the second step, a balance "between the vernacular and the conventions and traditions which give it order as a social manifestation." *See*: **B33**, **B53**, and **B101**

1944

B42   Yates. Peter. "Charles Ives." *Arts & Architecture* 61, no. 9 (September 1944): 20+.

A tribute to Ives on the eve of the composer's seventieth birthday. Yates considers the performance difficulties in Ives's music analogous to the difficulties attributed to such great works of Beethoven and Bach as the *Diabelli Variations* or the *Art of Fugue*. In his brief discussion of Ives's songs he writes that "since

Dowland, Byrd, and Purcell no other composer has so completely and adequately set forth in music the native fall and fluency of English speech."

1945

B43 "Institute of Arts Names 15 Members." *The New York Times,* December 28, 1945, page 13.

"Fifteen American artists, writers and musicians have been chosen for membership in the National Institute of Arts and Letters as recognition of works that 'survive temporary appeal,' it was announced yesterday. Membership in the institute is limited to 250 and the latest selections leave only ten vacancies....This year seven were chosen from the field of art, six from literature and two [Ives and Schuman] from music."

1946

B44 Lang, Paul Henry. "Hearing Things. Charles Ives." *The Saturday Review of Literature* 29, no. 22 (1 June 1946): 43-44.

In this critical assessment, Lang views Ives "as the first musician who realized the futility of Western European gropings for new music which at the same time held on to the post-Wagnerian faith." He asserts that "the curious primitivism of his symphonies is not due to lack of training and craftsmanship...but is a symbol of the lack of a center, of a focus, in the life of the young century." Lang attributes the "American tragedy" of Ives's failure to solve "the great problems of music" to the non-revolutionary tendencies in America which inhibited composers of Ives's revolutionary bent.

1947

B45 Lederman, Minna. "Some American Composers." *Vogue* 137 (February 1, 1947): 184-186+.

Ives, "the great discovery" of the age, is the featured composer in this survey of seven American composers (Ives, Copland, Harris, Thomson, Piston, Blitzstein, and Sessions). The article appeared within a few months after the demise of *Modern Music,* which Lederman had edited since its inception in 1924. In her sympathetic overview Lederman contrasts American and European responses to Ives: "To American purists Ives seems full of faults; to Europeans, from Mahler to Milhaud and Manuel Rosenthal, his freshness has been an endless fascination."

Portraits of Thoreau, "A Subject in a Charles Ives Sonata" and Hawthorne, "Another Charles Ives Subject" are included among a group of captioned photographs in subsequent issues of *Vogue*: "Musical Portraits," [15 April 1949, pp. 64-65] and "Charles Ives, American Composer" [1 May 1953, pp. 120-121; list of recordings on p. 55].

B46   "Ives, Charles Edward." *Current Biography 1947*, pp. 330-332. New York: H. W. Wilson Co., 1947.

Bibliographical entry based largely on Cowell (**B352**), Howard (**B37**), Rosenfeld (**B29**), and several other acknowledged references. The entry traces Ives's career and major events that mark a gradual public recognition, and includes quoted excerpts from various critical articles as well as Ives's writings and letters.

1948

B47   Moor, Paul. "On Horseback to Heaven: Charles Ives." *Harpers* 197 (September 1948): 65-73.

Moor writes an appreciative survey, in which he discusses Ives's health and lifestyle in the 1940s, his marriage of mutual devotion to Harmony, his political convictions, and his independence of European conventions. "Among progressive American musicians and critics, the neglect of Charles Ives has for years been the cause of a kind of group guilt-complex, for there is not the slightest doubt among authorities both here and in Europe that Ives is one of the richest and most remarkable talents this country has ever produced."

B48   Perkins, Francis D. "In Defense of Critics." [Letter to the editor in response to "On Horseback to Heaven," Moor 1948] *Harpers* 197 (December 1948): 14.

Perkins defends against the charge that "critics should share in the kind of group guilt complex suggested by Mr. Moor" and asks that "our best critical musicologists" more than overworked critics take on the task of "seeking out and proclaiming significant and thus far unknown scores" such as those by Ives.

1949

B49 "Charles E. Ives." *Life* 27, no. 18 (31 October 1949).

One week after Ives's seventy-fifth birthday, *Life* published the first professional photo of the composer, taken by W. Eugene Smith, and accompanied by a brief caption. [*See: Ives Remembered* (**B318**), pp. 42-44, for Smith's recollection of the photo session and a reproduction of this and two other Smith photos of Ives.]

B50 Kirkpatrick, John. "*Three Page Sonata; Some South-Paw Pitching; The Anti-Abolitionist Riots in Boston in the 1850's,* for Piano Solo. New York: Mercury Music Corp., 1949. *Three Harvest Home Chorales,* for Mixed Chorus (SATB) with Piano Accompaniment. New York: Mercury Music Corp. 1949. *Notes* 6, no. 3 (June 1949): 486-487.

In reviewing these keyboard works Kirkpatrick notes Cowell's careful editing but regrets that he omitted Ives's revealing marginalia. After supplying samples of Ives's marginal notes, Kirkpatrick explains why these "completely uninhibited moments" inspire a devotion "analogous to the hilarious reverence accorded to Beethoven's most outrageous bagatelles." He considers the *Harvest Homes Chorales* "one of Ives' most exasperating mixtures of exalted inspiration and cantankerous impracticality," and recommends that it is "worth the trouble" to create a notation that would facilitate the performance of the nearly impossible polyrhythms in the second Chorale, even if "Ives would undoubtedly disapprove of such coddling." *See:* **W76** and **W78:9 & 21**

B51 Taubman, Howard. "Posterity Catches Up with Charles Ives." *The New York Times Magazine* (23 October 1949): 15+.

Taubman focuses on Ives's belated recognition, which the author attributes to rhythmic difficulties that were "insoluble" to earlier conductors and soloists. Although Taubman does not think that the awards and performances of the 1940s have "yet matched Mr. Ives' accomplishments," he does believe that events of the recent past validate the title of his article. "It has taken America a long time to recognize that he is the most audacious pioneer in music this country has produced and that in his vast output...we have a living portrait of the land worthy to stand beside the literature of New England's flowering."

1950

B52   Ewen, David. "The Belated Discovery of Charles Ives." *Tomorrow*
9, no. 9 (May 1950): 10-14.

In this sympathetic but unoriginal overview of Ives, Ewen writes
that, rather than Ives's technical innovations, it is an "intrinsic
Americanism that gives Ives' music its significance and assures
its permanence in our cultural heritage."

B53   Mellers, Wilfrid. "American Music and an Industrial Community."
In *Music and Society*, pp. 191-203. New York: Roy Publishers,
1950.

Mellers offers a slightly new angle to his earlier stated views (**B33**
and **B41**). He now considers that Ives's "attitude to sound" shows
a healthy recognition "that distinctions between a noise and
musical sound can only be arbitrary." Nevertheless, Mellers
tempers this praise with a condescending qualifying remark: "At
the same time Ives's attitude is, in its literalness, naive because it
does not recognize that although such distinctions may be
arbitrary they are none the less necessary." He also reiterates his
view (albeit less directly than in his 1943 essay) that Ives, who
represents "the emergence of the vernacular," was unable to
integrate the vernacular with "the conventions and traditions
which give it coherence as a social manifestation." *See*: **B31**,
B41, and **B101**

B54   Yates, Peter. "Charles E. Ives." *Arts & Architecture* 67, no. 2
(February 1950): 13-17.

Yates dismisses those critics embarrassed by Ives's apparent
rejection of musical propriety and contends that, "the listener
fortunate enough to be able to hear several times in adequate
performance a major work by Ives will find in it...a durable
conception of whole form, the continuous variation of a thematic
nucleus without reference to any strict tonality, which has
become the central principle of twentieth century music in its
most developed styles."

1951

B55   Watt, Douglas. "Musical Events: Concert Records." *The New
Yorker* 27, no. 1 (17 February 1951): 97-99.

Review of several recent Ives recordings. Watt is more impressed
with "the feeling of participation he [Ives] gives the listener,"

especially in such short orchestral works as *The Unanswered Question* and *Central Park in the Dark* (Polymusic Records PRLP-1001), than with Ives's technical innovations. Although Watt considers Ives's output uneven and "sometimes hard to grasp," he credits "the simple, unsophisticated quality of his thought" with rescuing Ives's music from its overly complicated forms.

1952

B56   Goss, Madeleine. "Charles Ives." In *Modern Music-Makers: Contemporary American Composers*, pp. 14-33. New York: E. P. Dutton & Co., 1952.

Conventional and unoriginal essay on Ives's life and thought, but important as one of the earliest extended Ives profiles to be published in a book. Includes a list of Ives's compositions arranged by genre.

1953

B57   Slonimsky, Nicholas. "Musical Rebel." *Américas* 5 (September 1953): 6-8+.

A biographical and stylistic introduction to Ives. Slonimsky points out that the illegibility of Ives's scores does not obscure the clarity of Ives's musical thought. That Ives's ideas are willful is borne out by the composer's ability to explain "which note is the right one and which sharp or flat is in its proper place, even though some of his unpublished manuscripts date fifty years back." The essay includes a facsimile and transcription of a portion of the *Three-Page Sonata.*

1954

B58   Downes, Olin. "American Original." *The New York Times*, May 30, 1954, page 7; reprinted as "Charles Ives." *American Composers Alliance Bulletin* 4, no. 1 (1954): 17+.

In this obituary, Downes recounts his reaction to his first experience with Ives's music, the premiere performance of the *Fourth Symphony* (first and second movements) in 1927, and inserts a substantial portion of his review of that concert (**B598**). He also cites a second "episode" (*circa* 1942), in which the Russian Ballet de Monte Carlo rejected Ives as a Stravinsky-come-lately. Finally, Downes eulogizes Ives--"as thorny, unmalleable and vigorous a creative personality as American music has known."

B59 ____. "Composer's Need; Ives's Career Lacked Audience to Accept or Reject His Creative Experiments." *The New York Times*, June 6, 1954, section 2, page 7.

Downes echoes and quotes Copland's sentiment that Ives's music reflects the tragedy of the American composer (**B777**). Quoting Downes: "There is no doubt in our mind that he would have been a more completely integrated composer if artistic conditions of his place and time had been such as to concentrate his musical development and more harmoniously fuse his thoughts and emotions in ways to make the experience and its tonal realization one." Downes also recalls his meetings with Ives in the mid-1920s.

B60 Evett, Robert. "Music Letter: A Post-Mortem for Mr. Ives." *Kenyon Review* 16 (Autumn 1954): 628-636.

In this first substantial critical rejection Evett accuses Ives of incompetence, stylistic excesses, vulgarity, and making a "cult of disorder," and asserts that Ives's "later work" is "characterized by the four cardinal sins of recent music." Briefly, these sins inculde "impracticality" (i.e., making impossible demands on performers), "stylistic extravagance" (i.e, "whoring after novelty"), "standardlessness, which generally masks itself as catholicity of taste," and a "chauvinism," which glorifies the unpleasant fact that Ives "smelled like Whitman's armpits." Evett even discredits the rarely disputed claim that Ives anticipated twentieth-century musical innovations.

B61 Glanville-Hicks, Peggy. "Ives, Charles." In *Grove's Dictionary of Music and Musicians*, 5th edition, volume 4, page 560.

Although Glanville-Hicks characterizes Ives as "the archetypal ancestor of much that is peculiarly American in the present-day American school of American composers," the space allotted in this edition of *Grove's Dictionary* is surprisingly sparse. Superficial biographical and critical comments are followed by a grossly incomplete catalogue of works.

B62 Grunfeld, Frederic. "Charles Ives: Yankee Rebel." *High Fidelity* 4, no. 9 (November 1954): 34-36+; reprinted in *American Composer Alliance Bulletin* 4, no. 3 (1955): 2-5.

Grunfeld agrees that "there was ample evidence to support the contention of Henry and Sidney Cowell that Ives was 'one of the four great creative figures in music of the first half of the twentieth century' [along with Schoenberg, Stravinsky, and Bartók] **(B354)**. No doubt Grunfeld had early access to the Cowell biography, since he clearly relied upon it for this biographical survey. The article is most valuable for Grunfeld's independent critical survey of the first twenty years of Ives recordings.

B63   Helm, Everett. "Charles Ives, American Composer." *The Musical Times* 95 (July 1954): 356-361.

A considerable portion of this brief survey is taken up by musical illustrations from *"Concord" Sonata,* the *Fourth Violin Sonata,* and *Soliloquy,* but Helm writes little about these works. He adds to the conventional overview of Ives's career only when he fails to resist, when "sorely tempted," to compare Ives with Satie. He regards both Satie and Ives as "something less than adequately trained in the technical processes of music," but who nonetheless "possessed a fantasy and 'whimsy' that induced new trends of musical thought."

B64   Lyons, James. "A Prophet Passes." *The American Record Guide* 20, no. 10 (June 1954): 313-315+.

An obituary and critical review of several Ives recordings, including the then deleted performance of the *Second String Quartet* by the Walden Quartet **(D39)**. Although grateful for the "teasing glimpse" of Ives's output these recordings provide, Lyons cannot conceal his disappointment with their generally poor fidelity and his perturbation at some of the mediocre performances. Lyons singles out Walter Hendl's recording of *Three Places in New England* **(D25)** as "the kind of public relations that the music of Ives must have to get where it belongs--which is in the mind and the heart and the very sinew of our cultural life, and better late than never."

B65   Moore, Ralph Joseph, Jr. "The Background and the Symbol: Charles E. Ives: A Case Study in the History of American Cultural Expression." Senior essay, American Studies Department, Yale College, 1954. 184 pp.

An accomplished and surprisingly mature study for an undergraduate thesis. Moore's thoroughly researched and insightful discussion of Ives's years at Yale and the Yale milieu remains in many respects unsurpassed, even by Rossiter (**B215**), who acknowledges his debt to Moore's essay in a footnote. Moore is also unusually successful in placing Ives's thought within a cultural perspective, and he clearly explains how Ives, as a symbol of the American artist, has been used and distorted by both traditionalists and modernists. Perhaps no other essay captures more effectively what Ives, on the eve of his death, expressed (or failed to express) to American culture.

B66   Slonimsky, Nicholas. "Charles Ives--America's Musical Prophet." *Musical America* 74, no. 4 (15 February 1954): 18-19; reprinted in *Pan Pipes* 47 (January 1955): 20.

Slonimsky emphasizes Ives as a man who "anticipated every known musical innovation of the twentieth century" and discusses his father's influence. The first man to conduct *Three Places in New England* describes his rhythmic complexities to the second movement before noting the Ivesian paradox: "That his music is at once fantastically complex and appealingly simple."

B67   "Musical Whitman." *Newsweek* 43 (31 May, 1954): 78.

In this obituary (which includes a photograph) Ives is viewed as an unappreciated revolutionary, who chose the insurance business because "he wanted the means with which to write the kind of music he believed in."

B68   "Charles E. Ives Dies at 79; Music Won Pulitzer Prize." *New York Herald Tribune*, May 20, 1954, page 14.

An obituary that stresses the "Yankee flavor" of Ives's music as it reviews Ives's career and recognizes his stature. "The Yankee folk tunes of his New England background were combined with his vast musical knowledge and technical skill to create what were recognized, belatedly, as works of art."

B69   "Charles Ives, 79. Composer, Is Dead." *The New York Times*, May 19, 1954, page 31.

In this rather matter-of-fact obituary *The New York Times* attributes Ives's belated recognition and "prolonged obscurity" to his shyness, to the alleged performance difficulties, and especially to the precocious modernity of his music.

1955

B70   Chase, Gilbert. "Composer from Connecticut." In *America's Music*, pp. 403-428. New York: McGraw Hill Book Co., 1955; reprinted 1966 and 1987.

In this pioneering and influential text on American music, Chase devotes his longest chapter on a single individual to Ives and offers a sympathetic introduction to Ives's life and musical thought. He pays particular attention to Ives's musical innovations and New England influences before concluding with a programmatic guide to *"Concord" Sonata* illustrated by excerpts from Ives's *Essays* **(B660)** and the musical score.

B71   _____. "A Communication. The Music of Charles Ives." *The Kenyon Review* 17, no. 3 (Summer 1955): 504-506.

Spirited rebuttal to Robert Evett's attack on Ives the previous year in *The Kenyon Review* **(B60)**. Chase considers Evett's remarks "harsh...and offensive," but he confines his letter, not on Evett's "critical judgments, which may legitimately differ," but on his factual errors, "which are a matter of record."

B72   Downes, Olin. "Ives Memorial; His Scores and Papers Given to Yale." *The New York Times*, June 5, 1955, section 2, page 9.

Downes praises the efforts of Cowell, Harrison, Kirkpatrick, and the rarely-acknowledged musicologist, Joseph Braunstein, for classifying, ordering, and bringing together under one roof all of Ives's extant manuscripts. He also discusses some of the editorial problems that will face future students of Ives and commends the United States for giving such an "original and prophetic" composer "appropriate recognition and honor but a year after his death."

B73   Frankenstein, Alfred. Review of *Charles Ives and His Music*, by Henry and Sidney Cowell. *The Musical Quarterly* 41, no. 2 (April 1955): 253-256. *See:* **B354**

Frankenstein considers it "fitting" that Cowell, who more than any single individual brought Ives's music to the world, should join his wife in presenting the first full-length study, published within a year of Ives's death. Frankenstein notes that the Cowell biography is the first to consider Ives's business life, and that the Cowells relate Ives's story and the 'career' of his music "with great warmth and sympathy and with rich, arresting detail."

Nevertheless, he regrets that the book does not include more analysis of specific Ives works.

B74 Goldman, Richard Franko. Review of *Charles Ives and His Music*, by Henry and Sidney Cowell. *Notes* 12, no. 2 (March 1955): 217-218. *See*: **B354**

Goldman considers that the Cowell biography "illuminates its subject as few monographs on composers ever succeed in doing, and that it "speaks with authority as well as with clarity and with grace." As far as the book under review is concerned, Goldman finds fault only with its brevity, but he does have some reservations about their subject, a composer who never "came to terms with Mozart or with many other great phenomena of our common musical past."

B75 Lockspeiser, Edward. Review of *Charles Ives and His Music*, by Henry and Sidney Cowell. *The Musical Times* 96 (October 1955): 532-533. *See*: **B354**

Lockspeiser takes issue with the "wild over-estimation" of Ives's stature and the "indiscriminate" praise of Ives's music in the Cowell biography. He concedes that "there was something approaching genius in Ives's many-sided personality," but concludes that Ives "remains a composer of predominantly national significance, in whom one may see the origins of certain extravagances in the work of other American composers, notably the 'note-cluster' of the co-author of this study." Not surprisingly, considering his assertion that Ives was "not big enough to have been the Mussorgsky of American music," Lockspeiser regrets the analytic focus on such complex works as *Paracelsus* and *"Concord" Sonata* when they could have more appropriately "stressed the qualities of some of the smaller songs."

B76 Mellers, Wilfrid. Review of *Charles Ives and His Music*, by Henry and Sidney Cowell. *Music and Letters* 36, no. 4 (October 1955): 400. *See*: **B354**

Although he fails to share their "extragavant" claims regarding Ives's stature, Mellers praises the Cowells for their "lucid account of the experiential logic of Ives's technique." Mellers denies that Ives possessed a "cultural heritage," but considers his "remoteness from tradition" a positive phenomenon that made him "more radically, more excitingly prophetic than his great European contemporaries."

B77   Plinkiewisch, Helen E. "A Contribution to the Understanding of the Music of Charles Ives, Roy Harris, and Aaron Copland." Ed.D., Teacher's College, Columbia University, 1955. 183 pp.

Plinkiewisch offers a sympathetic but superficial appreciation and suggestions on how to teach several Ives works: *Harvest Home Chorales*; *Psalm 67*; *Third Symphony*; *"Concord" Sonata*; and four songs (*Serenity, Ann Street, Two Little Flowers*, and *Evening*). The fact that each composer appears in this thesis as an autonomous unit, explains its exclusion from the **Ives and His Contemporaries** category.

B78   Schonberg, Harold C. Review of *Charles Ives and His Music*, by Henry and Sidney Cowell. *Musical Courier* 151, no. 4 (15 February 1955): 45; reprinted in *Tempo* 36 (Summer 1955): 31-32. *See*: **B354**

Schonberg has high praise for this genius-confirming book: "The Cowells add nothing to the legend, nor do they take anything away. Their biography is factual and sympathetic; their analyses (in Part II of the book) of the music are understanding and unhysterical. For the first time in print the reader can get a very good idea of what made the man tick." Schonberg notes the Ivesian paradox of a "composer who wrote for the people but threw into their faces every possible technical reason for not playing his music." This review marks the first of numerous critically positive assessments of Ives by the future senior music critic of *The New York Times*.

B79   Schrade, Leo. "Charles E. Ives: 1874-1954." *The Yale Review* n.s. 44 (June 1955): 535-545.

Schrade examines the anomalous historical position and "the present conclusion that Charles E. Ives is the most remarkable, the boldest, and the most original composer this country has ever had." He does not attribute the paucity of Ives performances to difficulties in execution but to performer's rejection of his "simultaneous use of old and new," and he asserts that Ives's isolation disqualified him as "the father of modernism" in America. Like Carter (**B338**), Schrade considers the "wealth of rhythmic varieties" Ives's most "remarkable" innovation. He concludes by drawing parallels between the idiosyncratic aesthetics of Ives and Debussy.

B80   "Notes of the Day." *Monthly Musical Record* 85 (July-August 1955): 141-144.

In contrast to Mussorgsky, "the very archetype of semi-illiterate genius," the anonymous correspondent describes Ives as a man who "seems to have cared little how his music sounded." Another Russian, Scriabin, is offered as a more accurate parallel to Ives, because the two composers share "the same introversion, the same elaboration of musical texture, the same preoccupation with the transcendental." But although the writer concedes Ives's genius, he concludes that Ives's compositions "seem to us to be only the doodlings of a wealthy and likeable eccentric."

B81   "The Stuff of Success." [Review of *Charles Ives and His Music*, by Henry and Sidney Cowell.] *Newsweek* 45 (17 January 1955): 90-91. *See*: **B354**

This article, noteworthy in a weekly news magazine for its length, particularly so soon after Ives's death, is less a review of the Cowell biography than a biographical portrait of Ives that uses the Cowell study as its source. It does, however, describe this book as "not only a must for musicians but a personal document of surpassing interest for all who care about American culture."

1956

B82   Orr, C. W.   Review of *Charles Ives and His Music*, by Henry and Sidney Cowell. *The Music Review* 17, no. 2 (May 1956): 169-170. *See*: **B354**

Orr, in the two paragraphs he devotes to this book, allows insufficient space to support his condescension with reasoned argument. He does, however, allow himself enough space to reveal an extraordinary ignorance roughly proportionate to his antipathy. In a journal of this stature a review such as this is inexcusable.

1957

B83   Slonimsky, Nicholas.   "Ives, Charles." In *Die Musik in Geschichte und Gegenwart*, pp. 1574-1580. Translated by Wilhelm Pfannkuch. Kassel und Basel: Bärenreiter, 1957.

Biographical and stylistic overview of Ives largely derived from Slonimsky's earlier Ives portraits (**B27, B57,** and **B66**). Slonimsky's entry and list of works far exceeds Glanville-Hicks's recent *Grove's Dictionary* article in both substance and completeness (**B61**).

1958

B84 Kirkpatrick, John. "Ives's Transcendental Achievement." A talk given on the Fourth of July, 1958 at Tanglewood. Unpublished.

Introductory remarks to a program that included three songs arranged by Kirkpatrick for voice and strings (*Song for Harvest Season, Religion,* and *Hymn*), "Emerson" from *"Concord" Sonata,* three songs with piano (*Evening, Immortality,* and *General Booth*) and the *Second String Quartet.* Kirkpatrick argues that Ives's Transcendentalism was fundamental and pervasive and, although "best characterized by the *Essays*" (**B660**), by no means confined to *"Concord" Sonata.* He concludes that "perhaps the most radical of all Ives's transcendental impulses was his faith in his performers....Anybody else's inspiration, if whole-hearted and whole-souled would in some way have as much validity as his own."

B85 Schonberg, Harold C. "America's Greatest Composer." *Esquire* 50, no. 6 (December 1958): 229-235.

In this biographical and stylistic overview of Ives, Schonberg demonstrates his sympathy to Ives's music and its aesthetic underpinnings. According to Schonberg, Ives's "anticipations of virtually every technique of modern music was not rationalized," and Ives possessed "genuis" but "a terrible technique." Schonberg also observes that Ives's program music "had flavors and colors, rather than story content" and that "of all major twentieth-century composers, Ives and Bartók have the closest relationship."

B86 Taubman, Howard. "Forget Posterity." *The New York Times,* November 23, 1958, section 2, page 11.

Taubman contradicts Bernstein's remarks made at a New York Philharmonic preview that Ives was a "primitive." He expresses his regret that in contrast to Webern, who remained a musical professional, albeit a neglected one, Ives's musical development was greatly inhibited because he was denied "a place in the mainstream of American musical life" and felt compelled to withdraw from a professional musical life. Taubman hopes that we can learn a lesson from our neglect of Ives and our over-reliance on posterity and support our composers today, for example, Easley Blackwood.

1961

B87   Buhrman, Laurel Chenault. "An Analysis of the Music of Charles Ives." M.A. thesis, University of Oklahoma, 1961. 75 pp.

Biographical summary based exclusively on Cowell and Bellamann is followed by brief and superficial remarks on several songs from *114 Songs, General Booth, The Unanswered Question, Tone Roads No. 1, Second String Quartet, Second Symphony, Fourth Violin Sonata,* and *"Concord" Sonata.* In her introduction Buhrman explains that "the method employed in the explanations and charts is derived from Hindemith's system based on a study of acoustics." Twenty-seven musical illustrations and appallingly small bibliography.

B88   Hansen, Peter S. "Music in the United States." In *An Introduction to Twentieth Century Music,* pp. 77-84. Boston: Allyn and Bacon, Inc., 1961; reprinted in 1978 [pp. 86-96].

Ives is the only composer chosen to represent America in "Part One: 1900-1920" of this standard text. In 1961 Hansen briefly surveys *"Concord" Sonata* through Ives's "written introductions" (i.e., the *Essays* [**B660**]) and concludes that "the question of whether Ives' music achieves 'greatness' or not is a debatable one"; in the second edition he adds a brief discussion of the complex rhythms of Ives's *Fourth Symphony,* "the climactic example of his unique style," and notes that, alone among his contemporaries, Ives's music "continues to interest the musical world" and inspire "even young composers of the mid- seventies."

B89   Kirkpatrick, John. "Ives as Revealed in His Marginalia." *The Cornell University Musical Review* 4 (1961): 14-19.

Kirkpatrick writes at the outset that "the most entertaining part of the job [of compiling a comprehensive catalogue of Ives's manuscripts] was copying over a thousand memos." He then surveys Ives's marginal memos from 1892 to 1942 and provides a representative sampling of these private conversations, which offer valuable biographical information and illuminating commentary on Ives's compositional thinking. *See:* **B7**

B90   Mays, Kenneth Robert. "The Use of Hymn Tunes in the Works of Charles Ives." M.M. thesis, Indiana University, 1961. 130 pp.

Mays has selected four works in which Ives presents hymn tunes prominently (*Third Violin Sonata* and *Symphonies Nos. 2-4*). For each work he cites all statements of a hymn tune as they appear in the work and offers brief verbal descriptions at each occurrence "in vertical chart-form columns" under three categories: 1) "How the implied hymn tune is treated"; 2) "how the hymn tune quote is accompanied"; and 3) "how the example is organized tonally." Musical illustrations accompany nearly every description. Although he describes, for example, Ives's practice of combining "incomplete phrases of two different hymn tunes," Mays's failure to address critical or analytical issues greatly reduces the significance of his labor.

B91   Yates, Peter. "Charles Ives." *Arts & Architecture* 58 (1961): no. 2, p. 6; no. 3, p. 4; no. 5, p. 6.

An idiosyncratic study of Ives's aesthetic. Yates, who knew Schoenberg and corresponded at length with Ives's wife, Harmony, offers some insightful parallels between these two nearly exact contemporaries. Particularly provocative is Yates's reported conversation with Schoenberg, who "recalled gratefully that Ives, though already an ill man, came to greet him at a reception when the Schoenbergs, in flight from Nazi Germany, arrived in New York [1933]" (**B112** and **B225**). Yates conjectures that this meeting inspired Schoenberg's famous tribute to Ives (**B390**). He also writes about the significance of Gilman's famous 1939 review of *"Concord" Sonata* (**B670**).

1963

B92   Farberman, Harold. Jacket notes to *Pieces for Chamber Orchestra and Songs*. Cambridge CRS 1804 [1963] (**D11**).

Conventional biographical essay is followed by informative historical and analytical notes to the works recorded on the album. The descriptions of *Over the Pavements, Tone Roads Nos. 1 and 3, Hallowe'en,* the *Three-Page Sonata for Piano, The Cage,* and *General William Booth* contain useful formal capsules, and musical illustrations are provided for most of the works.

B93   Helm, Everett. Review of Ives's *Essays Before a Sonata and Other Writings,* edited by Howard Boatwright. *Musical America* 83, no. 2 (February 1963): 52. *See:* **B660**

Helm opens his two-paragraph review with the following unequivocal endorsement: "This book should be required reading for every person interested in American music--and we hope that this means every person practicing the art of music in America."

B94   Kirkpatrick, John. "What Music Meant to Charles Ives." *The Cornell University Music Review* 6 (1963): 13-18.

Kirpatrick's "revision of a talk given at Ithaca College, 22 May 1963" is a compilation, connected by brief remarks of excerpts taken mainly from portions of Ives's 1932 *Memos* (**B378**) that were not available to Henry and Sidney Cowell (**B354**).

B95   "Ives Revived." *Newsweek* 62 (7 October 1963): 65.

Review of recent concerts at Carnegie Hall and the Museum of Modern Art which featured Ives compositions, including *Three Quarter-Tone Pieces for Two Pianos, Robert Browning Overture,* and *"Concord" Sonata. Newsweek* emphasizes the growing appreciation for Ives since his death and reports that an increasing number of performances and recordings, for example Pappastavrou's rendition of *"Concord" Sonata,* attain "both breadth of vision and extraordinary technical virtuosity."

1964

B96   Clarke, Henry Leland. Review of Ives's *Essays Before a Sonata and Other Writings,* edited by Howard Boatwright. *The Musical Quarterly* 50, no. 1 (January 1964): 101-103. *See:* **B660**

Clarke writes that the *Essays* "do not bring us very close to the protagonists [Emerson, Hawthorne, the Alcotts, and Thoreau], nor to the particular notes of the sonata, but bring us right into the mind and heart of Ives as a human being." He also contrasts the conventionality of Jacob Abbott, the creator of Rollo (Ives's symbol of placid conformity), with his "rigorously unorthodox" contemporary, Bronson Alcott. Brief remarks about some of the "other writings" are followed by critical remarks about the format of the book, such as the absence of a comprehensive bibliography and an index and the presence of cumbersome "two-stage footnotes."

B97   Cohn, Arthur B. "Cambridge, CRI, and Vox, that Supremely Individual Creative Genius Chas. E. Ives." *The American Record Guide* 30, no. 9 (May 1964): 760-762+.

A review of five recordings representing a variety of Ives's orchestral, chamber, keyboard, and vocal works on three labels: *Pieces for Chamber Orchestra* (**D11**); *Washington's Birthday, Hallowe'en, The Pond,* and *Central Park in the Dark* (**D5**); *Thanksgiving* (**D20**); *The Fourth of July* (**D5**); and the two string quartets performed by the Kohon Quartet on Vox STDL-501.120.

Cohn expresses "doubt that the performances [on Cambridge] could be bettered" and that "the Kohons do wonders with the scores," but gives subdued praise for the CRI performances. An editor's note tells us that Cohn's "own Stringart Quartet gave its world premiere [of *Hallowe'en*] back in the early thirties." *See:* **W51a**.

B98   Dickinson, Peter. "Charles Ives: 1874-1954." *The Musical Times* 105 (July 1964): 347-349.

Dickinson's introduction portrays Ives as lacking the "technical sophistication" of the next generation of Americans, but a composer for whom "there is no longer any excuse for neglecting." He asserts that most of Ives's works are "not unreasonably difficult by contemporary standards," and that in his "totally unsophisticated approach to music" Ives "offers a fresh experience to both performer and listener."

B99   Hall, David. "Charles Ives: An American Original." *HiFi/Stereo Review* 13, no. 3 (September 1964): 43-58.

In this inaugural article of a biographical series on major American composers, Hall presents a thoughtful and richly illustrated overview of Ives's life and work. Of particular interest is Hall's history of Ives recordings that includes a listing of fourteen "essential recordings," a prelude to his comprehensive three-part discography that would follow in forthcoming issues. *See*: **B14**

B100   Helms, Hans G. "Der Komponist Charles Ives." *Neue Zeitschrift für Musik* 125, no. 10 (1964): 425-433.

Helms discusses how Ivesian techniques (e.g., tone clusters, "antiphonal music," and especially aleatory or "statistical" music) influenced composers such as Stockhausen, Brant, and Cage. But he concludes that it is not the "technical details in Ives that one can find again in today's music" ("nicht was an technischen Details man von Ives in der gegenwärtigen Musik wiederfinden kann") but the processes which he unleashed ("die Prozesse, die es auslöst") that are truly relevant to the present generation of composers.

B101   Mellers, Wilfrid. "Realism and Transcendentalism: Charles Ives as American Hero." In *Music in a New Found Land: Themes and Developments in the History of American Music*, pp. 38-64.

London: Barrie and Rockliff, 1964; reprinted in 1987 with a new forward.

The two "isms" of Mellers's chapter title represent "two qualities that lead us to the core of Ives's work as a whole. The first is its acceptance of life-as-it-is, in all its apparent chaos and contradiction....The second quality...is that the attempt to discover unity within chaos is in essence a transcendental act." Mellers cites examples from nearly a dozen songs that demonstrate Ives's realism and offers an extended analysis of *"Concord" Sonata* to show Ives as a Transcendentalist. The essay contains numerous imaginative insights, for example artistic parallels between Ives and Beethoven. Mellers asseses Ives as a "fitful genius" and historically important for possessing "the aural imagination" necessary to give "substance" to his radically experimental technique.

B102   Yellin, Victor Fell. Review of Ives's *Essays Before a Sonata and Other Writings*, edited by Howard Boatwright. *Journal of the American Musicological Society* 17, no. 2 (Summer 1964): 229-231. *See*: **B660**

Yellin effectively demonstrates stylistic connections between Ives's prose and music, for example, "similarities of phrasing, use of parenthetical expressions and quotations," and "the juxtaposition of the sublime with the ridiculous." He also articulates why he considers these characteristics more desirable in music than in prose. Remarkably, Yellin's review was the only writing on Ives published in this important journal of American musicology prior to Solomon's article in 1987. *See*: **B558**

1965

B103   Cohn, Arthur. "On Five Lables Simultaneously, More Music by Charles Ives." *The American Record Guide* 31, no. 10 (June 1965): 958-961.

Review of several recently released Ives recordings: the first collected performance under one conductor (Strickland) of the *Symphony "Holidays"* (**D19**); Sykes's anthology of several short piano pieces (**D53**); two complete performances of *Three Places in New England*, one conducted by Ormandy (**D26**) and the other by Hendl (**D25**), and a "historical memento" reissue of *The Housatonic at Stockbridge* conducted by Janssen (Everest LPBR-6118). Cited for special praise are Ormandy's "stunning" and rhythmically precise performance. Cohn also extends his appreciation for the first opportunity to hear what he unknowingly regards as "all the shorter piano music Ives ever produced."

B104 Riedel, Johannes. Review of Ives's *Essays Before a Sonata and Other Writings*, edited by Howard Boatwright. *Journal of Research in Music Education* 13, no. 1 (1965): 61-63. *See*: **B660**

Riedel tries to show through quotation that Ives's writing "about Emerson's style is also valid for his own" and that Ives's goal in writing is the same as Emerson's. He also views Ives's "verbal eccentricities ...as a genuine interpretation of the turmoil of the industrial and technological era we live in."

B105 Wilson, Donald Malcolm. "Metric Modulation. Part Two of a Thesis." D.M.A. dissertation, Cornell University, 1965, pp. 106-124.

In chapter three, "Metric Modulation in the Music of Charles Ives," Wilson adopts Cowell's "new and complete method of notating 'divisive,' or fractional, time-values" and Hindemith's "meter-signs with unconventional denominators" in order to unravel the rhythmic perplexities of Ives's *Over the Pavements*. He concludes "that the piano, percussion, and trombone pulses did not change speed as it would seem from the original notation, but, on the contrary, maintained themselves strictly through the point of modulation and in fact served as its foundation." Other examples of Ives's metric modulation are cited without discussion: *First Violin Sonata*; *Piano Trio*; *"Concord" Sonata*; *Robert Browning Overture*; and from *114 Songs*, nos. 3, 33, 44, 74, and 91. According to Wilson, Ives's works exhibit "the first application of metric modulation as a fully developed twentieth-century compositional technique."

1966

B106 Austin, William W. "Contemporaries in America, Australia, Japan." In *Music in the 20th Century*, pp. 57-61. New York: W. W. Norton, 1966.

Largely unsympathetic summary of Ives's adventure and achievement in this influential and highly acclaimed study. Despite praise for Ives's "extraordinary courage and self-reliance," Austin asserts that Ives's music possessed "no unity short of the unity of the cosmos." Also according to Austin, one needs to read Ives's prose and know the borrowed material in order "to guess what Ives is getting at," since Ives's "command of musical materials is deficient." For a critique of Austin's arguments see Burkolder's dissertation (**B284**). *See also:* **B141**

B107 Bryant, Sister Emily Marie. "The Avant-Garde Character of Charles Ives' Music Exemplified in Various Works." M.A. thesis, Mount St. Mary's College, Los Angeles, 1966. 112 pp.

Even within her small sampling of works (*Psalm 67*, "Lord of the Harvest" from *Three Harvest Home Chorales, Over the Pavements, The Unanswered Question*, the *Fourth Symphony* [first and second movements], and the *Second String Quartet*, Bryant is able to identify and illustrate a great number of avant-garde techniques, many of which she relates to medieval compositional practices as well as to the work of Ives's contemporaries and successors. Throughout her thesis Bryant acknowledges her debt to Howard Hanson's *Harmonic Materials of Modern Music* for a number of her melodic and harmonic interpretations. Most valuable is the extended analysis of the *Second String Quartet* and the summary of her interview with Herman Langinger, the man who engraved the 84-page second movement of the *Fourth Symphony* for the *New Music* publication of 1929 at $24 per page.

B108 Tenney, James. "Some Notes on the Music of Charles Ives." *Charles Ives Songs* (1966). FM 3344 and FM 3345 [**D66**]; reprinted in *Soundings: Ives, Ruggles, Varèse. Soundings* (Spring 1974): 63-64.

Tenney outlines seven avant-garde stylistic features present in Ives's music. Although he acknowledges that most of these innovations were also developed by Schoenberg and Webern, he notes "that Ives never really abandoned the more traditional procedures, as did his European counterparts" and that for Ives, "each new element was simply incorporated into a style that became, thereby, broader in its scope than that of any other composer of that period." In fact, the only counterpart to Ives, according to Tenney, "is the music of Bach, encompassing many disparate lines of development in the music of his predecessors, as well as his own innovations."

1967

B109 Kolodin, Irving. "Are My Ears On Wrong?" Program notes for New York Philharmonic, Lincoln Center for the Performing Arts, 1966-67. *See:* **W133a**.

Informative background on "the devious path" by which the seven songs performed by Hubert Linscott and Copland reached Yaddo in 1932 (**W133a**), and a useful chronological chart of "Landmarks in Ives' Artistic Career."

B110 McClure, John. "Charles Ives--Lonely American Giant." *The Gramophone* 44, no. 527 (April 1967): 516-517.

A tribute to Ives's ability to conquer creative isolation with enormous courage. McClure considers Ives's *114 Songs* as perhaps "the greatest collection of songs written since Brahms, and like *Sacre* and *Pierrot* and *Wozzeck*, one of the aesthetic pivots of the twentieth century." [As Director of Columbia Masterworks, McClure spearheaded his company's efforts to record a large number of Ives works.]

B111 Salzman, Eric. "Ives." In *Twentieth-Century Music: An Introduction*, pp. 143-147. Englewood Cliffs, NJ: Prentice-Hall, 1967; reprinted 1974 [pp. 128-131].

Brief but important critical assessment of Ives's aesthetic position and achievement. Salzman tries to dispel "the myth which depicts him as an untutored pioneer," and sees Ives's music both as "a direct and continuing influence...linked quite directly with certain recent avant-garde ideas," and as a "kind of traditionalist...able to encompass his vision of the totality of human experience." Virtually unchanged in the 1974 edition.

B112 Yates, Peter. "An Introduction to Charles Ives." In *Twentieth Century Music: Its Evolution from the End of the Harmonic Era into the Present Era of Sound*, pp. 252-270. New York: Pantheon Books, 1967.

According to Yates's psychological portrait of Ives, it was "the war, the collapse of all he had believed in, rather than worry about nonreception of his music, which precipitated his breakdown." Yates describes Ives's so-called "theoretical innovations" as "experimental," and asserts that "Ives liberated his technique from harmony, freeing dissonance and consonance impartially."

In addition to relaying his conversation with Schoenberg, in which Ives came to meet the German refugee in 1933 (**B91** and **B225**), Yates also recalls a conversation that took place in 1964 with Ruggles, who describes sitting next to Schoenberg at a performance of Ives's *The Unanswered Question*, "presumably in 1933." Yates's first appendix, "Ives's 'Anticipations,'" contains a reprint of Bryant's summary of Ives's seven "anticipations" that appear in the *Fourth Symphony* (second movement). *See*: **B107**

1968

B113 Brozen, Michael. "A Week for Charles Ives: Recitals by Esther Glazer/Easley Blackwood and Alan Mandel." *High Fidelity/Musical America* 18, no. 6 (June 1968): MA 17. *See*: **W59e**, **W77a**, and **W78b**.

Review of Town Hall recitals of the four Ives violin sonatas on March 21 performed by Glazer (violin) and Blackwood (piano) and Mandel's premiere on March 23 of *Five Takeoffs* and *Eight Studies*. After lamenting the fact that Ives's neglect prohibited his musical influence, Brozen expresses his view "that the morganatic marriage in his music of the sublime and the quotidian was consummated with the utmost artistry" and that "the music, particularly the Takeoffs, should have been part of our repertory long ago."

B114 Cohn, Arthur. "Ten Records--Keeping Up with Charles Ives." *The American Record Guide* 34, no. 5 (January 1968): 376-381+.

Review of ten Ives recordings: *String Quartets Nos. 1 and 2* with the Juilliard (**D38**) and Kohon (Turnabout TV-34157S) quartets and a reissue of the *Second Quartet* with the Walden Quartet (**D39**); three recordings of the *First Piano Sonata*, two by Masselos (**D52** and RCA LSC-2941) and one by Lee (**D51**); and a group of orchestral works that include Gould conducting the premiere recording of the *Orchestral Set No. 2* (RCA LSC-2959), Johanos conducting a complete recording of the *Holidays Symphony* (**D18**), and no less than three recordings of the *Robert Browning Overture*, Gould (same as above), Ormandy (Columbia MS-7015), and Strickland (**D14**).

Cohn rates the Walden performance the best of the three interpretations of the *Second Quartet*, despite its antiquated fidelity, and finds it difficult to chose a favorite from the three excellent performances of the *First Piano Sonata*. Among the orchestral performances Cohn singles out the "simply superb" Gould recording and the "artistry and virtuosity" coupled with a masterful "intrepretative analysis" of the Johanos performance.

B115 Drew, James. "Information, Space and a New Time-Dialectic." *Journal of Music Theory* 12, no. 1 (1968): 86-103.

Within the context of a broader survey Drew considers Ives a successful "pioneer in the use of multiplicity" (later "designated as 'layer-composition')." According to Drew, Ives's "fundamental theory was that each spatial dimension is self inclusive and is therefore of an autonomous nature."

B116 Eger, Joseph. "Ives and the Beatles." *Music Journal* 26, no. 9 (September 1968): 46+.

Imaginative, albeit largely unsubstantiated, attempt to explain the reasons underlying the popular appeal of Ives and the Beatles. Eger cites the "naive, childlike openness, and an individualism spiked with missionary zeal," "romantic rebellion," innovative use of sound resources, and optimistic response to life, despite "all the loneliness and separation from society," as characteristics shared by a solitary artist having his day in the sun and the unprecedentedly popular rock quartet.

B117 Price, Jonathan. "The Rough Way up the Mountain." *Yale Alumni Magazine* (April 1968): 28-37; reprinted in *Music Educator's Journal* 55, no. 2 (October 1968): 38-45 and in The Four Symphonies of Charles Ives, Columbia D3S 783 [1968] (**D17**).

A tribute to Ives's spirit partly through prose and partly through free verse. Price describes the significance of Ives's writings: "Like the music, it is not strictly sequential, or rather, one can follow several sequences through the material, all at once. For the main thing that strikes one on approaching Ives' music is its multiplicity."

B118 Rich, Alan. "The Ives Canon." *Saturday Review* 51, no. 17 (27 April 1968): 75+.

Review full of praise for two recently released Ives "packages," a four-disc set of the so-labelled *Complete Piano Music of Ives* performed by Mandel (**D48**), and a three-record issue of the four symphonies conducted by Farberman (Vanguard 10032/4). Rich suggests that listeners begin to explore the music presented here with *The Celestial Railroad*, which, when compared with the other versions of similar material in the "Hawthorne" movement from *"Concord" Sonata* and the second movement from the *Fourth Symphony*, demonstrate "that underneath the unruly inventiveness lay a core of imaginative craftmanship." .

B119 Salzman, Eric. "Charles Ives, American." *Commentary* 46, no. 2 (August 1968): 37-43.

Expanded version of Salzman's comments on Ives in *Twentieth-Century Music* (**B111**) and an excellent overview of Ives's career and musical thought that avoids discussion or analysis of specific works other than *The Unanswered Question.* Salzman writes that the "concept of open-endedness--of material found in the environment which could then constantly undergo change and transformation--was the most surprising and upsetting of all of Ives's prophetic notions," and that his "real originality lies in just the fact that he was not at all concerned with the problem of historical dialectic and change."

B120 "Charles Ives Society Founded in Holland." *Sonorum Speculum* 35 (Summer 1968): 13-16.

Announcement of the founding of The Charles Ives Society in Amsterdam. The Society, motivated by the conviction that Ives "has come to be one of the most important composers of the twentieth century through the non-conformity of his ideas and music," was formed for the expressed purpose of proselytizing Ives's name. Published in English and German on parallel columns.

1969

B121 Bernlef, J. and Reinbert de Leeuw. *Charles Ives.* Amsterdam: DeBezige Bij, 1969; pages 133-209 of De Leeuw's contribution, "Charles Ives--Zijn Muziek: Inleiding, Ives' Gebruik van Muzikall Material," in an English translation by Bertus Polman, reprinted without musical illustrations in *Student Musicologists at Minnesota* 6 (1975-1976): 128-191.

The first major biographical and stylistic study after the Cowells (**B354**). In his treatment of biographical and aesthetic matters Bernlef draws heavily on the earlier study as well as Ives's *Essays* and "Postface to 114 Songs" (**B660**). After Bernlef concludes with excerpts from Stravinsky, Schoenberg, and Cage's comments on the composer, De Leeuw discusses general stylistic features, Ives's use of musical material, and the mature symphonies, chamber music, piano sonatas, and several songs. He argues that the emphasis on Ives's avant-garde techniques "is partially why the essentials of his music are often ignored."

According to de Leeuw, the most important Ivesian stylistic features are his "continuous use of thematic transformation," his "extension" of harmonic language and harmonic counterpoint, his original treatment of rhythm and meter, and his use of "static, anti-thematic 'montage forms'" to replace "the dynamic development form of the tonal system." De Leeuw also describes what Burkholder would later refer to as "cumulative" setting (**B284** and **B297**), in which fragmentation precedes the full statement of a melody. The book concludes with a list of Ives's compositions based on the Kirkpatrick *Catalogue. See:* **B7**

B122   Evett, Robert. "Music: Shadow and Substance in Ives." *Atlantic* 223 (May 1969): 110-111.

Although he acknowledges the error of his earlier assumption that Ives's "lifework was too fragile a structure to support anything as cumbersome as the Ives cult as we now have it," Evett remains firm in his conviction that Ives was little more than an amateur who happened to possess some originality. He minimizes Ives's successes in such smaller works as *Charlie Rutlage*, maximizes what he views as Ives's glaring technical failures, and concludes by resisting (barely) the temptation "to damn Ives entirely on the basis of his irresponsible essays." *See:* **B60**

B123   Frank, Alan Robert. "The Music of Charles Ives: For Presentation in the Listening Program of the Secondary School." Ed.D., Teacher's College, Columbia University, 1969, pp. 114-250.

Frank emphasizes "the abundance of twentieth-century compositional devices" in his illustrated analyses of the following: *Washington's Birthday* and *Decoration Day* from Symphony *"Holidays," The Unanswered Question, Tone Roads No. 1, Three Harvest Home Chorales, The Pond, The Circus Band, General William Booth, Variations on America, The Varied Air with Protests*, and *Three-Page Sonata*. His aids to prospective secondary school teachers include: "(1) an explanation of the analyses themselves, (2) a methodology for the presentation of the music, (3) an index to the techniques employed by the composer, and (4) some analytical generalizations on his style."

B124   Frankenstein, Alfred V. "Charles Ives: *Essays Before a Sonata.*" In *Landmarks of American Writing*, ed. by Hennig Cohen, pp. 270-279. New York and London: Basic Books, Inc., 1969. *See:* **B660**

Frankenstein summarizes the content of the six *Essays Before a Sonata*. Generous quotations allow Ives to speak largely for himself.

B125 Henderson, Clayton Wilson. "Quotation as a Style Element in the
Music of Charles Ives." Ph.D. dissertation, Washington
University, 1969. 388 pp.

A useful introduction to the breadth and range of Ives's treatment
of borrowed melodies and the relationship between the borrowed
sources and Ives's transformations. The three appendixes, "Index
of All the Tunes Quoted," "Quoted Material in Specific Works,"
and "Musical Index of Quoted Sources" [171 total], although in
need of revision, remain especially valuable resources. *See*:
Henderson's forthcoming catalogue, *The Charles Ives Tunebook*.

B126 Hitchcock, H. Wiley. "Charles E. Ives." In *Music in the United
States: A Historical Introduction*, pp. 148-174. Englewood Cliffs,
NJ: Prentice-Hall, 1969; reprinted, 1974, third edition, 1988, pp.
161-186.

Hitchcock supports his view of Ives as "the most extraordinary
and significant American composer of the late nineteenth and
early twentieth centuries" by honoring him as the only composer
to merit a separate chapter. Hitchcock introduces Ives's musical
thought and surveys a large number of works that illustrate the
range of Ives's musical technique. The third edition includes an
overview of Ives's compositional output and an updated
bibliography. A succinct but useful reliable survey of Ives's
aesthetic and style.

B127 Jacobson, Bernard. "The 'In' Composers: Mahler, Ives, Nielsen,
Sibelius, Vivaldi, Berlioz--Are They Permanent Classics or Just
Temporary Fads?" *High Fidelity/Musical America* 19, no. 7 (July
1969): 54-57.

An attempt to explain the phenomenon of the "In" classical
composer, defined by Jacobson as "a temporary beneficiary of one
of the upturns of fashions." Among the seven composers
discussed, Jacobson considers Ives, along with Berlioz and
Nielsen, as less likely than Mahler and more likely than Liszt,
Sibelius, and Scriabin to graduate from In-ness and thereby
achieve artistic permanence. Jacobson's assessment of Ives's
popularity in 1969 has remained largely true in the late 1980s,
i.e., "interest on the part of composers and other specialists
rather than a movement in public taste."

B128 Mellers, Wilfrid. Review of Ives's *Essays Before a Sonata and
Other Writings*, edited by Howard Boatwright. *The Musical Times*
110 (July 1969): 744-745. *See*: **B660**

Mellers writes: "One cannot claim that Ives's prose is easy going, nor that it is as rewarding as his no less tough music....since his genius (and the word is not too strong) is musical, not literary....None the less, the greatness of the man shines through the muddle." He also praises the editor, Howard Boatwright, "on exemplary editing, and on the probity and relevance of his annotations."

B129 _____. Review of *Charles Ives and His Music*, by Henry and Sidney Cowell [2nd edition]. *The Musical Times* 110 (November 1969): 1144. *See*: **B354**

Mellers welcomes the paperback release of this "pioneering" biography, which "contains much information about the music which is not otherwise accessible." But because in the fifteen intervening years Ives had become "one of the most frequently recorded (and in the USA performed) of the major composers of the 20th century," Mellers considers the Cowell study "inadequate" for the present and calls for a more definitive biography.

B130 Riedel, Johannes, and Robert Oudal. "A Charles Ives Primer." Minneapolis: University of Minnesota, 1969.

Subtitled "a tentative introduction to music idioms as found in Charles Ives' music," the purpose of this primer is to present "characteristic usages of elements which would point the way for further exploration of Ives' style." Riedel and Oudal arrange their examples in five categories--rhythm, harmony, melody and cadences, and quotation--and provide a musical illustration chosen from various works by Ives and an aphoristic verbal explanation for each musical point.

B131 Ward, Charles. "The Use of Hymn Tunes as an Expression of 'Substance' and 'Manner' in the Music of Charles E. Ives, 1874-1954." M.A. thesis, University of Texas at Austin, 1969. 139 pp.

Ward's thesis is that in a large number of Ives's compositions "the text accompanying a hymn tune will, in many cases, provide significant information." He occasionally makes a strong case, e.g., "that there is a significant interrelationship between the extra-musical connotations provided by the text of the tunes used and the 'substance' of 'In the Night.'" Nevertheless, in his attempt to elevate Ives's retrospective programs to the status of motivic development, too often Ward advocates tenuous, unprovable textual or programmatic interpretations. His purely musical connections are more consistently convincing.

Works analyzed (sparsely illustrated) include: *The Unanswered Question*; "*In the Night*"; the two string quartets; symphonies (nos. 2-4); *First Piano Sonata*; the violin sonatas; *The General Slocum*; *Thanksgiving*; *Decoration Day*; and the *Second Orchestral Set*. Appendix A lists the seven hymnals that Ives is known to have used between 1888 and 1902. *See*: **B189**

B132 Woodham, Ronald. Review of Ives's *Essays Before a Sonata and Other Writings*, edited by Howard Boatwright. *Music and Letters* 50, no. 4 (1969): 526-527. *See*: **B660**

Woodham values Ives's writings for what they reveal about Ives as a person as well as a musician. He especially appreciates the total absence of "narrow dogmatism and smug arrogance which afflict some contemporary writers on music."

1970

B133 Davidson, Audrey. "Transcendental Unity in the Works of Charles Ives." *American Quarterly* 22, no. 1 (Spring 1970): 35-44.

In his attempt to answer the question, "What did unity mean to Ives?", Davidson asks us to "redefine unity in Ivesian terms" by examining the origins and significance of the following four points: "(1) unity as found in nature, (2) unity created by the wedding of dualisms (specifically those of substance and manner) (3) unity created by flashes of revelation, and finally, (4) unity which allows perfect freedom to exist within it." Clearly Davidson views the last of these points as the most important for Ives. Throughout his essay Davidson rejects attempts to define Ivesian unity according to "*Gestalt* psychology or conventional aesthetics."

B134 Drew, James. "Modern Music and the Debt to Charles Ives. Parts I and II." *Yale Reports* (27 December 1970 and 3 January 1971).

Drew posits that "Ives has influenced a certain kind of philosophical position that has produced a certain kind of composer in this country." He considers Ives's "polyphony of whole ideas," each retaining its autonomy and his original notion "to neutralize time" in order to free it from meter and goal-orientation (principles most prominently embodied in the *Fourth*

Symphony), as Ives's most important influences on composers of the 1960s and 1970s.

B135 Heaton, Charles Huddleston. Review of *Charles Ives: A Bibliography of His Music*, by Dominique-René De Lerma. *Music: The AGO/RCCO Magazine* 4 (September 1970): 44. *See*: **B5**

After describing the scope of this bibliography, Heaton illustrates De Lerma's complicated methodology by listing a sample entry and accompanying it with the necessary annotations.

B136 Hutchinson, Mary Ann. "Unrelated Simultaneity as an Historical Index to the Music of Charles Ives." M.M. thesis, Florida State University, Tallahassee, 1970. 145 pp.

Hutchinson defines "unrelated simultaneity" as "the concurrent expression of two or more unconnected, independent, and non-associable ideas." She tries to show how this concept gradually developed since the middle ages and to support a thesis that a scientific and philosophical movement towards relativity and indeterminacy have their aesthetic counterpart in the music of Schoenberg, Stravinsky, and Ives.

Through numerous examples drawn from various genres, Hutchinson espouses the view that Ives composed "music that better fits into the scheme and progression of history than much of the music of his contemporaries." But after she has denied any connectedness in Ives's heterogeneity, she is also unable to clarify why Ives made the compositional choices he did. Consequently, Hutchinson's thesis itself dissolves in its own disconnected and non-associable ideas.

B137 Johnson, Russell I. "A View of Twentieth-Century Expression." *Journal of Aesthetics & Art Criticism* 28, no. 3 (1970): 361-368.

Johnson tries to demonstrate through an examination of representative 20th century artists in various disciplines how "the creative products of man succeed in promulgating the clearest image of man at any moment in history." His musical representative is Ives, who by "merging past and present" through musical quotation to create "a flattening of time," parallels the artistic aims of contemporaries such as T. S. Eliot. Johnson thus argues that "the juxtaposition of the trivial and important with the historical and modern aspects of his music unites Ives with the visual and literary artists of the twentieth century."

B138 Kirkpatrick, John. Review of *Charles Ives: A Bibliography of His Music*, by Dominique-René De Lerma. *Notes* 27, no. 2 (September-December 1970): 260-262. *See*: **B5**

Kirkpatrick cites numerous examples to support his contention that this bibliography "betrays insensitivity to various kinds of distinctions." He challenges the usefulness of this book and asserts that De Lerma possesses insufficient knowledge of Ives's music and idiosyncratic compositional procedures.

B139 Noble, David W. "Freedom from Form: Progressivism in Architecture, Art, and Music." In *The Progressive Mind 1890-1917*, pp. 131-135. Chicago: Rand McNally & Co., 1970.

A misguided attempt to interpret Ives as a zealot and later a progressive, a Christ figure who "composed in isolation from a corrupt world in order to to save that world." Noble also incorrectly attributes the text to Ives's song, *West London*, quoted in full, to Ives himself rather than to Matthew Arnold.

B140 Rinehart, John McLain. "Ives' Compositional Idioms: An Investigation of Selected Short Compositions as Microcosms of His Musical Language." Ph.D. dissertation, The Ohio State University, 1970. 264 pp.

The compositional idioms Rinehart examines are "devices of serial ordering applied to the parameters of duration, pitch and intensity" in Part I, "aspects of polyphonic construction" (including polyphony of groups and spatial composition) in Part II, and in Part III, a discussion of Ives's integration of borrowed materials, the correspondence between Ives's comedic technique and Bergson's comedic theories, various degrees of aleatoric procedures, and Ives's "musical realism." For each idiom Rinehart cites examples as appropriate from the following fifteen compositions: *From the Steeples and the Mountains*; *Scherzo* from *A Set of Three Pieces*; *In the Inn*; *Scherzo: Over the Pavements*; *The Unanswered Question*; *Hallowe'en*; *Largo Risoluto Nos. 1 and 2*; *The Gong on the Hook and Ladder*; *Tone Roads Nos. 1 and 3*; *Vote for Names*; *Paracelsus*; *In Re Con Moto Et Al*; and *On the Antipodes*.

1971

B141 Austin, William M. "Ives and Histories." In *Bericht über den internationalen musikwissenshaftlichen Kongress Bonn 1970*, edited by Carl Dahlhaus et. al., pp. 299-303. Kassel: Bärenreiter, 1971.

In this brief but important essay Austin offers thoughtful responses to several challenging historical questions: "How can a historian today regard Ives as a central figure in a continuous line of developing musical thought? How...can a historian regard Ives in the context of American music? Can a historian still regard Ives as an "outsider?" Can a historian...ever provide a new central line of continuity for a group of people, national or professional, comparable to a traditional 'mainstream'?" As part of his response to the first question Austin injects a personal reference to his "fresh thinking" about Ives since the appearance of his text on 20th century music: "For me the line has emerged only since 1966, when I was regarding Ives as a representative minor figure in a pattern whose centers were Debussy and Stravinsky." *See*: **B106**

B142 Dujimic, Dunja. "The Musical Transcendentalism of Charles Ives." *International Review of the Aesthetics and Sociology of Music* 2, no. 1 (June 1971): 89-95. [Includes summary in Croatian.]

Although he perhaps overstates the pervasive role of Transcendentalism as a "continuous source" of "irreplaceable inspiration" in Ives's music, Dujimic presents an articulate definition of this philosophy and suggests useful parallels between Transcendentalism and Ives's aesthetic.

B143 Gligo, Niksa. "Prostornost i pokret u imanenciji glazbe." ["Space and Movement in the Immanence of Music.] Zvuk--Jugoslovenska Ruzicka Revija 111-112 (1971): 1-20.

Gligo discusses the music of Ives within the larger aesthetic context of what is often termed "spatial music." He argues that Ives in works such as *The Unanswered Question, Three Places in New England,* and the *Fourth Symphony,* succeeded in freeing himself from a tonal hierarchical perspective and independent layering of sound sources. Ives is thus shown to be a precursor of Varèse's *Poème électronique* and Xenakis's *Metastasis,* in which space becomes a necessary structural element. [English summary on page 20 does not mention Ives.]

B144 Rakhmamova, M. "Charl'z Ayvs." *Sovetskaya Muzyka* 35 (June 1971): 97-108.

Rakhmamova offers a sympathetic and generally accurate biographical and stylisitic survey that is noticeable for its avoidance of ideological argumentation. Relying heavily on the Cowell biography **(B354)** for its biographical data and discussion of *"Concord" Sonata*, Rakhmamova, in contrast to many European writers, considers Ives a thorough, albeit eclectic professional and an innovator with strong musical roots in the Transcendental school of nineteenth-century New England. He also compares Ives's *Essays* **(B660)** with Whitman's poetry, concluding that both men were successful in integrating a utopian philosophy into their art.

B145   Rosa, Alfred F. "Charles Ives: Music, Transcendentalism, and Politics." *The New England Quarterly* 44 (September 1971): 433-443.

A conventional introduction to selected compositions and political writings by Ives. Rosa demonstrates a sufficient knowledge of Trancendentalism, but does not succeed in showing that "Ives understood the Transcendental philosophy of anti-Lockeanism, intuition, Idealism, and the doctrine of correspondence." A lack of insight into Ives's music and several glaring errors (e.g., that Ives wrote few essays after World War I, when, in fact, he wrote all of his important musical writings after 1918), undermine the usefulness of Rosa's essay.

B146   Slonimsky, Nicolas. *Music Since 1900* (4th edition), pp. 64, 254, 256, 446, 523-524, 532-533, 549, 685, 813, 907, 975, 1070, 1150, 1199-1200, 1225, 1318-1348, 1432, 1439, 1445, 1464-1466, 1477, 1484, 1491, 1498. New York: Charles Scribner's Sons, 1971.

Slonimsky notes important Ives premieres and comments on programmatic and avant-garde features for most works. Specific Ives compositions are also cited throughout Slonimsky's index of 20th-century techniques as precursors of bitonality, dodecaphonic music, ethnic resources, metamusic, metric modulation, microtonality, polymetry, ragtime, sonic exuviation, and tone clusters. Also valuable is the inclusion of both sides of the Ives-Slonimsky correspondence (1929-1937).

1972

B147   Corner, Philip. "Thoreau, Charles Ives, and Contemporary Music." In *Henry Thoreau: Studies and Commentaries*, edited by Walter Harding, George Brenner, and Paul A. Doyle, pp. 53-81.

Rutherford, Madison, and Teaneck, NJ: Fairleigh Dickinson University Press, 1972; reprinted as "Thoreau and Ives with Specifics for This Time," pp. 15-39. In *Soundings: Ives Ruggles, Varèse. Soundings* (Spring 1974).

An attempt to create parallel ideological connections between Thoreau and Ives. Corner's principle technique is the juxtaposition of quotations by these two artists that refer to analogous concerns. He joins these quotations with gratuitious remarks and diatribes on contemporary musical and political life (e.g., "The line of hard work...is incompatible with the slick assurances and pretensions of study with Nadia Boulanger.") Unfortunately, as a result of this approach we learn far more about Corner than we do about Thoreau or Ives.

B148 Crunden, Robert M. Review of "Charles Ives and American Culture," by Frank R. Rossiter. *Yearbook for Inter-American Musical Research* 8 (1972): 181-184. *See:* **B148**

Review of Rossiter's unpublished dissertation. Crunden criticizes Rossiter's topical rather than chronological organization, his overquoting of secondary sources, "excessive" background on Yale in the 1890s, and several important omissions, especially a failure to recognize that other progressives shared Ives's artistic dilemma (i.e., the genteel versus the vernacular), and Rossiter's "regrettable neglect of religion." Despite the rigor of his critical response, Crunden praises Rossiter's originality, his "patient organization of the Ives material," and "the very great contribution to knowledge that the dissertation makes."

B149 Konold, Wulf. "Neue Musik in der Neuen Welt. Der Komponist Charles Ives." *Musica* 26, no. 3 (1972): 239-244.

Brief survey of Ives's life and musical style with an emphasis on such innovative stylistic techniques as collage (e.g., *The Fourth of July*) which influenced the composer, Alois Zimmermann. Konold also offers several parallels between Ives and his "friend" Mahler, and mentions in passing how Ives's use of folklore anticipated Bartók's similar interest.

B150 _____. "Schallplatten: Werke von Charles Ives." *Musica* 26, no. 3 (1972): 296+.

Konold reviews a large number of Ives recordings that recently entered the German market. With few exceptions (e.g., Bernstein's recording of the *Third Symphony*), he expresses only praise and respect for the technical and interpretative achievements embodied in the recordings that follow:

"The World of Charles Ives" (CBS S 77 406) [4 records]; *"Concord" Sonata* (Kirkpatrick); *String Quartets Nos. 1 and 2* **(D38)** (Juilliard Quartet); choral music and psalms (Gregg Smith Singers); *Three Places in New England, Washington's Birthday,* and *Robert Browning Overture* (Ormandy, Bernstein, Stokowski) **(D13, D26)**; *Symphony No. 2* and *Fourth of July* (Bernstein) **(D17)** ; *Symphony No. 3, Decoration Day, Central Park in the Dark, The Unanswered Question* (Bernstein) **(D1)**; *Symphony "Holidays"* (Johanos) **(D18)**; *Symphony No. 3* (Ormandy) (RCA LSC 3060-B); *Three Places in New England* (Thomas) (DG 2530 048); *String Quartets Nos. 1 and 2* (Kohon String Quartet); (Turnabout Vox TV 34 157 S); *From the Steeples and the Mountains* (Foss) **(D32)**; *Largo for Violin, Clarinet, and Piano* (DG 2 530 104); *Variations on America* (Zacher) (Wergo Wer 60 058); *"Concord" Sonata* and *Three-Page Sonata* (Szidon) (DG 2 530 215); *Orchestral Set No. 2* (Stokowski) (Decca SAD 22 117); *Three Places in New England* and *Symphony No. 3* (Hanson) (Philips 839 262 DSY); *Robert Browning Overture, The Unanswered Question, Set for Theatre Orchestra, The Circus Band March* (Farberman) **(D12)**; complete works for piano (Mandel) **(D48)**.

1973

B151 Helm, Everett. Review of *Charles E. Ives: Discography,* compiled by Richard Warren, Jr. *The Music Review* 34, no. 2 (May 1973): 175-176. *See*: **B17**

Despite Warren's exclusion of non-American non-commercially released recordings, Helm regards this list of 560 recordings a "labour of love and precision," and a "model discography." That one must travel to Yale University to hear deleted commercial recordings, however, since "copying is not permitted," Helm describes as "indeed, a fly in the ointment."

B152 Isham, Howard. "The Musical Thinking of Charles Ives." *Journal of Aesthetics and Art Criticism* 31 (Spring 1973): 395-404.

Isham remains unconvincing when drawing distinctions between Ives and Schoenberg, for example, that "the fundamental relational unit of Ives's musical language is not the *tone,* as it was for Schoenberg and his school, but the *sound."* He does, however, provide a thoughtful example in Berio's acknowledged Ives-influenced *Sinfonia* to support his central premise: "That in Ives's music and writings on music is to be found a style of musical thinking which forms the aesthetic foundation for new directions in the contemporary musical scene."

B153 Mandel, Alan. Review of *Charles E. Ives Memos*, edited by John Kirkpatrick. *Notes* 29, no. 4 (June 1973): 716-719. *See:* **B378**

Mandel demonstrates with a generous sample of quotations that the *Memos* illustrate Ives's originality, a "remarkable diversity in the range of his concerns and interests," the importance of the ideas behind the sounds, and "innumerable examples...of how Ives relates music to other aspects of life."

B154 Rossiter, Frank R. Review of *Charles E. Ives Memos*, edited by John Kirkpatrick. *Yearbook for Inter-American Music Research* 9 (1973): 182-185. *See:* **B378**

Rossiter discusses "two principal themes" explored in these *Memos*: Ives's "music itself--its nature and the influences that acted upon it" and "Ives's terrible musical isolation during the first two decades of this century." In contrast to the interpretation he offers in his biography, Rossiter here interprets Ives's isolation as an irony, with a potentially eager avant-garde audience "forming literally around the corner from Ives in New York," rather than as a tragedy. *See:* **B215**

B155 Vinay, Gianfranco. "Charles Ives e i musicisti Europei: Anticipazioni e dipendenze." *Nuova Rivista Musicale Italiana* 7 (July-December 1973): 417-429.

Substantially the same as the chapter, "Ives e i musicisti europei: affinita, anticipazioni e dipendenze," in Vinay's book, *L'America musicale di Charles Ives.* As suggested by the title, Vinay focuses on the degree to which Ives anticipated the musical language of the twentieth century. Of special interest are his comparisons and contrasts between Ives and Mahler (e.g., how these composers approached remembrance with nostalgia and anguish respectively), and stylistic analogies between the piano music of Ives and Debussy. Musical examples are excerpted from Hindemith's *Kammermusik No. 1*, Debussy's *Suite Bergamasque*, and Ives's *Robert Browning Overture* and *First Piano Sonata. See:* **B187**

B156 Wallach, Laurence. "The New England Education of Charles Ives." Ph.D. dissertation, Columbia University, 1973. 396 pages.

The most thorough study of Ives's musical education and compositional development in Danbury (1874-1893) and a solid introduction to Ives's further musical growth in New Haven and Yale (1893-1898). Wallach demonstrates an impressive grasp of primary sources such as letters, diaries, and contemporary newspaper accounts, and provides a thoughtful analysis or at least some discussion of nearly every early work whether complete or incomplete. He also devotes valuable chapters on the "decline of community music-making and the simultaneous rise of art-music in nineteenth-century America" and the life and musical career of Ives's father, George, and two slightly less successful chapters on "transcendental rhetoric" and "transcendental aesthetics."

Appendixes include a program from the Chicago World's Fair (1893), half of a *New York Herald* article (January 5, 1890) about Danbury's musical organizations, and transcriptions of fourteen unpublished works from the Danbury period (*New Year's Dance*; *Two Hymns*; *Psalm 42*; *"Jerusalem the Golden" Variations* [Var. 2]; *Postlude in F*; *Because of You*; *A Song in G*; *All Love* [two excerpts]; *The Year's at the Spring*; *I Think of Thee*; *Crossing the Bar*; *Psalm 139*; *Easter Carol*; and *God of My Life*) and three unpublished works that Ives composed while at Yale (*Fugue in Four Keys*; *Organ Fugue in C Minor*; and *Pre-First Violin Sonata* (first movement).

1974

B157 Buechner, Alan. "Ives in the Classroom: A Teaching Guide to Two Compositions." *Music Educator's Journal* 61, no. 2 (October 1974): 64-70.

Introduction to Ives for high school or college music appreciation courses. Buechner has selected two works, the *Variations on America* for organ and the Finale to the *Second Symphony*, and provides useful step-by-step lesson plans and descriptive analytical outlines for each work.

B158 Chase, Gilbert. "Charles Ives and American Culture." *High Fidelity/Musical America* 24, no. 10 (October 1974): MA 17-19.

Chase discusses two contrasting conceptions of "culture": 1) culture as equivalent to "the Genteel Traditions's ideals of dignity, refinement, and purity"; and 2) culture as "the *manmade part of the human environment*." He contends that Ives's cultural perspective corresponds to the latter conception and "that there is a common root for his view of art and that of the cultural anthropologist." Chase cites this and other reasons to explain "why Charles Ives is the first American composer to have seriously engaged the interest of cultural historians."

B159 Cooper, Frank. "The Ives Revelation: Columbia's Contribution to the Ives Centennial." *Music: The AGO/RCCO Magazine* 10 (October 1974): 30+.

Review of Columbia's centennial album, *Charles Ives: The 100th Anniversary* (M4 32504). Cooper focuses on Record IV, "Ives Plays Ives," a record he considers nothing less than "the most important piece of documentation in the history of American music." He also values Ives's performance as an artistic document and expresses the opinion that none of the greatest Ives interpreters "has matched this combination of purely musical tone, cantabile phrasing and rhythmic ease."

B160 Corner, Philip. "Charles Ives," In *Soundings: Ives, Ruggles, Varèse. Soundings* (Spring 1974): 135-197.

In idiosyncratic and occasionally provocative but undeveloped and somewhat diffuse personal observations, Corner offers separate treatment to *The Unanswered Question, On the Antipodes, Some Southpaw Pitching, Anti-Abolitionist Riots,* and *Three-Page Sonata.* Corner notes Ives's use of a twelve-tone row in this last work. (earlier he discussed Ives's use of C major), and inserts asides on performance indeterminacy in the *First Piano Sonata* and ostinatos in the *Second String Quartet* and *Over the Pavements.*

B161 Cott, Jonathan. "Charles Ives, Musical Inventor." *The New York Times,* October 29, 1974, page 21+.

In this thoughtful centennial tribute Cott uses Ives's quotations from Emerson to "explain why Ives...never thought of using his technical discoveries ...as the foci of new musical systems." He also considers several philosophical issues: That "Ives's method of simultaneous presentation discloses nothing less than a world of profound synchronicity," and that Ives's music "anticipates the future because it originates from a perspective that sees time as laid out, simultaneously not successively, in space."

B162 Cowell, Sidney. "Ivesiana: 'More Than Something Just Usual.'" *High Fidelity/Musical America* 24, no. 10 (October 1974): MA 14-16; reprinted as the "New Forward" in the 1983 Da Capo Press

edition of *Charles Ives and His Music* by Henry and Sidney Cowell.
See: **B354**

Sidney Cowell explains how Seeger's and Ruggles's original
antipathy for Ives's music delayed Henry Cowell's direct exposure
until 1927 (when it precipitated an immediate positive response).
She relates her observations of her visits (with her husband) with
Charles and Harmony Ives in New York or West Redding after
1940, especially the conversations between Mr. Cowell and Mr.
Ives on how to create musical explosions and ways to continue
the *Universe Symphony*.

B163   Crunden, Robert. "Charles Ives' Innovative Nostalgia." *The Choral
Journal* 15, no. 4 (December 1974): 5-12.

Original overview of Ives's career and thought. Crunden shows
how Ives's business, political, and musical ideology parallels the
views of Progressive Era figures such as John Dewey. In his
central argument Crunden argues that Ives's "nostalgia and its
values can lead to music that is truly innovative."

B164   Dickinson, Peter. Review of *Charles Ives: Memos*, edited by John
Kirkpatrick; Ives's *Essays Before a Sonata and Other Writings*,
edited by Howard Boatwright; *Charles E. Ives: Discography*, by
Richard Warren; and *L'America Musicale di Charles Ives*, by
Gianfranco Vinay. *The Musical Times* 115 (November 1974): 947-
948. *See*: **B378, B660, B17,** and **B187**

Dickinson focuses almost exclusively on the *Memos*. He
discusses the genesis and historical importance of this volume
and expresses the opinion that as editor, "Kirkpatrick has
provided a body of information which no serious student or
performer can do without." Following this assessment Dickinson
points out that "its copious organization and planning--in ironic
contrast with Ives's own haphazard attitude--is also a landmark
in musical documentation."

B165   _____. "New York, New Haven." *The Musical Times* 115
(December 1974): 1067+.

Concise summary of the Ives Centennial Conference held in New
York and New Haven, October 17-21, a conference Dickinson
views as "well balanced between critical discussion and lively
concerts, with some first performances and new arrangements."

B166   Geselbracht, Raymond. "Evolution and the New World Vision in
the Music of Charles Ives." In *Journal of American Studies*, edited

by Dennis Welland, Vol. 8, no. 2, pp. 211-227. London: Cambridge University Press, 1974.

Geselbracht discusses one of Ives's central aesthetic positions: That Nature "through its principle of evolution, moves from chaos toward integration." He then tries to show how an evolving interpretation of Nature influenced Ives's musical compositions throughout his career. For example, Geselbracht describes the dialectic between the "lyric motive" and the "epic motive" in *"Concord" Sonata* as appropriately resolved "in a quiet communion with Nature" in the movement dedicated to the nature-loving Thoreau. *On the Antipodes* reveals that after World War I Ives could see Nature as an enemy as well as friend, an agent of evil as well as the divine.

B167 Goldman, Richard Franko. "American Music: 1918-1960. (i) Music in the United States, Charles Ives." *New Oxford History of Music*, Band 10, pp. 574-582. London, New York, Toronto: Oxford University Press, 1974.

Sympathetic overview that depicts Ives as a composer who possessed "an imagination coupled with intellect" and "the independence that can come only from tradition and discipline, the solid base over which the most diverse elements can be assimilated and made into a new unity." Traditional emphasis on Ives's technical innovations, precocious modernity, and independence from Europe.

B168 Gray, Michael H. Review of *Charles E. Ives: Discography*, by Richard Warren. *Notes* 31, no. 1 (1974): 63-64.

In a single paragraph of a review devoted to ten recently published discographies Gray lauds Warren's Ives discography, "which assembles an enormous amount of pertinent information in an ideally concise and accessible format....a standard for its subject, and a standard for discographic publications."

B169 Henderson, Clayton W. "Ives' Use of Quotation." *Music Educator's Journal* 61, no. 2 (October 1974): 24-28.

An introduction to Ives's technique of borrowing that includes musical illustrations to show specific transformation devices, a graph on the "architectonic structure" of the first place in New England, and general remarks on several of Ives's compositional approaches to pre-existent thematic material. *See*: **B125** and **B170**

B170 _____. "Structural Importance of Borrowed Music in the Works of Charles Ives: A Preliminary Assessment." In *Report of the Eleventh Congress of the International Musicological Society Held at Copenhagen, 1972,* edited by Henrik Glahn et. al., Vol. I, pp. 437-446.

Useful introduction to Ives's use of borrowed material. Henderson offers a wide-ranging summary of Ives's "principal designs and/or figures in works containing quotations" (rhapsodic/improvisatory style, chorale-oriented, rondo, verse and refrain/chorus, ternary form, arch, and cyclic use of quotation). He also presents five graphs and abundant musical examples that illustrate these designs in various Ives works, including the *Third Violin Sonata, Thanksgiving, Three Places in New England* ("St. Gaudens"), *First Piano Sonata,* and the *Fourth Symphony. See*: **B125** and **B169**

B171 Hitchcock, H. Wiley, ed. *Charles Ives Centennial Festival-Conference.* Program Booklet. New York: G. Schirmer and Associated Music Publishers, 1974.

Informative background notes on the works performed at the Ives Centennial Festival-Conference held at New York and New Haven, October 17-21. Also included are capsule biographies of the participants and seventeen International Views of Ives. *See*: **B253**

B172 Kerr, Hugh H. "Report from Miami: Ives Centennial Festival, 1974-75." *Current Musicology* 18 (1974): 41-42.

In this newsletter Kerr describes in some detail the participants and program for this ambitious festival (October 1974 to May 1975). Scheduled highlights included "the performance of substantially all of Charles Ives's known compositions" and "the projected world premiere of portions of Ives's unpublished 'Universe Symphony.'"

B173 Kirkpatrick, John. Review of *From the Steeples and the Mountains,* by David Wooldridge. *High Fidelity/ Musical America* 24, no. 9 (September 1974): MA 33-36.

A stinging attack on what Kirkpatrick describes as "an exciting historical novel with the illusion of authenticity." Kirkpatrick challenges Wooldridge on dozens of factual and interpretative statements and devotes a lengthy paragraph to rebutting the author's "allegations against Parker" (especially the alleged failures of Ives's teacher during his student days in Germany).

As a result of Wooldridge's practice of presenting "on almost every page...imagined possibilities masquerading as apparent certainties," Kirkpatrick seriously doubts the legitimacy of "the few scoops which, if true, contribute valuable data, chiefly the Messerklinger story [p. 150], and the correspondence between Parker and H. E. Wooldridge about Mahler [pp. 205-206]." *See*: **B193**

B174 Konold, Wulf. "Arkadien in Neuengland: Zum hundersten Geburtstag von Charles Edward Ives. *Musica* 28, no. 5 (1974): 468-469.

Konold argues that Ives's musical prophecies have had a greater influence on composers in the 1970s such as Cage than the serialism of Schoenberg. According to Konold, Ives's emphasis on process rather than system is especially relevant to contemporary musical thought.

B175 McLendon, James Wm., Jr. "Expanding the Theory: Charles Edward Ives--Theologian in Music." In *Biography as Theology: How Life Stories Can Remake Today's Thoelogy*, pp. 140-169. Nashville and New York: Abingdon Press, 1974.

Thoughtful Ivesian survey based on the Cowell biography (**B354**) and Ives's *Essays* (**B660**) and *Memos* (**B378**). After stating his premise that, "as with every source, Ives took what the Transcendentalists gave him and recomposed it as his own," McLendon offers several reasonable conclusions as to how Ives reinterpreted Transcendentalism in his aesthetic, political, and business philosophy. He then focuses on Ives's broad "musico-theological vision" as it is revealed in the composer's evolving treatment of "Beulah Land" (from the *First String Quartet* to the *Fourth Symphony*).

B176 Morelli, Giovanni. Review of *L'America Musicale di Charles Ives*, by Gianfranco Vinay. *Rivista Italiana di Musicologia* 9 (1974): 316-322. *See*: **B187**

Morelli notes how Vinay shares Cowell's view (**B354**) that Ives used borrowed material for structural purposes, and not capriciously as argued by Kurt Stone (**B521**). He also discusses Vinay's examination of Cage's published response to Ives (**B325-326**) and concludes that Ives's influence on Cage and other experimentalists demonstrates an impact that goes beyond the "private laboratory of a reclusive maestro" ("laboratorio privato serale di un maetro eluso").

B177   Morgan, Robert P. "Let's Hear It from Charlie Ives!" *High Fidelity* 24, no. 10 (October 1974): 79-81.

Review of Columbia's 5-record 100th anniversary album (Col. M4 32504), Serebrier's performance of the *Fourth Symphony* (**D6**), Ormandy's *Second*, and the Zukofsky-Kalish reinterpretation of the Violin Sonatas (**D35**). Particularly valuable are Morgan's remarks on Ives as an interpreter of his own music (fourth record of the centennial album). He considers the Serbrier performance "unquestionably the clearest, most precise, and most decisive that we have on disc," although it "does not in any way 'displace' the Stokowski edition" (**D7**).

B178   Norris, Christopher. "American Pioneer." *Music and Musicians* 23, no. 2 (October 1974): 36-38+.

Norris offers a centennial review of Ives in which he considers "the best of Ives" those works such as the *Robert Browning Overture* that depart from the "usual track of large-scale inspiration." Because Ives did not develop his avant-garde techniques into "a whole compositional programme," Norris laments the exaggerated emphasis commonly placed on their historical importance.

B179   Perry, Rosalie Sandra. *Charles Ives and the American Mind.* Kent, Ohio: Kent State University Press, 1974; revised version of "Charles Ives and American Culture." Ph.D. dissertation, University of Texas at Austin, 1972. *See:* **B206** and **B208**

Despite the absence of a central thesis, several significant unsubstantiated claims, and the overstatement of such issues as the pervasiveness of Transcendentalism in Ives's life and thought, this book is nevertheless replete with interesting and original observations. Perry credits Parker perhaps with too much influence on Ives's aesthetic development [most effectively challenged by Burkholder (**B296**)], but she places the musical legacy of Ives's music professor in clearer perspective than most studies. She also comments thoughtfully on Ives's musical rhetoric and the importance of stream of consciousness and religion in the development of his unique aesthetic. The published edition includes a foreword by Gilbert Chase that focuses on the gradual recognition of and scholarly interest in Ives, especially after 1960.

B180   Porter, Andrew. "Songs His Father Taught Him." *The New Yorker* 50, no. 37 (4 November 1974): 187-190+.

Acknowledging that he "borrowed freely" from Rossiter's dissertation, Porter reviews the Ives "legend" and Ives's psychological complexities. He also echoes Carter's "doubt whether Ives' direct vernacular quotations are from music strong enough to bear the weight with which he charged them." At the outset of his essay Porter cites the *BMI Orchestral Survey* of 1972-73 that shows that Ives's total of 467 orchestral performances "surpasses not only those of all compatriots but also of Bartók, Prokofieff, and Shostakovich." This mark of success convinces Porter that Ives "hardly needs champions now." The highly critical tone of this essay provides sufficient evidence that Ives could not count on Porter, one of "new" music's most articulate spokesmen, to support his posthumous struggle to achieve an unambiguously positive artistic reputation. *See:* **B215** and **B668**

B181 Rich, Alan. "Must We Now Praise Famous Men?" *New York* 7, no. 43 (28 October 1974): 95-96.

Rich's "note of dissent" is perhaps the essay most critical of Ives to appear during the centenary year. He acknowledges as "technically deserved" Ives's recognition as the discoverer of "many of the musical tricks that years later were to become fair territory for important contemporary composers," and he grants Ives "a certain degree of respect" for some of his smaller works and songs. But Rich disputes the idea that Ives possessed "an artistic overview that makes the trickery justified and important," and he denies that Ives's experimentalism "suggested further explorations." He concludes by comparing Ives to other "accidental innovators" (such as Gesualdo) "whose place in the history of genuine innovation is somewhat akin to that of the chimpanzee who eventually types out *Gone With the Wind.*"

B182 Saal, Hubert. "Connecticut Yankee." *Newsweek* 84 (4 November 1974): 71.

A brief survey of some highlights of the Ives Centennial, including the "Mini-Festival" at Lincoln Center, the Miami Festival, and especially the "movable five-day Ivesian feast" in New York and New Haven. According to Saal, Ives "was immeasurably the greatest American composer and, with Stravinsky and Schoenberg, a seminal figure in twentieth-century music."

B183 Salzman, Eric. "Charles Ives--A Centennial Keepsake Album from Columbia." *Stereo Review* 33, no. 3 (September 1974): 122-123.

Salzman precedes his overview of the five-record Centennial Album (Columbia M4 32504) by quickly dispelling some of the conventional Ivesian myths. He concludes that Ives was "the last representative of a great tradition of American music of which he was also, apart from his father, the only member."

B184 Schonberg, Harold C. "Natural American, Natural Rebel, Natural Avant-Gardist." *The New York Times Magazine* (21 April 1974): 12-13+.

A highly readable and for the most part reliable overview of Ives's career and the career of his music that incorporates well-chosen and well-integrated quotations. Schonberg stresses "the dichotomy between the kind of music he wrote and the kind of world he was trying to express," and the nostalgic retrospection over the more often recognized avant-garde vision. Particularly insightful is an insert, "Ives at the keyboard," on which Schonberg discusses the recently released recording of Ives's piano playing (Columbia M4 32504), describes Ives's romantic and emotional interpretative approach, and concludes that Ives was "a better and more imaginative pianist than any who have played the 'Concord' to date." The most extended essay on Ives by one his most ardent and influential supporters.

B185 Tick, Judith. "Ragtime and the Music of Charles Ives." *Current Musicology* 18 (1974): 105-113.

In this survey of Ives's transformation of ragtime Tick "refutes Copland's contention that 'serious composers became aware of the polyrhythmic nature of Afro-American music only in its jazz phases.'" She argues that Ives "carried certain tendencies in popular ragtime to great extremes," but she also points out historical precedents for several of Ives's seemingly radical notions. The essay contains musical examples from Joplin's *School of Ragtime* and Ives's *Over the Pavements, First Piano Sonata,* and *Third Violin Sonata.*

B186 Tilmouth, Michael. Review of *Charles E. Ives: Memos,* edited by John Kirkpatrick. *Music and Letters* 55, no. 1 (1974): 112-113. *See:* **B378**

Throughout this review Tilmouth considers these *Memos* "something of a hotch-potch and perhaps for that reason no bad reflection of Ives the man and (part-time) musician." Nevertheless he concludes with the salvo that Kirkpatrick's accomplishment is "a major contribution to what we know of Ives as man and musician."

B187 Vinay, Gianfranco. *L'America Musicale di Charles Ives.* Torino [Turin]: Giulio Einaudi, 1974. *See:* **B164, B176, B213, B219-220**

The most substantial Ives study in Italian and one of the few published book-length studies in any language. Vinay bases his biographical material largely on the Cowell biography (**B354**), and devotes much attention to the Transcendental influences on Ives. His sixth chapter is derived (with only a few alterations) on the essay published in *Nuova Rivista Musicale Italiana* the previous year (**B155**). In discussing Ives's musical syntax Vinay focuses on three topics: layering and contrapuntal heterophony; the use of quotation; and Ives's unique interpretation of sonata form and thematic growth. In this latter section Vinay also briefly surveys the piano sonatas and the violin sonatas. Finally, Vinay tries to summarize the nature of Ives's Transcendental musical language and the distinctions Ives made between "manner" and "substance." The book contains a chronological catalogue of works but no musical illustrations.

B188 Wallach, Laurence. Review of *Charles E. Ives: Memos*, edited by John Kirkpatrick. *The Musical Quarterly* 60, no. 2 (1974): 284-290.

Well-balanced and informative review of this indispensable resource which Wallach rightly considers "the closest thing we have to an autobiography...especially valuable for the scrupulously objective way that documentary material is presented [by Kirkpatrick]." Although disturbed by the overabundance of bitter aphorisms, Wallach for the most part understands and symphathizes with Ives's extreme and ubiquitous defensiveness. He considers "most significant" the fact "that Ives lays down clear terms for listening to and evaluating his music," and concludes that "the overall picture of his *oeuvre* seems less anarchic and more structured once one is aware of the composer's own criteria."

B189 Ward, Charles. "Charles Ives: The Relationship Between Aesthetic Theories and Compositional Processes." Ph.D. dissertation, University of Texas at Austin, 1974. 190 pp.

Thoughtful study of Ives's aesthetic.
Chapter 1: A review of Ives's philosophical commitment to

idealism and faith in the "moral goodness" of man as espoused in the *Essays* (**B660**).
Chapter 2: How Ives viewed technique and experimentation as subordinate to the "substance" of a musical work.
Chapter 3: How Ives translated artistic intuitions and ideas into musical sounds.
Chapter 4: "Like Berlioz, Ives thought of music as representational in the sense of displaying the dramatic implications of human experience."
Chapter 5: Without rejecting the musical importance of quotation, Ward emphasizes the symbolic (textual and programmatic) potential of the borrowed materials Ives selected.

B190 _____. "Charles Ives's Concept of Music." *Current Musicology* 18 (1974): 114-119.

Throughout this essay Ward returns to Ives's often-cited diatribe, "My God! What has sound got to do with music!" as indicative that "Ives's concept of music was metaphysical in the highest transcendental sense." Ward then tries to show with only partial success, despite his clear summary of Thoreau's ideas on music, that the "roots" of Ives's musical philosophy can be *directly* linked to the man Ives described as a "great musician...because he did not have to go to Boston to hear 'the Symphony.'"

B191 Westenburg, Richard. "Charles Ives." *Music/The AGO-RCCO Magazine* 8, no. 10 (1974): 26-29.

Conventional overview of Ives's career and thought that emphasizes Ives's reliogiosity. Includes liberal quotations from Bellamann, Carter, Mellers, and especially Ives's *Essays* (**B660**).

B192 Wooldridge, David. *From the Steeples and Mountains: A Study of Charles Ives.* New York: Alfred A. Knopf, 1974. *See:* **B173, B197, B209, B213, B234, B242, B264, B397**

Without doubt the most controversial Ives biography. Although Wooldridge bases his study on primary documents and quotes generously from Ives's letters and marginalia, his failure to document a barrage of interpretations greatly diminishes the book's value. His hypothesis that Harmony Ives had a hysterectomy ten months after their marriage was subsequently verified by Sidney Cowell, but his conjectures that "Ives wasn't allowed to sleep with her again" remains merely an unsubstantiated guess, and his claim that "Ives must have started to play the stock market" as an explanation for why the composer stopped composing has been discredited by Burkholder (**B296**). In his review Kirkpatrick vehemently disputes more than fifty additional "facts" (**B173**).

Particularly provocative is Wooldridge's reported conversation with Messerklinger, a timpanist who had played under Mahler in Munich, and who provides a plausible recollection that Mahler conducted Ives's *Third Symphony* in Munich in 1910. Wooldridge's idiosyncratic and seldom documented biography also contains numerous original observations about Ives and his work. Taken with the necessary salt, this frustrating and often justifiably criticized profile remains a valuable source.

B193 Wooldridge, David, and John Kirkpatrick. "The New Ives Biography: A Disagreement." *High Fidelity/Musical America* 24, no. 12 (December 1974): MA 18+.

Wooldridges's rebuttal to Kirkpatrick's aggressively negative review of *From the Steeples and Mountains* (**B173**) and Kirkpatrick's counterattack. Of the sixty "sample" errors cited in Kirkpatrick's review, Wooldridge acknowledges the validity of four and accuses Kirkpatrick of "misreadings, false assumptions, and willful misrepresentations" of fifty others.

The last word in this often-personal exchange of unpleasantaries is given to Kirkpatrick, who responds to Wooldridge's challenge on numerous points of fact and several of interpretation. Kirkpatrick chastizes Wooldridge repeatedly for his "presentation of conjecture as fact" and for his unwillingness to acknowledge "the obligation to reveal and clarify distinctions between the possible, probable, or certain."

B194 "Ives the Innovator." *Time* 104, no. 19 (4 November 1974): 85+.

Although *Time* finds Ives's music as difficult and complex as any music in the literature and "easier to praise than to listen to," the weekly news magazine with the largest circulation states without equivocation that "Ives is generally acknowledged as the greatest, certainly the most original of America's composers." Despite inevitable over-simplifications and some questionable conclusions, e.g., that Ives's quotations of popular music "can be said to have prophesied pop art," these three-plus columns add up to a remarkable centennial tribute.

1975

B195   Anderson, William. "Editorially Speaking: Composer Charles Ives
Enters History." *Stereo Review* 34, no. 3 (March 1975): 4.

In this sardonic post-centennial editorial Anderson explicates
Schoenberg's often printed or invoked "Sacred Text" (**B390**), and
concludes that Ives did not deserve this panegyric "to his
unassailable artistic virtue." Although Anderson expresses
"admiration for the splendid craft," he remains highly critical of
Ives's "essentially unlovable" music and clearly considers Ives a
much over-rated composer.

B196   Austin, William W. *"Susanna," "Jeanie," and "The Old Folks at
Home": The Songs of Stephen C. Foster from His Time to Ours*, pp.
317-330. New York: Macmillan Publishing Co., 1975.

Austin offers a rich interpretative discussion of Foster's meaning
in the life and work of Ives. In explaining the contexts of the five
Foster songs that Ives incorporated into numerous works, Austin
devotes most of his attention to the *Second Symphony*, the
"Thoreau" movement from *"Concord" Sonata*, "The St. Gaudens in
Boston Common" from *Three Places in New England*, and "Elegy
for Our Forefathers" from the *Second Orchestral Set* (which until
as late as 1947 was entitled *Elegy for Stephen Foster*). But he
does not neglect other important Foster reminiscences in works
such as the *Trio for Violin, Cello, and Piano, Third March, The
Things Our Fathers Loved, Some Southpaw Pitching*, and the
Theater Orchestra Set.

B197   Davenport, Guy. "Ives the Master." *Parnassus: Poetry in Review*
3, no. 2 (Spring-Summer 1975): 374-380.

Apparently unmoved by or oblivious to Kirkpatrick's
overwhelmingly negative review (**B173**), Davenport opens his
essay with an unequivocally laudatory assessment of
Wooldridge's controversial Ives biography (**B192**), a book which
Davenport considers to be "the only book on Ives worthy of its
subject." Davenport then offers parallels between Ives and
various literary figures, lists several reasons to explain Ives's
"classic American obscurity," and concludes that "Ives aligns with
the most significant art of his time."

B198   Eiseman, David. "George Ives as Theorist: Some Unpublished
Documents." *Perspectives of New Music* 14, no. 1 (Fall-Winter
1975): 139-147.

Informative discussion and convincing interpretation of George
Ives's unfinished and unpublished pedagogical article on music
theory and other evidence of his influence on his son as revealed
in the *Memos* (**B378**). Eiseman concludes that "Charles's own
writings refect the same resistance to tradition, the same open-
mindedness toward possibilities, the same reliance upon the ear
as the ultimate judge."

B199 Fleming, Shirley. "Of Ives, Elephants, and Polish Independence;
A Five Day Festival Covers It All. *High Fidelity/Musical America*
25, no. 2 (February 1975): MA 26-29.

Review of the Ives Centennial proceedings (New York and New
Haven, October 17-21, 1974). Although Fleming briefly reviews
the Festival concerts, she devotes the majority of her report to a
summary of the content of the papers and panels presented.
Rather than taking sides on the frequently contradictory ideas
expressed, Fleming tries to show that like an elephant, Ives "is
whatever you want to make of him." According to Fleming, a
central unanswered Ivesian question raised by this conference is
"whether Ives was the sophisticated and highly self-aware
innovator which so many claim, or a happy-go-lucky
experimenter who plucked inventions almost casually out of a
rich imagination but backed away from pursuing them
intellectually to their fullest implications."

B200 Harrison, Max. Review of *Charles Ives Remembered*, by Vivian
Perlis, and *Charles E. Ives: Memos*, edited by John Kirkpatrick.
Composer (London) 55 (Summer 1975): 37-38. *See*: **B318** and
B378

In this brief review of these two important books Harrison asks us
to think of Ives as a 19th-century composer, "too much having
been made of his anticipation of tone-rows, multiple orchestras,
etc." Harrison also writes that Ives's caricatures of contemporary
classics such as Stravinsky's *Le Sacre du Printemps* (described by
Carter [**B668**]), prove that "Ives was as inept at criticism as most
composers."

B201 Helms, Hans G. "Charles Edward Ives--Ideal American or Social
Critic?" *Current Musicology* 19 (1975): 37-44; reprinted in
German as "Charles Edward Ives--idealer Amerikaner oder
Sozialkritiker?" *Beiträge zur Musikwissenshaft* 20, no. 1 (1978):
16-22.

Report on the Ives Centennial Festival-Conference (New York and New Haven, October 17-21, 1974). Helms argues vigorously but without much support that Ives should be interpreted as a socialist, a pacifist, and a man who "related ideas about music as a functioning political force in the class struggle." He criticizes the Conference for failing to discuss "Ives's socio-economic critique" and interprets Ives's writings and music through a Marxist looking glass. Helms's Ivesian view prompted a vigorous rebuttal by Taruskin. *See*: **B217**

B202 Henahan, Donal. Review of *Charles Ives and His America*, by Frank R. Rossiter. *The New York Times Book Review*, November 30, 1975, section 7, pages 41-42. *See*: **B215**

Henahan attributes Rossiter's basic premise to Thomson's famous Ives essay (**B403**), but credits Rossiter with offering some new ideas on "the psychosexual dynamics of art." Although Henahan devotes most of his review to these dynamics, even obliquely endorsing "the facile theory beloved of amateur psychiatrists" of Ives as "a repressed homosexual," he concludes that "all that counts finally is what comes of the conflicting forces and psychic demons struggling within each artist, and [that] it is the inevitability and the desirability of such conflict that studies such as Rossiter's seem to undervalue."

B203 Kaufman, Charles H. Review of *Charles Ives Remembered*, by Vivian Perlis, and *Charles Ives and the American Band Tradition*, by Jonathan Elkus. *Notes* 34, no. 2 (1975): 273-275. *See*: **B318** and **B579**

Kaufman is the only reviewer of *Charles Ives Remembered* to seriously question Perlis's editorial practices. A comparison between interview excerpts released on the Columbia Records centennial album bonus record (M4 32504) and the published transcriptions reveals the following: "In many instances material has been left out in the transcription, the order of statements has been shifted, what might be construed as somewhat offensive material has been deleted or changed, and, in at least one instance, there is an outright error." Kaufman also finds little to praise in Elkus's "somewhat overblown" pamphlet.

B204 Lamb, Gordon H. "Interview with Robert Shaw." *The Choral Journal* 15, no. 8 (1975): 5-7.

Shaw recalls his experiences as a conductor of several Ives works, both for chorus and for orchestra. In contrast to most conductors who tend to exaggerate the difficulties in conducting Ives, Shaw relates that "There were never any problems, I think, in the *Harvest Home Chorales* or in the *Fourth Symphony* that couldn't be reconciled simply by telling the forces what you are doing." He also speaks of the Ives practice "in which fragmentation precedes assembly or statement" (designated "cumulative settings" by Burkholder (**B284**), and finds the origins of this practice as early as Ives's *First Symphony*.

B205 Leuchtmann, Horst. Review of *Charles Ives in seiner Kammermusik für drei bis sechs Instrumente,* by Ulrich Maske. *Neue Musikzeitung* 24, no. 4 (1975): 15. *See:* **B585**

Leuchtmann praises Ives's variety and modernity and considers Maske's analysis of twenty-one chamber works "an important contribution for the history of the new music" ("ein wichtiger Beitrag für die Geschichte der Neuen Musik").

B206 Mellers, Wilfrid. "The Sound of Democracy." Review of *Charles Ives Remembered,* by Vivian Perlis, and *Charles Ives and the American Mind,* by Rosalie Sandra Perry. *The Times Literary Supplement* (January 24, 1975): 81. *See:* **B319** and **B179**

Meller concludes that while Perry's study "provides valuable documentary evidence about the mind and art of this great American, it is Dr. Perlis's book that best enables us to understand why Ives 'stays news.'" In his attempt to clarify why Ives did not pursue music as a professional composer Mellers writes that "the producer-consumer relationship inherent in commercial concert-promotion was extraneous to his view of art." He also explains a paradox that is "latent in all true art of our time," that if Ives's "common men" had been able to hear his music, "they would have been outraged, because their ideas as to what music 'ought' to be were conditioned by what they themselves were not--that is, by genteel European tradition."

B207 Morgan, Robert P. Review of *Charles Ives and His America,* by Frank R. Rossiter. *Yearbook for Inter-American Musical Research* 11 (1975): 225-228. *See:* **B215**

Morgan finds much to praise in Rossiter's "fascinating portrait of Ives and his time," but he criticizes the author for failing to place Ives's musical thought within a musical context. Morgan practices what he preaches on several occasions. *See:* **B256** and **B406**.

B208 Muser, Frani. Review of *Charles Ives Remembered*, by Vivian Perlis, and *Charles Ives and the American Mind*, by Rosalie Sandra Perry. *The Musical Quarterly* 61, no. 3 (July 1975): 485-490. *See:* **B318** and **B179**

Summary, or "composite portrait," through a liberal use of quotation, of Perlis's "meticulously edited and handsomely presented" oral history, a work which "joins with distinction" the *Memos* (**B378**), the *Essays* (**B660**), Kirkpatrick's *Catalogue* (**B7**), and the Cowell biography (**B354**). Muser is highly critical of Perry and supports the view that her study "fails to present any fresh material about Ives" since it is marred by "errors of fact and arbitrary interpretations."

B209 Norris, Christorpher. Review of Charles Ives: A Portrait, by David Wooldridge. Music and Musicians 23, no. 12 (August 1975): 37. See: B192

Despite his annoyance with Wooldridge's "peculiarities of style," Norris considers this biography the best book to appear in response to the Ives centenary. After citing specific instances of Wooldridge's insights into such matters as Ives's reading tastes and the meaning of his marginal notes, Norris concludes, in stark contrast to Kirkpatrick (**B173**), that this book "is large-minded, truthful and informed, with a breadth of knowledge which one rarely finds in musical biographies."

B210 ____. Review of *Charles E. Ives: Memos*, edited by John Kirkpatrick; *Charles Ives Remembered*, by Vivian Perlis; and *Charles Ives and the American Band Tradition*, by Jonathan Elkus. *Music and Musicians* 23, no. 7 (26 March 1975): 26-27. *See:* **B378**, **B318**, and **B579**

Norris finds that Ives's persistent defensiveness in his *Memos* belies "that famous independence of spirit and indifference to opinion." He accepts unquestioningly Carter's recollections of Ives in Perlis's oral history, and praises Elkus, who "throws out hints enough for a dozen books or theses."

B211 Palisca, Claude. "Report on the Musicological Year 1974 in the United States." *Acta Musicologica* 47, no. 2 (1975): 285-286.

Palisca cites the unique features of the Ives Centennial Festival-Conference (October 17-21), including the noted composers in attendance and special performances (several based on new editions), and quotes from Hitchcock's summaries of selected papers. He concludes that "doubters had to admit that the best works...possess a richness of poetic allusion and an infinity of meanings that shift with each hearing," but that "many long-time admirers of Ives had to concede that some of his music is rather lightweight."

B212 Perrin, Peter. "The Composer as Historian." *Arts Canada* 198-199 (June 1975): 58+.

In his discussion of several composers of various nationalities, Perrin singles out Ives as the representative American "historian in music." Among numerous works that recall specific historical places and events or conjure a more generalized nostalgia, Perrin regards Ives's "greatest achievement as historian" to be *"Concord"* *Sonata*, "the noblest piece of music ever written in the Western Hemisphere." Although Perrin's essay provides excellent public relations for Ives enthusiasts, it does not contribute to our understanding of "the greatest composer North America has produced so far, music's only equivalent to Melville."

B213 Prausnitz, Frederik. Review of *Charles Ives Remembered*, by Vivian Perlis; *Charles Ives: A Portrait*, by David Wooldridge; *Charles Ives and the American Band Tradition*, by Jonathan Elkus; *L'America Musicale di Charles Ives*, by Gianfranco Vinay; and *Charles E. Ives: Memos*, edited by John Kirkpatrick. *Tempo* 114 (September 1975): 28-30+. *See*: **B318, B192, B579, B187, B378**

Prausnitz considers the Perlis interviews "valuable," since they "provide the reader with a sense of depth and perspective so far lacking in available Ives literature." Like most reviewers, he views Wooldridge's "free-wheeling scholarship, matched by a densely capricious style" less favorably, and to substantiate his criticisms, he refutes "almost every factual statement" of a paragraph in which Wooldridge mentions actions taken by Prausnitz. He treats Elkus cursorily but favorably and states that Vinay's "impressive Italian treatise" should be translated into English. In his comments on the *Memos*, Prausnitz expresses his wish that Kirkpatrick write "a really searching biographical study of Ives."

B214 Rodgers, Harold A. "Lenox Arts Center: "Ives." *High Fidelity* /*Musical America* 25, no. 12 (December 1975): MA 26-27.

Review of the August 20-24 premiere of *Meeting Mr. Ives*, by Richard Dufallo and Brendan Gill. Concise description of this "theater piece built around the music of Charles Ives," in which each scene "relates to a specific Ives score."

B215 Rossiter, Frank R. *Charles Ives and His America.* New York: Liveright, 1975; revised and expanded version of "Charles Ives and American Culture: The Process of Development, 1874-1921." Ph.D. dissertation, Princeton University (Department of History), 1970. *See*: **B148, B202, B207, B227, B231, B233-234**, and **B250**

The most thoroughly researched published biographical study of Ives. Rossiter presents informative background chapters on the cultural milieu of nineteenth-century Danbury and Yale before devoting separate chapters to a sociological and psychological analysis of Ives's multiple roles as composer, businessman, "political and social thinker," and "self-conscious artist in isolation." In the second part of the biography, which post-dated his dissertation, Rossiter traces the gradual and eventual meteoric rise of Ives's recognition and fame between the largely indifferent response to the *"Concord" Sonata* and accompanying *Essays* in 1921 (**B660**) to the wide acclaim Ives received on the eve of his centennial in 1974. The interpretation of the political and social climate and its influence on Ives's music is particularly convincing.

Several of Rossiter's conclusions remain controversial, for example his use of psychosexual theories to explain why Ives used dissonance, avant-garde techniques, and the vernacular, and his tragic interpretation of Ives's isolation. Readers should also be advised that, although Rossiter discusses the aesthetic foundation of Ives's music, he does not attempt to analyze the music itself. Nevertheless, Rossiter's study remains the most important biographical publication on the composer since the pioneering work of Henry and Sidney Cowell in 1955 (**B354**).

B216 Schwartz, Elliott. "Directions in American Composition Since the Second World War: Part I--1945-1960. *Music Educator's Journal* 61, no. 6 (February 1975): 29-39.

In one portion of this article (pages 34-35), Schwartz briefly discusses Ives's influence on Carter (who also "assigned roles...to the members of a chamber group") and Brant (who followed Ives's "spatial placement of performers throughout the hall"), and cites an unspecified linkage from Ives to Cage.

B217 Taruskin, Richard. Letter in reply to Hans G. Helms, "Ives--Ideal American or Social Critic?" *Current Musicology* 20 (1975): 33-40.

An impassioned as well as articulate rebuttal to Helms's review of the Ives Centennial Festival-Conference (**B201**). According to

Taruskin, Helms's article constitutes an "exploitation of cultural treasures toward inappropriate and illegitimate ends." He accuses Helms of "semantic abuse" and offers numerous well-argued correctives to Helm's distortion of Ives's life and thought.

B218 Tilmouth, Michael. Review of *Charles Ives Remembered*, by Vivian Perlis. *Music and Letters* 56, no. 2 (1975): 214-215. *See:* **B318**

Tilmouth considers the Carter and Herrmann remarks the most important portion of this book, since they alone reveal "understanding coupled with genuine criticism." The value of the remaining reminiscences is for the most part lost on Tilmouth, and he concludes with an appeal for "a close and critical scrutiny of the music, especially if extravagant claims are to be made for it."

B219 Tonietti, Tito. Review of *L'america musicale di Charles Ives*, by Gianfranco Vinay. *Nuova Rivista Musicale Italiana* 9 (January-March 1975): 137-140. *See:* **B187**

Although he finds fault with Vinay's publisher for not allowing musical examples to clarify the author's musical observations, Tonietti considers this book an important contribution to Ives studies. Tonietti praises Vinay's outline of Ives's cultural and social roots and his frontier-style American mixture of sentimentality and violence that links Ives to Emerson, Melville, the Alcotts, Whitman, and Hawthorne, as well as to nature. He also appreciates that Vinay clarifies Ives's departure from the vernacular tradition to confront the academic tradition and Ives's ability to link his music with his philosophical theories.

B220 Victor, Michèle. Review of *L'america musicale di Charles Ives*, by Gianfranco Vinay. *Musique en Jeu* 17 (January 1975): 120. *See:* **B187**

Victor criticizes Vinay for stressing the superficial connections between Ives and his European contemporaries rather than pursuing a more fruitful comparison between Ives and the avant-garde Varèse and Cage and electronic composers who built on Ives's work. He also regrets that Vinay quotes liberally from literature, but does not support his tentative musical analyses with musical examples.

B221 Walker, Donald R. "The Vocal Music of Charles Ives." *Parnassus: Poetry in Review* 3, no. 2 (Spring-Summer 1975): 329-344.

Thoughtful critical survey of Ives's choral and song output.
Walker discusses the compositional implications of Ives's
"'harmonist's' orientation," and offers an enlightening overview of
the special textural procedures and structural types in Ives's
choral music. He also summarizes Ives's song production during
each of three principal compositional phases.

B222   Wallach, Laurence. "The Ives Conference: A Word from the Floor."
Current Musicology 19 (1975): 32-36.

In this overview of the Ives Centennial-Festival Conference, where
"everyone seemed to have his or her own Charles Ives," Wallach
summarizes the paradoxical approaches presented, and points
out how "contradictory quotations of Ives's writings were invoked
to prove all points," and how the conference illustrated "the
frustrations of performing Ives."

B223   Williams, Jonathan. "A Celestial Centennial Reverie for Charles
E. Ives." *Parnassus: Poetry in Review* 3, no. 2 (Spring-Summer
1975): 350-373.

Williams attempts to transfer the content of Ives's *Essays* **(B660)**
into "new forms," i.e., blank verse. His arrangement follows Ives's
chapter titles.

B224   Wooldridge, David. "Charles Ives and the American National
Character: 'Musical Spirit of '76.'" In *Papers of the First American
Music Conference*, pp. 51-64. Keele University, England, 1975;
reprinted in *South Florida's Historic Ives Festival, 1974-1976*,
edited by F. Warren O' Reilly, pp. 27-29.

Wooldridge offers harsh indictments against many Ives
enthusiasts and critics alike ranging from Carter, whose "attack
on the 'Concord' Sonata has become a classic in musical
misunderstanding that seriously undermines his own reputation
as a distinguished composer" **(B668)**, as well as "the
anecdotalists...who, by their very anecdotes, betray themselves as
never having given even summary attention to Ives's music in
their lives." Among his examples Wooldridge returns to his earlier
published attacks of the distortions by all concerned of *Decoration
Day* and of the spurious but more salable "reconstructed" edition
of the *Second Symphony* **(B192)**. Wooldridge vindicates himself
when he condradicts Cowell's oft-repeated anecdote that has Ives
listening to the *Second Symphony* premiere "on the maid's little
kitchen radio" **(B354)**. He is correct when he asserts that Vivian
Perlis's interview with Will and Luemily Ryder, Ives's Redding

neighbors, in *Charles Ives Remembered* "corroborates my own account [based on a conversation with Mrs. Ryder] in every respect" **(B318)**.

B225 Yates, Peter. "Charles Ives: An American Composer." *Parnassus: Poetry in Review* 3, no. 2 (Spring-Summer 1975): 318-328.

Yates asks a series of questions about Ives such as, "Why the middle initial?" [Answer: "He signed his name like an American businessman"], and offers some valuable observations based on his communication with those who knew Ives. Most interesting is Yates's story, allegedly told to him directly by Schoenberg, "who clearly remembered Ives' appearance," that when the Austrian and his family arrived in New York (1933), "Ives, although unwell, went to a reception for them and gave Schoenberg a check." Yates assigns a 1944 date to Schoenberg's famous panegyric to Ives, following the Evenings on the Roof concerts in Los Angeles that honored the seventieth birthdays of the two composers. *See*: **B91** and **B112**

B226 Yellin, Victor Fell. "Charles Ives Festival-Conference." *The Musical Quarterly* 61, no. 2 (1975): 295-299.

Yellin describes the Festival-Conference as "much more an historical than a musical event." He considers Rossiter's **(B259)** and Forte's **(B251)** papers "the two most successful" and discusses each, and he raves about the New York concert in which Masselos and Kirkpatrick performed the sonatas they premiered: "In short the Kirkpatrick-Masselos-Ives concert was one of those musical experiences one cherishes with the same fervor as the lucky ones who were at the Giants-Dodgers playoff game of 1951."

1976

B227 Blum, Stephen. Review of *Charles Ives and His America*, by Frank R. Rossiter. *The Musical Quarterly* 62, no. 4 (October 1976): 597-603. *See*: **B215**

One of the most severe critiques of this most-often lauded biography. Blum faults Rossiter for many interpretations, especially his attempt to manufacture dichotomies between "form" and "content" or between the "cultivated" and "vernacular" musical traditions, when they did not exist for Ives. He also criticizes Rossiter for failing to recognize Ives's values: "As a symptom of this neglect, he makes no mention of some writers to whom Ives frequently referred (such as Horace Bushnell and John Ruskin) or of one philosopher whose work reveals remarkable analogies with that of Ives (C. S. Peirce)."

B228 Bolcom, William. "The Old Curmudgeon's Corner." *Musical Newsletter* 4, no. 4 (1976).

Bolcom takes two recent critical reviews of Ives's music [one by Alan Rich (**B181**), the other by Andrew Porter (**B180**)] to task for responding "to the storm of *critical praise* of Ives rather than to the man and his music." He chastizes Rich for his easy and uncritical acceptance of Mozart, and compares Porter's essay to Mark Twain's famous essay on Fenimore Cooper. But since Porter does not go as far as Twain, Bolcom offers more examples of Ives's musical sins before offering his personal and original defense of the "crusty old American...who wrote exactly what he was."

B229 Buchau, Stephanie von. "Meeting Mr. Ives." *Opera News* 40 (May 1976): 39-40.

A cursory and negative critique of this musical show based on the life and music of Ives. According to Mr. Buchau, the co-authors (Brendan Gill and Richard Dufallo)," debased the composer by using Muzak to support a series of thin, undramatic skits."

B230 Childs, Barney. "Some Anniversaries." *American Society of University Composers Proceedings* 9 and 10 (1976): 13-27.

Childs uses Ives as a "springboard" to introduce a discussion of America's cultural state during three crucial epochs, "the 1890s, World War I, and the 1960s." He suggests three approaches to understanding the composer, "Ives' musical position," Ives's "thought and his philosophical speculations," and "Ives as a figure of what we might choose to call the American Myth." Childs, who writes that Ives's use of borrowed material was "for a largely evocative purpose not related to meta-musical commentary," asks us "not to over-intellectualize some of the immediacies of his work."

B231 Chase, Gilbert. Review of *Charles Ives and His America*, by Frank R. Rossiter. *High Fidelity/Musical America* 26, no. 7 (July 1976): MA 38-39. *See:* **B215**

Chase, not at all bothered by the absence of musical discussion, praises Rossiter for his successful efforts to convey "the broad context of musical biography *as history*," and for writing a book that "compels us to rethink and remake our image of Ives, without diminishing his greatness."

B232 Cordes, Joan Kunselman. "A New American Development in Music: Some Characteristic Features Extending from the Legacy of Charles Ives." Ph.D. dissertation, Louisiana State University, 1976. 144 pp.

After acknowledging the anti-eclectic and pro-dodecaphonic climate that dominanted the mainstream of music history for the first half of the twentieth century, Cordes discusses a large group of American composers (e.g. Cage, Crumb, Rochberg, Martirano, Silverman, Druckman, Bolcom, and Albright) to show that eclecticism has become the dominant feature of the "so-called American style." Cordes's dissertation "points to the similar stylistic and conceptual bases that relate these contemporary composer to Ives, and it considers the philosophical and cultural conditions that have accommodated the emergence of these characteristics."

The central eclectic conceptual bases include the combining of disparate musical elements, a concern with interrelationships of composers and other music, and the use of indigenous materials. Cordes also explores a range of related issues: the belated acceptance of heterogeneity, interest in the creation of new sound materials, spatial placement of sound, and a new emphasis on a reinterpretation that does not deny the melodic-harmonic tradition.

B233 Craft, Robert. Review of *Charles Ives and His America*, by Frank R. Rossiter. *The Sunday Times* of London. November 28, 1976, page 40. Reprinted as "Ives's World" in *Current Convictions: Views and Reviews.*" New York: Alfred A. Knopf, 1977. *See:* **B215**

Craft lauds Rossiter "as a historian of the social castes" in Danbury, Yale, and New York, but challenges his musical and psychological interpretations. Craft, who does not think it plausible that Ives could not have known about Cowell's "sexual proclivities," asserts that "Ives's hatred of effeminacy protests too much, and that fears for his own masculinity might be considered among the reasons for his reclusiveness." He also does not understand how Rossiter could deny the sensuousness in Ives's music. Craft concludes by challenging Rossiter's opinion that Ives's isolation was harmful to his artistic development: "Ives could not have begotten this music under other conditions, and we should rejoice that he had the courage to persevere on his lonely path."

B234 Dickinson, Peter. Review of *Charles Ives Remembered*, by Vivian Perlis; *Charles Ives: A Portrait*, by David Wooldridge; *Charles Ives and His America*, by Frank R. Rossiter; and *Charles Ives and the American Band Tradition*, by Jonathan Elkus. *The Musical Times* 117 (November 1976): 910-911. *See*: **B318, B192, B215**, and **B579**

Dickinson focuses on the Wooldridge and Rossiter biographies. Although he finds Wooldridge's idiosyncratic style and undocumented facts and theories frustrating, He advises "that students of the subject cannot afford to neglect it even though its assertions must be treated with caution." Of *Charles Ives and His America* Dickinson writes that our understanding of Ives's cultural context "is immeasurably enhanced by Rossiter's detailed study."

B235 Helms, Hans G. "Charles Ives--Hommage zum 100. Geburtstag; 1. Zur Physiognomie eines revolutionären Komponisten und Citoyen; 2. Zum Phänomen der ungleichzeitigkeit kompositorischer Konzeptionen und ihrer technischen Realiserbarkeit!" *Student Musicologists at Minnesota* 6 (1975-1976): 95-127.

Among the works discussed in this essay Helms views *From the Steeples and the Mountains*, a work that is both dodecaphonic and aleatory, as especially representative of Ives's diversity and subsequent influence on composers such as Stockhausen, Serocki, Cage, and Brown. Helms also compares Ives's politically motivated socialist art to Eisler's, and, on the evidence of a heavily marked and annotated volume of Ruskin's work that he found in Ives's West Redding house in 1970, considers Ruskin as great an influence on Ives's aesthetic philosophy as the Concord Transcendentalists. These and other provocative ideas remain undeveloped and unsubstantiated before Helms concludes his essay by asserting that Aloys Kontarsky is the first pianist to thoroughly understand Ives's precisely notated intentions, an assertion which he believes supported by the fact that Kontarsky's recording of "The Alcotts" matches Ives's recording of this movement down to the second.

B236 Kirkpatrick, John. "Thoughts on the Ives Year." *Student Musicologists at Minnesota* 6 (1975-1976): 218-224.

Brief comments on several works performed during the Ives "year" (which actually began in October 1973 and lasted until October 1975). Kirkpatrick writes that he "was hardly prepared for the dignity of the two surviving student fugues for organ," savors the "spell-binding magic" of *Sunrise*, Ives's last work (composed in 1926), and offers his latest reactions to *"Concord" Sonata* and the Violin Sonatas. He concludes with his personal assessment that Ives's "power of spiritual transcendence is...the strongest cumulative impression of the Ives year."

B237 Lyles, Jean Caffey. "Charles Ives's America." *Christian Century* 93 (23 June 1976): 589-591.

Considering his probable readership, it is surprising that Lyles, in this conventional overview of Ives, pays scant attention to religiosity in Ives beyond the following: "The strong religious strain that runs through all his compositions...is unmistakable."

B238 Morgan, Robert P. "American Music and the Hand-Me-Down Habit." *High Fidelity/Musical America* 26, no. 6 (June 1976): 70-72.

Morgan discusses "the prominent role played by quotation in so much of American music," using recent recordings by Heinrich, Bloch, and Harris, and two of Ives as representative examples [the Ormandy interpretation of *"Holidays" Symphony* (RCA ARL 1-1249) and Hadassah Sahr's performance of *"Concord" Sonata* (Critics Choice CC 1705)]. Unlike the works of Heinrich, Bloch, and Harris, in which American subject matter is treated superficially, Morgan writes that in *"Holidays" Symphony* and *"Concord" Sonata*, "the whole logic of the musical development is transformed through the use of pre-existing music."

B239 Quackenbush, Margaret Diane. "Form and Texture in the Works for Mixed Chamber Ensemble by Charles Ives." M.A. thesis, University of Oregon, 1976. 125 pp.

A study of nineteen individual short chamber and small orchestral works (or movements), seven of which subsequently resurfaced as songs for voice and piano. Quackenbush is faithful to her stated purpose, to study "what sorts of musical material Ives employs, and how he organizes this material." Following brief descriptive "program notes" for each work that frequently acknowledge Rinehart's 1970 study **(B140)**, Quackenbush concludes with a general "discussion and comparison of the particular formal and textural concepts" underlying these compositions.

Works analyzed include: *Song for Harvest Season; The Pond; Like a Sick Eagle; Allegretto Sombreoso; Adagio Sostenuto; Scherzo: The See'r; The Rainbow; Set for Theater or Chamber Orchestra; From the Steeples and the Mountains; Scherzo: All the Way Around and Back; Scherzo: Over the Pavements; Calcium Light Night; Tone Roads Nos. 1 and 3; Central Park in the Dark; The Unanswered Question;* and *The Gong on the Hook and Ladder.*

B240   Shirley, Wayne. "Ives as an Innovator." In *South Florida's Historic Ives Festival, 1974-1976,* edited by F. Warren O'Reilly, pp. 50-52.

Spirited defense of Ives from Carter's charges (**B318** and **B668**) "that most of his radicalism may have been grafted onto his music years after its technical date of completion." Shirley acknowledges that Ives had in fact "jacked up the dissonance level" in some works, including *Three Places in New England, "Concord" Sonata,* and *The Unanswered Question* but concludes "that this question is of interest primarily to the historian." Shirley argues his case that in these latter-day dissonant works (and many others) "the startling qualities, the things which make the works prophetic of the music to be written during the century they usher in, are woven so deeply into the work that the work could not exist without them."

B241   Slonimsky, Nicolas. "Working With Ives." In *South Florida's Historic Ives Festival, 1974-1976,* edited by F. Warren O'Reilly, pp. 35-37.

In this anecdotal essay Slonimsky recalls his early encounters with Ives and his solution to the rhythmic problems of "Putnam's Camp" from *Three Places in New England.* Slonismky suggests that psychiatrists could learn much from Ives's "words of approbation and of opprobrium" and notes that a recording of *Three Places* "got into a detective novel, *Funeral in Berlin* [as] a crucial clue." He concludes with a priceless excerpt from his correspondence with Ives in which the composer explains his preference for pencil over pen because with his shaky hand he can "steer it with less vibrato." *See:* **B66, B255,** and **B489**

B242   Tilmouth, Michael. Review of *Charles Ives: A Portrait,* by David Wooldridge. *Music and Letters* 57, no. 2 (1976): 173-175. *See:* **B192**

The "atrocious journalese" would disturb Tilmouth less, "if Mr. Wooldridge had much that was really new to say about Ives." Since "a considerable amount of space is allocated to the denigration of Parker," Tilmouth devotes a considerable percentage of his review to refuting Wooldridge on this point. The only "measure of reasonableness" credited to Wooldridge is his treatment of Ives's creative demise after World War I.

B243 Wickstrom, Fred. "Ives and Percussion, A Forerunner on All Fronts." In *South Florida's Historic Ives Festival, 1974-1976*, edited by F. Warren O'Reilly, pp. 57-58.

After crediting Ives for making "demands upon the performing percussionist not made on him again until the late '50's in American Jazz," Wickstrom criticizes the composer for his uncanny ability "to notate a [percussion] passage that was the most difficult to reproduce the sound he heard in his head," and for his poor understanding of "the acoustics of percussion." He also notes the importance of the percussion in Ives's extensive use of metric modulation, a technique which succeeded in destroying "the traditional bipartite feeling of pulse in music." Wickstrom's examples are taken from *Three Places in New England* and the *Fourth Symphony*.

1977

B244 Blum, Stephen. "Ives's Position in Social and Musical History." *The Musical Quarterly* 63, no. 4 (October 1977): 459-482.

Blum states that his essay "is based upon the premise that Ives's writings, music, and actions constituted different types of responses to problems faced by other composers, European and American, of the nineteenth and early twentieth centuries." According to Blum, Ives's music "has resisted the types of analytic method employed by Carter and Thomson," who have concluded that Ives was incompetent and illogical in his handling of form. The major example Blum employs to contradict this view is the *Piano Trio*, in which Ives also offers a "reinterpretation of conflicts between variants of two melodic progressions in several harmonic contexts."

B245 Brooks, William. "Ives Today." In *An Ives Celebration: Papers and Panels of the Charles Ives Centennial Festival-Conference*, edited by H. Wiley Hitchcock and Vivian Perlis, pp. 209-223. Urbana: University of Illinois Press, 1977.

An examination of Ives from a structuralist perspective, in which "the relationships between behavioral events may reveal more clearly the workings of an individual or culture than the contents or characteristics of the events taken by themselves." Drawing on structural anthropologist Claude Lévi-Strauss's metaphor, Brooks explores the extent to which Ives can be thought of as a *bricoleur*, a person capable of "devising solutions with efficiency and even elegance from the materials at hand." Brooks also compares the work and philosophical underpinnings of Ives and Buckminster Fuller. After briefly distinguishing between the cyclic process evident in Ives's sketches and Beethoven's linear sketches, Brooks espouses the view that cyclic processes are more relevant to our present world than linear ones.

B246 Brown, Earle and Vivian Perlis, Co-chairs. "Ives Viewed from Abroad." In *An Ives Celebration: Papers and Panels on the Charles Ives Centennial Festival-Conference*, edited by H. Wiley Hitchcock and Vivian Perlis, pp. 45-63 and pp. 227-256. Urbana: University of Illinois Press, 1977.

An international panel of composers offers a spectrum of reactions to Ives. On one end of the spectrum Guido Baggiani of Italy expresses his view that although he considered Ives "a real composer," he also did not think that Ives knew "exactly what he was doing." [In his personal statement (p. 228) Baggiani gives a useful listing of Ives's performances between 1957 and 1974 on Italian radio network (RAI).] Similarly, Ilhan Usmanbas of Turkey did not consider Ives "an accomplished composer but one who shows us some possibilities in music." In contrast, Hans G. Helms said that in Germany Ives "is not regarded as an exotic being; he is regarded as the composer that he was, one of the great composers of the century and of musical history." Similarly, the following short, often personal, prepared statements of each panelist printed as Appendix I, depict a considerable range of contemporary foreign views on Ives:

Andriessen, Louis, "*Anachrony I* and Charles Ives," p. 227; Baggiani, Guido, "Ives and Our Music Today," pp. 228-230; Beckwith, John, "Reflections on Ives," pp. 230-232; Bernlef, J., "On Charles Ives and 'Wild Gardening,'" pp. 232-238; Cadieu, Martine, "Charles Ives, or America of the 'First Romance,'" pp. 238-241; Clarkson, Austin. "Charles Ives Here-and-Now-and-After," pp. 241-243; Dickinson, Peter, "On Charles Ives," 243-246; Helms, Hans G., "Some Reflections on Charles E. Ives," pp. 246-248; Hoffman, Alfred, "A Great Visionary Musician," pp. 248-249; Ionnidis, Yannis. "On Charles Ives," p. 250; Jolas, Betsy,

"Charles Ives," pp. 250-251; Rasmussen, Karl Aage, "Thoughts on Ives," pp. 251-252; Rijavec, Andrej, "Charles Ives in Yugoslavia," pp. 252-254; Usmanbas, Ilhan, "Random--and Provocative--Thoughts on Ives," pp. 254-256.

B247 Bruce, Neely. "Ives and Nineteenth-Century American Music." In *An Ives Celebration: Papers and Panels of the Charles Ives Centennial Festival-Conference*, edited by H. Wiley Hitchcock and Vivian Perlis, pp. 29-43. Urbana: University of Illinois Press, 1977.

Bruce compares Morrison Foster's 1896 collection of songs composed by his brother, Stephen, and Ives's 1922 song collection, a comparison that reveals "a number of significant similarities" in their thinking. Examples chosen by Bruce for comparison include stylistic irregularites and nonconformities (admittedly "much more extreme" in Ives), bell imitations, self-quotation, the use of additional instrumental parts, and even the enormous range of quality exhibited in the two collections. Bruce also draws "similar comparisons" between Ives and other nineteenth-century music, concluding that "the more one examines nineteenth-century music in this country, the more 'Ivesian' it becomes."

B248 Clarke, Gary E. "Charles Edward Ives." *Essays on American Music: Contributions in American History*, pp. 105-131. Westport, CT: Greenwood Press, 1977.

Clarke portrays Ives "as a logical product of his age and locality," a Transcendentalist and a pragmatist. In his biographical treatment Clarke emphasizes the importance of the "George Ives-Horatio Parker synthesis" as well as his New England heritage in explaining the many Ivesian discrepancies, e.g., nineteenth-century traditions and twentieth-century visions; in his musical discussion he emphasizes the philosophical underpinning or the programmatic element of a work. Clarke defends Ives "as a careful artist who considered the implications of every note of his music" against critics such as Thomson (**B403**), who harshly espouse the opposite view. He also contradicts Ives's feigned indifference to recognition (exemplified by his caustic remarks upon receiving the Pulitzer Prize in 1947) when he tells us that the award "was framed and hung in the study of Ives's West Redding home along with the framed certificate of the National Institute of Arts and Letters."

B249   Crunden, Robert M. "Charles Ives's Place in American Culture."
In *An Ives Celebration: Papers and Panels of the Charles Ives
Centennial Festival-Conference*, edited by H. Wiley Hitchcock and
Vivian Perlis, pp. 4-15. Urbana: University of Illinois Press, 1977.

Crunden's central argument is that "Ives had many precursors in
America, and there were many individuals whose creative careers
paralleled his; they simply were not chiefly engaged in music, and
they remain little known to musicologists." Continuing this line
of thought Crunden suggests that we should view Ives "as a
'progressive' American, who seems strange and out of place to us
only because other progressives [such as John Dewey or Woodrow
Wilson] did their innovating in other disciplines, like educational
psychology, politics, or business administration." For an essay
that treats Ives as a man isolated from his contemporary
progressives see Rossiter's essay (**B259**), which follows in this
collection.

B250   Emmerson, Simon. Review of *Charles Ives and His America*, by
Frank R. Rossiter. *Music and Musicians* 25 (January 1977): 28.
See: **B215**

Surprisingly, Emmerson finds Rossiter "refeshingly free from
over-emphasized Freudian interpretation of the underlying sexual
problems of Ives' relationships." After reviewing some of Ives's
"fundamental contradictions" discussed by Rossiter, Emmerson
expresses his dissatifaction only with the final chapter,
"Recognition since 1939" and epilogue, "An Interpretation." He
acknowledges the controversy that Rossiter's study has generated
but concludes that "for those for whom this adds to the
appreciation of the music (as it does for me) the book is
invaluable."

B251   Forte, Allen. "Ives and Atonality." In *An Ives Celebration: Papers
and Panels of the Charles Ives Centennial-Festival Conference*,
edited by H. Wiley Hitchcock and Vivian Perlis, pp. 159-186.
Urbana: University of Illinois Press, 1977.

After characterizing atonal compositions "by the occurrence of
musical configurations that are reducible to note collections or
sets that normally are not found in traditional tonal music," Forte
offers numerous isolated examples as well as a more detailed
examination of a single work (*Maple Leaves*) to show that
atonality is "the primary connection between Ives and modern
European music." Through the use of set theory Forte attempts
to replace "the catchwords *polyharmony, polytonality,* and the

like" with a more precise and therefore more helpful methodology. The parallels Forte draws between Ives and Schoenberg (and in one appropriate example between Ives and Berg) dispersed throughout the essay are especially enlightening.

B252 Hitchcock, H. Wiley. *Ives*. London: Oxford University Press, 1977. *See*: **B262-263** and **B265**

In this clearly and succinctly written 95-page monograph organized by genre Hitchcock offers insightful commentary on a large number of Ives works. Hitchcock, a master of the helpful generalization, is particularly impressive at conveying the musical principles as well as the central biographical and programmatic contexts underlying a work. Sixty-two musical examples support specific musical points cited in the text. Below is a list of the works either illustrated or discussed for at least one full paragraph. [Asterisks mark those works discussed for three or more pages.]

Songs: S*low March, Down East, Serenity, Two Little Flowers, On the Counter, Walking, Charlie Rutlage, Like a Sick Eagle, Mists, *On the Antipodes, Soliloquy, Song for Harvest Season, Feldeinsamkeit, Evening, Maple Leaves, *General William Booth Enters into Heaven.*
Choral: *Psalms 67, 150, 54, 24*, and **90, Processional: Let There Be Light, *Harvest Home Chorales, The Celestial Country, The Boys in Blue, Lincoln the Great Commoner.*
Keyboard: *America Variations, *Three-Page Sonata, Varied Air and Variations, Three Quarter-Tone Pieces, *First Piano Sonata, *"Concord" Sonata.*
Chamber: *Violin Sonatas Nos. 2, 3*, and *4, String Quartets Nos. 1* and *2, Trio for Violin, Cello, and Piano, From the Steeples and the Mountains, Hallowe'en.*
Orchestral: *Over the Pavements, Theatre Orchestra Set, The Unanswered Question, Central Park in the Dark, Symphonies Nos. 1, 2, 3*, and *4, Robert Browning Overture, Three Places in New England, Second Orchestral Set, Universe Symphony.*

B253 Hitchcock. H. Wiley, and Vivian Perlis, ed. *An Ives Celebration: Papers and Panels on the Charles Ives Centennial Festival-Conference*. Urbana: University of Illinois Press, 1977. *See*: **B266, B271, B273**, and **B281**

This anthology, a major secondary resource, includes an impressive and varied array of essays on Ives by William Brooks, Neely Bruce, Robert M. Crunden, Allen Forte, Robert P. Morgan,

Frank R. Rossiter. A large portion of the book is devoted to the following panel discussion topics: "Ives Viewed from Abroad," chaired by Earle Brown; "Editors' Experiences" and "On Performing the Violin Sonatas," chaired by Alan Mandel; "Three Realizations of *Chromâtimelôdtune*," chaired by John Kirkpatrick; "Conductors' Experiences," moderated by John Mauceri; and "Five Composers' Views," organized by Roger Reynolds. Each essay and panel discussion has been given a separate entry in this Bibliography. *See*: **Appendix 4**

B254 Mandel, Alan, Chair, with Lou Harrison, John Kirkpatrick, and James Sinclair. "Editors' Experiences." In *An Ives Celebration: Papers and Panels on the Charles Ives Centennial Festival-Conference,* edited by H. Wiley Hichcock and Vivian Perlis, pp. 67-85. Urbana: University of Illinois Press, 1977.

Three men with considerable experience editing Ives offer insights into the difficulties of this task and a number of solutions. When it came to evaluating the many versions of *"Concord" Sonata,* Kirkpatrick depicts Ives as a man who "had a kind of scorn for what he had done in the past." Kirkpatrick's own view is that in many cases "Ives's first idea was best." In a provocative tangential comment Kirkpatrick acknowledges that Ives would "probably have kicked me out of the house" for restoring the fugue (which Ives had reworked into the third movement of the *Fourth Symphony*) to its original position where it opened the *First String Quartet.* Sinclair discusses the editing problems in restoring Ives's chamber version of *Three Places in New England* (published by C. C. Birchard in 1933), "to its original full-orchestra form" (published by Mercury in 1976), and Harrison discusses the background of the premieres of Ives's *Third Symphony* and the *First Piano Sonata* before briefly commenting on his editorial work, and expresses his hope for "a collected edition that would consist of super reproductions with modern photographic enhancements of even the faintest pencil marks."

B255 Mauceri, John, Moderator, with Lehman Engel, Gunther Schuller, James Sinclair, Nicholas Slonimsky, Gregg Smith, and Arthur Weisberg. "Conductors' Experiences." In *An Ives Celebration: Papers and Panels on the Charles Ives Centennial Festival-Conference,* edited by H. Wiley Hitchcock and Vivian Perlis, pp. 113-126. Urbana: University of Illinois Press, 1977.

A theme that emerges from this discussion is that despite Ives's improvisatory approach to performance, including the recently released recordings of Ives playing his own music, his scores, particularly those requiring orchestral forces, are rhythmically "absolutely dead accurate" (Schuller) and his "notation always proves to be about as wise and musical a notation as it could be" (Smith).

B256 Morgan, Robert P. "Spatial Form in Ives." In *An Ives Celebration: Papers and Panels on the Charles Ives Centennial Festival-Conference,* edited by H. Wiley Hitchcock and Vivian Perlis, pp. 145-158. Urbana: University of Illinois Press, 1977.

In this important essay Morgan makes a strong case that Ives wrote "music based largely on relationships that are simultaneous, reciprocal, and reflective in nature rather than successive, sequential, and unidirectional," i.e., "spatial" as opposed to "temporal." He shows how Ives uses a traditional technique such as fragmentation in "Hawthorne" from *"Concord" Sonata* to create a non-traditional and "multidimensional framework in which relationships can be established simultaneously in both directions," and he argues that the historical importance of Ives's approach "suggests the possibility of a new historical alignment, within which Ives would occupy a much more central postion than the one currently accorded him." *See*: **B406**

B257 Reynolds, Roger, Organizer, with Charles Dodge, Lou Harrison, Salvatore Martirano, and Gordon Mumma. "Five Composers' Views." In *An Ives Celebration: Papers and Panels on the Charles Ives Centennial Festival-Conference,* edited by H. Wiley Hitchcock and Vivian Perlis, pp. 187-208. Urbana: University of Illinois Press, 1977.

Each of the composers independently prepared a "statement" designed "to achieve a controlled counterpoint of spatial, aural, and visual experiences." Reynolds articulated the view shared by the others when he says that "what strikes me most about Ives is his willingness to incorporate...anything of interest from the real world, whether sounds, or ideas, or images." Similarly, when Dodge acknowledges a "kinship" between his work and Ives rather than a direct Ivesian influence, he also represents the sentiments of this group.

B258 Robinson, David B. "Children of the Fire: Charles Ives on Emerson and Art." *American Literature* 48 (January 1977): 564-576.

Robinson offers a great many parallels between Ives and the Transcendentalists, especially Emerson. In fact, he concedes only one important conflict between their otherwise identical "conceptions of organic form" in Ives's rejection of economy as desirable in either nature or art. While Robinson's connections between Ives and the Transcendentalists are often plausible, he does not ultimately succeed in convincingly demonstrating that these connections are linked by cause and effect. He also overstates Emersonian influences when he writes that, "Ives was not intimidated by tradition so long as he had Emerson's authority for support." [For a more balanced perspective on the Transcendental influences on Ives see Burkholder, **B296**.]

B259 Rossiter, Frank R. "Charles Ives: Good American and Isolated Artist." In *An Ives Celebration: Papers and Panels of the Charles Ives Centennial Festival-Conference,* edited by H. Wiley Hitchcock and Vivian Perlis, pp. 16-28. Urbana: University of Illinois Press, 1977.

In contrast to Crunden's essay linking Ives to the Progressive movement during the decades prior to World War I (**B249**), Rossiter writes that Ives had "little connection" with this movement and considers the remarkable fact "that his interest in and knowledge of some its most important aspects were so minimal." Rossiter argues that in his "one-man revolt carried on in strict privacy" Ives denied potentially sympathetic critics an opportunity to see his work and concludes that "in both his musical life and his larger cultural life Charles Ives succumbed to enormous social pressures that committed him inexorably to a life of narrow conventionality." Rossiter develops these ideas at far greater length in *Charles Ives and His America* published one year after this centennial paper was first delivered. *See:* **B215**

B260 Sive, Helen R. *Music's Connecticut Yankee: An Introduction to the Life and Music of Charles Ives.* New York: Atheneum, 1977.

Despite overgeneralized psychological explanations, for example, that Ives's "unusual two-sidedness...allowed him on one hand to be a strong nonconformist, and on the other to adjust quite well to rules and accepted modes of behavior," and her inability to explain "the particular and wonderful way" that Ives had of "illustrating the vastness of man's experience," Sive's mastery and clear exposition of the basic facts of Ives's life make this an excellent book-length [141 page] biographical survey effectively designed for young readers.

B261 Vinay, Gianfranco. Review of *Charles E. Ives: Memos*, edited by John Kirkpatrick. *Nuova Rivista Italiana di Musicologica* 11, no. 2 (April-June 1977): 270-274. *See:* **B378**

A clear explanation as to how these *Memos* capture Ives's disdain for those who found his music difficult or unplayable and his preoccupation with philosophical or representational program music. Vinay also offers a useful summary of the contents of the twenty-one appendixes.

1978

B262 Banfield, Stephen. Review of *Ives*, by H. Wiley Hitchcock. *Music and Letters* 59, no. 3 (1978): 346-347. *See:* **B252**

After briefly noting the central items of Ives bibliography from the Cowell biography in 1955 (**B354**) to the considerable amount of Ives material published since 1972, Banfield writes that Hitchcock "fills a remaing gap" with his "useful, uncomplicated handbook to a complicated output." Banfield regrets that Hitchcock avoids "critical evaluation," and that he does not "appraise musical excellence" for the benefit of those like Banfield who believe that Ives's "work is no style and all idea," and for others who "still regard him as a charlatan."

B263 Dickinson, Peter. Review of *Ives*, by H. Wiley Hitchcock. *The Musical Times* 119 (March 1978): 239

Dickinson writes: "This kind of technical appraisal, not, of course, exhaustive, is exactly what students of Ives and of 20th-century music now need. In spite of the book's compactness, Hitchcock manages to provide new insights about Ives on almost every page, valid both for the experienced listener and the novice."

B264 Elliot, J. H. Review of *Charles Ives: A Portrait*, by David Wooldridge. *The Music Review* 39, nos. 3-4 (August-November 1978): 286-287. *See:* **B192**

An uncritical assessment of Wooldridge's controversial study. In contrast to most reviewers, especially Kirkpatrick (**B173**), Elliot writes that "we are given many relevant facts, and the author's occasional speculations appear convincing if they are not necessarily conclusive."

B265 Harrison, Max. Review of *Charles Ives: A Discography*, by Charles Warren; *Charles Ives and the American Band Tradition*, by Jonathan Elkus; and *Charles Ives*, by H. Wiley Hitchcock.

Composer (London) 62 (Winter 1977-1978): 48-50. *See*: **B17**, **B579**, and **B252**

Although Harrison appreciates the detail of Warren's discography, he regrets the fact that his alphabetical listing makes it impossible to chart chronologically "the slowly increasing number of Ives recordings." He finds Elkus's perspective as a "practical musician...a useful conterbalance, even on this limited terrain, to the more aesthetically or sociologically inclined studies of Perry (**B179**), Rossiter (**B215**) and others," and Hitchcock's book best suited to "concentrated studies in particular compositional procedures" such as the piano studies and *Harvest Home Chorales.*"

B266   Helm, Everett. Review of *An Ives Celebration*, edited by H. Wiley Hitchcock and Vivian Perlis. *Fontes Artis Musicae* 25, no. 3 (1978): 278-279. *See*: **B253**

According to Helm, "Ives has become a cult, and this dubious distinction becomes neither the man nor his music." He is thus disturbed by the laudatory praise which "verges on fatuity" in this uncritical "celebration" of Ives, a book that "does more to confuse than to enlighten."

B267   Josephson, Nors S. "Charles Ives: Intervallische Permutationen im Spätwerk." *Zeitschrift für Musiktheorie* 9, no. 2 (1978): 27-33.

Josephson states his thesis and purpose clearly at the outset: "Ives's orchestral and chamber music compositions from the years 1906 to 1926 show an increasing use of intervallic constructions and permuations: tendencies, which shift in many of these works directly in stylistic closeness to the Debussy and Schoenberg circle. The goal of this investigation is to explore the sytematic intervallic organization of Ives's late works and moreover to establish that there is a consistent stylistic development in his creative work." ["Ives' Orchester-und-Kammermusik-kompositionen aus den Jahren 1906-1926 zeigen eine zunehmende Verwendung intervallischer Konstruktionen und Permutationen: Tendenzen, die manche dieser Werke in die unmittelbare stilistiche Nähe der Debussy-under Schoenberg-Kreise rücken. Ziel dieser Untersuchung ist es, die intervallische Organisation mehrerer dieser Ives'schen Spätwerke systematisch zu untersuchen und ausserdem eine konsequente stilistische Entwicklung innerhald seines Schaffens festzustellen."]

Works discussed and graphed for their intervallic permutations include: *Serenity; Central Park in the Dark; Second Orchestral Set*

("Elegy to Stephen Foster" and "From Hanover Square North");
Three Places in New England ("St. Gaudens"); *Tone Roads No. 1*;
"Thoreau" from *"Concord" Sonata*; *Universe Symphony* (end of
section C); *The Rainbow*; *Decoration Day*; *Symphony No. 4* (fourth
movement); *Third Orchestral Set* (first and third movements);
Three Quarter-Tone Pieces ("Chorale"); *Peaks*; *A Sea Dirge*; and
Sunrise.

B268 Slonimsky, Nicholas. "Ives, Charles Edward." *Baker's
Biographical Dictionary of Musicians* (6th edition), pp. 804-806.
New York: Schirmer, 1978.

Slonimsky allows himself only occasional hyperbole in this
generally straightforward biographical account, when he asserts
at the outset that Ives's "individual genius created music so
original, so universal, and yet so deeply national in its sources of
inspiration that it profoundly changed the direction of American
music." Of special interest is Slonimsky's statement that "in the
number of orchestral performances, in 1976 Ives stood highest
among modern composers on American programs." The entry
concludes with lists of works, Ives's writings, and selected
bibliography.

B269 Sofonea, Traian. "Charles Ives: un grande compositore americano
che operò con slancio messianico in campo assicurativo."
Separate from *Generali*, 6 serie, no. 35-36, Trieste, 1978. Yale
Collection, ML 410 I95 S68+.

Straightforward biographical survey of Ives's dual careers in
music and business based on the Cowell (**B354**) and Rossiter
(**B215**) biographies, *Charles Ives Remembered* (**B318**), and Ives's
The Amount to Carry (**B375**).

1979

B270 Ballantine, Christopher. "Charles Ives and the Meaning of
Quotation in Music." *The Musical Quarterly* 65, no. 2 (April
1979): 167-184.

Ballantine considers "the complex dialectic between the quoted
fragment, its new treatment, and its new context" and, "in a realm
far removed from that of ordinary musicological discourse,"
demonstrates connections and parallels between dream theory
and symbolism and Ives's quotation process. He distinguishes
between examples where the quoted material uses words (e.g.,
West London) with those independent of words (e.g., *Second String*

Quartet), and describes how three levels of meaning (abstract, programmatic, and music-philosophical) can be applied to *Central Park in the Dark* and *Washington's Birthday*. He also discusses other compositions (e.g., "Hawthorne" from *"Concord" Sonata*) where the quoted material serves "to connote a generalized American experience."

Ballantine concludes by challenging Marshall's assertion that "melodic similarities undoubtedly influenced his decisions to combine these particular tunes" (**B651**): "One could as easily argue that Ives needed these tunes for their significance and he therefore sought for melodic similarities, possibilities of contrapuntal combination, and so on."

B271 Banfield, Stephen. Review of *An Ives Celebration*, edited by H. Wiley Hitchcock and Vivian Perlis. *Music and Letters* 60, no. 2 (April 1979): 216-217. *See:* **B253**

Banfield asks musicians "to adopt some of the procedures of literary criticism if their commentaries are to prove fruitful." He considers the comments of novelist and music critic Martine Cadieu's parallels between Ives and Proust [pp. 238-241], the only acceptable response to this challenge. After praising the papers presented by Crunden (**B249**) and Bruce (**B247**) and lamenting the fact that "some of the panel discussions fail to return to life on the printed page," Banfield devotes a final dense paragraph to Forte's paper, "Ives and Atonality" (**B251**). He credits Forte with a "fertile power of observation," but focuses on Forte's "perversely abstract labelling" and misinterpretation, and concludes that "all this seems to me to have the scope of a nut attacking a sledgehammer, to be largely misguided, and to suggest that...Professor Forte's ears are 'on wrong.'"

B272 Buechner, A. C. "Die Welt des Charles Ives, Protagonist der amerikanischen Musik." *Österreichische Musikzeitschrift* 34 (February 1979): 75-89.

Introductory biographical survey with some discussion with musical examples of *Three Places in New England, Fourth Symphony* (fugue), *Variations on America, Psalm 67*, and "The Alcotts" from *"Concord" Sonata*. Emphasis on Ives's innovations, quotations, and a tragic isolation that prohibited his influence on the next generation of American composers.

B273 Emmerson, Simon. Review of *An Ives Celebration*, edited by H. Wiley Hitchcock and Vivian Perlis. *Music and Musicians* 27 (June 1979): 44. *See:* **B253**

Emmerson praises Brooks's essay (**B245**), in which Ives is viewed from a structuralist rather than the usual Transcendentalist perspective, and several valuable panels on editing Ives (**B254** and **B568**). He faults the "often too literally transcribed" discussions and the fact that "questions requiring whole books to answer were dismissed or misunderstood," and he objects to the presumption of knowledge needed to follow several of the lecturers, especially Forte's paper on "Ives and Atonality" (**B251**), despite its "scratching at a very important surface." Emmerson also dismisses the "Five Composers' Views" (**B257**) and "Essays from Foreign Participants" (**B246**) as either "totally out of place" or "irrelevant."

B274 Kingman, Daniel. *American Music/A Panorama*, pp. 454-481. New York and London: Schirmer, 1979; second edition, 1987.

A generally reliable survey of Ives's "life and career" is followed by a brief discussion of "nine songs, arranged in an approximate order of difficulty and dimension" [full texts are printed with those songs marked by an asterisk]: *A Christmas Carol; At the River; The Greatest Man; *Tom Sails Away; *The Cage; West London; *Majority; *Charlie Rutlage;* and *General William Booth Enters into Heaven.* In subsequent portions of his essay Kingman perhaps overstates the conclusions that Ives's work, "even his 'pure' music," is "fundamentally" programmatic and that Ives's music revealed growing "remoteness from the realistic arena of performance."

B275 Pavlyshyn, Stepanikila Stefanivna. *Charlz Aivz [Charles Ives].* Moscow: Vsesoyuznoe izdatel'stvo "Sovetskii Kompozitor" [All-Union Publishers "Soviet Composer"], 1979. 184 pp. Available in the United States only in the Library of Congress (LC 80-475199).

This difficult-to-obtain book is the major study of Ives's music in Russian. Pavlyshyn follows an introductory chapter on "Ives and American Musical Culture" with individual chapters on Ives's symphonic works, instrumental chamber works, vocal works, and features of his style. Appendixes include a list of Ives's music and a bibliography of literature in various languages.

1980

B276 Lück, Hartmut. "Provokation und Utopie: Ein Porträt des amerikanischen Komponisten Charles Edward Ives." *Neuland* 1 (1980): 3-15.

Survey of Ives's life and thought with an emphasis on Transcendental influences. Works surveyed include *Three Places in New England*, *"Concord" Sonata*, and the *Second String Quartet*. The provocation of the title refers to Ives's musical rebellion, the utopian vision embodied in the *Universe Symphony*. A discography of recordings readily available in Germany in 1979 follows.

B277 Zimmermann, Walter. "Self-Reliance." *Neuland* 1 (1980): 54-58.

Zimmermann cites parallels between Ives and various essays by Emerson, particularly *Self-Reliance* (1841). According to Zimmermann, Emerson's central thoughts form a perfect description of Ives's experimental musical style. Zimmermann also draws some distinctions between American Transcendentalism and European Idealism based in part on the enormous size disparities between their respective geographies.

1981

B278 DiYanni, Robert. "In the American Grain: Charles Ives and the Transcendentalists." *Journal of American Culture* 4, no. 4 (1981): 139.

According to DiYanni, the nineteenth-century influence on Ives was "philosophical rather than musical." He then asserts that "from the philosophical currents circulating in mid-nineteenth-century America, Ives drew not a theory of composition, but a set of ideas, coherent if unsystematic, about the nature, forms and purposes of art and life." Excellent encapsulated survey of Emerson's and Thoreau's influences on Ives's thought and the parallels between Ives and these two Transcendentalists. In addition to *"Concord" Sonata* "and its related works" DiYanni describes specific Transcendental influences on five additional works: "The Housatonic at Stockbridge" from *Three Places in New England*, *Symphonies Nos. 2* and *4*, *The Unanswered Question*, and the *Universe Symphony*.

B279 Feder, Stuart. "Charles and George Ives: The Veneration of Boyhood." *The Annual of Psychoanalysis* 9 (1981): 265-316.

A skillfully argued examination into Ives's childhood, "insofar as it may be studied through the methods of applied psychoanalysis." Feder focuses on "Ives's unique relationship with his father and its role not only in Ives's career choice, character, and style but in the nature of his music as well." In the process he explores suggested meanings for the suprising absence of Ives's mother in Ives's writings, the "scant reference to the maternal in any of Ives's music," and the sparse references to Ives's mother (who died in 1929) in the secondary literature on Ives.

A major part of Feder's essay is devoted to a discussion of the significance of Ives's repeated espousal of "the ear as the masculine organ of creativity" and his provocative theory that Ives's "fantasy of origin was that of the immaculate conception in and through this ear." Through his psycho-biographical analysis of several musical examples (*Fourth Violin Sonata, The Unanswered Question,* and *The Pond*) Feder supports the hypothesis of Sidney Cowell who wrote in her collaborative biography with her husband that "it is not too much to say that the son has written his father's music for him" (**B354**). *See:* **B291, B475, B557,** and **B816**

B280 Julien, Jean-Rémy. Review of *An Ives Celebration,* edited by H. Wiley Hitchcock and Vivian Perlis. *Revue de Musicologie* 67, no. 1 (1981): 118-119. *See:* **B253**

In this thoughtfully-argued essay Rabinowitz advocates the need Julien reminds French readers of Henry Prunières's review of Ives's *Three Places in New England* (**B481**), in which the distinguished critic wrote of Ives's poor assimilation of Schoenberg, a composer then completely unknown to Ives. For Julien, *An Ives Celebration* signals that Ives, judged by Copland as the first American composer of major importance, has become vindicated by history, and is now taking his revenge on critics such as Prunières.

B281 Rabinowitz, Peter J. "Fictional Music: Toward a Theory of Listening." In *Theories of Reading, Looking, and Listening,* edited by Harry R. Garvin, pp. 193-208. Bucknell Review, 26, no. 1. Lewisburg: Bucknell University Press, 1981.

In this thoughtfully-argued essay Rabinowitz advocates the need for a theory of listening "which takes account of both programmatic and stylistic elements, but which, is in addition, alert to the relationship between the knowledge and experience of the audience." Before explaining his "central term," which he labels "*fictional* music," Rabinowitz draws careful distinctions between "*primary*" music ("music that is simply what it appears to be," e.g., a Bach fugue), and "*imitative* music" ("music that somehow presents itself as something it is not," e.g., when the clarinet in Beethoven's *Sixth Symphony* "'pretends' for a moment that it is a cuckoo."

Rabinowitz goes on to describe *fictional music* as "music that pretends to be a different performance of some other music" (e.g., the New York Philharmonic "pretending to be a small-town band playing a traditional tune under different circumstances") as a special type of imitative music, and he explains further that musical borrowings such as those employed by Ives, "may be either fictional or nonfictional, for they may or may not be presented as if they were some other musical performance." After asserting that Ives was "the first composer to treat fictional music as a major weapon in his aesthetic arsenal...with a sophistication and variety that few have equaled since," Rabinowitz concludes that "our whole evaluation of Ives as composer...will depend largely on our placement of his music," i.e., whether or not we understand its fictionality.

B282   Rossiter, Frank. "The 'Genteel Tradition' in American Music." *Journal of American Culture* 4, no. 4 (1981): 107-115.

Rossiter cites two manifestations of the "genteel tradition" of late-nineteenth and early twentieth-century American composers: Their desire to gain their musical training in Europe and "their disdain for the culture of the American masses, a culture that seemed to them sordid, trashy and commercialized." He then compares the careers of Daniel Gregory Mason (1873-1953), who exemplified the genteel tradition, and Ives, who revolted from it. Although Ives followed the vernacular and modernistic roads not taken by Mason, Rossiter convincingly shows that the Mason's conservative book, *Contemporary Composers* (1918) directly influenced Ives's assessments of Strauss, Debussy, Elgar, Wagner, and ragtime in his *Essays* (**B660**). Rossiter concludes that Mason and Ives ultimately share "the same idealistic aspiration toward the transcendental and spiritual in music, the same prudish fear of sensual and physical appeal, the same insistent moralizing about composers and their compositions..."

B283   Schoffman, Nachum. "Serialism in the Works of Charles Ives." *Tempo* 138 (September 1981): 21-32.

Schoffman succeeds with his intention "to demonstrate the presence of purposeful serialism, and to present some evidence of

Ives's attitude towards it." After citing a rich array of twelve-tone rows, chord series, duration series, series in other elements (e.g., tempo and dynamics), serialism in several elements at once, and palindromic constructions, he concludes with an interpretation that Ives "saw immediately that serialism, although it solves the problem of the organization of non-tonal musical materials, is dangerous if used too consistently--that it is too easy."

1983

B284 Burkholder, J. Peter. "The Evolution of Charles Ives's Music: Aesthetics, Quotation, Technique." Ph.D. dissertation, University of Chicago, 1983; Chapters 1-4 reprinted as *Charles Ives: The Ideas Behind the Music.* New Haven and London: Yale University Press, 1985 **(B296)**; Chapter 5 reprinted as "'Quotation'and Emulation: Charles Ives's Uses of His Models." *The Musical Quarterly* 71, no. 1 (1985): 1-26 **(B297)**. [A revised and expanded version of the remaining chapters (Chapter 6-12) will appear in the forthcoming volume, *The Evolution of Charles Ives's Music,* also by Yale University Press. This entry focuses on Chapters 6-12.]

The most important work on Ives's aesthetic, style, and development. In addition to his successful and comprehensive effort to create a workable vocabulary of Ives's stylistic characteristics and a brilliant survey of the primary and secondary literature on Ives, Burkholder has written a convincingly argued reevaluation that places Ives in the mainstream of twentieth-century European musical thought. The following summary remarks can only suggest the richness and significance of this study.

Part II, "Ives's Uses of Existing Music." **Chapter 6**, "Ives and the Art of Paraphrase." A demonstration of how Ives developed a unique approach to melodic transformation. **Chapter 7**, "Cumulative Settings." Burkholder explores the manner in which "a complex form virtually unique to Ives which develops motives from the tune or presents important countermelodies before the theme itself is presented whole at the end," grows out of paraphrase. **Chapter 8**, "Quodlibet, Collage, and Patchwork." An explanation of more complex Ivesian techniques.

Part III, "Techniques: Traditional Roots and Contemporary Parallels." **Chapter 9**, "The Paradigm for Ives's Evolution." A discussion of "the unifying process which underlies all aspects of Ives's growth as a composer, i.e, a progressive intensification or exaggeration of musical techniques and assumptions he inherited from both classical and vernacular musical traditions of the late 19th century." **Chapter 10**, "Layering and Articulation, Process and Form," and **Chapter 11**, "Harmony, Melody, and Rhythm." Burkholder demonstrates that Ives preserves the principal of "harmonic function, whether the harmonic order has any direct relation to normal procedures of tonality or not." **Chapter 12**, "Generative Systems, Organic Unity, and Economy of Means." Burkholder contrasts the private research function of Ives's experimental works with the more "public" concert music. In his conclusion he reviews and then removes various obstacles that have inhibited Ives's admirers and detractors alike from reevaluating Ives as a "peer of Schoenberg and Stravinsky rather than as an amusing oddity."

Principal works discussed:
Chaper 6: *First Quartet* and *Second Symphony* [these first important works to exhibit Ives's paraphrase technique are discussed at greater length than any others in the dissertation]; *Housatonic at Stockbridge, Down East, The Side Show, Religion, Evening,* and *Variations on Jerusalem the Golden*. Chapter 7: *Third Symphony.* Chapter 8: *First Piano Sonata* ["good example of Ives's retrospective programs"], *The Last Reader.* Chapter 10: *Central Park in the Dark* and *On the Antipodes.* Chapter 11: *Romanzo di Central Park, Majority,* and *General William Booth.* Chapter 12: *Robert Browning Overture* and *Fourth Symphony.*

B285   Conn, Peter J. "Innovation and Nostalgia: Charles Ives." In *The Divided Mind: Ideology and Imagination in America, 1898-1917,* pp. 230-250. Cambridge: Cambridge University Press, 1983.

Conn stresses compatibility and historical precedents when considering such paradoxes as Ives's "moralized conception of commerce" and the unusual combination of experimentalism and traditionalism found in his music. Using Pound as his principal example of this second point, Conn espouses the view that "the casual coincidence of technical experimentation--often leading to explosive originality of form--with some reactionary ideaology or other describes not only Ives's music but the work of the makers of modernism as well."

In noting that "Ives's devotion to 'the people' seems to have forged the link, in his own imagination, between his musical and business careers," Conn points out the irony of Ives's present neglect by "the common man" and his acceptance and recognition "precisely from the professional musicians and the academicians whose predecessors had tormented his creative years." Musical examples briefly discussed are *"Concord" Sonata* and *"Holidays" Symphony*, including a facsimile of *Thanksgiving*.

B286 Gingerich, Lora Louise. "Processes of Motivic Transformation in the Keyboard and Chamber Music of Charles E. Ives." Ph.D. dissertation, Yale University, 1983. 281 pp.

The most thorough motivic analysis of the *Three-Page Sonata*, the *Fourth Violin Sonata*, and the *First Piano Sonata* (first, third, and fifth movements). Gingerich conveys with conviction how the *Three-Page Sonata* "is saturated with Bach's name, and that Ives applies an organized network of transformations to the B-A-C-H motive," and in her detailed and sophisticated motivic analysis of the *First Piano Sonata* she shows how Ives made his motivic transformations coherent and yet "free from any chronological temporal framework." Complex, albeit precise, terminology is greatly aided by copious musical illustrations.

B287 Hamm, Charles. "The Search for a National Identity." *Music in the New World*, pp. 424-437. New York and London: W. W. Norton, 1983.

Although he considers Ives "the most talented composer of his generation" and successful "in writing truly American music where his peers had mostly failed," Hamm for the most part finds Ives's works more "remarkable" than great. He discusses no work at length, but does include musical examples to illustrate Ives's use of hymns, Foster, and ragtime in the *First Piano Sonata* and the *First String Quartet*. It is also significant that in contrast to earlier texts on American music by Chase (**B70**), Mellers (**B101**), and Hitchcock (**B126**), Hamm's survey does not honor Ives with a chapter of his own.

B288 Harvey, Mark Sumner. "Charles Ives: Prophet of American Civil Religion." Ph.D., Boston University Graduate School of the History of Religion, 1983. 421 pp.

Briefly defined, "civil religion is the public religious dimension 'expressed in a set of beliefs, symbols, and ritual'; and 'institutionalized in a collectivity'" [small quotes are excerpted from the writing of Robert Bellah, who developed this concept in 1967]. Again quoting Bellah, civil religion is "a set of religious beliefs, symbol, and rituals growing out of the American historical experience, interpreted in the dimension of transcendence." Harvey espouses the view that Ives and his music is "symbolic, in a prophetic mode, of the relation of civil religion and ethos in America." The Ives works Harvey chooses to demonstrate his thesis are *Lincoln, The Great Commoner, Three Places in New England, Orchestral Set No. 2,* and the *"Holidays" Symphony.*

Perhaps the most useful chapter to most students of Ives is Chapter V, in which Harvey examines the separate influences of denominational and evangelical Christianity on Ives, and the significance of Ives's choice of sacred choral texts. Also in this chapter Harvey provides an informative survey of Ives's borrowed material, vernacular as well as religious.

B289   Starr, Lawrence. "The Early Styles of Charles Ives." *19th Century Music* 7 (Summer 1983): 71-80.

Starr suggests at the outset that "the very confusion of the early output, far from being a cause for consternation, is the key to a fuller understanding of Ives's later work." He shows examples of Ives's "radical manner" and "conservative manner" that appeared in the early works before 1902, and points out that "whether traditional or radical, they tend strongly toward internal stylistic homogeneity." After 1902 Ives "decided to do within individual pieces what he tried to do with successive pieces before 1902." Starr views as an "essential, logical connection" the evolution from Ives's early internal homogeneity to the "extraordinary preoccupation with internal heterogeneity" in his mature works.

1984

B290   Davis, Peter G. "Ives Thrives." *New York* 17, no. 14 (2 April 1984): 58. *See:* **W21c**.

Enthusiastic report on a twelve-hour Wall-to-Wall Ives marathon performed at the Symphony Space on March 17 by numerous solo and chamber artists and at least two orchestras. Like earlier appreciations of Ives, Davis emphasizes the "boldly original" music, "anticipating almost every avant-garde technique in the book." An idea more representative of post-Centennial thought on Ives is Davis's remark that his "most ferociously dissonant experiments were at least in part an attempt to prove his masculinity." Davis concludes that "the composer's greatest scores have found a secure niche in the repertory," and is comforted by the thought "that Ives in all probability, is here to stay." *See:* **B295**

B291 Feder, Stuart. "Charles Ives and the Unanswered Question." *The Psychonanalytic Study of Society* 10, edited by Werner Münsterberger, L. Bryce Boyer, and Simon A. Grolnick, pp. 321-351. Hillsdale, NJ and London: The Analytic Press, Lawrence Erlbaum Associated, 1984.

Feder asserts that "ideas referring to the ominous presence of death in life and its unknown aftermath" are manifest throughout Ives's work, particularly at various crisis periods such as at the time of his first heart attack in 1906, his wife's hospitalization in 1909, and following his own more serious attack in 1918. He offers brief but informative discussions of *Immortality, Two Little Flowers, Like a Sick Eagle, Mists, Disclosure, Spring Song, Evidence, Charlie Rutlage, General William Booth Enters Into Heaven, Evening, Sunrise,* and a more detailed psychoanalysis of *Premonitions, The Pond, The Unanswered Question,* and the third movement of the *Fourth Violin Sonata.* A common if not invariable thread revealed in these works is a two-part or "question and answer" form, "the first of which is associated with uncertainty and death, the second with confidence and the future." *See:* **B279, B475, B557,** and **B816**

B292 Milligan, Terry G. "Charles Ives: Musical Activity at Yale (1894-98). *Journal of Band Research* 19, no. 2 (1984): 39-50.

In this serviceable survey of Ives's "tridimensional experience" at Yale--classroom studies with Parker, organist position at Center Church, and music for social occasions such as fraternity shows--Milligan offers a familiar one-sided indictment of Parker's role, "probably the least enjoyable and also the least important in relation to Ives' music." He also inexplicably neglects to mention either of the two major works Ives completed at Yale, the *First Symphony* and *First Quartet.*

B293 ____. "Charles Ives: Musical Activity at Poverty Flat (1898-1908)." *Journal of Band Research* 20, no. 1 (1984): 30-36.

Informative but unoriginal biographical survey of Ives's social, business, and musical career between his graduation from Yale and his marriage. During these years Ives lived at three addresses in New York City, each dubbed Poverty Flat, with a total of fifteen to twenty fellow bachelors comprised of medical and law students and young businessmen, including his future brother-in-law, David Twichell. Milligan displays liberal quotations from the *Memos* (**B378**), but does not discuss or even mention most of the major compositions Ives was working on during these years.

B294   Sales, Grover. "The Strange Case of Charles Ives or, Why Is Jazz Not Gay Music." *Gene Lees Jazzletter* 4, no. 5 (December 1984): 1-8.

Sales devotes two pages (pp. 4-5) of his provocative, albeit unsubstantiated and ultimately unconvincing, hypothesis on Ives's relationship to the "feminized culture" associated with classical music. He concludes that Ives's "vision of a virile male-centered democratic American art music actually came to realization, quite unselfconsciously [*sic*], in black America during his own lifetime."

B295   Stone, Peter Eliot. "Charles Ives Wall-to-Wall." *High Fidelity/Musical America* 34, no. 8 (August 1984): MA 25-26. *See:* **W21c**

Review of the twelve-hour Ives marathon performed at New York's Symphony Space on March 17. Highlights included a group of Ives songs sung by DeGaetani and accompanied by Kalish; the Lang Trio performing the *Trio for Violin, Cello, and Piano* (which "foreshadows the compositional attitudes of Elliott Carter"); the New York premiere of the *Four Ragtime Dances* performed by the New England Ensemble (**W21c**); the Chamber Orchestra of New England under Sinclair performing *Three Places in New England*; Dennis Russell Davies performing the *First Piano Sonata*; Stephen Drury performing *"Concord" Sonata*; and a moving performance of *The Unanswered Question* "based on a new edition of the work that corrects errors in the 1953 printed edition and includes alternate versions of some details as reflected in a 1906 shortscore sketch and in Ives's first (1934) orchestration of the work." *See*: **B290**

1985

B296   Burkholder, J. Peter. *Charles Ives: The Ideas Behind the Music.* New Haven and London: Yale University Press, 1985. *See*: **B298, B302, B305-306, B308, B313,** and **B315**

In the first of two volumes based on his remarkable dissertation (**B284**, Chapters 1-4), Burkholder offers "the first detailed history of Charles Ives's aesthetics." He successfully challenges, refutes, and reassesses the long established and prevailing myths and partial truths that have been accepted without rigorous examination, particularly the exaggerated significance attributed to Transcendentalism in Ives's aesthetic and musical development. One of the most impresive accomplishments of Ives scholarship.

B297 ____. "'Quotation' and Emulation: Charles Ives's Uses of His Models." *The Musical Quarterly* 71, no. 1 (1985): 1-26. *See*: **B284**, Chapter 5

After introducing five principal techniques that Ives uses with existing music--modeling, paraphrasing, cumulative setting, quoting, and quodlibet--Burkholder focuses on the first technique: "*modeling* a work on an existing one, assuming its structure, incorporating a small portion of its melodic material, or depending upon it as a model in some other way." After demonstrating a historical context and precedent for modeling, he then shows how Ives employs modeling in several works throughout his career from *Holiday Quickstep* (1887), *Slow March* (1887 or 1888), and *Turn Ye, Turn Ye* (?1890), to *Serenity* (1919), *On the Counter* (1920) [a parody of *A Song for Anything* (1892)], and *West London* (1920). Burkholder supports his original thesis that Ives's modeling, as a technique clearly distinguishable from "quotation," was "one of the seminal techniques for his musical method, one which appears very early and has important ramifications for his later compositions."

B298 Echols, Paul E. "Ives as Ideator." Review of *Charles Ives: The Ideas Behind the Music*, by J. Peter Burkholder. *Newsletter of the Institute for Studies in American Music* 15, no. 1 (November 1985): 5. *See*: **B296**

Echols considers Burkholder's study "a good and timely addition to the growing body of scholarly work on Ives" and "the most useful look to date at Ives's development as a musical thinker." He eagerly anticipates the forthcoming second volume on Ives's music and suggests that Burkholder also explore Ives's "fascinating and successful" third career, "disseminating his music and nurturing his image as a composer."

B299 Hamm, Charles and Peter Winkler. Interview with Charles Hamm. *Review of Popular Music* 1 (1985): 8-10 [Newsletter of The International Association for the Study of Popular Music].

During several controversial question and answer exchanges Hamm sharply rebukes Ives, his "present heavy," for failing to "integrate, specifically the contemporary popular music of his time," and for his rejection of "the cultures that were producing it." According to Hamm, it was not a "racist" Ives but the populists Copland and Gershwin who "demonstrated that classical music could make sense in the context of American culture." Hamm, who is "no longer convinced" of Ives's greatness, also brands Ives "as much an elitist as Babbitt."

B300 Kinney, Arthur. Review of *Three American Originals: John Ford, William Faulkner, and Charles Ives* by Joseph Reed. *Modern Fiction Studies* 31 (Summer 1985): 411-413. *See*: **B361**

Kinney is largely sympathetic to this book with its "wondrous display of dexterity," despite "the fact that there are no easy conclusions for Reed, and not many parallels or many comparisions to be made either." He also acknowledges that "on the whole, it is Ives who gets short shrift," but considers Reed's short analysis of two songs "illuminating."

B301 Ward, Keith. "Charles Ives and the Oversoul." Paper presented at the Mid-Atlantic Chapter Meeting of the American Musicological Society, February 3, 1985.

Useful definition of Emerson's Over-Soul and an introduction to three symbolic applications of this concept in Ives's music, which "appear within layered texture, an Ivesian trademark symbolizing the organic, multifarious nature of existence." The paper includes musical examples from the "allegorical...wandering chromatic line" in "In the Night" (*Set of Pieces for Theater or Chamber Orchestra*) and an interpretation of Ives's musical depiction of darkness in *Central Park in the Dark*.

1986

B302 Alexander, Michael J. Review of *Charles Ives: The Ideas Behind the Music*, by J. Peter Burkholder. *Tempo* 157 (June 1986): 35-37. *See*: **B296**

In this somewhat hostile review, Alexander finds considerable fault with what he considers Burkholder's "total lack of cultural perspective" and absence of a "sound methodological basis." With seeming regret he manages to force himself to commend the author for the biographical chapters 5-8.

B303 Chmaj, Betty E. "The Journey and the Mirror: Emerson and the American Arts." In *Prospects 10: An Annual of American Culture*

Studies, edited by Jack Salzman, pp. 353-408. Cambridge University Press, 1985 (1986).

Detailed analysis of the major themes Emerson explored in his *American Scholar* (1837) address and a discussion of Emerson's considerable influence on American architecture, literature, painting, and music, "on which the impact of these ideas has been conspicuous." Chmaj devotes major attention to Emerson's Double Consciousness, introduced in the essay, *The Transcendentalist* (1841-43), and symbolized by the metaphor of the journey and the mirror. She argues that the most profound realization of Emerson's Double Consciousness occurs on pages 5 and 6 of the published score of *"Concord" Sonata* ("Emerson" movement). More briefly discussed are *The Unanswered Question* and the *Fourth Symphony,* two works by Ives, "the true Emerson of American music," that illustrate his Emersonian characteristics.

B304 Field, Corey. Review of *Three American Originals: John Ford, William Faulkner, and Charles Ives,* by Joseph Reed. *Notes* 42, no. 4 (June 1986): 783-785. *See:* **B361**

Field measures Reed's success "more by the amount of further thought he invites and creates than by the concrete answers he proposes." She faults Reed for failing to make any musical observations in his discussion of Ford's films "beyond pointing out the use of folk songs also used by Ives," and especially laments the absence of any mention of the "Ivesian" dance scene in Ford's *The Grapes of Wrath.*

B305 Mellers, Wilfrid. Review of *Charles Ives: The Ideas Behind the Music,* by J. Peter Burkholder. *Times Literary Supplement* (7 February 1986): 143. *See:* **B296**

Mellers writes that Burkholder exaggerates the difficulties in understanding Ives and objects to the segregation of the music from the ideas. He also criticizes Burkholder, whom he believes "unnecessarily knocks down a few Aunt Sallies" when debunking the myth of Ives's pervasive Transcendentalism, "for the point is surely not that Ives borrowed this or the other from the Transcendentalists, but simply that he stands, in his religious and philosophical heritage, for a comparable fusion of the physical with the metaphysical." He credits Burkholder with clarifying the "apparently contradictory strands" of Ives, and acknowledges the perceptiveness of the author's description of Parker as "a liberating agent" through whom "Ives became more deeply and widely aware of the traditions of art music--European in orgin, yet capable of American metamorphosis."

B306 Rossiter, Frank. Review of *Charles Ives: The Ideas Behind the Music,* by J. Peter Burkholder. *The American Historical Review* 91, no. 4 (October 1986): 1007. *See:* **B296**

Rossiter acknowledges Burkholder's book as an "important study," and credits the author with providing "a useful periodization of Ives's artistic life." He remains unconvinced by some of the "evidence for the influence of various figures on Ives," but registers his primary disappointment with what he considers an "incomplete presentation of the social context of Ives's life."

B307 Winters, Thomas Dyer. "Additive and Repetitive Techniques in the Experimental Works of Charles Ives." Ph.D. dissertation, University of Pennsylvania, 1986. 333 pp.

The most substantial analytical study of Ives's shorter avant-garde or experimental works. Winters devotes chapters to each of three techniques (wedge-palindrome, ostinato, and imitation) that Ives employed frequently in his experimental works for chamber ensemble, piano, and chorus. [He defines "wedge-palindrome as any technique which progressively and systematically modifies one or more musical parameters...and then restores the parameter(s) in a mirror-image design."] In a forcefully argued and clearly explicated thesis Winters asserts that "Ives was able to amplify and extend their [the three techniques] unifying properties to all levels of the musical hierarchy. In sum, the combination of systematic repetition and predictable change inherent in these designs helps furnish the skeletal organization necessary for the syntax of Ives's eclectic style to emerge as a coherent musical language." In the final chapter Winters "evaluates several examples from Ives's larger works--the *Second String Quartet, Fourth of July,* and 'The Housatonic at Stockbridge" from *Three Places in New England*--to discover how these techniques are used within a nonexperimental environment."

The experimental works discussed are:
Chamber: *Fugue in Four Keys on The Shining Shore; From the Steeples and the Mountains; Scherzo for String Quartet; Hallowe'en; Largo Risoluto Nos. 1 and 2; All the Way Around and Back;* "In the Cage" and "In the Night" from *Set for Theater or Chamber Orchestra; The Unanswered Question ; Central Park in the Dark; Over the Pavements; Set No. 1; The Gong on the Hook*

and Ladder; Tone Roads Nos. 1 and 3; In Re Con Moto Et Al.
Choral: *Psalms 24, 25, 54, 67, 90, 100, and 135; Three Harvest Home Chorales.*
Piano: *Three-Page Sonata; Set of Five Take-offs; Studies Nos. 2, 5-9, and 20-23.* [The above works are indexed on pp. 332-333.]

1987

B308   Block, Geoffrey. Review of *Charles Ives: The Ideas Behind the Music,* by J. Peter Burkholder. *The Journal of Musicology* 5, no. 2 (Spring 1987): 308-311.

"The successful refutation and clarificaton of the Transcendental Ives is only the most prominent of the myths that Burkholder puts to rest." Particularly valuable additional contributions include Burkholder's reassessment of "Parker's positively crucial role in shaping Ives's musical development within the European art tradition" and his pioneering examination of the roles that John Griggs [Choir Director at Center Church in New Haven], William Lyon Phelps [Ives's English professor at Yale], and Harmony Ives played in Ives's aesthetic development. "Nearly every chapter is rich in ideas about Ives that help us to understand the misconceptions surrounding the composer's complex story."

B309   Crutchfield. Will. "Why Our Greatest Composer Needs Serious Attention." *The New York Times,* May 10, 1987, section 2, page 19+.

Thoughtful assessment of Ives inspired by Bernstein's "withdrawal" of the *Fourth Symphony* and Christoph von Dohnanyi's forthcoming New York performance of this work with the Cleveland Orchestra. Crutchfield outlines the present danger that "without careful and continuing exposure to the music itself, in the hands of discriminating and excellent performers, the composer's reputation can slip into the phantom world of second-hand opinions and witticisms." He also responds with equanimity to Carter's famous criticisms of Ives and offers a non-partisan defense of Ives's musical values, including his "transgressing the values (absolute values for many, though unexpressed as such) of order, economy, coherence and plan," and the meaning of Ives's quotation.

B310   Lambert, J. Philip. Review of Ives *Three Improvisations,* transcribed and editied by Gail and James Dapogny (Associated, 1984) and *The Unanswered Question,* critical edition by Paul C.

Echols and Noel Zahler (Peer, 1985). *Notes* 44, no. 2 (December 1987): 352-355. *See:* **W83** and **W28:1**

Thoughtful, balanced, and adequately detailed critical review of two important Ives editions. Lambert writes of the *Three Improvisations* that "following the score while listening to the recording [made by Ives in 1938] highlights a great many nuances of pianistic style that could influence a performance of any Ives work." He considers the present edition of *The Unanswered Question* most useful "in providing a thorough history of the work's evolution and making available all source information on this twentieth-century classic." *See:* **B573**

B311 Mortenson, Gary C. "Father to Son: The Education of Charles Ives." *Music Educator's Journal* 73, no. 7 (March 1987): 33-37.

Conventional overview with appropriate paragraph-length quotations from *Ives Remembered* (**B318**), *Memos* (**B378**), "Some 'Quarter-Tone' Impressions" (**B727**), the Conductor's Note to the *Fourth Symphony* (**B379**), and the Cowell (**B354**) and Rossiter (**B215**) biographies. In assessing Ives's studies with Parker, Mortenson "can sympathize with both the teacher and the student in what must have been a strenuous relationship from the start." He attributes Ives's "withdrawal from composition" to his "frustration for the public's lack of understanding" and hypothesizes with insufficient substantiation that Ives's "world became too complicated for him to understand, and his childhood too distant to easily recall."

B312 Pearsall, Ronald. "Ives in Performance." *The Music Review* 47, no. 1 (February 1986/7): 24-28.

Cursory summary of selected Ives performances mainly between 1925 and 1931. Includes a brief discussion and some quotations from various reviews of the 1931 Parisian programs in which *Three Places in New England* was performed. *See:* **B479-484**

B313 Schubert, Giselher. Review of *Charles Ives: The Ideas Behind the Music*, by J. Peter Burkholder; and *Charles Ives: Ausgewählte Texte*, edited by Werner Bartschi. *Neue Zeitschrift für Musik* (January 1987): 63. *See:* **B296**, **B660**, **B771**, and **B378**

Although Schubert does not feel that Burkholder fulfilled the expectations generated by his title, he does offer modest praise for his contribution to Ives biography. The second book marks the first appearance in German of Ives's major writings (*Essays*, "Postface to the 114 Songs," and *Memos*). Felix Meyer contributed what Schubert describes as a fluid, readable and much-appreciated German translation.

B314 Solomon, Maynard. "Charles Ives: Some Questions of Veracity." *Journal of the American Musicological Society* 40, no. 3 (Fall 1987): 443-470.

In this important article, surprisingly the first on Ives to appear in this journal, Solomon challenges several fundamental assumptions about Ives's role as an innovator. He introduces his subject by exploring the "strong element of self-deception here, rising from Ives's need to idealize his relationship with his father," and goes on to review how Ives's defense of George Ives's precocious modernism led him to conceal and subsequently deny other musical influences.

Solomon describes various claims in the *Memos* (**B378**) "as a brief to establish Ives's priority as a modernist innovator, an audacious and pathetic attempt, backed almost entirely by the composer's own words and little, if any external circumstantial documentation." He then explores his "central issue--the veracity of the datings of Ives's music" through an examination of several mansucripts in which Ives "added many of his notations retrospectively," notations which Solomon concludes are often "self-serving, in conflict with other datings, or patently false." Examples, several with accompanying facsimiles, include: *The American Woods Overture*; *The Majority*; *Washington's Birthday*; "Putnam's Camp" from *Three Places in New England*; *Rock of Ages*; *Psalm 67*; *The Unanswered Question*; *The Celestial Country*; *Piano Trio*; and *Robert Browning Overture*. Solomon also seriously challenges the "contradictory datings" in Ives's various chronological lists compiled between 1930 and 1950.

Regrettably according to Solomon, Ives "apparently did not understand" that his artistic achievement did not depend on his priority as an innovator. Ives's desire for musical hegemony thus led to his tampering with the evidence, "a systematic pattern of falsification sufficient for the prudent scholar to withhold acceptance of Ives's datings pending independent verification of his assertions and scrupulous testing of the evidentiary trail that he left on his autographs." *See*: **B558**

B315 Swartz, Anne. Review of *Charles Ives: The Ideas Behind the Music*, by J. Peter Burkholder. *American Music* 5, no. 2 (Summer 1987): 222-223. *See*: **B296**

Swartz briefly praises Burkholder's "elaboration of numerous literary and artistic sources for Ives's thought, his ability to integrate these influences with Ives's own divergent philosophical ideals as seen in his writings, and his skill in relating these strands of thought to various phases of Ives's career."

IVES AND HIS CONTEMPORARIES

General
See also: **B356**

B316   Stambler, Bernard. "Four American Composers." *The Juilliard Review* 2, no. 1 (Winter 1955): 7-16.

Stambler discusses the careers of Ives, Copland, Barber, and Schuman and how their respective careers reflect evolving conditions in American cultural life. Like many others Stambler considers Ives's creative isolation at the turn of the century "a tragic expression of the experience of the artist." He applauds the situation fifty years later: "It is a less torturing problem today to know what it means to be an American composer."

B317   Perlis, Vivian. "Ives and Oral History." *Notes* 28, no. 4 (June 1972): 629-642.

Perlis describes the genesis of the Ives Oral History Project and offers highlights from nearly sixty interviews of Ives's family, friends, business associates, and musical contemporaries. Nearly complete transcripts of these interviews appear in book form as *Charles Ives Remembered* (**B318**) according to the categories presented in this article. Perlis concludes by underlying the urgent need for additional oral history projects and summarizing present and future prospects in this area.

B318   _____. *Charles Ives Remembered: An Oral History.* New Haven and London: Yale University Press, 1974. *See:* **B200, B203, B206, B208, B210, B213, B218**, and **B234**

"The only extensive biographical oral history of an American composer" [in 1974], these fifty-eight transcribed interviews constitute one of the most important sources in the Ives literature. Much of this information, arranged usefully into four categories, "Youth and Yale Years," "Insurance," "Family, Friends, and Neighbors," and "Music," cannot be obtained from any other source. Particularly valuable are the many detailed personal reminiscences of Ives as family man, friend, and business associate, and the first-hand reports on the historical and aesthetic genesis of many Ives works. Among the more illustrious interviewees not listed among Ives's contemporaries below are Nicolas Slonimsky, Lehman Engel, Goddard Lieberson, Louis Untermeyer, and John Kirkpatrick.

Henry Adams [1838-1918]

B319 Frantz, Donald Howe, Jr. "Search for Significant Form, 1905-1915: An Evaluation of the Symbols of Tradition and Revolt in American Literature, Painting, and Music." Ph.D. dissertation, Religion, University of Southern California, 1960. 355 pp.

Ambitious but ultimately unsatisfactory inter-disciplinary study of the work and thought of Adams, Einstein, Prendergast, Ives, and Hocking. Frantz proposes at the outset "to offer some evidence that some of the art in question (American literature, painting and music, 1905-1915) embodies the essence of religion." While drawing useful parallels, for example, between Adams and Hocking, Frantz does not possess the musical expertise with which to develop significant relationships between Ives and these contemporaries. Consequently his discussions of Ives's works too often reveal inaccuracies or a superficial understanding. Despite these deficiencies, Frantz offers some thoughtful observations on the complementary nature of art and religion.

B320 Larson, Gary O. "Charles Ives and American Studies." *Student Musicologists at Minnesota* 6 (1975-1976): 237-249.

Larson describes Henry Adams's autobiography, published in 1906, as "a statement concerning the passing of traditional values before the assault of technological innovations." He notes that both Adams and Ives share "the theme of multiplicity" and that both reject "the artificial order," but that Adams departs from Ives in his view that "chaos, the law of nature, had defeated order, the dream of man."

Samuel Barber [1910-1981]
See also: **B316**

B321 Ramey, Phillip. "A Talk with Samuel Barber." *Songs of Samuel Barber and Ned Rorem.* New World Records 229 [1978].

After dismissing the notion of an American song tradition in the previous question, Barber admits to being "unfashionable" when he speaks of Ives as "an amateur, a hack who didn't put pieces together well." When Copland expressed the Tanglewood decision that "Ives is a great composer," Barber left the class and drove away.

John J. Becker [1886-1961]
See also: **B318** and **B356**

B322 Becker, John J. "Charles E. Ives, Musical Philosopher."
Northwest Musical Herald (January 1933) [Yale Collection Box 56,
folder 2, typeset on 6 pages].

Although he describes Ives as "the father of the ultra-modern
group of composers" and does not hesitate to point out precocious
technical innovations, Becker emphasizes Ives's "spirituality" and
"philosophical contemplation of God and man." He considers
Ives's *"Concord" Sonata* and *Fourth Symphony* as particularly
profound musical illustrations of these noble characteristics.

B323 _____. *"Essays Before a Sonata."* *Music News* 42 (February
1950): 22-23.

This article consists almost entirely of paragraph-length
quotations from various chapters in Ives's prefatory essays
(**B660**), out of print in 1950. According to Becker, *"Concord"
Sonata* "reflects the soul of a great man and composer, a fine
musician and a philosopher," and "no composer has written a
more beautiful book with a more deeply moving message."

B324 _____. "Charles E. Ives." *Etude* 74 (May-June 1956) 11+; (July-
August 1956) 14+.

A summary of Ives's career. Becker introduces his subject with
excerpts from Rosenfeld (**B29**) and *Time Magazine* (**B675**), and
throughout the essay intersperses generous excerpts from
Bellamann's article on the *Fourth Symphony* (**B497**) and Ives's
political and aesthetic writings (**B371-374** and **B380**). As he did
in 1933 (**B322**), Becker appreciates Ives, "not only as a great
composer but as the living last symbol of a great man," and
places the greatest value on Ives's "deeply moving spirituality."

B325 Gillespie, Don. "John Becker, the Musical Crusader of St.
Thomas College." In *Student Musicologists at Minnesota* 6 (1975-
1976): 31-65; revised as "John Becker, Musical Crusader of Saint
Paul." *The Musical Quarterly* 62, no. 2 (April 1976): 195-217.

An overview of the career of John Becker, who was the earliest
and foremost "Midwest spokesman" for Ives, Cowell, Ruggles, and
Riegger and their efforts to create "an American music with
experimental tendencies drawn from our own American
experience rather than from Europe." Within this larger focus
Gillespie discusses the origins and development of the Ives-

Becker friendship and musical collaboration from 1931 until Ives's death in 1954.

Henry Bellamann [1882-1945]
See also: **B318** and **B652**

B326 Bellamann, Henry. "The Music of Charles Ives." *Pro Musica Quarterly* (March 1927): 16-22; reprinted by Robina C. Clark in the *Danbury Evening News*, June 6, 1927.

Historically important as one of the earliest assessments of Ives's work. Bellamann is the first of innumerable writers to contrast the positive influence of George Ives's "profound investigations" with the "inhospitality of academic authority" that marked Parker's "frosty hostility" to Ives's "Bolshevism." While he acknowledges Ives's extraordinary originality, Bellamann also recognizes that the twenty-year evolution of Ives's music from conventional to avant-garde idioms "owes to the music of the past what every soundly made work owes to predecessors." Bellamann's perception that Ives wrote "slowly and carefully, allowing ideas to come to leisurely maturity, exerting at all times a most exacting self-criticism," would later be challenged as Ives's work habits became better known.

B327 _____. "Charles Ives: The Man and His Music." *The Musical Quarterly* 19, no. 1 (January 1933): 45-58.

One of the earliest biographical and critical assessments of Ives to appear in a major scholarly journal. Bellamann describes Ives's dual career and the paradox of a businessman who writes the avant-garde music of a "wild-eyed revolutionary inhabiting the regions of Bohemia." Unlike most contemporary writers on Ives and in contrast to his own earlier remarks (**B326**), Bellamann acknowledges the positive influence of Horatio Parker, Ives's music professor at Yale. Bellamann also offers some perceptive general remarks on Ives's style (*"Concord" Sonata* and *Fourth Symphony*) and discusses numerous adventurous details from the *114 Songs* (*The White Gulls, September,* and *December* are illustrated). Although Bellamann departs "profoundly" from Ives's "aesthetic premises," he unquestionably admires Ives's "sincerity, the loftiness of his aims, the human sympathy, the consummate mastery of technique, and the prodigious musical erudition back of it."

B328 Parthun, Paul. "Concord, Charles Ives, and Henry Bellamann." In *Student Musicologists at Minnesota* 6 (1975-1976): 66-86.

In this informative overview of Bellamann's musical and literary career, Parthun discusses and tries to remedy "the chronological confusion surrounding the premiere of '*Concord.*'" He also demonstrates the historical importance of Bellamann's support for Ives and describes their mutual friendship between 1920 and Bellamann's death in 1945.

Arthur Berger [1912-]
See also: **B318** and **B776**

B329 Berger, Arthur. "The Young Composer's Group." *Trend* 2 (April-June, 1933): 26-28.

Berger writes about a group of young American composers, most of whom are making "an effort to restore the balance between tradition and novelty" (in favor of the former). This group adopted Ives as their mentor, "a 'find' worthy of exploitation," much as *Les Six* adopted Satie. Berger notes an important distinction, however, between the two sets of relationships: "While the Six-men en masse accepted Satie as a model for their musical expressions, only two of the present Group [Heilner and Moross] have done so with Ives."

B330 ____. "Contemporary Music Society." *New York Herald Tribune,* April 26, 1949, page 18. *See:* **W62d, W76a, WW133c,** and **B714**

Review of Masselos's premiere performance of *Three-Page Sonata* that took place the previous evening at the Museum of Modern Art (**W76a**). Berger praises only the "jazz" portion of this work as well as the *Third Violin Sonata* and the song, *Walking,* also performed at this International Society for Contemporary Music concert: "It is the only part that has any meaning for me, for the whole has very little profile, least of all the profile of a sonata movement."

B331 ____. "Ives in Retrospect." *The Saturday Review* 37, no. 31 (July 31, 1954): 62-63.

Berger believes that "to scorn Ives for his conservatism would be to commit the error of those who overevaluated him for his early use of dissonance." Nevertheless he argues that Ives's reputation as an innovator is undeserved and suggests the possibility that Ives was a musical conservative at heart, who used dissonance as "a coating to be applied or left off at will."

B332 ____. "His Aim Was to Be Solely American." Review of *Charles Ives and His Music*, by Henry and Sidney Cowell. *The New York Times Book Review*, January 9, 1955, section 7, pages 3+. *See:* **B354**

Berger shows his respect for the dedication of the Cowells, but does not share their high praise for Ives. According to Berger, Ives is "in some ways a primitive, which accounts for both his charm and crudity," and he goes on to deny that Ives achieved an "integration of forms and materials." Furthermore, Berger believes that Ives could have profited from the European training he so willfully avoided and that the seemingly happy situation of Ives's present recognition fails to diminish the reality of "the unhappy story of a man who came too early to enjoy the support that an avant-garde group of compatriots would have given him."

Marc Blitzstein [1905-1964]
See also: **B566**

B333 Blitzstein, Marc. "Ives." *La Revue Musicale*, Paris (February 1936) [Yale Collection Box 55, folder 6, with translation].

Blitzstein laments the fate of the avant-garde American composer at the hands of a conservative public: "Perhaps the most tragic example is that of Charles Ives, a New England musician magnificently gifted, who has completely stopped composing since 1921. His *114 Songs*, his choral and orchestral works reveal a bold and profound talent, and a singularly prophetic vision....He is a true 'original' who launched in his music flashes of ideas that have taken history many years to comprehend. But a composer, even when he is a genius, cannot write for himself alone; without a public he is deprived of support."

John Cage [1912-]

B334 Cage, John. "History of Experimental Music in the United States." In *Silence*, pp. 67-75. Middletown, CT: Wesleyan University Press, 1961.

In the single paragraph [pp. 70-71] that he devotes to Ives in this essay (first published in the *Darmstadter Beiträge* in 1959), Cage attributes no value to Ives's prophetic use of harmony and rhythm or his use of Americana, but recognizes the importance of Ives's experiments with musical space, collage, and indeterminacy.

B335 ____. "Two Statements on Ives." In *A Year From Monday: New Lectures and Writings*, pp. 36-42. Middletown, CT: Wesleyan University Press, 1967.

In these two revealing statements from 1964 and 1965 respectively, Cage expands on the points he introduced in his earlier comments on Ives (**B334**). He explains that his late interest in Ives corresponded to his evolving interest in indeterminacy and clarifies why he feels that Ives's decision to enter the insurance business revealed a weakness. In his present delight with "everything" he hears by Ives, Cage tempers his earlier objection to Ives's American aspects, since "in view of 'pop art' they are pertinent."

B336 Kostelanetz, Richard. *John Cage*, pp. 12, 25, 100-102, 130, 162-165, 167, 177, 202, 204. New York and Washington: Praeger Publishers, 1970.

In response to a question on how music can enhance the appreciation of our environment Cage offers a deliberate "misinterpretation" of Ives's remark "that any man, sitting on his porch looking out toward the mountains with the sun setting, could hear his own symphony." Cage also expands on Ives's enjoyment of complexity and performance liberties and places his own HPSCHD in the "tradition" of Ives's experimental and spatially oriented, unfinished *Universe Symphony*.

Elliott Carter [1908-]
See also: **B668**

[**B337-343** have been reprinted in *The Writings of Elliott Carter-- An American Composer Looks at Modern Music*, compiled, edited, and annotated by Else Stone and Kurt Stone. Bloomington & London: Indiana University Press, 1977. Page numbers in brackets after each citation refer to this volume.]

B337 Carter, Elliott. "Ives Today: His Vision and Challenge." *Modern Music* 21, no. 4 (May-June 1944): 199-202 [pp. 98-102].

In the five years since his negative assessment of the *"Concord" Sonata* (**B668**), Carter has softened his criticisms, but he is still troubled by Ives's practice of quotation and by "the amount of detail left to the interpreter's discretion." Carter singles out for special comment Ives's use of simultaneous tempi in several orchestral scores, considers Ives's *Essays Before a Sonata* (**B660**) "a little masterpiece," and advocates a "real demonstration" of Ives's music in the form of more performances.

B338 _____. "An American Destiny." *Listen* 9, no. 1 (November 1946): 4-7 [pp. 143-150].

In this character study Carter discusses Ives's careers in business and music and provides examples of many of Ives's endearing personal idiosyncracies such as his extreme modesty and generosity, his desire to retain "amateur status" in music, his originality, and his high ideals.

B339 _____. "The Rhythmic Basis of American Music." *The Score* 12 (June 1955): 29-31 [pp. 160-166].

Carter discusses "the American composer's relationship to jazz," and the work of four composers (Harris, Copland, Sessions, and Ives) who were able to incorporate jazz techniques into classical American music. Most remarkable of these figures, according to Carter, was Ives. Not only had Ives composed most of his music prior to the dissemination of jazz in the 1920's, he also "went one step further than the composers mentioned above." Carter then specifies and illustrates three of Ives's most radical rhythmic practices, which, although described by Cowell as early as 1930, had not become a major concern to American composers at the time of Carter's article.

B340 _____. "Shop Talk by an American Composer." *The Musical Quarterly* 46, no. 2 (April 1960): 189-201; reprinted in *Problems of Modern Music*, edited by Paul Henry Lang, pp. 51-63. New York: W. W. Norton, 1962 [pp. 199-211].

Within a question and answer format Carter responds to the final question, "What do you think of Charles Ives now?" He expresses his unwavering admiration for Ives the man, despite his misgivings towards Ives's music, mainly the "undifferentiated confusion" and "frequent reliance on musical quotations for their literary effect." Carter remains most interested in how Ives represented the "special conflicts" of the American composer.

B341 _____. "Expressionism and American Music." *Perspectives of New Music* 4, no. 1 (Fall-Winter 1965): 1-13; revised version reprinted in *Perspectives on American Composers*, ed. Benjamin Boretz and Edward T. Cone, pp. 217-229. New York: W. W. Norton, 1972 [pp. 230-243].

Carter writes about American composers who have adopted some of the aesthetic and musical techniques of European expressionism. According to Carter, Ives's adapted translation of Hegel reveals his closeness to expressionist thought, but the "extreme heterogeneity" of his music contradicts Schoenberg's "more acceptable attitude" represented in the latter's desire for "inner cohesion."

B342 _____. Interview. In *Charles Ives Remembered: An Oral History*, by Vivian Perlis, pp. 131-145. New Haven and London: Yale University Press, 1974 [pp. 258-269].

An expansion of Carter's personal recollection of Ives (**B668**). In an attempt to dispel the myth that Ives had not heard contemporary music, Carter mentions a number of works that he heard in concert with Ives in the 1920s. Again Carter wonders when Ives's earlier music "received its last shot of dissonance and polyrhythm," and despite his acknowledgment of critical error on his part regarding *"Concord"* Sonata and his unwavering fascination for "the polyrhythmic aspect" and "multiple layering" in Ives's music, Carter reiterates his dissatisfaction with Ives's practice of quotation, a practice which leads occasionally to a "disturbing lack of musical and stylistic continuity."

B343 _____. "Documents of a Friendship with Ives." *Parnassus: Poetry in Review* 3 (Summer 1975): 300-315; reprinted in *Tempo* 117 (June 1976): 2-10 [pp. 331-343].

The documents in the title of this article are letters and sketches of letters between Carter and the Iveses, beginning with Ives's letter of recommendation on behalf of Carter's freshman application to Harvard (1926) and concluding with Harmony Ives's acknowledgement of Carter's letter of condolence (1954). In addition to filling several lacunae of his earlier published personal recollections, Carter discusses the "disastrously traumatic" personal effect precipitated by his own negative 1939 review of *"Concord"* Sonata (**B668**). He also outlines the "practical actions to further Ives's cause" that he undertook when his earlier musical admiration for his former mentor returned in the 1940s.

B344 Edwards, Allen. *Flawed Words and Stubborn Sounds: A Conversation with Elliott Carter*, pp. 29, 32, 39-41, 43, 45-46, 62-63, 65, 91, 117n, 121. New York: W. W. Norton, 1971.

At various times throughout this conversation book Carter recollects his personal memories of Ives and restates a number of the views expressed in his articles (**B337-343** and **B668**). Of particular interest is Carter's reply to a question on Ives (page 65) where, in direct contrast to his regretted condemnation of Ives's *"Concord"* Sonata in 1939 (**B668**), he describes the motivic and harmonic materials of the "Emerson" movement as "highly organized" and "closely interconnected."

Winston Churchill [1871-1947]

B345 Davidson, Colleen. "Winston Churchill and Charles Ives: The Progressive Experience in Literature and Song." In *Student Musicologists at Minnesota* 3 (1968-1969): 168-194, and 4 (1970-1971): 154-180.

Davidson argues that the careers and creative work of the American novelist, Winston Churchill, and Ives demonstrate a parallel Progressive Era ideology. For each artist an early "romantic disposition" evolved into increasingly political artistic commentary and a belief in the salvation of a "social gospel," and a final period of disillusionment with war and the non-perfectibility of man that resulted in thirty years of "isolation and silence." Six novels of Churchill and twelve songs of Ives illustrate this thesis.

Aaron Copland [1900-]
See also: **B777**

B346 Copland, Aaron. *Music and Imagination*, pp. 99-100 and 111-113. Cambridge, MA: Harvard University Press, 1952.

Copland briefly discusses Ives in two of his six Charles Eliot Norton Lectures at Harvard University. In his fifth lecture, "Musical Imagination of the Americas" [pp. 99-100], he compares Ives with Villa-Lobos, noting their similar "lack of restraint" and "lack of self-criticism." In the final lecture, "The Composer in Industrial America" [pp. 111-113], Copland stresses the significance of Ives's "acceptance of the vernacular." Copland admires "the comprehensiveness of Ives's musical mind," despite his lapses in "formal coherence." This latter lecture concluded with a performance of Ives's *First Piano Sonata* by its first interpreter, William Masselos. *See:* **W64c**

B347 _____. "A Businessman Who Wrote Music on Sundays." *Music and Musicians* 9, no. 3 (November 1960): 18.

"Excerpt from the talk on American composers given in London....transcribed by the United States Information Service." In the Ives portion of his talk, Copland weighs the pros and cons of Ives's decision to enter the insurance field rather than to become a professional composer. Although Copland acknowledges that Ives had the means to publish his compositions at his own expense, he expresses his regret that the almost total absence of public performances during his creative years prohibited Ives from a critical audience response, "a real test that every artist needs."

Henry Cowell [1897-1965]
See also: B633

B348   Cowell, Henry. "Four Little Known Modern Composers." *Aesthete Magazine* 1 (August 1928): 1 [quoted excerpt in Yale Mss. 14, Box 55, second folder, page 14].

"No one has carried the harmony of rhythm as far as Ives; and he is motivated not by instincts of creating, nor the possible improvement of technical resources, but uses his new means because they are the only way of producing the exalted state of musical flow he requires in his larger works, such as in at least two movements of the Fourth Symphony." [The other three composers are Chavez, Slonimsky, and Weiss.]

B349   ____. "Music: Three Native Composers." *The New Freeman* 1 (May 3, 1930): 184-186.

Cowell writes that Ives, Ruggles, and the promising young Harris had created original American compositions without incorporating jazz themes into their music. He also explores European and American biases and misconceptions regarding native American composers and explains how Ives used the sounds of his native music "the way it was played, not the way it was written" as the foundation for an authentic American style.

B350   ____. "American Composers. IX: Charles Ives." *Modern Music* 10 (November-December 1932): 24-33.

Cowell discusses how Ives incorporates idiosyncratic features of American band and church traditions into an original musical style. He emphasizes Ives's avant-garde features such as the latitude Ives frequently allows performers and his unprecedented rhythmic and contrapuntal complexities. The essay concludes with a comparison between the "astonishingly favorable reviews" of the past and the "more recent criticisms" which find Ives out of style. Cowell is confident that Ives, "one of the leading men America has produced in any field," eventually will find the audience he deserves.

B351   ____. "Charles E. Ives." *Disques* (November 1932): 374-376 [Yale Collection Mss. 14, Box 56, folder 1].

Cowell considers the irony that Ives, the American composer most truly independent of the European tradition, was unknown in his own country until "Europeans recognized that here was the most potent and original figure they had been shown in American music, and said so in loud print." According to Cowell, it is Ives's ability to "synthesize almost every possible musical material," including American popular music, to create an art which encompasses, "almost the entire range of human experience," that truly marks his greatness.

B352   ____. "Charles E. Ives." In *American Composers on American Music: A Symposium*, edited by Henry Cowell, pp. 128-145. Stanford, CA: Stanford University Press, 1933; reprinted New York: Frederick Ungar, 1962.

Cowell follows the organization and much of the wording of the article published in *Disques* the previous year (**B351**). But with its greater clarity, specificity, and the benefit of musical illustrations, this expanded article is an improvement on its predecessor and is historically important as one of the first studies that grapples with the essential features of Ives's style.

B353   ____. "The Music and Motives of Charles Ives." *Center* 1 (August-September 1954): 2-5.

At the outset of his first published article on Ives after the composer's death the previous May, Cowell reveals his unequivocally positive assessment of Ives: "There can be little doubt that he was the greatest American composer of his epoch...the only American composer of originality and broad scope." Of special interest is Cowell's overstated but generally accurate assertion (somewhat softened in his forthcoming biography (**B354**) that "Ives' quotations are never exact."

B354   Cowell, Henry, and Sidney Cowell. *Charles Ives and His Music*. New York: Oxford University Press, 1955; 2nd edition enlarged and reprinted 1969; unabridged reprint of the 2nd edition. New York: Da Capo Press, 1983. *See*: **B73-76, B78, B81-82, B129,** and **B369**

This first full-length biographical and musical study of Ives, one of the most important books in the Ives literature, was begun in 1947 with the composer's consent and completed before Ives's death in May 1954. Despite "endless cross-fertilization," the authors explain that Sidney [Henry's wife since 1941] wrote most of the "life" portion and Henry the "music" portion. Although the Cowells allow Ives to speak for himself from his *Memos* (**B660**) "wherever possible," it should be noted that according to Kirkpatrick's Appendix 1 ("Extant leaves of the *Memos*, concordance with the Cowell book"), the biographical information is based on "less than one-sixth" of the Ives *Memos* published with Kirkpatrick's annotations and appendixes in 1972 (**B378**).

Henry Cowell articulates the essential features of Ives's musical style through a separate examination of various musical parameters (polyphony, harmony, melody, rhythm, form, and instrumentation and voice writing). He then offers a more detailed exploration of three works, *Paracelsus, "Concord" Sonata,* and the incomplete *Universe Symphony.* The Cowells place great emphasis on the prophetic nature of Ives's music, and it is largely on the basis of his anticipation of twentieth-century techniques that they consider Ives, along with Schoenberg, Stravinsky, and Bartók "to be one of the four great creative figures in music of the first half of the twentieth century." The enlarged and reprinted edition contains "a new forward, a postscript, and an updated list of works, bibliography, and discography," but no revisions in the main text.

B355 Cowell, Henry. "Charles Ives." *Perspectives USA* (Autumn 1955): 38-56.

In this biographical and stylistic summary of his collaborative biography with his wife Sidney, Henry Cowell adds a paragraph on Ives's importance around 1950 to younger film, theater, and avant-garde composers, and a paragraph on Balanchine's 1954 ballet, *Ivesiana.* The article includes a musical reprint of *Paracelsus* with a greatly abbreviated discussion.

B356 Mead, Rita H. "Henry Cowell's New Music 1925-1936: The Society, the Music Editions, and the Recordings." Ph.D. dissertation, City University of New York, 1978; reprinted in *Studies in Musicology,* no. 40. Ann Arbor: UMI Research Press, 1981.

A valuable source that offers a detailed account of the performance, publication, and recording history of the many Ives works linked with Henry Cowell and *New Music,* such as the publication of the second movement of the *Fourth Symphony* in 1929 and the first recording of an Ives work, *Washington's Birthday,* in 1934. Includes much discussion and substantial quoted excerpts from the Ives-Cowell correspondence (1927-1954).

B357 ___. "Cowell, Ives, and *New Music*." *The Musical Quarterly* 66, no. 4 (October 1980)): 538-559.

In this focused and detailed summary based on her dissertation (**B356**), Mead outlines the publication history of the Ives works that first appeared in Cowell's *New Music* and assesses Ives's anonymous and indispensable role as the principal financial supporter of this quarterly (1927-1954). She argues convincingly that only the fortuitous combination of Cowell's "dynamism" and Ives's financial sustenance enabled *New Music* to issue "score after score in an amazing variety of styles by every major American composer of the twentieth century."

B358 ___. "The Amazing Mr. Cowell." *American Music* 1, no. 4 (Winter 1983): 63-89.

Mead summarizes the circumstances leading up to the publication of Ives in *New Music* from the *Fourth Symphony* (second movement) in 1929 to the *Eighteen* [sic] *Songs* in 1935. [Other Ives works published in *New Music* include the *Theatre Orchestra Set* (1932), *Lincoln, the Great Commoner* (1932), *The Fourth of July* (1932), and *34 Songs*.] Especially provocative is her statement "that Cowell's initial contacts with Ives were probably motivated more by financial interests than aesthetic."

E. E. Cummings [1894-1962]

B359 Coakley. John Pius. "The Artistic Process as Religious Enterprise: The Vocal Texts of Charles Ives and the Poetry of E. E. Cummings." Ph.D. dissertation, Brown University, 1982. 316 pp.

Coakley argues that "man's search for purpose and meaning...has a distinctive religious dimension" that is especially pronounced when artists such as those under investigation reveal "a distinctive religious sensibility." His "central concern" is "disclosing how Ives's and Cumming's respective approaches to their art can be called a religious enterprise." He examines the religious dimension in their work through a study of each artist's "comments on his craft," Ives's vocal lyrics, and Cumming's poetry and (to a much lesser degree), painting.

For the most part Coakley keeps his subjects separate, especially in the Ives chapters, though he does attempt some integration in his final chapter ("Coda"). The wide-ranging nature of Coakley's religious interpretation of Ives's texts is exemplified by comments such as the following: "Ives was always a deeply spiritual man, for whom composition was a kind of religious practice even when it was not related to church material." Musical examples include sketch facsimiles of *Two Little Flowers*, *On the Counter*, *On the Antipodes*, *La Fède*, and *Psalm 90*.

Claude Debussy [1862-1918]

B360 Gibbens, John Jeffrey. "Debussy's Impact on Ives: An Assessment." D.M.A. dissertation, University of Illinois at Urbana-Champaign, 1985. 152 pp.

In this path-breaking study Gibbens offers rich documentation of Debussy's introduction and "inexorable rise" in American musical life after 1901. He also offers a well-articulated response to various probing questions. "How much did Ives know about Debussy at the peak of his productivity or later...? How early did he become aware of Debussy, either by reputation or through hearing his music? What impact did this awareness have, either influential or provocative, on his musical thought and practice that may be either documented or inferred? What parallels exist between the two composers and how might they enhance our views of both?"

In his analysis of Ives's song, *Grantchester*, which incorporates the opening theme from Debussy's *Prelude to the Afternoon of a Faun* [the only contemporary quotation used by Ives], Gibbens demonstrates that "from the first chord onward Ives logically prepares for the statement of the Debussy theme and, when it enters, supports it contrapuntally with related material. After exploring the "apparent link between *Grantchester* and two of Ives's major instrumental works" [the *Second String Quartet* and *Fourth Symphony*], he goes on to discuss "a list of mature Ives works which are concerned with imagery and subjects close to Debussy's preoccupations...[and] which demonstrate the clearest evidence that Ives knew Debussy's work, reinterpreted certain of its features and rejected others" [*The Pond, Thoreau, Yellow Leaves, Mists, Down East, Tom Sails Away, Incantation, Maple Leaves, Premonitions, The Housatonic at Stockbridge, From "The Swimmers," The Indians, The New River, Evening, Sea Dirge*, and *Sunrise*]. Finally, Gibbens explores his thoughtful argument "that, in both composers, preexisting material is used to interpret traditional and present-day musical experience in terms of an as-yet-unattained, transcendental human experience." Forty-four musical illustrations follow the text.

Isadora Duncan [1878-1927]
See: **B409**

Thomas Eakins [1844-1916]
See: **B370**

Albert Einstein [1879-1955]
See: **B319**

William Faulkner [1897-1962]

B361 Reed, Joseph W. *Three American Originals: John Ford, William Faulkner, and Charles Ives.* Middletown, CT: Wesleyan University Press, 1984. *See:* **B300** and **B304**

An interdisciplinary attempt to explore the careers and canons of three American artists and their respective art forms--film, fiction, and music. While searching for the commonality among these distinctive personalities, Reed explores what it means to be an American artist. Although he often fails to hit his intended mark in his *ménage à trois*, Reed's shot, to quote from Ives's *Essays* (**B660**), does not "rebound and destroy the marksman." The only work discussed at any length is the song, *A Song--for Anything.*

John Ford [1895-1973]
See: **B361**

Robert Frost [1874-1963]

B362 Booth, Earl Walter. "New England Quartet: E. A. Robinson, Robert Frost, Charles Ives and Carl Ruggles." Ph.D. dissertation, University of Utah, 1974. 203 pp.

An interdisciplinary study that provides thoughtful and demonstrable relationships and parallels between music and literature. Although he relies heavily on Cowell (**B354**) and Yates (**B112**), and his poetic analysis surpasses his musical analysis in sophistication, Booth offers numerous original analogies between words and music. He also explains clearly how each of these four artists worked as a "solitary representative of the New England Emersonian vision" within a twentieth century context. His brief discussion of the forty songs that Ives set to his own poetry helps to compare Ives's brand of Transcendentalism and concept of nature with his literary contemporaries.

George Gershwin [1898-1937]

B363   Starr, Lawrence. "Ives, Gershwin, and Copland: Reflections on the Strange History of American Art Music." Paper presented to the College Music Society, Vancouver B.C., November 8, 1985.

Starr focuses on the "meaningful connections" between two markedly contrasting musical figures, Ives and Gershwin. He argues that both composers understood "a new American art music had to come to terms with an unprecedented variety of available materials and techniques and forged them into an artistic unity," and stresses their mutual adoption "of the native vernacular music with which they had grown up, combining these with other materials and techniques, many derived from European art music." He also answers the question, "Shouldn't a wildly pluralistic culture be described by a wildly pluralistic music?" resoundingly in the affirmative and criticizes American scholarship for deprecating Ives and Gershwin for their heterogeneity and pluralism. In the context of these issues Starr considers Copland's attempt "honestly to represent and reflect his native culture" (after rigorous European exposure and training).

Lou Harrison [1917-]
See also: B254, B257, B318, B615, and B649

B364   Harrison, Lou. "Ruggles, Ives, Varèse." *View* (November 1945); reprinted in *Soundings: Ives, Ruggles, Varèse*. *Soundings* (Spring 1974): 1-4.

After denouncing the proliferation of musical commercialism, Harrison asserts that a prominent characteristic of American music is that "its finest thinking and finest writing practitioners have for a long time been amateurs." Harrison briefly but emphatically laments that "it is now 1945 and not one of the major orchestra works has yet been played in full in America. Harrison himself would remedy this situation the following year, when he would lead the New York Little Symphony with the premiere of *Third Symphony. See:* **W3a**

B365   ____. "On Quotation." *Modern Music* 23, no. 3 (Summer 1946): 166-169.

Harrison cites parallels between Ives's quotation technique with that of Mahler (**B384**) and parallel "work procedures" between Ives's music and the novels of James Joyce. Surprisingly, when considering his insightful remarks on Ives's *First Piano Sonata*

(B649) and the Violin Sonatas **(B615)**, Harrison does not qualify the assertion that Ives states borrowed material from beginning to end without development or embroidery.

B366   _____. "The Music of Charles Ives." *Listen* 9, no. 1 (1946): 7-9.

Harrison laments the fact that Ives and other important composers "have endured ignorance and ignominy shocking to think about," and points out that the historical significance of Ives's technical innovations was "allied to the high range of his expression." He then discusses the artistic strengths of Ives's symphonies, *"Concord" Sonata*, the *Second String Quartet*, the violin sonatas, and various other works that deserve far more frequent performances.

B367   _____. "Such Melodies and Clutter: Thoughts Around Ives, 1974." *Parnassus: Poetry in Review* 3, No. 2 (Spring-Summer 1975): 316-317.

Poetic centennial tribute to the "wondrous variety" of Ives's music, "the divine 'clutter' of it all--the fertility of such mess." Harrison delights that "in our era of cheerful and fertile intellectual chaos," we are able to appreciate the "exuberant variety and liveliness" of Ives's day and can "wholeheartedly rejoice in Mr. Ives' bewildering munificence."

Bernard Herrmann [1911-1975]
See also: **B318** and **B410**

B368   Herrmann, Bernard. "Charles Ives." *Trend* 1 (September-November 1932): 99-101.

Herrmann writes with partisan zeal in this critical assessment of Ives. He attributes more logic to Ives's music than either Schoenberg's or Stravinsky's because it is "not built upon a set of mystical incantations...or upon a group of artificial neo-classic rules." He also asserts his unequivocal conviction that the Ives *Fourth Symphony* is "one of the greatest ever penned...the great American symphony that our critics and conductors have cried out for."

B369   _____. "Yankee Composer." Review of *Charles Ives and His Music*, by Henry Cowell. *Saturday Review* 38, no. 3 (January 15, 1955): 27-28. *See*: **B354**

Only the first paragraph of this review pays lip service to the Cowells's "remarkable achievement" in their "splendid book."

Instead, Herrmann presents a personal and critical assessment of Ives by a man who "was fortunate in knowing Ives for many years." He has the highest regard for Ives's rare personal qualities as well as his musical contribution and places great emphasis on the significance of Ives's "American quality" as a source of Ives's greatness and the principle cause for his neglect outside of the United States.

William E. Hocking [1873-1966]
See: B319

Winslow Homer [1836-1910]

B370 Koppenhaver, Allen J. "Charles Ives, Winslow Homer, and Thomas Eakins: Variations on America." *Parnassus: Poetry in Review* 3, no. 2 (Spring-Summer 1975): 381-393.

In this comparative study of two painters and Ives, Koppenhaver tries to demonstrate "likenesses and what they tell us about the American experience as well as what they tell us about Ives." His assertions that these three artists "certainly were not obviously influenced by European art," and that Ives (like Homer and Eakins) was "essentially self-taught" should be qualified, if not altogether refuted. Less arguable parallels include: "Their realism and love of American things"; "their strong show of masculinity and love of athletics"; and their common artistic isolation.

Charles Ives [1874-1954]
See also: **B660, B727, B771-B772, B777** and **Appendix 3**

B371 Ives, Charles. "Stand by the President and the People" [August 6, 1917]. In *Essays Before a Sonata, The Majority, and Other Writings by Charles Ives*, selected and edited by Howard Boatwright, pp. 225-231. New York: W. W. Norton, 1970. *See*: **B660**

Ives's first appeal (unpublished) for direct government. He argues that the disproportionate power in the hands of "corporate lawyers, and the type of men that now dominate the United States Senate," have corrupted America's representative democracy. Ives sees Wilson, the man who "has done more than any other President to voice the sentiments of the people rather than of politicians," as America's best hope to re-establish democratic principles. Ives would develop his plan for direct democracy at length in "The Majority." *See*: **B373**

B372   _____. "A People's World Nation" [1918; additions in early 1940s]. In *Essays Before a Sonata, The Majority, and Other Writings by Charles Ives*, selected and edited by Howard Boatwright, pp. 225-231. New York: W. W. Norton, 1970. *See:* **B660**

In Ives's People's World Nation (based in part on President Wilson's aborted plan for a League of Nations) "each country will be free to live its own native life, and the people free to work out for themselves their own problems in a fair, open-minded 'will-of-the-people way.'" Included in its structure Ives proposes "in place of national armies throughout the world, A People's World Nation Army Police Force...to stop all criminal acts of any country."

B373   _____. "The Majority" [1919-1920]. In *Essays Before a Sonata, The Majority, and Other Writings by Charles Ives*, selected and edited by Howard Boatwright, pp. 134-138. New York: W. W. Norton, 1970. [In introducing "George's Adventure," Appendix 9 of the *Memos*, Kirkpatrick writes that Ives began "The Majority" "in a form borrowed from Plato, but then forsook dialogue and rewrote it as a long essay. Later he reworked some of the dialogue into the following short story." *Charles E. Ives: Memos*, edited by John Kirkpatrick. New York: W. W. Norton, 1972.] *See:* **B660** and **B378**

In Ives's most extensive essay on politics and society the composer develops the ideas outlined in "Stand by the President and the People" (**B371**). Like Rousseau, Ives espouses the idealistic conviction that the Majority, i.e., the people, are innately good. Ives goes one step further in his assertion that the Majority is *always* right. Under his radical but simple plan laws would be created by a direct majority vote of the people, thus reducing Congress to a "clerical machine."

Countering objections to this plan, Ives considers potential dangers less frightening than current realities and expresses his conviction that "if there be virtue" in Minority ideas, those outvoted "can rest assured that they will eventually be accepted, or, at least tried out by the Majority." Among his other proposals Ives advocates the limitation of individual income and property in order to inhibit powerful Minority interests from thwarting the Majority will.

B374   _____. "Concerning a Twentieth Amendment" [1920]. Includes "A Suggestion for a Twentieth Amendment," "Correspondence with William H. Taft," and "Letter to Editors." In *Essays Before a Sonata, The Majority, and Other Writings by Charles Ives*, selected and edited by Howard Boatwright, pp. 200-214. New York: W. W. Norton, 1970. *See:* **B660**

Ives translates his ideas for direct government of the people, developed at length in "The Majority" **(B373)**, into a proposed Twentieth Amendment to the Constitution.

B375   _____. "The Amount to Carry--Measuring the Prospect." *Eastern Underwriter*, September 17, 1920, part 2 (Life Insurance Salesmanship Edition), pp. 35-38; issued by Ives & Myrick, printed c. 1921-1923. Sections I-III and IX reprinted with "Correspondence with Darby A. Day," February 7, 1920, in *Essays Before a Sonata, The Majority, and Other Writings by Charles Ives*, selected and edited by Howard Boatwright, pp. 232-242. New York: W. W. Norton, 1970. *See:* **B660**

The subtitle reveals the subject matter of Ives's principal published essay on life insurance: "Suggested Presentation, Selling Plans and Formulas Which Will Guide and Assist the Agent in Making Proper Adjustments of Insurance Protection to Carrying Ability and Needs." Below the subtitle Ives writes: "The subject matter relating to practical agency work begins in Section IV, Part 4" [not included in *Essays* **(B660)**].

Ives's working premises are that "life insurance is doing its part in the progress of the greater life values" and that "the manner of selling is becoming more and more scientific." He also accepts it as a given that "a life insurance policy is one of the definite ways of society for toughening its moral muscles, for equalizing its misfortunes."

B376   _____. "College Athletics." [Letter to the Editor from Another Yale Graduate]. *The New York Times*, May 14, 1922, section 8, page 8.

In response to a letter from a Yale Graduate that appeared two days earlier in *The New York Times*, Ives disputes the notion that athletics won the last war and suggests that Yale in 1922 might possess "a stronger individualism," despite its greatly diminished success in athletics.

B377   _____. "'Broadway' (Not a Continuation of 'Main Street')." Ives & Myrick, Managers of the Mutual Life Insurance Co. of New York, 46 Cedar Street, New York. Printed, by request, from Agency Bulletins July-September 1922. Reprinted in Appendix 10 of *Charles E. Ives: Memos*, edited by John Kirkpatrick, pp. 229-235. New York: W. W. Norton, 1972. *See:* **B378**

An original didactic parable describing two kinds of insurance agents, the "casual opportunist" who "took immediate advantage of a chance opportunity" and "made a man of responsibility take a kind of policy more suited to his needs [$5,000] than the one he had in mind" [$2,500], and a "systematic opportunist" who by careful preparation, psychological insight, and personal conviction, convinced the same client that he needed a $42,000 policy.

B378   ____. *Memos* [1931-1932; with corrections, revisions, and additions 1933-1934]. *Charles E. Ives: Memos*, edited by John Kirkpatrick. New York: W. W. Norton, 1972. [Excerpts from the *Memos* arranged by subjects ("On Critics," "On 'Great' Music," "On War and Nationalism," "On Making Recordings," "On Celebrity Performers," "On the Reactions of Others to His Work," "On Provincialism," "On Labels," "On Music and Musicianship," and an "Ode to a Music Critic" appeared in "The Old Yankee Iconoclast Strikes Again--Posthumously. Memos by Charles E. Ives," *High Fidelity* 21, no. 10 (october 1971): 66-72.] *See:* **B153-154, B164, B186, B189, B200, B210, B213, B261**, and **B396**

This invaluable source contains all the extant Memos that Ives wrote and dictated in the early 1930's, only three-fifths of which were available to the Cowells when they prepared their biography (**B354**). The dust jacket notes succinctly summarize the principal contents: "Part One, '*Pretext*,' sets forth Ives's aims, his view on music, critics, and criticism. In Part Two, '*Scrapbook*,' Ives discusses his music. Part Three, '*Memories*,' is devoted to biographical and autobiographical remembrances." Ives devotes separate sections of the *Scrapbook* to each of his symphonies, the orchestral and theater sets, the two piano sonatas and the four violin sonatas, the *Second String Quartet*, *Thanksgiving Prelude and Postlude*, *Men of Literature Overtures*, *Hallowe'en*, *Three Quarter-Tone Pieces for Two Pianos*, and various other works including college marches and take-offs.

In addition to the meticulously thorough and extraordinarily useful annotations throughout the text, Kirkpatrick offers a "Chronological Index of Dates" and no less than twenty-one appendixes: "Lists of Ives's music, other writings of Ives that round out the Memos, material clarifying Ives's relationship with people who influenced him, and a play and a story Ives thought had operatic possibilities."

1. Extant leaves of the *Memos*, concordance with the Cowell book; 2. Ives's earlier Lists of Works (1929-35); 3. Ives's later Lists of

Works (1937-50); 4. The *114 Songs* and their reprints; 5. Ives's note on the *67th Psalm*; 6. Ives's scholastic record (1894-98), Chadwick's visit to Parker's class (1898), and the footnote to *Ich grolle nicht*; 7. Memos about the *Concord Sonata* (1935); 8. Questionnaires about the *Concord Sonata* (1935); 9. *George's Adventure* and *The Majority* (1919); 10. *Broadway* (1922) (**B377**); 11. Letter to John Tasker Howard (1930); 12. *Ode to a Music Critic*; 13. George Edward Ives (1845-1894) and his family; 14. Henry Anderson Brooks (c. 1855-1906?); 15. John Cornelius Griggs (1865-1932); 16. Joseph Hopkins Twichell (1838-1918); 17. Poverty Flat, 1898-1908; 18. Julian Southall Myrick (1880-1969); 19. Harmony Twichell (1876-1969); 20. *Major John Andre* by Lyman Brewster (1832-1904); 21. *The Red Patrol* by Sir Gilbert Parker (1862-1932).

B379   ____. "Music and Its Future." In *American Composers on American Music: A Symposium*, edited by Henry Cowell, pp. 191-198. Stanford, CA: Stanford University Press, 1933; reprinted New York: Frederick Ungar, 1962. Excerpted from "The Fourth Symphony for Large Orchestra [Conductor's Note for the Second Movement]. *New Music* 2, no.2 (January 1929). Reprinted in *Symphony No. 4*. Performance score edited by Theodore A. Seder, Romulus Franceschini, and Nicholas Falcone, pp. 12-14. Preface by John Kirkpatrick. New York: AMP, 1965.

Sensitive to practical as well as philosophical considerations, Ives discusses the relationship between perceived sound and its musical space, especially how we perceive dynamic, pitch, and rhythmic levels or complexities from varying distances. Among his conclusions Ives writes "that in any music based to some extent on more than one or two rhythmic, melodic, harmonic schemes, the hearer has a rather active part to play" and that, although "money may travel faster than sound in some directions," it places second "in the direction of musical experimentation or extension."

B380   ____. "Letter to Franklin D. Roosevelt" [January 6, 1938] and "Memoranda" [1935-1938]. In *Essays Before a Sonata, The Majority, and Other Writings by Charles Ives*, selected and edited by Howard Boatwright, pp. 215-224. New York: W. W. Norton, 1970. *See:* **B660**

Ives urges the passage of the Ludlow Amendment to the Constitution, which would require unequivocal Majority acquiescence before the United States could enter a war. At the time Ives wrote this letter and accompanying Memoranda, he thought that a referendum would reduce the potential for war; he was also influenced by the fact that the amendment represented the will of the Majority, 73% of which approved its adoption. *See:* **B373**

James Joyce [1882-1941]
See also: **B365**

B381 Dickinson, Peter. "A New Perspective for Ives." *The Musical Times* 115 (October 1974): 836-838.

Dickinson discusses "a change in the cultural balance of power" in literature and music in favor of the United States and cites examples of Ives's posthumous influence on several British composers (Tippett, Musgrave, Crosse, Holloway, and Vaughan Williams). After noting the absence of a British musical parallel to Ives, Dickinson enumerates historical and artistic parallels between Ives and Joyce, especially their shared practices of incorporating "recollections of childhood and youth" and their prevalent use of quotation.

Ernst Krenek [1900-]

B382 Krenek, Ernst. "Charles Ives, 1874-1954." *Schweizerische Musikzeitung* 95, no. 4 (April 1955): 141-144.

After a biographical and stylistic overview based on the Cowell biography, Krenek offers an evaluation of Ives's achievement, in which he views with ingenuous astonishment Ives's foresight upon his graduation from Yale to understand the impossibility of a musical career and praises Ives's innovations and unwillingness to compromise. He concludes that Ives was a tragic symbol, perhaps victim, of American culture, whose strength of character surpassed his narrow achievement. Krenek's article also can stand as a symbol for the subtle condescension with which American composers are often viewed by Europeans.

Edward MacDowell [1860-1908]

B383 Davis, Ronald L. "MacDowell and Ives." In *A History of Music in American Life Vol. II: The Gilded Years, 1865-1920*, pp. 108-138. Huntington, NY: Robert Krieger Publishing Co., 1980.

Only the opening and closing paragraphs of this chapter contain any direct comparisons between these two composers. The remainder of Davis's essay consists of two independent, conventional and uninspired but generally reliable biographical surveys.

Gustav Mahler [1860-1911]
See also: **B365**

B384 Morgan, Robert P. "Ives and Mahler: Mutual Responses at the End of an Era." *19th Century Music* 2 (1978): 72-81.

An imaginative comparative examination of these two musical contemporaries. Unlike most writers on Ives, Morgan, without dismissing the significance of Ives's independence from Europe and his American identity, places Ives squarely in the European tradition, and he argues persuasively that both composers "shared common assumptions regarding the materials and techniques, as well as the underlying aesthetic, of musical composition." Among numerous wide-ranging issues in this important essay Morgan explores Ives's and Mahler's similar approach to musical quotation and handling of form, and their mutual "interest in exploiting space."

B385 Daugherty, Michael Kevin. "Goethe and Emerson, the Link between Aesthetic Theories and Compositional Processes of Gustav Mahler and Charles Ives." M.A. thesis, Yale University, 1982. 67 pp.

An attempt to "clarify the extent to which two very special composers shared common beliefs concerning the purpose of musical composition." Daugherty argues that "the comparison of Goethe's ideas about art and literature with those of Emerson casts illumination upon Mahler's and Ives' aesthetic perspective as a whole." To support this thesis he offers numerous parallels between Goethe and Emerson as well as between the two composers, especially as exhibited in Mahler's *Ninth Symphony* and Ives's *Fourth.* Included within the text are ample musical illustrations from both "biographical" works.

Darius Milhaud [1892-1974]
See: **B318**

Jerome Moross [1913-]
See also: **B318**

B386 Moross, Jerome. "Some Thoughts on Ives." In *South Florida's Historic Ives Festival, 1974-1976*, edited by F. Warren O'Reilly, p. 38.

Brief retrospective of Moross's early first exposure to Ives at the age of fifteen (1928) and his championing of Ives during his own developing stages as a composer (1930-1936). He briefly relates that "Cowell had introduced me to Ives and I saw him a number of times in the years 1933-36." In the light of subsequent challenges (e.g., **B558, B360**, and **B668**), it is worth noting that Moross "never quite believed his statements that he hadn't heard *any* works by this or that composer, but whether he had or not isn't really important." Moross asserts that "two-thirds of Ives' music is of extraordinary quality," and concludes by singling out four additional composers as deserving far more attention than they have previously received: Ornstein, Cowell, Riegger, and Gilbert.

Maurice B. Prendergast [c. 1860-1924]
See: **B319**

Edwin Arlington Robinson [1869-1935]
See: **B362**

Dane Rudhyar [1895-1985]
See: **B318**

B387 Rudhyar, Dane. "The Birth of the Transcendental Movement and Its Manifestations in Music and the Modern Dance." *New Mexico Daily Examiner* (21 August 1938).

Rudyar equates Transcendentalism with the movement at the turn of the century "toward creative freedom in the arts manifested as a search for a new technique," and "for new formal relationships between...melodic lines and tonalities"; he brands the new-classicism that dominated the musical scene after 1920 as "a form of cultural Fascism." Rudhyar considers Ives to be the most Transcendental of composers, and predicts that he "will some day rank as one of the most significant figures in modern music, the greatest American-born composer of this day."

Carl Ruggles [1876-1971]
See also: **B318** and **B362**

B388 Seeger, Charles. "Charles Ives and Carl Ruggles." *Magazine of Art* 32 (July 1939)): 396-399 and 435-437.

Seeger contrasts the similarities in background and artistic purposes between Ives and Ruggles with their "diametrically opposed technical methods"--Ruggles's "stylization" and

"Schoenberg tendency" and Ives's unique *mélange* of styles, his predilection for American roots over European and his theory of "musical perspective," i.e., "a systematic ordering of the relationships between various levels in a composition." While he acknowledges the important contributions of both composers, Seeger makes it abundantly clear that future composers in the "genteel" tradition would "sing America" better by writing more accessible music incorporating "the musical vernacular of plain, everyday America."

Muriel Rukeyser [1913-1980]

B389   Rukeyser, Muriel. "Ives." In *A Turning Wind: Poems*, pp. 115-120. New York: The Viking Press, 1939. [Yale 56/3]

In this poetic tribute to Ives, Rukeyser emphasizes Ives's New England ambience and his ability to translate life into art: "He gathers the known world totally into music, passion of sense, perspective's mask of light into suggestions inarticulate gesture, invention."

Arnold Schoenberg [1874-1951]
See also: **B723**

B390   Schoenberg, Arnold. Panegyric to Charles Ives [1944].

The Cowells included the following footnote in their biography (**B354**): "After the death of Arnold Schoenberg in 1951, his widow mailed to Mr. and Mrs. Ives a sheet she found among his papers on which he had written the following, apparently in 1944: 'There is a great Man living in this Country--a composer. He has solved the problem how to preserve one's self-esteem and to learn. He responds to negligence by contempt. He is not forced to accept praise or blame. His name is Ives.'" One of the most frequently printed statements on Ives. *See*: **B91** and **B225**

B391   Moor, Paul. "Two Titans: Schoenberg and Ives." *Theatre Arts* 34 (February 1950): 49-51+.

Writing not long after their seventy-fifth birthdays Moor focuses on how Schoenberg and Ives as old men have responded to their neglect. He contrasts Schoenberg's "venom towards the world," brought about in part by his belief that composers (e.g., Copland) actively conspired against performing his music, with Ives's "fine appearance of not giving a damn." Moor argues that both composers "deserve far better" from the general public and expresses his desire that both will someday receive the recognition that is their due.

B392 Middleton, Richard. "Ives and Schoenberg: An English View." *Saturday Review/World* 2, no. 1 (September 21, 1974): 39-41.

Middleton offers a useful comparative examination of these two composers who were born several weeks apart in 1874. Unlike many writers, he considers Ives as well as Schoenberg "sophisticated in the sense of possessing both acute aural sensitivity and constructive skill." He also compares the musical philosophies of each composer, and manages in non-technical language to cite specific similarities and differences in their individual treatment of musical materials.

B393 Fisher, Fred. "Ives and Schoenberg: The Impulse to Greatness." *Connecticut Review* 8, no. 2 (April 1975): 82-88.

Fisher notes that both Ives and Schoenberg attempted unsuccessfully "to communicate with an audience on comparatively down-to-earth terms" early in their careers. Just as "Ives in 1902 attempted to court public favor with a New York performance of a cantata" without success, Schoenberg also served a failed residency as "music director and composer in a Berlin cabaret modeled after the high-spirited cafes and cabarets of Paris' Montmartre." After "this early taste of defeat," which might "be taken as another common bond between Ives and Schoenberg," Fisher argues that as a consequence both composers embarked on "a gradually increasing commitment to the credo of radicalism."

B394 Schwarz, Boris. "Schoenberg--und Ives--Tagunen in den USA." *Österreichische Musikzeitschrift* 30 (January-February 1975): 67-68.

A summary of Ives and Schoenberg centennial festivals and conferences in Washington, D.C., New Haven, and New York, and an announcement of new Schoenberg research centers in California. Schwarz makes only one stylistic comparison between these composers when he states that Schoenberg's dissonance is the result of a principle in contrast to Ives's use of dissonance for purely coloristic and programmatic purposes.

Charles Seeger [1879-1982]
See: **B318, B388** and **B601**

Elie Siegmeister [1909-]

B395 Siegmeister, Elie. "The Case of Ives." *Music Today* 4, no. 1 (June-August 1961): 1-2.

Siegmeister recalls with nostalgia his "thrill of discovery" when he first heard the seven Ives songs performed at Yaddo in 1932. After a brief outline of Ives's historical importance and eventual recognition, he interprets the present general musical neglect of Ives as a retreat from the celebration of life that so marked Ives's music.

B396 ____. Review of *Charles E. Ives: Memos*. *High Fidelity/Musical America* 23, no. 3 (March 1973): MA 29-31. *See*: **B378**

Articulate summary of what the *Memos* reveal about Ives accompanied by a generous sample of Ivesian quotations. Although he berates him slightly for overzealous editing, Siegmeister nevertheless would like to see Kirkpatrick receive "an American equivalent for the French Legion of Honor" as a reward for his extraordinary scholarly achievement. Siegmeister goes as far as to rank this edition of Ives's *Memos* as "perhaps one of the most important music books of recent years" and "required reading for every composition student *before* he is inoculated with electronitis and alleatoromania."

B397 ____. Review of *From the Steeples and the Mountains*, by David Wooldridge. *Notes* 31, no. 2 (December 1974): 291-293. *See*: **B192**

Siegmeister offers more than faint praise for Wooldridge's "insights in the inner nature of Ives the man and his penetrating interpretations of the music" and recommends the biography as "required reading for anyone interested in Ives or in American music." He considers equally misguided those (such as Virgil Thomson) who view Ives "as an amateurish, irresponsible composer of quaint backwoods trifles (**B403**), or (the avant-gardist view) as a forerunner of the present Establishment school, solely concerned with complex techniques, inventions, and mechanics." Siegmeister also registers his alarm and negative reaction to Wooldridge's sudden and not infrequent metamorphoses "from a Dr. Jekyll of careful scholarship to a Mr. Hyde of wild-eyed speculation."

B398 _____. "Charles Ives: American Expressionist and Populist." In
South Florida's Historic Ives Festival, 1974-1976, edited by F.
Warren O'Reilly, pp. 39-43.

An articulate and well-argued point-by-point rebuttal to
substantial attacks on Ives's "casual" and "unoriginal" music and
"crippled" character respectively by Thomson (**B403**), Carter
(**B668**), and Porter (**B180**). Siegmeister observes that "the parallel
between many of Ives' compositions with the work of certain
contemporaries who have come to be called 'expressionsists'
is...inescapable," and in his final argument he describes Ives "as
America's first musical populist."

Wallace Stevens [1879-1955]
See also: **B707**

B399 "Some Imperishable Bliss." The Ambassador of the United States
Insurance Company (August 1966): 18-19.

Introduction for readers in the insurance field to the unlikely
careers of Ives and Stevens, both of whom achieved phenomenal
success as insurance executives while producing innovative
masterpieces in music and poetry, respectively. To answer the
question, "Why insurance?" the anonymous author quotes
Professor Peter Fingesten: "The creative mind is drawn to
freedom, to challenge, to risk...and Insurance is one of the rare
worlds where they are all found."

Igor Stravinsky [1882-1971]

B400 Stravinsky, Igor, and Craft, Robert. *Expositions and
Developments*, pp. 92, 97-99, 104. Garden City, NY: Doubleday,
1962.

In response to Stravinsky's remark [p. 92] that he shares an
approach to jazz in *Histoire* "perhaps not so unlike that of, say,
Ives's Third Violin Sonata," rather than Berg's jazz, Craft asks
Stravinsky to share his "thoughts about Ives's music" [pp. 97-99].
After pointedly informing Craft that Ives was performed outside of
the East Coast before World War II [he first heard Ives in Los
Angeles in 1942], Stravinsky speaks of how he "respected Ives as
an inventive and original man" and "wanted to like his music,"
and his consequent disappointment when he found all but the
shorter pieces such as *Tone Roads* "badly uneven in quality,
however, as well as ill-proportioned and lacking strength of style."
Although Stravinsky cautions us not to regard "Ives as a mere

historical phenomenon, 'The Great Anticipator,'" he focuses his discussion of Ives's music exclusively on the musical prophecies, including the "music exploiting polytonality almost two decades before *Petroushka!*"

B401 ____. *Themes and Episodes,* pp. 15-16, 48, 106, 154. New York: Alfred A. Knopf, 1966.

Stravinsky asks himself "What is a masterpiece," and tries to answer with "a very small example"--Ives's *Decoration Day* [pp. 15-16]. He mentions the "genuineness of feeling" and "rhythmic and harmonic imagination," and again discredits the exaggerated importance of Ives's "anticipations" **(B400)**. Soon Stravinsky finds himself at the end of a paragraph in which he has singled out for praise numerous specific references in the score passages, unable to answer his question but nonetheless willing to maintain his conviction that "*Decoration Day* is a masterpiece, one of Ives's greatest." While assessing Stokowski's conducting [p. 154], Stravinsky also refers to Ives's *Fourth Symphony* as an "astounding work."

B402 ____. *Retrospectives and Conclusions,* pp. 30-32. New York: Alfred A. Knopf, 1969.

In response to Craft's query whether he had heard Ives's *Fourth Symphony,* Stravinsky praises the "astonishing achievement" of the second movement. On the whole, however, he considers *Three Places in New England* to have "more consistently good music." Again he cites the musical prophecies before discounting them, this time as "of less moment than my discovery in him of a new awareness of America." After discussing his general lack of identification with America, Stravinsky issues his final published comment about Ives: "The time has come to turn criticism around and rather than continue to emphasize his isolation, consider his share in the ideas of the century."

Virgil Thomson [1896-]
See also: **B442, B718,** and **B738**

B403 Thomson, Virgil. "The Ives Case." *The New York Review of Books* 14, no. 10 (May 21, 1970): 9-11; reprinted in *American Music Since 1910,* pp. 22-30. New York: Holt, Rinehart and Winston, 1971 and in *A Virgil Thomson Reader,* pp. 460-467. Boston: Houghton Mifflin, 1981.

Although he acknowledges "delicious moments and even perfect whole pieces," Thomson is "somewhat unimpressed by the Ives output in general." He even regards Ives's anticipation of twentieth-century techniques merely as a "historical curiosity." Thomson theorizes that upon retirement Ives intended to copy out the vast output that he had hurriedly composed during the years of his double life, and interprets Ives's unexpected physical infirmities and creative malaise "as an acceptable, though unplanned, consequence of the total strategy." That Ives divided his energies between "God and Mammon" Thomson regards as "maiming" to Ives's artistic production and an American tragedy.

Michael Tippett [1905-]

B404 Tippett, Michael. "The American Tradition." *American Musical Digest* 1 (October 1969): 21 [abridged from *The Listener* (England), June 5, 1969].

Tippett regards *Three Places in New England* as "possibly Ives's best single work" and expresses his regret that "this is not yet in the repertoire of any first-class English orchestra." He also praises Ives, along with Gershwin and Copland, for incorporating the "enormous stock of common sounds and experiences" available to an American composer.

Edgard Varèse [1883-1965]
See also: **Appendix 6, no. 11**

B405 Dahlhaus, Carl. "Aussenseiter der Neuen Musik: Charles Ives und Edgard Varèse." In *Bericht über den internationalen musikwissenschaftlichen Kongress Bonn 1970*, edited by Carl Dahlhaus et. al., p. 299. Kassel: Bärenreiter, 1971.

Dahlhaus draws a parallel between these two "Genies der Antizipation," Ives anticipating the improvisational character of much music composed in the 1960s (including Cage) and Varèse influencing the future course of electronic music.

B406 Morgan, Robert P. "Rewriting Music History: Second Thoughts on Ives and Varèse." *Musical Newsletter* 3, no. 1 (January 1973): 3-12 and no. 2 (April 1973): 15-23 and 28.

One of the most provocative and important articles in the Ives literature. Morgan seriously challenges the "prevailing philosophy of twentieth-century music" and makes a compelling argument that Ives and Varèse rather than Stravinsky and Schoenberg "represented the true center of twentieth-century music history." In the first part of this two-part article Morgan focuses on Ives. Among the many issues he explores with enormous insight and originality are Ives's innovations and use of quotation. He also provides an eloquent defense against those who accuse Ives of technical incompetence. Equally remarkable is Morgan's ability to elucidate the historical and artistic significance of musical procedures.

B407 Small, Christopher. "Words on Music--Ives and Varèse." *Music in Education* 37, no. 362 (1973): 187-188.

Within the context of reviewing Boatwright's edition of Ives's *Essays Before a Sonata and Other Writings* (**B660**), Kirkpatrick's edition of Ives's *Memos* (**B378**), and Ouellette's biography of Edgard Varèse, Small makes several modest connections between the two composers, e.g., that both were misunderstood in their lifetime and that the European Varèse, like Ives, was "American by adoption and conviction (since America is as much a state of mind as a county)."

Anton Webern [1883-1945]
See: **B619**

William Carlos Williams [1883-1963]

B408 Johnston, Walter E. "Style in W. C. Williams and Charles Ives." *Twentieth Century Literature* 31 (Spring 1985): 127-136.

Johnston notes several biographical and numerous stylistic similarities between Williams and Ives. He considers that each artist used "dissonance to defeat 'normal' expectation and open the music/poem to a new freedom of devlopment." He also observes that both Williams and Ives share "the attention to the common thing, the appeal to nature, the hostility to genteel tradition" and that Williams and Ives share a common posthumous fate, in that their styles have not entered the "public vocabulary." He concludes that "for all their concern for rediscovering the concrete 'American' experience, the dissonance leads to self-discovery but not to any larger vision of community."

Frank Lloyd Wright [1869-1959]

B409 Geselbracht, Raymond H. "Transcendental Renaissance in the Arts: 1890-1920." *The New England Quarterly* 48 (December 1975): 463-486.

In separate sections Geselbracht discusses the philosophical underpinnings of Wright, Ives, and Isadora Duncan. He notes significant common denominators among these disparate artists, most notably their incorporation of nature into their creative work. He argues, for example, that "implicit in Ives's thought is the belief that if man does continue to ask to confront--if he does, that is to say, continue nature's dialectic of evolution--he will in time become perfect, united in communion with infinite spirit." According to Geselbracht, each of these artists achieved "authenticity flowing from a union of soul with nature, unaffected by the mandates and expectations of the past." His summary of Wright's aesthetic is especially helpful.

Symphonies (General)

B410 Herrmann, Bernard. "Four Symphonies by Charles Ives." *Modern Music* 22, no. 4 (May-June 1945): 215-222.

The first published survey of Ives's four symphonies. Although Herrmann's pioneering sketch is cursory and contains a number of factual errors (e.g., that the Finale of the *Fourth Symphony* "uses no themes, quotations or motives, no harmonic or rhythmic patterns"), it exudes an extraordinary sympathy and respect for this body of work. Contains provocative but insufficiently substantiated references to parallels between Ives and Mendelssohn, Raff, Tchaikovsky, Edmund Rubbra (*First*), Prokofiev (*Second*), Gesualdo, Bach (*Third*), and Varèse (*Fourth*), and musical illustrations on nearly every page.

B411 Myers, Betty Dustin. "The Orchestral Music of Charles Ives." M.M. thesis, Indiana University, 1951. 90 pp.

The first dissertation on Ives's orchestral music. Myers focuses her descriptive survey on the four symphonies, but she also surveys the *"Holidays" Symphony*, the two orchestral sets, the *Set for Theater or Chamber Orchestra*, and *Three Outdoor Scenes* (*The Pond, Hallowe'en*, and *Central Park in the Dark*). While Myers praises his rhythmic and harmonic innovations and his "sincerity," she criticizes Ives for his stylistic inconsistencies, his lack of melodic originality, and his technical incompetence. The appendixes contain transcriptions of two brief letters from Henry Cowell on Ives's behalf in response to several of the author's queries (December 15, 1950 and May 12, 1951).

B412 Gerschefski, Peter E. "A Critical Analytical Study of Two Works by Charles Edward Ives." M.A. thesis, University of Southern California, 1959. 141 pp.

Biographical summary precedes separate and combined analytical remarks on the *Second Symphony* and *Three Places in New England* arranged under various topics (form, harmony and tonality, melody [themes], polyphony, complexities and stabilizing forces, orchestration, and pre-existent material). Although superceded by Burkholder (**B284**) and Stein (**B490**) in its examination of thematic interconnectedness, Gerschefski's illustrations of the thematic transformations of "The British

Grenadiers" in "Putnam's Camp" (*Three Places*) remains useful. He considers a number of technical "weaknesses" in the *Second Symphony* but acknowledges that in mature works such as *Three Places* Ives "always manages to insert some sort of stabilizing factor which tightens the organization and strengthens the sense of direction."

B413 Stone, Kurt. "Reviews of Records." *The Musical Quarterly* 50, no. 1 (January 1964): 114-118.

Review of *Washington's Birthday, Hallowe'en, The Pond, and Central Park in the Dark*, performed by the Imperial Philharmonic of Tokyo, conducted by William Strickland (**D3**). Stone, who focuses on the works rather than the performances, issues a negative assessment of Ives's stature. While acknowledging Ives's "uncommonly bold vision," he asserts as "fact," that Ives's "prophetic imagination was coupled with a rather pronounced lack of professional skill, a skill without which it is usually impossible to develop any musical ideas (let alone bold visions) into convincing compositions." Stone judges *Hallowe'en* "a great little piece" for the most part because "the familiar tunes have been replaced by purely musical phenomena."

B414 Goodfriend, James. "Charles Ives: Making Up for Lost Time." *HiFi/Stereo Review* 17, no. 1 (July 1966): 72.

Review of two recordings, RCA LSC 2893 (*First Symphony, Variations on America*) and Columbia MS 6843 (*Third Symphony, Decoration Day, The Unanswered Question*, and *Central Park in the Dark*). Of the *First Symphony* Goodfriend, paraphrasing (and colloquializing) Schumann's famous critical prophecy regarding Chopin writes: "Albeit the materials were trite, it is almost inconceivable that any musician who came across the score would not have said, "By golly, a genius." He praises both recordings, but cites the Ozawa/Peress interpretation of *Central Park in the Dark* for special praise. *See*: **B437**

B415 Raynor, Henry. *The Music Review* 27, no. 4 (1966): 331. *See*: **W4i** and **W7e**

Review of the August 24 performance of a "good performance by Prausnitz and the New Philharmonica [*The Fourth of July*], and the *Fourth Symphony*, incoherently played by Gunther Schuller and the BBC Symphony Orchestra." Raynor regrets the "fashionable" comparison recently offered between Ives and Mahler, since he believes that Ives, unlike Mahler, "does not just disdain finesse; he doesn't know it, and his ambitions outrun his technique." *See:* **B365, B384,** and **B472**

B416   Kirkpatrick, John. Jacket notes to the First Recording of the *Second Orchestral Set,* Morton Gould conducting the Chicago Symphony Orchestra, RCA LSC-2959 [1967].

In brief but authoritative notes Kirkpatrick describes programmatical and borrowed elements of the *Second Orchestral Set* and "Putnam's Camp" from *Three Places in New England.* The notes also contain a slightly more detailed musical summary of the third work recorded on this album, *Robert Browning Overture.*

B417   Salzman, Eric. "Charles Ives: Music Big as Life." *HiFi/Stereo Review* 19, no. 2 (August 1967): 65-67.

Review of two recordings: RCA LSC 2959 (*Orchestral Set No. 2, Robert Browning Overture,* and "Putnam's Camp" from *Three Places in New England*), conducted by Morton Gould, and Columbia MS 7015 (*Three Places in New England, Washington's Birthday,* and *Robert Browning Overture*), conducted by Stokowski and Bernstein. After an emphatic rebuttal to the notion that Ives was "an untrained American primitive," Salzman espouses his view that Ives's most "revolutionary idea...was the overthrow of the old notion of 'manner' or 'style' and the acceptance of all kinds of experience as valid material for a far-reaching and, yes, even profound conception of musical relevance." Of the *Orchestral Set No. 2* premiere recording Salzman writes that "all of the material is entirely transformed into one of Ives' most austerely beautiful works." He cites for special commendation Stokowski's interpretation of the *Robert Browning Overture* and Bernstein's reading of *Washington's Birthday* (both on **D13**).

B418   Goodman, John. "An Urbanized Thoreau." *New Leader* 51 (23 September 1968): 23-24.

Goodman focuses on two Ives characteristics, "polyphonic confrontations" and the use of borrowed material. He writes admiringly that Ives possessed the "technical mastery needed to avoid excessive wit or vulgarity, twin pitfalls for any art that relies heavily on borrowings," and compares Ives's symphonies favorably to Eliot's *The Waste Land.* Goodman concludes with some remarks on a number of recently released orchestral recordings: the four symphonies conducted by Farberman (Vanguard VCS 100-32/34; *"Holidays" Symphony* conducted by

Bernstein (Columbia MS-7147), and Ormandy's *First Symphony* and *Three Places in New England* (**D26**).

B419   Shirley, Wayne. "The Challenge of Ives Brings a New Round of Challengers." *High Fidelity/Musical America* 18, no. 6 (June 1968): 80-81.

Review of the *Symphonies Nos. 1-4* (with *Hallowe'en*) conducted by Farberman (Cardinal VCS 10032/34) and the Ormandy interpretation of the *First Symphony* [with *Three Places in New England*] (**D26**). Shirley writes that the symphonies, in contrast to *"Holidays* and the two orchestral sets, "all employ some sort of organic development," and he illustrates this point with an example from each. He then evaluates the recordings under review in relationship to other available recordings and offers specific reasons for his preferences: *First* (Ormandy) [1967], *Second* (Farberman) [1968], *Third* (Hanson--Mercury SR-90149) [1959], and *Fourth* (Stokowski--Columbia MS-6775 9) [1965] (**D7**).

B420   Eiseman, David. "Charles Ives and the European Symphonic Tradition: A Historical Reappraisal." Ph.D. dissertation, University of Illinois, 1972. 279 pp.

Eiseman rejects the widely held view of Ives "as a peculiarly American composer who rejected all European musical tradition and devoted himself to experimentation and radical innovation." He follows a musically illustrated survey of 19th-century symphonic trends with an examination of Ives's exposure to these trends through the traditional musical education he obtained from his father and Parker. He also examines the range of musical offerings in Danbury, Yale, and New York before Ives withdrew from professional musical life in 1902. Using Ives's first two symphonies as prime specimens, Eiseman provides a detailed and richly illustrated examination of Ives's enormous and multi-faceted debt (structural, harmonic, and thematic) to the European tradition. An appendix presents full programs of the New Haven Symphony Orchestra's sixteen programs performed while Ives was at Yale.

B421   Kolter, Horst. "Zur Kompositionstechnik von Charles Edward Ives." *Neue Zeitschrift für Musik* 133, no. 10 (October 1972): 559-567.

Kolter writes that ostinato technique is the means by which Ives integrates his heterogeneous compositional fabric. Ives demonstrates this technique most pervasively and with greatest sophistication in the *Fourth Symphony*, but "the same technique of rhythmic integration ("derselben rhythmischen Integrationstechnik") can be observed earlier to a lesser degree in the *Robert Browning Overture*. Kolter also discusses a function of Ives's ostinatos that is identical to that used by composers of the so-called Second Viennese school.

B422 Echols, Paul. "The Music for Orchestra." *Music Educator's Journal* 61, no. 2 (October 1974): 29-41.

Echols briefly and clearly outlines the range of Ives's enormous output of fifty-eight symphonic works, "including pieces that were left incomplete, were set down merely as preliminary sketches, or have been lost." He then selects special features of *Symphonies Nos. 1-3, Three Places in New England,* and the *Theater Orchestra Set* and illustrates them with full-score (and full-page) excerpts. In addition to useful publication data we learn that Ives quoted "Columbia, the Gem of the Ocean" "in no less than eighteen separate works" and that he added the final eleven-note tone cluster to his *Second Symphony* not long before its publication in 1951. *See:* **B296** and **B448** for other references to this last point.

B423 Hall, David. "Two New Symphonies by Charles Ives." *Stereo Review* 33, no. 5 (November 1974): 134-135.

Review of two Ives symphonic recordings, the *Fourth* conducted by Serebrier (**D6**) and the *Second* conducted by Ormandy (RCA ARL 1-0663). Hall devotes most of his review to the Serebrier *Fourth,* which he compares quite favorably with the pioneering recording by Stokowski (**D7**). Although the Serebrier recording lacks some of Stokowski's "visceral excitement," Hall cites specific instances in which "the clarity of texture" and the absence of "certain compromises" are definite improvements. According to Hall, Stokowski "provided a vivid initial topographical map of the piece, the Serebrier recording a searching and illuminating further exploration." In his assessment of the Ormandy *Second,* Hall praises its "interpretive path midway between Herrmann and Bernstein," but rejects the sound of glossy strings and genteel brass and percussion.

B424 Josephson, Nors S. "Zur formalen Struktur einiger später Orchester-werke von Charles Ives (1874-1954)." *Die Musikforschung* 27 (1974): 57-64.

Josephson divides Ives's orchestral works or individual movements into six convenient but slightly artificial categories:

tradition-bound works (e.g., *Symphonies Nos. 1 and 2)*; small experimental chamber works (e.g., *The Unanswered Question*); "quasi-impressionistischem" works (e.g., "The Housatonic at Stockbridge" from *Three Places in New England*); abstract works (e.g., *Robert Browning Overture*); programmatic works (e.g., *Decoration Day*); and finally, a group of free through-composed cyclical works (e.g., "From Hanover Square North At the End of a Tragic Day" from the *Second Orchestral Set*. Josephson provides simple formal outlines of four representative examples, discusses over-lapping material in various works, and concludes with an undeveloped comparison between the musical language of Ives and Berg.

B425 Magers, Roy Vernon. "Aspects of Form in the Symphonies of Charles E. Ives." Ph.D. dissertation, Indiana University, 1975. 375 pp.

A somewhat prolix survey of musical form in Ives's four symphonies. Although he offers a broad view of form ("all interrelationships of all elements and events in a composition"), Magers remains unconvincing when he summarizes and evaluates Ives's formal successes and failures. Valuable features include Figure 23, "Material from the 'Hawthorne' Movement of the Concord Sonata in the Second Movement of the Fourth Symphony," and Magers's programmatic interpretation of the relationship between Hawthorne's story, "The Celestial Railroad," and the *Fourth Symphony* (second movement).

B426 Serebrier, Jose. "Ives for Orchestra." *The Instrumentalist* 29 (February 1975): 40-41.

After describing the painstaking and time-consuming rehearsals that were required in order to prepare the London Philharmonic Orchestra for its recording of the Ives *Fourth Symphony* (**D7**), Serebrier suggests several works that could be performed by young musicians: the *First* and *Third* Symphonies, the third movement of the *Fourth* ("and possibly the first movement"), William Schuman's arrangement of *Variations on America*, *Decoration Day*, *The Unanswered Question, Hymn, The Rainbow*, and for band, *The Circus Band, A Son of a Gambolier*, and again the *Variations on America* (arr. Schuman).

B427 Ellison, Mary. "Ives' Use of American 'Popular' Tunes As Thematic Material." In *South Florida's Historic Ives Festival, 1974-1976*, edited by F. Warren O'Reilly, pp. 30-34.

Ellison uses the *Third Symphony* and *Three Places in New England* to support her argument "that the quoted material used by Ives is, in most cases, related to the general melodic structure of the composition." Includes musical examples from these two works.

B428 Curtis, William D. "Symphony No. 4; Central Park in the Dark, conducted by Seiji Ozawa." *The American Record Guide* 40, no. 1 (October 1977): 32-34.

This extremely negative review of this Ozawa recording (**D2**) concludes at the outset that this is a "sorely disappointing record." It goes on to elucidate how "Ozawa, with the apparent collaboration of DG's engineering staff, has nearly succeeded in making the work sound dull."

B429 Fuhrmann, Peter. "Ist seine Zeit gekommen? Charles Ives: Sinfonien Nr. 1-4." *Opernwelt* 18, no. 6 (1977): 48.

More a reflection of European attitudes towards Ives than a review of the Ives *Symphonies 1-4, Three Places in New England, The Unanswered Question, Central Park in the Dark*, the *Symphony "Holidays*," and *Variations on America* (CBS 77 424). Although he acknowledges Ives's anticipation of twentieth-century techniques and refers to the praise bestowed on Ives by Mahler and Schoenberg, Fuhrmann nevertheless concludes that Ives's time has *not* arrived.

B430 Badolato, James Vincent. "The Four Symphonies of Charles Ives: A Critical, Analytical Study of the Musical Style of Charles Ives." Ph.D. dissertation, Catholic University of America, 1978. 225 pp.

A stylistic overview of the four Ives symphonies. Although he shows Ives's motivic organicism, Badolato more often describes than analyzes. Nevertheless, he augments his descriptions (more substantial regarding melody than to form or harmony) with copious and useful musical illustrations.

B431 Kavanaugh, James Vincent. "Music and American Transcendentalism: A Study of Transcendental Pythagoreanism in the Works of Henry David Thoreau, Nathaniel Hawthorne, and Charles Ives." Ph.D. dissertation, Yale University, 1978. 261 pp.

In Pythagoreanism "the universe is ordered by a divine harmony whose sensuously perceptible form is the harmony of earthly music." Kavanaugh defines Transcendental Pythagoreanism as "a reformulation of classical Pythagorean cosmology in terms of the philosophic idealism of Emersonian Transcendentalism." He considers Ives's music "the logical culmination of Thoreau's and Hawthorne's Transcendental Pythagoreanism in that the composer "attempted to express in music the idea of Harmony of the Universe."

Even without musical illustrations Kavanaugh successfully explores Ives's technical means to achieving this end, "the representation of earthly and cosmic 'soundscapes' through spatial separation of instrumental ensembles in *The Unanswered Question* and *Central Park in the Dark*, the *Fourth Symphony*, and the *Universe Symphony*. He also offers thoughtful parallels between Ives and Mahler, and Ives and Scriabin. Surprisingly, judging from the bibliography, Kavanaugh's valuable contribution to our understanding of what Morgan describes as "spatial music," is indebted neither to Morgan's essay (published in 1977) (**B256**) nor to Drew's writings on this subject (**B115** and **B134**).

B432 Barry, Malcolm. "Modern." Concert Reviews. *Music and Musicians* 27, no. 12 (August 1979): 47.

Review of performances by the orchestral group, Kaleidoscope, conducted by David Robertson at St. John's, Smith Square [*The Unanswered Question* and *Third Symphony* (May 11); *Tone Roads Nos. 1 and 3*; and *Washington's Birthday* from *Symphony "Holidays"* (May 30). Barry's review is notable for its harshly negative assessment of Ives's work as a whole: "He remains a provincial, a bywater even in the history of American music, and the publicity efforts on his behalf...cannot disguise the undisciplined poverty of much of his invention." The exceptions that prove the rule are the "tough" *Tone Roads*, which "rob much of the avant-garde of the 1920s of originality."

B433 Schwarz, Robert K. "Reviews: *Symphony No. 3; Orchestral Set No. 2*." *High Fidelity/Musical America* 35, no. 8 (August 1985): 62.

Review of Thomas's recording of two Ives symphonic works (**D10**). Schwarz briefly places the new edition of the *Third Symphony* in historical perspective and praises its "subtle changes in instrumentation." High praise also for Ives's "carefully juxtaposed" rather than "savagely layered" treatment of quotations and for Thomas's performance of "penetrating intelligence." Of the two performances Schwarz writes: "Instead of the incoherent jumble that so often passes for Ivesian performance, one is treated to readings that constantly clarify the intertwining musical lines and bring out the inner voices."

B434 Stout, Alan. "Review of Charles Ives Symphonies Nos. 2 and 3." *American Music* 3, no. 4 (Winter 1985): 499-501.

The fact that Thomas's recording of the *Second Symphony* (**D15**) is uncut as well as the first to use Goldstein's new critical edition, does not inhibit Stout from finding serious fault with Thomas's interpretation (especially his excessive "rhythmic espressivo"). Ironically, Davies, in his interpretation of the *Third Symphony* (**D22**), did not use *its* new edition, which contains more audible alterations than than the *Second*, but Stout otherwise judges this interpretation "almost a complete success."

First Symphony [W1]

B435 Deane, James G. "Capital's U.S. Fete Includes Fifteen Premieres." *Musical Courier* 147 (July 1953): 29. *See:* **W1a**

"WASHINGTON.--The year's American Music Festival at the National Gallery of Art numbered seven concerts and no less than 15 world premieres, including--oddly enough--that of Charles Ives' First Symphony. The Ives work, in D minor, was completed in 1898, the year he was graduated from Yale. It is striking, even if a bit long-winded, and its neglect seems unaccountable."

B436 Cohn, Arthur. "From RCA Victor: After 68 Years, the First Symphony of Chas. E. Ives." *The American Record Guide* 32, no. 11 (July 1966): 1032-1033.

Positive review of the symphony and its performance by Gould (RCA LSC-2893). Cohn points out the enormous disparity between the symphony's conventionality and an Ives polytonal choral work that dates from the same year. Although he believes that the finale "limps because it is mucilaged by sequence," Cohn also writes that "the subject material, especially for the first three movements, is real art," and that the opening of the second movement possesses "Mahlerian depth."

B437 Salzman, Eric. "New Stereo Discs for a Further Look at Ivesian Questions and Answers." *High Fidelity* 16, no. 4 (June 1966): 70-71.

Review of two Ives recordings: Morton Gould conducting the *First Symphony*, *Variations on America* [arr. Schuman], and *The Unanswered Question* (RCA LSC 2893), and Bernstein conducting the *Third Symphony*, *Central Park in the Dark*, *Decoration Day*, and *The Unanswered Question* (Columbia MS 6843). Salzman devotes the most attention on the premiere recording of the *First*

Symphony, the work itself and its performance. He argues that this work illustrates "the case for Ives's mastery of tradition" and concludes that "it is hard to understand why Ives was not immediately recognized as the freshest, ablest, and most remarkable talent of his day."

B438 Willis, Thomas. "Premiere Recording of Ives' First Symphony." Jacket notes to phonograph recording of Charles Ives, *Symphony No. 1*. LSC-2893 [1966].

Willis, a music critic of *The Chicago Tribune*, recalls that the November 1965 "premiere" of Ives's *First Symphony* (**W1c**) (also with the Chicago Symphony Orchestra under Morton Gould), was "sandwiched between two redoubtable inhabitants of the standard repertory aviary--the Waltz from Tchaikovsky's *Swan Lake* and Sibelius' *The Swan of Tuonela*." Willis reviews the standard story of the conflict between Ives and his Yale professor, Parker, and briefly describes the "sweet, surprising and sometimes beautiful work" that emerged from "all this cross fire and countercurrent."

Second Symphony [W2]

B439 Cowell, Henry. "Review of Second Symphony, First Performance." *The Musical Quarterly* 37, no. 3 (July 1951): 399-402. *See*: **W2a**

Cowell recalls the day in 1949 when Ives showed him some manuscripts and photostat sheets of the *Second Symphony* with the comment, "This old thing...maybe you'd look at it." Although he praises the work as "a finely wrought symphony, full of feeling and vitality," Cowell compares its historical position to the place of *Verklärte Nacht* in Schoenberg's oeuvre. Both works represent only an "embryonic state" of the exploratory avant-garde works to follow.

B440 Downes, Olin. "Symphony By Ives Is Played In Full." *The New York Times*, February 23, 1951, page 33. *See*: **W2a**

Review of the February 22 premiere of Ives's *Second Symphony*, Leonard Bernstein conducting the New York Philharmonic. Downes gives Bernstein "eternal credit" for taking the initiative in realizing this event, but despite his enthusiasm for the work's "immense structure" and the "unique inspiration" and "noble elevation of thought" of the slow movement, Downes admits his inability to categorize and his reluctance to judge it.

B441 Sabin, Robert. "Bernstein Conducts Ives Symphony No. 2." *Musical America* 71, no. 4 (March 1951): 32-33. *See:* **W2a**

Sabin describes this symphony as "a loose, scattered work with episodes of academic imitation cheek by jowl with superb music." With the intent to praise he notes the "Mahleresque freedom" of the opening movement, but considers Ives's handling of his material, presumably in contrast to Mahler, "long-winded and unnecessarily repetitious." The folky "scramble of harmonies and rhythms" that concludes this "utterly sincere" work "makes wonderful sense." Concerning the performance Sabin writes only that "Mr. Bernstein conducted it with both love and technical mastery."

B442 Thomson, Virgil. "Music: From the Heart." *New York Herald Tribune*, February 23, 1951, page 16. *See:* **W2a**

Review of the February 22 premiere of Ives's *Second Symphony*, Leonard Bernstein conducting the New York Philharmonic. Thomson warmly receives both Bernstein's performance and Ives's symphony, the latter a "landscape piece with people in it," and concludes that the symphony "is unquestionably an authentic work of art, both as structure and as communication."

B443 "Announcement of Premiere." *International Musician* 49 (March 1951): 10. *See:* **W2a**

"In its first performance anywhere as a whole, Charles Ives' Symphony No. 2 was presented by the New York Philharmonic-Symphony on February 23 [*sic*]. Says Ives of the work, 'It expresses the musical feeling of the Connecticut countryside around here (Danbury and Redding) in the 1890's, the music of the country folk. It is full of the tunes they sang and played then, and I thought it would be sort of a bad joke to have some of these tunes in counterpoint with some Bach tunes.'"

B444 F.A.K. "Carnegie Hall. N.Y. Philharmonic-Symphony, Leonard Bernstein. Ives--Symphony No. 2." *Musical Courier* 143, no. 9 (15 March 1951): 12. *See:* **W2a**

Review of the *Second Symphony* premiere (February 22). "The score--and mainly the beautifully tense first movement--are filled to the brim with richest motivic life, and the master of the organ bench is evidenced in every measure by the sovereign and convincing handling of the polyphonic design. That it should have taken half a century to bring about a first performance of this highly representative work is one of the curious cases of neglect in America's musical history." [Other works on the program included works by Mozart (three German Dances, the Overture to *Don Giovanni*, and the piano concerto K. 453 conducted from the keyboard by Bernstein), and Coplands's *El Salon Mexico*.]

B445   "Scores: Symphony No. 2 by Charles Ives." *Musical Courier* 143, no. 9 (1 May 1951): 29.

"A strongly nationalistic score, a little less 'primitive' than some of the other Ives works, but intensely melodic, filled with Americanisms, and also with the unanticipated, daring touches that are never absent from the composer....The Second Symphony may lack polish, to a certain extent, but it is a strangely moving and beautiful work."

B446   "Yankee Music." *Time* 57, no. 19 (5 March 1951): 72+. *See*: **W2a**

Review of the Carnegie Hall premiere of the *Second Symphony*, a work that is judged "much easier going than the sometimes bewildering *Third*." *Time* quotes Downes's *New York Times* review ("unique inspiration and a noble elevation of thought") **(B440)**, Thomson's *Herald Tribune* verdict ("unquestionably an authentic work of art") **(B442)**, and reprints most of Ives's remarks cited above in the "Announcement of Premiere" **(B443)**.

B447   Phillips, Burrill. "Symphony No. 2 for Large Orchestra. New York: Southern Music Publishing Co., 1951." *Notes* 9, no. 3 (June 1952): 499-500.

Phillips prepares those who associate Ives exclusively with the avant-garde for the "distinct surprise to find music by Ives that sounds nostalgic." For Phillips "the most curious feature of the work is the juxtaposition of the two slow movements, 3 and 4," a juxtaposition that succeeds in achieving "a perfectly satisfactory kind of balance." He shows his high regard for the conservative Ives when he concludes that "there is every reason for this work to have a wide circulation and gain adherents for a phase of Ives' style not too well known at present."

B448   Frankenstein, Alfred. "American Music at Home." *The Juillard Review* 3, no. 1 (Winter 1955-56): 3-7.

Although he devotes only one paragraph to Ives, this article is significant for the first appearance in print of the often-cited observation that Ives, in an act of rebellion from his Brahmsian model, inserted for his final chord in the *Second Symphony* a tone cluster that included "all the notes of the chromatic scale except B; the symphony had opened in B minor, and Ives carefully avoided the one note which for Brahms would have been essential." Frankenstein did not know that Ives added this tone cluster years after he had completed the rest of the symphony. *See*: **B296** and **B422**

B449 Lang, Paul Henry. "Hidden Wonder in Ives' Scores." *New York Herald Tribune*, October 12, 1958, section 4, page 5.

Review of the October 3 New York Philharmonic preview concert in which Bernstein introduced and conducted Ives's *Second Symphony*. Lang devotes his article to a rebuttal of Mr. Bernstein, who, "following a commonly accepted view, introduced this original, bold, and altogether sophisticated musician as an 'American primitive.'" Lang also expresses the view that when performers go beyond such "innocuous" works as the Ives *Second* and perform the "great works" of Ives, "we shall discover an American composer compared to whom many of those who were born when Ives quit composing appear as primitives, indeed."

B450 Sargeant, Winthrop. "Music Events: Opening Concert." *The New Yorker* 34 (11 October 1958): 168-171.

Review of a New York Philharmonic performance of Ives's *Second Symphony*, introduced and conducted by Bernstein. Sargeant writes favorably of the concert as a whole, in which "the orchestra played with a sort of tautness and responsiveness that has shown only intermittently during the past few decades." He considers this symphony "one of the finest compositions ever to emerge from the mind of an American composer," and takes issue with those who praise Ives for his innovations rather than his intrinsic worth. Finally, he chastizes Bernstein for speaking of "one of the most sophisticated of composers and a master of the technique of his craft" as a "primitive."

B451 Trimble, Lester. "Music: Opening Program of New York Philharmonic." *The Nation* 187 (25 October 1958): 299-300.

A review of Bernstein's opening concert of the 1958-59 season which featured Ives's *Second Symphony*. Trimble praises the "simple sincerity and expressiveness" of the second movement and Bernstein's "sensitive, affectionate and thoroughly graceful performance." He also expresses his regret that Ives was denied the opportunity to hear his music performed during the creative years when he easily could have corrected "a thousand measures which do not quite come off."

B452 Bernstein, Leonard. Jacket notes to the phonograph recording, *Symphony No. 2.* [1960] **(D17)**.

Bernstein writes that "the real measure of his [Ives's] greatness is that those works of his that do not rely on such experimentation-- works which employ the normal procedures of music as he found them [e.g., the *Second Symphony*] for all their simplicity and easy listenability, succeed in carrying a strongly personal and original message." He praises and cites examples of Ives's "awkward, primitive style," and lists a number of references to other composers that have been challenged by other writers such as Frankenstein **(B453)** Charles **(B458)**, and Burkholder **(B462)**. The notes also contain historical background to the work and a descriptive summary of each movement by David Johnson.

B453 Frankenstein, Alfred. "From Bernstein and the Philharmonic-- Ives's Second Symphony Grandly Conceived." *High Fidelity* 10, no. 7 (November 1960): 75-76.

Frankenstein describes this symphony in glowing terms as the "the first American symphony to set beside Schumann and Brahms," and "the most successful fusion he [Ives] was ever to make between his favorite type of thematic mataerial and the European symphonic tradition." He informs us that the set of 24 photographs included with the album (not included in the current issue of this recording, **D17**) "is by far the most extensive Ives iconography ever published," and suggests that Bernstein, who "gets away with" his performing liberties, exaggerates to excess when he cites a list of symphonic quotations that should be viewed as "accidental resemblances of the kind that occur in the work of every great composer."

B454 Salzman, Eric. "Records: Ives. His Symphony No. 2 Is Really Sophisticated." *The New York Times*, September 25, 1960, section 2, page 21.

In this review of Bernstein's recording of the *Second Symphony* **(D17)** Salzman refutes the widely held notion that considered this eclectic work "stitched together with great skill and smoothness" and its composer "a kind of musical Grandma Moses." According to Salzman, Ives "was no more of a dilettante musician than Wallace Stevens was a dilettante poet." He also praises Ives's integration of "the classics" that are "fitted in with the kind of skill

and smoothness that make them seem right and appropriate."
Bernstein receives demerits for "several injudicious cuts" and for
taking liberties that deprive the symphony of some of its proper
seriousness.

B455 "Radical from Connecticut." *Time* 76, no. 8 (22 August 1960): 36.

Assessment of Ives prompted by the release of Bernstein's
recording of the *Second Symphony* (**D17**) emphasizes Ives's
background, his precocious anticipation of musical techniques,
and unusual double career. *Time* describes the symphony as "a
passionate, lyrical piece" with "unmistakable echoes of the great
German romantics" juxtaposed with Ives's "variations" on
American popular music.

B456 Schonberg, Harold C. "Stubborn Yankee." *The New York Times*,
March 5, 1961, section 2, page 9.

Schonberg describes Ives's "remarkable" *Second Symphony* as a
"flawed" work and "one of the few examples of real nationalism
that American music has produced." He considers Ives to be a
"very bad technician," but a composer who "was able to express,
in his unorthodox way, a vision of himself and a vision of America
that no composer has come remotely close to approaching."

B457 Cohn, Arthur. "Bravo, Mr. Bernstein! Bravo, Columbia." *The
American Record Guide* 28, no. 4 (December 1961): 302-303.

Cohn laments the lack of recordings of Ives's music and considers
the present recording (**D17**) "a matter of special jubilation" that
has "somewhat erased" Columbia's "sin of deleting the 'Concord'
Sonata." Without meaning any criticism of Bernstein's great
achievement in recording "one of Ives' masterpieces," Cohn has
trouble removing the thought that "Ives sounds best when he is
performed with a small amount of less-than-professionalism."

B458 Charles, Sydney Robinson. "The Use of Borrowed Materials in
Ives' Second Symphony." *The Music Review* 28, no. 2 (May 1967):
102-111.

One of the first articles to argue that Ives selected his borrowed
material for musical as well as programmatic purposes. After
pointing out the pitfalls in distinguishing borrowed from non-
borrowed material, Charles shows how "different borrowed
melodies, a college song and a hymn, with a single common
melodic element...are used in similar formal positions in two
movements." She classifies Ives's treatment of quotation into

three categories: 1) "quotations which have little or no structural importance"; 2) quotations "which are structurally essential, but only within the framework of a single movement"; and 3) "material which is used in more than a single movement." Finally, Charles notes that Ives "spared no effort to unify the Symphony by recurring thematic links drawn from borrowed and unborrowed material alike." An important article that anticipated Marshall's similar study by two years. *See:* **B651**

B459   Sterne, Colin. "The Quotations in Charles Ives's Second Symphony." *Music and Letters* 52, no. 1 (January 1971): 39-45.

Sterne subtracts "Blessed Assurance" and adds "Beulah Land" and "Nettleton" to Kirkpatrick's list of American quotations for this symphony (**B7**). Unlike Kirkpatrick, Sterne cites a list of European symphonic references. He also provides measure numbers for the most important quotations from both American and European sources. Sterne is prone to somewhat fanciful interpretations, for example when he suggests that Ives quotes the "Down in de cornfield" portion of Foster's "Massa's in de cold ground," because "he accepts the fact that he is a 'cornfield' composer in a 'cornfield' country," and that the composer reveals himself as "a verdant freshman, bringing in the sheaves from an American cornfield, betting his money on the bobtail nag while somebody else bet on the bay." Of more tangible interest is the first of two musical illustrations, in which one can see clearly a subtle but unequivocal melodic connection between the "Down in de cornfield" phrase and the main theme of the first and fourth movements.

B460   Greenfield, Edward. "Ives from England." *High Fidelity/Musical America* 22, no. 4 (April 1972): 20.

Greenfield describes how Herrmann retrieved the *Second Symphony* manuscript personally from Walter Damrosch's office and then prepared his own edition that restores several passages deleted from the Bernstein recording.

B461   Kolodin, Irving. "Ives by His Prophet, Bernard Herrmann." *The Saturday Review* 55, no. 37 (9 September 1972): 57-58.

Review of the Herrmann recording (London SPC 21086), the background of which was discussed by Greenfield above (**B460**). Kolodin ironically criticizes Herrmann's "vitality and insight" for revealing the shallowness of a dilettantish Ives, "whose extraordinary talent was never subjected to the discipline that produces mastery."

B462 Burkholder, J. Peter. "'Quotation' and Paraphrase in Ives's Second Symphony." *19th-Century Music* 11, no. 1 (Summer 1987): 3-25.

The most substantial historical and stylistic study of this work. In his reassessment of Ives's borrowed material Burkholder offers "three essential points": (1) "What is involved here is not *quotation* but *paraphrase*, the reworking of existing music through variation, ornamentation, omission, repetition, transposition, elision, and interpolation"; (2) "Ives's borrowed material is not inserted into an existing framework, but forms the very basis of the music"; and (3) "Ives uses his sources in a thoroughly systematic way." In his expansion of this latter point Burkholder notes that "every one of his themes paraphrases an American tune" and that "at the same time, many transitional sections, including at least one in each movement paraphrases transitions or episodes in the music of Bach, Brahms, or Wagner."

Burkholder discusses and illustrates for each movement all the borrowed vernacular material [he discusses Ives's preliminary sketch material for the most part in unillustrated, albeit substantial, footnotes]. He also offers a detailed survey of Ives's numerous Classical references, definite borrowings and possible allusions. In an elegantly argued thesis he writes that "borrowing transition sections from well-known European compositions and weaving them through paraphrase into the fabric of his own music allows him to emphasize what is lacking in American vernacular music" and helps him to achieve "the integration of American melody with European form."

Third Symphony [W3]

B463 Downes, Olin. "Tardy Recognition." *The New York Times*, April 14, 1946, section 2, page 5. *See:* **W3a**

The recent premiere of Ives's *Third Symphony* (**B464-465**) prompts Downes to discuss Ives's belated recognition. He recalls his first exposure to Ives at the 1927 premiere of Ives's *Fourth Symphony* (first and second movements) (**B498**) and his first reactions to *"Concord" Sonata* when he attended its premiere in 1939. Although Downes has some reservations about the coherence of Ives's forms, his exposure to the *Third Symphony* has strengthened his belief that Ives is a "significant creative spirit" who has been neglected by American performers and audiences far too long."

B464   Simon, Robert A. "Late-Season Harvest." *The New Yorker* 22, no. 14 (18 May 1946): 97-98. *See:* **W3a**

Review of the April 5 premiere of Ives's *Third Symphony*, Lou Harrison conducting the New York Little Symphony at Carnegie Chamber Music Hall. Simon notes the "nonderivativeness of this music" and rates Harrison "as a director of uncommon abilities." He prophecies that this "concise and restrainedly eloquent work...will soon find its way into current orchestral repertory."

B465   Straus, Noel. "Symphony by Ives in World Premiere." *The New York Times*, April 6, 1946, page 10. *See:* **W3a**

Review of the April 5 premiere of Ives's *Third Symphony*, Lou Harrison conducting the New York Little Symphony at Carnegie Chamber Music Hall. Straus laments the forty-year time lag between the composition and first performance of this symphony, which "possessed a freshness of inspiration, a genuineness of feeling and an intense sincerity that lent it immediate appeal and manifested inborn talents of a high order." Straus is critical only of the work's formal looseness and sameness in orchestration, but even this latter reservation is tempered by his praise of Ives's "orchestral sonorities."

B466   Bales, Richard. "Charles Ives: Third Symphony. *Notes* 5, no. 3 (June 1948): 413.

In his review of the Arrow Music Press publication (1947) Bales finds fault only with the monotony created by Ives's over-emphasis on the strings in the slow movements. He notes the "astonishing modernism" which "stands out in bold relief against the compositions of prominent European composers of the early 1900's," and concludes by assessing the work as a "true gem" that "deserves a real place in the repertoire."

B467   Cowell, Henry. "Symphony No. 3." *The Musical Quarterly* 42, no. 1 (January 1956): 122-123.

Review of the first commercial recording of this symphony (Vanguard VRS-468), issued in 1955. Cowell recommends the work highly even to those "who find Ives's work as a whole rather difficult to enjoy," and praises Reginald Stewart and the Baltimore Little Symphony for "a wholly satisfactory performance, brilliant but warm, live but lyrical."

B468 Rhein, J. von. "Chicago: the CSO's Adventurous Autumn." *Ovation* 4 (March 1984): 26.

Review of Tilson Thomas's guest performance, in which he conducted the Ives *Third* with the Chicago Symphony using the more complete new critical edition. "The restoration of these so-called 'shadow parts' makes the symphony a more complex, allusive, sophisticated piece, bringing it more in line with the visionary world of the Symphony No. 4, and Thomas rightly approached it as an example of Emersonian romanticism dressed up in its best Yankee bib-and-tucker."

A Symphony: New England Holidays [W4]

B469 Citkowitz, Israel. "Experiment and Necessity--New York, 1932." *Modern Music* 10, no. 2 (January-February 1933): 110-114.

Citkowitz devotes one paragraph of his critial survey of the most recent New York concert season to an assessment of *Washington's Birthday*. He finds "genuine poetry" in the opening section and "musical appeal" in the "scramble of village bands" [presumably the "Barn Dance"], but he indicts Ives for failing to integrate his "dissociative effects" into a "continuous, self-sufficient musical fabric."

B470 Copland, Aaron. "Scores and Records." *Modern Music* 14, no. 4 (May-June 1937): 230-233.

Among the scores and records Copland reviews is the *New Music* 1936 publication of *Washington's Birthday*. "What unique things Ives was doing during that period! [1913] And what a shocking lack of interest to this very day on the part of our major symphonic organizations in this true pioneer musician. A score like his can best be judged from actual performance. What is most striking from a mere 'reading' is the contrast between the 'homely' program attached to the piece and the incredibly complex means for achieving it."

B471 Rich, Alan. "Contemporary Music Society." *Musical America* 81, no. 4 (April 1961): 65. *See*: **W4h**

Review of the New York premiere (March 1) of *Decoration Day*, Jonel Perlea conducting the Manhattan School Orchestra at Hunter College. Rich sets the stage for his reaction to this work by introducing himself as a person who has strongly "resisted the Ives legend." *"Decoration Day* came close" to altering this view. "Certainly no dilettante could have turned out the long, haunting and beautifully-scored piece of quiet impressionism which begins it...No, this is a real piece of music, and now I must go back and re-think my whole position."

B472   Blyth, Alan. "Pop Celebration." *Music and Musicians* 15, no. 2 (October 1966): 42. *See:* **W4i**

Review of the British premiere of *The Fourth of July* at the Promenade Concerts, August 24. Although Blyth without a score is not sure "how much of Ives' rumbustious, almost raucous score" he heard, he concludes that Frederik Prausnitz conducting the New Philharmonica "appeared to do justice." *See:* **B415**

B473   Orga, Ates. "Anglo-American." *Music and Musicians* 16, no. 4 (December 1967): 46. *See:* **W4j**

Review of the London Symphony Orchestra program (September 29) conducted by Copland, a program that included *Decoration Day*. Although this work "proved less dramatic or revolutionary than Ives' experiments in general," Orga regards it as "a beautifully scored evocation of a rural ceremony at the turn of the century," and a work that "can stand repetition."

B474   Shirley, Wayne. "Ives's 'Holidays': A Glorious 'Fourth,' and No Anticlimax." *High Fidelity/Musical America* 17, no. 9 (September 1967): 79-80.

Review of the "first complete integral recording of '*Holidays*'" (**D18**). Shirley considers the openings of *Washington's Birthday* and *Decoration Day* "some of Ives's most moving and evocative music," and praises Johanos's performances which "can stand up to Bernstein's and in places surpass them." He also praises Turnabout's "natural" recording practices, which aim to recapture a "concert hall sound rather than an X-ray picture of just what every individual instrument is doing at every moment in the score."

B475   Feder, Stuart. "Decoration Day: A Boyhood Memory of Charles Ives." *The Musical Quarterly* 66, no. 2 (April 1980): 234-261.

Feder, a psychiatrist who applies the "psychoanalytic method" to Ives's life and work, here analyzes the special psychological relationship between Ives and his father, George, and explores the profound influence he had on Charles's psychic and creative life. He states that "Ives's life-long 'collaboration' with George was part of a mourning process," and suggests that when he had reached the age at which his father died, Charles himself had completed a long, only partly conscious, mourning period, and could therefore no longer compose. One of several important articles by Feder that share this thesis. In this article Feder offers a convincing interpretation of the program and musical realization of *Decoration Day*, "an unusually specific instance" of Charles's musical memorialization of his father. *See*: **B280**, **B291**, **B557**, and **B816**

B476 Maisel, Arthur. "The Fourth of July by Charles Ives: Mixed Harmonic Criteria in a Twentieth-Century Classic. *Theory and Practice* 6, no. 1 (1981): 3-32.

"Adapting Heinrich Schenker's model of tonal music," Maisel tries to show that *The Fourth of July* "is built upon a structural framework involving a bass arpeggiation and an upper-voice descent in the background." Most of the article is devoted to a detailed discussion of numerous Schenkerian middleground grafts. Maisel interprets Ives's brand of atonalism as a logical outgrowth of the chromaticism and whole-tone harmonies of Mussorgsky, Brahms, and Wagner, but he also observes non-historical parallels with Schoenberg's *Kammersymphonie*. He concludes that "Ives used pitches and harmonies consistently" in this work and that "as in traditional tonal music, the pitches function with respect to each other in predetermined ways."

B477 Nelson, Mark D. "Beyond Mimesis: Transcendentalism and Processes of Analogy in Charles Ives' The Fourth of July." *Perspectives of New Music* 22, no. 1-2 (1984): 353+.

Nelson applies Ives's Transcendental ideas to the philosophical and musical characteristics of *The Fourth of July*. He posits that Ives created four categories of "musical analogs" which serve to describe "acoustical events," "natural phenomena," "psychological phenomena," and "non-programmatic musical unity which constitutes an analogy to the Divine Oneness pervading the Transcendental Universe." According to Nelson, "the entire composition constitutes an integrated analogy to the psychological experience of a cherished event." Nelson's interpretations, e.g., "clearly, Ives has meticulously organized a wealth of musical materials such that they simultaneously unfold in a manner analogous to the chemical processes underlying an explosion," are frequently imaginative and engrossing.

B478 Shirley, Wayne. "The Second of July." Forthcoming.

In this important manuscript study Shirley discusses Ives's sketch-score of *The Fourth of July*, "in ink with many pencil changes and additions." Throughout he refers to the ink version (1911-1913) as *The Second of July*, a reference to the date John Adams mistakenly predicted as the celebration date for Independence Day. With insight and imagination he considers *The 2nd* as an independent composition from the pencil annotations which he dates "from soon after the drafting of *The 2nd* rather than from the final preparation of a copyist's score during the late 1920's."

After noting that *The 2nd* is "rhythmically squarer" and less complex texturally" than *The 4th*, Shirley identifies the various changes, which mainly take the form of additions (e.g., the addition of the 'minor tune from Todd's Opera House' [from *Old Home Day*]), and which result in the obscuring of "important formal landmarks of *The 2nd*." Thus "*The 2nd* has a fairly clear form, with points of demarcation and recapitulation...In *The 4th* these points of demarcation have been ruthlessly downgraded." Shirley concludes that "Ives seems to have drafted *The 2nd* knowing that he was going elaborate it" and that as a result of these elaborations Ives "turned a radical but somewhat mechanical piece into a masterwork."

First Orchestral Set [W5]
(A New England Symphony; Three Places in New England)

B479 Hale, Philip. "Mr. Slonimsky in Paris." *The Boston Herald*, July 7, 1931, page 14; reprinted in *Memos*, pp. 13-14. *See:* **W5b**

In his editorial indictment of the American avant-garde Hale contends that the composers selected by Slonimsky for performance in Europe "were not those who are regarded by their fellow-countrymen as leaders in the art, nor have they all been so considered by the conductors of our great orchestras." Hale's remarks prompted an angry letter from Ives to Slonimsky's Boston manager, A. H. Handley, and eventually served as the "Pretext"--a rebuttal to "Aunt" Hale, "a nice and dear old lady in Boston (with pants on, often)"--that metamorphosed into Ives's *Memos. See:* **B378**

B480 Le Flem, Paul. "M. Slonimsky à dirigé tout un programme de musique américaine." *Comoedia* (Paris), June 8, 1931, pp. 1-2; excerpt reprinted in **B378** and **B485**. *See:* **W5b**

Review of a Parisian concert on June 6 which included Ives's *Three Places in New England* and works of other Pan Americans. "Among them one Charles Ives seems to have created before the 'Sacre du Printemps,' a style which, by its audacities, places its author among the pioneers. He appears among his compatriots as the one most spontaneously gifted, whose daring, sometimes awkward, is never in contradiction with the aspiration of his feeling."

B481 Prunières, Henry. "American Compositions in Paris." *The New York Times*, July 12, 1931, section 8, page 6; excerpt reprinted in **B378**. *See*: **W5b**

Although he finds "some germs of originality" among the diverse "embryonic" American works performed in two Parisian concerts, Prunières, who assumes that Ives must have been influenced by Stravinsky and Schoenberg, expresses praise only for Ives's *Three Places in New England*:

"If it be true that Charles Ives composed his 'Three New England Scenes' before acquaintance with Stravinsky's 'Le Sacre du Printemps,' he ought to be recognized as an originator. There is no doubt that he knows his Schonberg, yet gives the impression that he has not always assimilated the lessons of the Viennese master as well as he might have. The second part, with its truculent parody of an American march in the Sousa vein and the unloosing of its percussion achieves a picturesque effect. The third part presents a typical American theme with pretty orchestral effects. The composer is manifestly a musician."

B482 Schloezer, Boris de. "La Vie musical à Paris." *Les Beaux-arts* (Brussels), June 26, 1931, p. 1; excerpt reprinted in **B378** and **B485**. *See*: **W5b**

"The 'Trois Coins de la Nouvelle Angleterre' shows Ives to be 'un veritable procurseur, un talent audacieus.' He is different from the others. His music has a 'saveur' peculiarly his own."

B483 Schmitt, Florent. "Les Concerts. Divers Musique Américaine." *Le Temps* (June 20, 1931); excerpt reprinted in **B378**. *See*: **W5b**

Schmitt mistakenly criticizes Ives, "un musicien très erudit double d'un philosophe," ("a very erudite musician who doubles as a philosopher") along with his fellow Americans for his dependence on the innovations of Stravinsky and Schoenberg, and for treating musical materials in a "bizarre and sometimes indiscrete" ("bizarres et parfois indiscretes") manner. Somewhat surprisingly, Schmitt notes that he is acquainted with *"Concord" Sonata*, Ives's "celebration" of the writings of Emerson, Hawthorne, and Thoreau.

B484 Weiss, Adolph. "In Defense of Native Composers." *The New York Times*, July 26, 1931, section 8, page 7.

In a letter to the Edtior dated July 18 the Secretary of Pan-American Composers Inc. responds to Prunières's recent attack (**B481**). Weiss contends that Prunières "does not do justice to the importance" of the Parisian performances on June 6 and 11 [in which *Three Places in New England* was performed at the former concert]. To support this view he quotes positive excerpts from three critics who reviewed these concerts: Paul Le Flem of *Comoedia* (**B480**); Emile Vuillermoz of *Excelsior*, and Paul Dambly. *See*: **B378**

B485 Salzedo, Carlos. "The American Left Wing." *Eolus* 11 (April 1932): 9-29.

Salzedo lists the Pan American concerts from its inception in April 1928 through the forthcoming three-day Havana festival the following September. He also includes a generous sampling of Parisian music critics, de Schloezer (**B482**), Le Flem (**B480**), and Emile Vuillermoz (*Excelsior*, June 15, 1931), each of whom reviewed a performance of *Three Places in New England* and singled out this work for its individuality and anticipation of the avant-garde. *See*: **B378**

B486 Daniel, Oliver. "New Recordings." *American Composers Alliance Bulletin* 3, no. 1 (1953): 17.

Review of the American Recording Society Orchestra (i.e., Vienna Symphony Orchestra recording of *Three Places in New England* (**D25**). Daniel rates Walter Hendl's conducting "a superb job" and the Ives work "unquestionably one of his best."

B487 Cohn, Arthur. "Playing and Conducting that Simply Could Not Be Bettered." *American Record Guide* 37, no. 3 (November 1970): 148-151.

Rave review of Tilson Thomas's debut recording, a coupling of *Three Places in New England* and Ruggles's *Suntreader* (**D2**) performed by the Boston Symphony Orchestra. Cohn offers an unusual assessment when he describes the orchestration of Ives and Ruggles as "*beautifully* incorrect" with a wonderful imbalance, even muddiness," that "conveys the composers' musical ideas exactly."

B488 Sinclair, James B., editor. Preface to Charles Ives *A New England Symphony: Three Places in New England.* Full orchestration restored and edited by James B. Sinclair. Bryn Mawr, PA: Mercury Music Corporation, 1935 and 1976. [Preface dated 27 January 1975].

In his Preface Sinclair discusses the genesis, sources, and performance history of this work. He shows that when Ives rescored *Three Places* in 1929 for Slonimsky's chamber orchestra, he made extensive compositional changes to the 1914 orchestral version (now about 75% missing). His solution as editor was to combine "the original coloring [from 1914] with the compositional revisions of 1929."

B489 Slonimsky, Nicholas. "Charles Ives As I Remember Him." *The Choral Journal* 15, no. 5 (1975): 15-16.

Slonimsky recalls the day Ives introduced him to the score of *Three Places in New England*: "By just looking at a few pages of the score I somehow intuitively felt that here was a revelation of a genius." He goes on to describe his role in persuading C. C. Birchard to publish the work and to explain how Slonimsky's notational alterations that were incorporated into the Birchard score reflect his "special method of notating his bi-manual conducting." Included is a facsimile of an exuberant note from Ives to Slonimsky (February 26, 1930). [Slonimsky concludes the article by noting that all of Ives's letters to him have been republished in *Music Since 1900* (4th edition) **(B146)**]. *See also:* **B66, B241,** and **B255**

B490 Stein, Alan. "The Musical Language of Charles Ives' Three Places in New England." D.M.A. dissertation, University of Illinois, 1975. 173 pp.

After background chapters on Ives's life and philosophy, Stein summarizes the origins and the program of *Three Places in New England.* In the following richly illustrated analysis he discusses melodic, rhythmic, and formal elements separately for each movement. He clearly and succinctly explains how Ives unified his borrowed material and the "intervallic consistency" between the opening and closing movements. Stein's chapter on rhythmic considerations and his distinction between rhythmic layering and transformation in the latter two movements is also useful.

B491   Hansen, Chadwick. "One Place in New England: The Fifty-Fourth
Massachusetts Volunteer Infantry as a Subject for American
Artists." *Student Musicologists at Minnesota* 6 (1975-1976): 250-
271; reprinted as "The 54th Massachusetts Volunteer Black
Infantry as a Subject for American Artists." *Massachusetts
Review* 16 (Autumn 1975): 745-759.

Hansen explores the historical background to the program of
Ives's first place in New England, "The 'St. Gaudens' in Boston
Common" (subtitled "Col. Shaw and his Colored Regiment"). He
reviews Saint-Gaudens's struggle to create and erect his statue of
the Shaw Memorial (unveiled in 1897), and discusses artistic
treatments of this theme preceding Ives's prefatory poem and
musical depiction of "The Black March" that opens his *Three
Places in New England.* Hansen conludes that "Ives had found a
subject worthy of his music."

B492   DeMuth, Jerry. "Aaron Copland/Charles Ives." *Down Beat* 46 (3
May 1979): 31.

Record review of Copland's *Appalachian Spring* and Ives's *Three
Places* with Dennis Russell Davies conducting the St. Paul
Chamber Orchestra (**D24**). DeMuth focuses almost exclusively on
the glories of digital sound, but offers the pertinent observation
that this is "apparently the first recording of Ives' reduction of his
score for chamber orchestra."

B493   Hall, David. "Copland and Ives." *Stereo Review* 42, no. 5 (May
1979): 108.

Record review of Davies coupling of Copland and Ives (**D24**). Hall
praises the "intensely poetic and rhythmically vital
interpretation," "the superbly clean recording," and "the amazing
feat of textural compression that Ives achieved in his chamber
scoring."

Second Orchestral Set [W6]

B494   Dettmer, Roger. "La Berganza in Lovely Debut." *Chicago
American* (February 20, 1967). *See:* **W6a**

Review of the February 18 premiere performance of the *Second
Orchestral Set,* Morton Gould conducting the Chicago Symphony
Orchestra in Orchestra Hall. Dettmer considered the Ives "pure
treat [and any number of tricks]." He continues: "The first
movement is a murmurous elegy based on 'Yes, Jesus Loves Me.'
The second is polyrhythmic jazz ['third-stream' indeed, before

Gunther Schuller was ever born], whose tune turns out to be 'Bringing in the Sheaves.' The finale is a crescendo, hair-raising in intensity for the reason that it is so deliberately developed, which culminates in hallucinogenic band music." Incidentally, the review clarifies that La Berganza did not have to share the stage with Ives; her local recital debut occurred the following day.

B495 Lowe, Steven. "Buffalo Philharmonic." *High Fidelity/Musical America* 19, no. 8 (August 1969): MA 12. *See:* **W6b**

Review of the New York premiere of this work, May 7 at Carnegie Hall, with Lukas Foss conducting the Buffalo Philharmonic. Lowe writes: "Foss drew a torrential outpouring of sound from the orchestra that at times bordered on the terrifying...but in creating this sonic boom the complex Ivesian writing was virtually impossible to unravel."

B496 Stiblij, M. "Berlinske Svecane Nedelije 1969." *Zvuk; Jugoslovenska Muzicka Revija* 101 (1970): 50. *See:* **W6c**

A Berlin Philharmonic performance of the *Second Orchestral Set* conducted by Lucas [*sic*] Foss prompts a brief discussion of Ives's attempt to link literary-political ideas with surprising and humorless musical-technical turns. According to Stibilj, external symbolic material such as the sinking of the *Lusitania* which inspired the third movement of the *Second Orchestral Set* cannot be truly captured musically, although it can lead to an "impressive musical work."

Fourth Symphony [W7]

B497 Bellamann, Henry. Program Notes to Ives's *Fourth Symphony*. *Pro Musica Program*, January 29, 1927.

Often-quoted summary of the programmatic content and the aesthetic and musical characteristics of Ives's *Fourth Symphony*. The notes also reveal that Bellamann was probably the first in print to recognize the inter-connectedness of Ives's borrowed material: "Most auditors would be surprised to discover that many of the hymn tunes are in a pentatonic scale (fourth and seventh either omitted or used sparingly on weaker accents). This characteristic makes it quite natural to interweave them, and is at the same time productive of atonal aspects of the musical development." Unless Bellamman is in error, we also can infer from these notes that in 1927 the fugue preceded the present second movement.

B498 Downes, Olin. Review of Ives's *Fourth Symphony. The New York Times*, January 30, 1927, section 1, page 28; substantially reprinted in *The New York Times*, May 30, 1954, page 7 and "Charles Ives," in *American Composers Alliance* 4, no. 1 (1954). *See*: **W7a**

Review of the January 29 premiere of Ives's *Fourth Symphony* (first and second movements). Downes offers his positive reaction to his first hearing of this work, which, although it "is not nearly as compact, as finished in workmanship, as smart in tone," he preferred to the Debussy and Milhaud works presented at the same concert. After paraphrasing Bellamann's program notes (**B497**), Downes continues with his assessment: "There is something in this music; real vitality, real naiveté and superb self-respect....And then Mr. Ives looses his rhythms. There is no apology about this, but a gumption, as the New Englander would say, not derived from some 'Sacre du Printemps,' or from anything but the conviction of a composer who has not the slightest idea of self-ridicule....It is genuine, if it is not a masterpiece, and that is the important thing."

B499 Gilman, Lawrence. Review of Ives's *Fourth Symphony. New York Herald Tribune*, January 31, 1927, page 11. *See*: **W7a**

Review of the 1927 premiere of Ives's *Fourth Symphony* (first and second movements). Gilman was not surprised to read in Bellamann's program notes (**B497**) that Ives had been using his "modernistic devices" years before this belated premiere, "for this symphony has a sureness of touch which is not that of a neophyte learning an unfamiliar technique." Gilman expresses his disappointment that the complete symphony was not performed.

B500 "Recent Publications. New Music (January 1929)." *Musical Courier* 98, no. 10 (March 7, 1929): 46.

Review of the recently published *New Music* edition of Ives's *Fourth Symphony* (second movement). The *Musical Courier* cannot "perceive any sign in this music of an expression of what he feels to be Americanism" and concludes with the following negative assessment of Ives: "The reviewer does not pretend to be able to read this score and to form any mental picture of its sound, but his memory of it from the Pro Musica performance (**W7a**) is that its was just simply awful, from beginning to end."

B501 Whitmer, T. Carl. "New Music." *The Musical Forecast* (March 1929): 5-6.

Sympathetic review of the *New Music* publication of the second movement of Ives's *Fourth Symphony*. In contrast to the prevailing critical view in Ives's lifetime (and frequently beyond), Whitmer characterizes Ives as "exacting to the nth degree in self-criticism." He also considers this movement "one of the most stirring, stunning pieces of rhythmic polyphony in contemporary music...a marvel of inner hearing, to say nothing of adroitness of management."

B502 Downes, Olin. "A Lonely American Composer." *The New York Times*, January 29, 1939, section 9, page 7.

Several days after Kirkpatrick premiered Ives's *"Concord Sonata"* **(W65a)** Downes recalls the next most recent Ives premiere, that of the *Fourth Symphony*, in 1927. After quoting at length from his review of the symphony premiere **(B498)**, he offers reasons to explain, "Why have we not heard this symphony again?" He attributes Ives's neglect primarily to Ives's personality, "the highly original, insouciant and independent character of the mysterious Mr. Ives, who actually has not the slightest interest in publicizing or promoting himself." Downes is convinced, however, that "his music will make its own way once the public knows it."

B503 Briggs, John. "Notes on the Program." *New York Philharmonic Program* (1965): 17+. *See:* **W7d**

Informative program notes in which Briggs identifies the crucial role of the Fleisher Collection of Philadelphia's Free Library in preparing the work for performance. He also offers a play-by-play guide to Ives's borrowed material.

B504 Cohn, Arthur. "A Divine Document--The Ives Fourth." *The American Record Guide* 32, no. 3 (November 1965): 220-222.

Review of the Stokowski premiere recording **(D7)**. Cohn summarizes the career of the *Fourth Symphony*, and writes about his own involvement with and admiration for this work, a photostat of which was sent to him by Mrs. Ives in 1942. He then describes and gives examples of the immense calligraphic and musical difficulties that faced editors, performers, Stokowski, and his two assistant conductors. Although he might prefer "further clarification between massed bands of sonority," he "appreciates the honesty of the Stokowski presentation."

B505 Franceschini, Romulus. "A Postscript on Ives's Fourth." *The American Record Guide* 32, no. 3 (November 1965): 223.

Fransceschini, staff member of "the Fleisher Collection, where Ives's Fourth Symphony was prepared for performance," writes that "musical progress has only just begun to catch up" with Ives, and lists parallels between Ives's music and the avant-garde of the 1960s. He also cites examples to show that Ives's complexities and ambiguities "are all capable of solution...if performers will only take the trouble of finding out what is in the music."

B506 Frankenstein, Alfred. "Ives's Fourth Symphony--An 'Unplayable' Work Gets Played." *High Fidelity/Musical America* 15, no. 11 (November 1965): 83-84.

In this review of the Stokowski recording (**D7**) of Ives's *Fourth Symphony* Frankenstein focuses entirely on the music of this "great if inconsistent work." He discusses the program, which he writes, "of all the Ives 'programs,' makes the least sense," and reviews some of the central musical features of each movement. He concludes with this assessment of the finale: "In many ways, this may well be the most original and important movement in any of the symphonies by America's greatest composer."

B507 Gould, Glenn. "The Ives Fourth." *High Fidelity/Musical America* 15, no. 7 (July 1965): MA 96-97; reprinted in *The Glenn Gould Reader*, edited and with an introduction by Tim Page, pp. 185-189. New York: Alfred A. Knopf, 1984. *See:* **W7d**

Review of the April 26 Carnegie Hall premiere performance, Stokowski conducting the American Symphony Orchestra. Gould explains at the outset that he writes not with "proper qualifications as a reviewer of Charles Ives's music," but as a representative of "that larger audience for which any exposure to Ives is still a rather special and, often as not, puzzling experience." He quotes from Leonard Marcus's program notes, which describe a "moving" rather than a musical "experience." For Gould, "Ives is extraordinarily short on the organic cell-motive continuations of the Austro-German tradition." He does, however, concede that Ives possessed "an infallible sense of climax sustained through carefully managed marginal points and, just as in Berg's theatre music, guides them toward brilliantly conceived dissolves."

B508 Hall, David. "Premiere and Cultural Turning Point: Charles Ives' Fourth Symphony: An Account of the History and Preparation of the Score, the Problematic Rehearsal, and the First Performance of an Almost Legendary Work." *HiFi/Stereo Review* 15, no. 1 (July 1965): 55-58. *See:* **W7d**

Surprisingly, this overview lives up to the all-encompassing claims. Hall considers the April premiere of the *Fourth Symphony* an event that "is likely to figure in our music-history books as a kind of belated cultural turning point." He also briefly discusses programmatic and musical features for each movement.

B509 ____. "A Masterwork Takes Its Rightful Place." *HiFi Review* 15, no. 5 (November 1965): 81-82.

Review of the Stokowski premiere recording (**D7**). Hall praises the fact that, in contrast to *"Concord" Sonata* and the *"Holidays" Symphony* , both of which had ten year lapses between premiere performances and first recordings, "we can be thankful that Columbia recorded the Ives Fourth three days after the premiere and has now released the disc only a few months later." After summarizing the symphony's program, Hall lauds its musical realization: "The immensely complex meters and textures of this remarkable work come through with astounding clarity, brilliance, and power."

B510 Jacobson, Bernard. "Premiere of Ives' Fourth." *Music and Musicians* 13, no. 11 (July 1965): 43. *See:* **W7d**

Concise summary of the performance history and philosophic message of Ives's *Fourth Symphony*, concluding with the following critical evaluation: "In short, this a magnificent and endlessly absorbing symphony. If it is not a masterpiece, that would be because there is a certain lack of focus in the projection of its philosophical message, an absence of any one moment that gathers up the several threads in one revelatory knot. But part of Ives' point is probably that life is like that."

B511 Kirkpatrick, John. "Preface to Charles Ives, Symphony No. 4." New York: Associated Music Publishers, 1965.

Kirkpatrick first provides a "chronological account" of those works which were reused to some extent in the *Fourth Symphony* along with other important works that have a separate evolution. He then summarizes the symphony's genesis and reprints some of Henry Bellamann's 1927 program notes ("obviously based on conversations with Ives, and revealing a different order of movements") **(B497)**. Finally, Kirkpatrick traces the musical progress of each movement, liberally providing musical quotations and rehearsal numbers, and outlines the performance and publication history of the work between 1927 and 1965.

B512 Kolodin, Irving. "Music to My Ears." *The Saturday Review* 48, no. 20 (15 May 1965): 32+. *See*: **W7d**

Review of the April 26 Carnegie Hall premiere performance, Stokowski conducting the American Symphony Orchestra. Kolodin admires Ives's "conceptions," even though he concludes that some of the composer's tonal "muddiness" was unintended. "Even such a master of aural perspective as Stokowski seemed to be fighting hard to achieve the transparency that was wanted." Despite these reservations, Kolodin considers the symphony to have "a consistency of substance as well as a profundity of mood that are rarely to be found with such concentration elsewhere in his orchestral works."

B513 Sargeant, Winthrop. "Musical Events: Fourth Symphony Performed by American Symphony Orchestra." *The New Yorker* 41, no. 12 (8 May 1965): 169+. *See*: **W7d**

Review of the April 26 premiere performance, Stokowski conducting the American Symphony Orchestra at Carnegie Hall. Sargeant considers it "a disservice to the memory of the late Charles Ives to hail him as a precursor of all the tiresome subsequent things," and regards Ives as "an isolated artist" rather than "a link in a chain." He also recognized that Ives's "obscuring of various melodic motifs is deliberate, artful, and designed to represent experiences." Praising Ives as "original" and "one of the few distinctly American personalities in symphonic music," Sargeant can only think of two *great* original composers (Berlioz and Debussy) and is unsure whether or not future generations will come to regard this American original as a great composer.

B514 Schonberg, Harold C. "A Complex Score Is Ives' No. 4." *The New York Times*, April 25, 1965, section 2, page 13. *See*: **W7d**

Preview of the Ives *Fourth* on the eve of its premiere. Schonberg provides background on the performance history of this original "masterpiece" and the gradual unravelling of the editorial nightmare that was needed before it could be performed. Schonberg is struck by the Ives "dichotomy," the fact that "all this advanced musical apparatus is used to recreate the American past."

B515 _____. "Complex and Yet Simple." *The New York Times*, May 2, 1965, section 2, page 11; reprinted as "Ives: Complex and Yet Simple" in *Facing the Music*, pp. 129-131. New York: Summit Books, 1981. *See:* **W7d**

In this retrospective several days after the premiere of Ives's *Fourth Symphony*, Schonberg addresses the impact that isolation had on Ives's music. He concludes that exposure to an audience would not have caused Ives to compose "a different kind of music." In his preface to the reprint of this article in his collection, *Facing the Music*, Schonberg acknowledges the error of his prediction that the Stokowski recording of Ives's *Fourth* (**D7**) "most likely will be the only available recording for years to come." *See:* **D6**

B516 ____. "Music: Stokowski Conducts Ives's Fourth Symphony in World Premiere After 50 Years." *The New York Times*, April 27, 1965, page 29. *See:* **W7d**

Review of the April 26 Carnegie Hall premiere of Ives's *Fourth Symphony*, Stokowski conducting the American Symphony Orchestra. Schonberg asserts that in order to understand the work, one must know about Ives's Transcendentalist philosophy as well as the popular tunes borrowed and transformed by Ives. Nevertheless, Schonberg does not think that the score's complexities inhibit its direct emotional appeal. Despite the "frequent awkwardness" and other minor problems, Schonberg considers the Ives *Fourth* a masterpiece with "tremendous personality and authentic stature."

B517 "The Transcendentalist." *Newsweek* 65 (10 May 1965): 101-102. *See:* **W7d**

Conventional biographical overview of Ives's unusual double career and belated recognition. The reviewer depicts the Ives *Fourth* as a "circus-like symphony, with breath-taking action high up on the trapeze, clowning around the perimeter, while all three rings churn wildly in separate entertainments."

B518 "Cantankerous Yankee." *Time* 85, no. 19 (7 May 1965): 56. *See:* **W7d**

Review of Stokowki's April 26 premiere performance at Carnegie Hall. Despite some quipping about the "musical snorts and snickers, hiccups and heehaws," and the additional conductors called on "to help referree such rowdy goings-on as 27 different rhythms being played at the same time," this *Time* sketch of Ives's

Fourth Symphony displays a genuine appreciation for the musical depth of this work: "The *Fourth Symphony* was a masterpiece, another great work from what an increasing number of people believe is America's greatest composer."

B519 Drew, David. "Charles the First." *New Statesman* 72 (30 September 1966): 489-490.

While recognizing that Ives's anticipation of avant-garde techniques is not a negligible achievement, Drew takes the view that "any reputation based solely on chronological precedence is subject to steady erosion." Drew is especially critical of Ives's decision to insert the fugue from his *First String Quartet* as the third movement of the *Fourth Symphony.* He also compares Ives's heterogeneity unfavorably to Mahler's, asserting that Ives "packs everything in because he still lacks a scale of values by which he may decide what to leave out."

B520 Hopkins, Bill. "Rootless Ives." *Music and Musicians* 15, no. 3 (November 1966): 44.

Review of the BBC Symphony Orchestra performance (September 13) conducted by Gunther Schuller in a performing version (presumably the conductor's own) which "excluded an important part for chorus." According to Hopkins, Ives's significance "lies chiefly in his historical and social position, and in the freedom of his aesthetic outlook," and his "principal shortcoming...is his self-conscious lack of real stylistic roots." He regards Ives's program as unoriginal whenever it was not vague or sentimental, the fugue unworthy of "a fully fledged composer," and the second movement "cacophonous." A strong candidate for Slonimsky's *Lexicon of Musical Invective.*

B521 Stone, Kurt. "Ives's Fourth Symphony: A Review." *The Musical Quarterly* 52, no. 1 (January 1966): 1-16.

An extensive critical examination of the symphony and its premiere recording by the man who served as Editor-in-Chief of Associated Music Publishers which published the work. Stone shares Carter's disdain for Ives's use of borrowed material and argues that "the most interesting and by far the most successful areas in Ives's aggregative compositions are found in the background activities," activities which "operate with composed (*not* borrowed) thematic ideas" (**B668**). According to Stone, Ives's musical references "have no apparent musical relevance to the whole of the work, nor do they even have any musical interrelationship among themselves. They seem to have been chosen largely for their non-musical connotations."

Stone also writes that Ives's program has "little application or relevance to the symphony as a composition--the impact of the music as such is much stronger." He shares Ives's own high regard for the fourth movement, which "generates a deeper emotional communication than perhaps any other work of his," and which Stone regards as "one of the most remarkable, most profoundly moving pieces of music ever written by an American composer." In his "last analysis" of the symphony Stone writes: "Its many self-contradictions in taste, artistry, and spirit seem to me to be too serious and too powerful to permit wholehearted acceptance." Several years later Gordon Cyr would vigorously oppose Stones's thesis. *See:* **B525**

B522   Sullivan, Timothy. "An Approach to Analysis of the Second Movement of Symphony No. 4 by Charles E. Ives and An Essay on Composition Based on Observations on the Same Work." Senior Essay, Yale University, 1966. 56 pp.

Sullivan asks how we should experience the multiple texural tapestries of this movement: "Should there be an attempt to experience them as separate though interacting entities, or should there be an attempt to combine them, and digest them as one thing?" In partial answer to his question Sullivan hears "downbeats" of isolated sound emerging occasionally from the "harmonic and rhythmic staticity." He then devotes considerable attention to those "details" which help "ascertain why these things occur and...what it is that contributes to the overall thrust of the movement."

B523   Walsh, Stephen. "Folk Songs in Counterpoint." *Music and Musicians* 14, no. 12 (August 1966): 28.

Review of the Stokowski recording (**D7**). Walsh discusses Ives's "free contrapuntal framework--an intense web of unrelated melodic strands which move more or less independently of one another." He equates Ives's use of "commonplace melodies" with Mahler's "process of 'bringing the world' into his music." Although he gives Stokowski "enormous credit" for recording the work, Walsh prefers to withhold judgment of the performance until he has seen a score. He concludes: "The Fourth Symphony is not, I'm sure, Ives' masterpiece, but it is extraordinarily compelling--music which holds the attention absolutely and which could easily become popular in the way Tchaikovsky first became popular 60 or so years ago."

B524 Call, William. "A Study of the Transcendental Aesthetic Theories of John S. Dwight and Charles E. Ives and the Relationship of These Theories to Their Respective Work as Music Critic and Composer." D.M.A. dissertation, University of Illinois, 1971. 229 pp.

Call outlines the history of American Transcendentalism and shows how this movement influenced the critical writings of Dwight and Ives's *Essays* **(B660)**. He then tries to demonstrate how Ives's Transcendental theories can be applied to the fourth movement of the *Fourth Symphony*. Call's analysis of this movement, which applies Schenkerian principles, is perhaps its most detailed formal, harmonic, and motivic analysis in print. In contrast, Call only sparsely acknowledges the Ives secondary literature, and makes almost no attempt to consider the symphony as a whole.

B525 Cyr, Gordon. "Intervallic Structural Elements in Ives' Fourth Symphony." *Perspectives of New Music* 9, no. 2 and 10, no. 1 (1971): 291-303.

An important article in which Cyr discards the "literary, patriotic, or metaphysical umbrella" to explain Ives's choice of quotation and, after crediting the pioneering analysis of Cowell **(B354)** and Marshall **(B651)** argues instead that Ives's borrowed material in this symphony possesses a "unifying thread in some common *musical* property." He supports this view with a convincing array of musical quotations that share "a *tendency* toward that form of the pentatonic scale equivalent to the diatonic collection minus the fourth and seventh degrees."

Cyr also provides compelling arguments that Ives was "aware" of what he had wrought, and that he shared Stravinsky's and Schoenberg's "concern for the interval as a prime factor in pitch-organization." For the most part Cyr succeeds in his attempt to contradict such writers as Stone **(B521)**, who have concluded that Ives "doesn't really know what he is doing, that the formal plan of his work, if successful, is the result of a fluke, not of his conscious design."

B526 Brooks, William. "Unity and Diversity in Charles Ives's Fourth Symphony." *Yearbook for Inter-American Musical Research* 10 (1974): 5-49.

The most thorough and sophisticated analysis in print of the first movement of the Ives *Fourth*. Brooks first outlines the sectional diversity in orchestration, tonality, meter, and melody. He then examines unity in Ives's handling of formal procedures, and argues that formal principles "are related by the sytematic negation of their traditionally conclusive character." In the next stage of his analysis Brooks presents the movement "as a lamination made from many coextensive layers of material" (seven families of layers all together), both in their diversity and their unity, and makes an engrossing comparison between Ives's superimposition of families of layers and "conventional contrapuntal music."

Brooks shows how "every pair of tunes is connected, no matter how distinct they may appear individually," and he also brings home Ives's request that his listeners take an active role when he writes that, "a person approaching this network is required to choose from an extraordinary diversity of options." Twenty-five diagrams and eighteen musical examples help Brooks to demonstrate his impressive argument.

B527 MacDonald, Malcolm. "Ives Symphony No. 4." *Gramophone* 52, no. 688 (October 1974): 688.

Review of the London Philharmonic recording conducted by Serebrier (**D6**). Although Macdonald denies this work "masterpiece" status, he does acknowledge that Ives has created "a good ration of moving music and a great deal of entertaining music." He praises Serebrier's "effective" interpretation for not being a "carbon copy of Stokowski's" (**D7**), and he notes that "the impact of his [Serebrier's] performance as a whole is notably enhanced by its recorded quality."

B528 Serebrier, José, and John Kirkpatrick. "Charles Ives' Fourth." *Symphony News* 25, no. 5 (1974): 11-12.

Serebrier and Kirkpatrick discuss the opposition generated by the stylistic disparity of the third movement and summarize several of the editorial and performance difficulties and their solutions. Kirkpatrick concludes by relating Ives to Debussy: "Like Debussy, Ives was against school-book form, and in search of a new kind of freedom. He was constantly revising and changing things. And not only his music."

B529 Serebrier, José. "Ives the Most Difficult Ever." *Music Journal* 32, no. 7 (September 1974): 14-15+.

Serebrier, who was one of Stokowski's assistants at the 1965 premiere and the first to record the work without assistants (**D6**), relates the musical and extra-musical problems he faced (e.g., obtaining and editing the parts, rehearsal scheduling and strategy), when he prepared his London Symphony Orchestra recording of the *Fourth Symphony*.

B530 ____. "Charles Ives--A Composer For All Directions." *Stereo Review* 35, no. 1 (July 1975): 48-51.

A discussion of the performance problems posed by the *Fourth Symphony*. Serebrier explains how it is possible to dismiss two conductors through sectional rehearsals and special recording techniques such as overdubbing, and argues that "*one* conductor can obtain more precise results than seven" (or three). He also cites examples of how quadrophonic recording techniques solve many problems (e.g., spatial separation) that are insoluble in live performance.

B531 Brooks, William Fordyce. "Sources and Errata List for Charles Ives' Symphony No. 4, Movement II." D.M.A. dissertation, University of Illinois, 1976. 170 pp.

Although the main text of this important dissertation comprises a modest forty pages, it constitutes the most thorough source study in print of this movement. Brooks summarizes the content of twenty-one sources that begin with sketches in 1910 and end with the Associated Music Edition published in 1965, and offers sophisticated but cautious interpretations of their relative and absolute chronology. The bulk of the dissertation is devoted to a systematic listing of selected errata (i.e., "only the most glaring of the discrepancies") that Brooks discovered when checking the Associated Music score against Ives's "ink copy" and other sources.

B532 Kenyon, Nicholas. "Holland Festival (Hague Residentie Orchestra)." *Music and Musicians* 25, no. 2 (October 1976): 52+. *See:* **W7f**

Review of the Holland Festival American Bicentennial performance of the Ives *Fourth*, with Cristobal Halffter conducting the Hague Residentie Orchestra at the Concertgebouw. Kenyon devotes a paragraph to the performance of "this vast collage of violent parody and (one presumes) utter seriousness," and criticizes the performance for sacrificing freedom and serenity for rigid control. The *Fourth* was one of thirty Ives works performed at this festival.

B533 Magers, Roy V. "Charles Ives's Optimism: or, The Program's Progress." In *Music in American Society 1776-1976*, edited by George McCue, pp. 73-86. New Brunswick, New Jersey: Transaction Books, 1977.

According to Magers, Ives's optimism is "one of his characteristic attitudes that lies at the very core of his existence as an American individual and composer." After drawing on Ives's writings to support this thesis, Magers expresses his view that "the central image evoked by texts associated with quoted hymn tunes is that of the wandering Pilgrim seeking his way toward the heavenly home." Magers devotes the rest of his essay to show that the "Program's Progress" of the *Fourth Symphony* conveys a metaphor of the Pilgrim's Progress as he searches for a union with God.

B534 Smith, William A. "Leopold Stokowski: A Re-evaluation." *American Music* 1, no. 3 (1983): 23-37.

Smith devotes several pages of his re-evaluation (pages 29-33) to Stokowski's linkages with Ives, especially the *Fourth Symphony*. He offers a useful summary of Stokowski's ten-year effort to perform and record this work and an interpretation that "much in this music and in Ives's attitudes and writing creatively parallels the values and beliefs Stokowski had lived by."

B535 Rathert, Wolfgang. "Charles Ives Symphonie Nr. 4, 1911-1916." *Neuland* 3 (1983-1984): 226-241.

The most substantial non-English survey of this work. In separate sections Rathert summarizes the genesis of the symphony, discusses its program, and analyzes its form, motivic-thematic inter-connections, quotations, and ostinati. Finally, Rathert selects several passages of the second movement for a more detailed examination. Interestingly, Cyr's article (**B525**) is cited only in a footnote in which Rathert dismisses his interpretation of penatatonic basic cells as banal ("eine Banalität"), since "all folk and popular songs are fundamentally pentatonic" ("alle Volkslieder und 'popular songs' sind im Grunde pentatonisch.")

B536 Lipkis, Laurence Alan. "Aspects of Temporality in Debussy's 'Jeux' and Ives' 'Symphony No. 4' Fourth Movement." Ph.D.

dissertation, University of California at Santa Barbara, 1984. 27 pp.

Lipkis's thesis, unfortunately undeveloped, is that Debussy's *Jeux* and Ives's *Fourth Symphony* (fourth movement) "each make temporal demands upon the listener that are radically different from those made by traditional Western music to that point." For the most part Lipkis considers these works separately and makes almost no attempt to compare them. He considers the "battery unit" and the "frequently chaotic complexity of the polyphony" as the central "impediment to normal temporal perception." Nevertheless, he concludes that "the determining factors in our aural perception of the works....is an overriding sense of organic growth and structural drama in the movement that enables us to hear the ending as a logical, intensely satisfying climax."

B537 Serebrier, José. "The Everest of Symphonies." *BMI* 4 (1984): 36-37.

Serebrier relates his personal involvement with the Ives *Fourth*, which antedates by nearly ten years the time he assisted Stokowski for the premiere performance and recording (**D7**) until twenty years later, by which time he had performed and recorded the work singlehandedly (**D6**).

B538 Brooks, William. "A Drummer-Boy Looks Back: Percussion in Ives's Fourth Symphony." *Percussionist* 22, no. 6 (1984) 4-45.

In this thoughtful examination of the role of percussion in the second and fourth movements of the *Fourth* Brooks states at the outset that Ives "treats the entire orchestra as though it were a percussion ensemble." After supporting this thesis, Brooks summarizes the role percussion played in Ives's life and work, and explores in detail the problems celesta, bells, and non-pitched percussion instruments face in this symphony. He also offers a detailed discussion of Ives's intentions for his "battery unit" in the fourth movement, and suggests a combined facsimile and "performance" score for the second and fourth movements that can show Ives's philosophical intent without neglecting a practical solution. An indispensable article for anyone who wants to conduct or play a percussion part in this symphony.

Universe Symphony [W9]

B539 Austin, Larry. "Reconstruction of Ives' Universe Symphony." In *Desert Plants/Conversations with 23 American Musicians*, by

Walter Zimmermann, pp. 207-220. Vancouver: A.R.C. Publications, 1976.

Zimmermann interviews composer Larry Austin about the problems in reconstructing Ives's *Universe Symphony* for performance. Austin describes the difficulties in transcribing and realizing Ives's sketches for this purposefully unfinished work. At every turn he was confronted by Ives's contradictions and unresolved issues. Many of the performance difficulties (e.g., simultaneous and multiple tunings and polyrhythms) could be solved with a computer. Austin also discusses his creative role in creating his three *Fantasies* on the work. The article includes some transcriptions and a facsimile of "Section B (Present)." *See*: **B540**

B540 ____. "Charles Ives's Life Pulse Prelude for Percussion Orchestra: A Realization for Modern Performance from Sketches for His Universe Symphony." *Percussionist* 23, no. 6 (1985): 58-84.

Austin discusses the nine sketch pages (of a total of thirty-six) that Ives left for the *Life Pulse Prelude* of his unfinished *Universe Symphony*. He states his purpose clearly at the outset: "In the nine sketch pages devoted specifically to the *Life Pulse Prelude*, Ives actually notated half of one of the planned ten cycles of music, which in the latter half, he specifies in exact palindromic reverse. Thus, one complete cycle was realized by Ives, himself. The other nine cycles are described in structural but not notational detail. With this and the structural outline provided by Ives, I have attempted to realize the entire *Life Pulse Prelude* with credible sensitivity to Ives's intent. What follows is a detailed explication of my interpretation of the *Life Pulse Prelude* sketches [transcription of each are included], the method of their realization for modern performance, and obervations on what I term 'the *Life Pulse Prelude* effect.'" An important article for anyone wishing to approach this mysterious Ives composition. *See*: **B539**

OTHER MUSIC FOR SYMPHONY ORCHESTRA
Robert Browning Overture [W15]

B541 "First Performances." *ACA Bulletin* 6, no. 2 (1957): 21. *See*: **W15a**

This announcement of the premiere pereeformance, October 14, 1956 at Carnegie Hall, Leopold Stokowski conducting the Symphony of the Air contains excerpts from four reviews: Louis

Biancolli of the *New York World Telegram and Sun*; Miles
Kastendieck of the *New York Journal American*; Francis D.
Perkins of the *New York Herald Tribune*; and Howard Taubman of
The New York Times [all reviews dated October 15].

B542 Trimble, Lester. "Review of Robert Browning Overture, by Charles
E. Ives." *The Musical Quarterly* 43, no. 1 (January 1957): 90-93.

Trimble is unsure how to interpret the complexities of this score,
especially the seemingly conflicting approaches in Ives's
orchestration (i.e., using instrumentation alternately to obscure
and clarify the same thematic material). Nevertheless, Trimble
concludes that "even when the analytical part of one's mind
cannot be sure just what is going on, the music possesses such
an air of utter authority, and the expressive reactions it evokes
are so powerful and unarguable, that one comes away convinced
that the Overture is truly a great work of art."

B543 Flanagan, William. "Charles Ives' 'Robert Browning Overture.'
"*HiFi/Stereo Review* 16, no. 5 (May 1966): 69-70.

Review of recording premiere of this work with William Strickland
conducting the Polish National Radio Orchestra **(D14)**. Despite
his enthusiasm for the *Overture*, Flanagan is not yet ready to
canonize Ives and expresses "suspicion that certain avant-garde
factions--who, granted, have perhaps been most powerfully
effective in creating Ives' present prestige...have made him rather
a sort of poetic justification for their own musical extremism."
Flanagan also quotes and comments on Trimble's review **(B542)**
included with "David Halls's wonderfully informative program
notes."

B544 Jacobson, Bernard. "American Symphony Orchestra: Stokowski."
High Fidelity/Musical America 17, no. 3 (March 1967): MA 16.
See: **W15a**

Review of the December 19, 1966 Carnegie Hall performance,
with Stokowski conducting the American Symphony Orchestra.
Jacobson contrasts Ives's *Robert Browning Overture* with the New
York premiere of Cowell's *A Thanksgiving Psalm*. While he
considers the Cowell naive and primitive, he praises the Ives as "a
thoroughly sophisticated work...an uncannily precise symbol for
the personal flavor of Browning."

B545 Hüsken, Renate. "Charles Ives' Robert Browning Overture."
Neuland 1 (1980): 16-24.

Hüsken briefly discusses the genesis of this work and then examines Browning's relationship to music and a number of parallels between Ives's and Browning's work and their reception. An analysis follows in which she outlines the *Overture's* form and discusses its motivic unity. In the course of the analysis Hüsken cites a parallel between Wagner's *Ring* and Browning's *Ring and the Book*, and makes a convincing argument that Ives may have considered this when he derived the main melodic material in his overture from a *Leitmotiv* (often referred to as "Siegfried" or "The Hero to Come").

B546 Hilliard, John Stanley. "Part I: Two Pieces for Orchestra (Original Composition Not Part of Microfilm Copy); Part II: Charles Ives' Robert Browning Overture: Style and Structure," pp. 73-225. D.M.A. dissertation, Cornell University, 1983.

The most thorough analytical examination of this work. Hilliard offers a detailed and richly illustrated formal and motivic analysis of the whole work, harmonic discussions of the twelve-tone chord (probably music's first), the opening, and adagio portions, and a chapter on "Contributions of Texture to Structure." As a result of his manuscript study, Hilliard notes "several critical errors in the printed score which affect the thematic understanding of the total work," especially two missing accidentals in the structurally crucial opening thematic material (which "proved to contain the melodic cells which generated the main three themes").

MUSIC FOR CHAMBER OR THEATRE ORCHESTRA
Miscellaneous

B547 Whallon, Evan. *The Unanswered Question*, for chamber orchestra. (Performable also as chamber music.) New York: Southern Music Publishing Co., 1953; *Calcium Light Night*, for orchestra. (New York: New Music Edition, American Music Center, 1953. *Notes* 11, no. 4 (September 1954): 607. *See*: *The Gong on the Hook and Ladder*

Review of first published editions of these works. Whallon contrasts the "unpretentious music" of *The Unanswered Question* with its "quiet beauty in the instrumental combination" and *Calcium Light Night*, "more pretentious, more difficult to perform and considerably less 'available' to the listener." He could not have known that he was describing not *Calcium Light Night* but *A Gong on the Hook and Ladder*, which had been inserted mistakenly in *New Music*, unbeknownst to its editor, Henry Cowell. *See*: **B356-357**

B548 Helms Hans G. "Über statistisches Komponieren bei Charles Ives." *Neue Zeitschrift für Musik* 127, no. 3 (March 1966): 90-93.

Helms discusses three short orchestral works (*Tone Roads No. 3, The Unanswered Question,* and *Over the Pavements*) that illustrate Ives's "statistical [i.e., aleatory] composition." He explains that in this type of composition "the musical work should not be an invariable object or thing, but a changing process" ["das musikalische Werk soll kein invariantes Objekt oder Ding sein, sondern ein veränderlicher Prozess"]. Furthermore, this process achieves its fulfillment through a free, imaginative performance.

B549 Burk, James. "The Wind Music of Charles Ives." *The Instrumentalist* 24 (October 1969): 36-40.

Overview of Ives's wind literature based for the most part on Kirkpatrick's *Catalogue* (**B7**). Some of Burk's information has been superceded by Kirpatrick's revisions (**B8**), particularly the discovery of several works (e.g., *Holiday Quickstep* and *Country Band March*). The article also contains facsimiles of the remains of Ives's first known work for band, *Schoolboy March,* and a portion of *All the Way Around and Back.*

B550 Schuller, Gunther. Jacket notes for "Calcium Light Night." Columbia MS 7318 [1970].

Informative background notes that emphasize the avant-garde nature of the short orchestral works performed on this album. The album includes the following works: *Sets Nos. 1-3; Tone Roads Nos. 1 and 3; From the Steeples and the Mountains;* Ives's arrangements of *The Rainbow* and *Ann Street; Scherzo: Over the Pavements; The Pond; All the Way Around and Back;* and Schuller's arrangement of *Chromâtimelôdtune.* Among the twenty individual pieces are "a number of compositions [seven] never before recorded or even previously performed."

B551 Shore, Jay. "Record: Calcium Light Night." *The Rolling Stone* 84 (10 June 1971): 46.

Review of Schuller's recording of Ives's short orchestral works (Columbia MS 7318), perhaps the only Ives recording discussed in a rock-oriented journal. "Unless one is well-versed in musical wit, ironic orchestration and unusual colors, much of Ives' magic can be missed...The playing is clean and warm and could only come from people appreciattive of Ives." *See:* **B550**

B552   Miller, Philip L. "Gunther Schuller--A Very Right Man to Interpret Ives." *The American Record Guide* 37, no. 6 (February 1971): 353.

In this review of Schuller's "Calcium Light Night" recording (Columbia MS 7318) Miller cites the six "ostensible duplications" on Cambridge CRS-1804 (four works) **(D11)** and Nonesuch H-71222 (two works) **(D31)**. He then uses the considerably reconstructed *Chromâtimelôdtune* (included on the Nonesuch), which "hardly sounds like the same piece as heard in the two recordings," to point out the "instructive" value of comparing versions. *See*: **B550**

B553   Battisti, Frank, and Donald Hunsberger. "The Wind Music of Charles Ives." *The Instrumentalist* 28 (August 1973): 32-34.

Brief background information on *Intercollegiate March, March Omega Lambda Chi, Country Band March, Calcium Light Night, The See'r*, and *Ann Street*. The co-authors include a personal communication from James Sinclair regarding *Country Band March* and Ives's description of piano drumming in *Calcium Light Night* (excerpted from *Memos* **[B378]**). The article concludes with a slightly longer annotated list arranged in the following categories: Existing Band Pieces, Band Arrangements, Wind Ensemble Pieces, Wind Ensemble Arrangements, and Pieces for Voice(s) with Wind Accompaniment.

B554   Singleton, Kenneth. Jacket notes to "Old Songs Deranged, Charles Ives Music for Theater Orchestra." Columbia M 32969 [1974].

Brief but useful notes for each of the fourteen selections included on this album, thirteen of which are premiere recordings. The selections include *Country Band March, The Swimmers, Overture and March: "1776,"* and *Holiday Quickstep* (edited by James Sinclair); *Mists, Charlie Rutlage, Evening, Marches II and III, An Old Song Deranged, Gyp the Blood or Hearst!? Which is Worst?!, Remembrance* (edited by Singleton); *Fugue in 4 Keys on "The Shining Shore"* (realized by John Kirpatrick); and the previously recorded *Chromâtimelôdtune* in a realization by Singleton.

B555   Milligan, Terry Gilbert. "Charles Ives: A Study of the Works for Chamber Ensemble Written Between 1898 and 1908 Which Utilize Wind Instruments." D.M.A. dissertation, University of Texas at Austin, 1978. 169 pp.

Milligan advocates a broader interpretation of wind music and therefore includes more than twice the total of Ives works in this category (25) than the nine cited in Kirkpatrick's *Catalogue* (**B7**). Nevertheless, Milligan confines his list to those chamber ensemble pieces that necessitate a conductor. Useful summary of Ives's Poverty Flat years (1898-1908), where Ives lived with various other Yale alumni at three addresses between graduation and his marriage to Harmony. Some analysis of *From the Steeples and the Mountains, Scherzo: Over the Pavements,* and *Central Park in the Dark. See:* **B293** and **B556**

B556 ____. "Charles Ives: A Survey of the Works for Chamber Ensemble Which Utilize Wind Instruments." *Journal of Band Research* 18, no. 1 (Fall 1982): 60-68.

Encapsulated descriptions (including instrumental combinations), chronology, and compositional circumstances of the twenty-five works discussed at greater length in Milligan, 1978.

B557 Feder, Stuart. "Calcium Light Night and Other Early Memories of Charles Ives." In *Fathers and Their Families,* edited by S. Cath, A. Gurwitt, and L. Gunsberg. Hillsdale, NJ: The Analytic Press (in press, December 1986). [Presented at the New York Psychoanalytic Society Meeting, December 10, 1985.]

Although he acknowledges "that conflict and resultant ambivalence to his father proved at length to be a strong motivating element in Charles' choices in life," Feder emphasizes here the "relatively unambivalent, pre-competitive, pre-conflictual phase of life" in order to explore "certain significant early childhood memories which the composer Charles Ives had of his father, George. As examples of works that show Ives's "reconstruction of memory" of his early childhood Feder uses *The Pond* and *Calcium Light Night.*

The brevity necessitated by the fact that this paper was delivered at a conference does not allow Feder the space to substantiate several conclusions, for example, the "Mollie Ives would have had to be an extraordinarily sensitive and responsive mother," but he does explore possible consequences of "the separations that Charles Ives experienced in the third year of life from an immensely significant object," i.e., his father, who was away for "at least six months" during this formative period. In addition to provocative psychoanalytic insights, the essay includes some previously neglected material on George Ives based on *The Danbury Evening News* and manuscript material for *Calcium Light Night.* Part of a longer study, still in manuscript entitled, *My*

Father's Song: The Story of Charles and George Ives, Vol. I. See:
B280, B291, B475, and **B816**

B558   Solomon, Maynard. "Charles Ives: Some Psychonalytic
Implications." Presented at the New York Psychoanalytic Society,
December 10, 1985, as a Response to Stuart Feder, "'Calcium
Light Night and Other Early Memories of Charles Ives.'"
Unpublished mansucript.

Invaluable as the only response by a psychiatrist-historian to
Stuart Feder's singificant psychoanalytic studies of Ives,
especially **B557.** In contrast to earlier studies of Feder (**B280,
B291, B475,** and **B816**), Solomon remarks at the outset that
"Ives was never able to complete--or perhaps, even to begin--the
process of mourning for his father, whose figure looms over the
composer's biography." He also points out that "autobiographical
writings are notoriously subject to distortions, deception, and
special pleadings" and asks us to question Ives's idealization of
his father and his autobiographical neglect of his mother.

Solomon suggests that the problem in dating *Calcium Light Night*
calls into question "Feder's attempt to connect the work with a
period of blocked creativity in 1905 and with Ives' courtship with
his future wife in 1906." When discussing *The Pond,* Solomon
does not question the presence of Ives's father, but he suggests
an alternative interpretation. According to Solomon, the work
serves less to "memorialize the male parent" than to express "a
desire to reach the mother by way of the father." *See:* **B314** and
B557

Holiday Quickstep [W17]

B559   "Amusements--The German Dramatic Association." *The Danbury
Evening News,* January 17, 1888, page 3. *See:* **W17a**

The first review of a work by Ives: "The feature of the evening, in
the musical line, was the rendition of the 'Holiday Quickstep,'
composed and arranged for an orchestra by Charlie Ives, a
thirteen-year-old son of George E. Ives. Master Ives is certainly a
musical genius, being an accomplished performer on several
instruments, as well as composer and arranger. The 'Holiday
Quickstep' is worthy of a place with reproductions of much older
heads, and Master Charlie should be encouraged to further
efforts in this line. We shall expect more from this talented
youngster in the future."

B560   Sinclair, James B., ed. "Preface" to published edition. Merion Music, 1975.

Historical background, list and description of sources, and notes. Preface also quotes the *Danbury Evening News* review (17 January 1888), the first known newspaper reference to Ives as a composer. *See:* **B559**

Fugue in Four Keys [W20]

B561   "Premiere." *Music Educator's Journal* 60 (April 1974): 125. *See:* **W20a**

Announcement of the March 8 premiere of Ives's *Fugue in Four Keys: "On the Shining Shore"* performed by the Chicago Civic Orchestra.

Overture & March 1776 [W22]

B562   Snapp, Kenneth. "Build a Band--And Educate It, Too." *The Instrumentalist* 32 (September 1977): 52-53.

Historical background and brief analysis of Ives's *Overture and March "1776."* Snapp's purpose is to prepare a band to peform this work by informing them of Ives's musical materials and to help them understand the spirit behind the music. *See:* **B563**

Country Band March [W23]

B563   Sinclair, James B., ed. Charles Ives *"Country Band" March for Theater Orchestra*; *Overture & March "1776"*. Merion Music, Inc. 1976. [Notes are dated 1975 in both publications].

Historical commentary and editorial notes, the latter including an "index of tunes quoted," "table of correlative measures" between this march and "Putnam's Camp" from *Three Places in New England*, a "description of sources," and "footnotes to the score." *See:* **B562**

B564   Dickinson, Peter. "Ives Source. Country Band March for Theatre Orchestra," *The Musical Times* 125 (May 1984): 278.

Review of Sinclair's newly-published edition that "describes sources and is informative about quotes as well as relating Country Band March (1903) to Putnam's Camp (1912) in a table covering every bar." Of the work itself Dickinson comments on how Ives's march "reflects the context of amateur music" and how

"Ives tried to notate this kind of informality more scrupulously than anyone else, even later composers responding to jazz."

Scherzo (Over the Pavements) [W25]

B565 Stevens, Halsey. *Scherzo: Over the Pavements.* For chamber orchestra. Performable also as chamber music. New York: Peer International Corp., 1954. *Notes* 12, no. 2 (December 1954): 326.

Review of the first published edition of *Scherzo: Over the Pavements.* Stevens is sympathetic to the "lively rhythms and odd instrumental colors" that would make the work "well worth hearing, but, "risking the ridicule of the aficionados," he questions the "curiosity" of Ives's "harmonic thought" in which "one cannot be certain of misprints."

The Pond [W26]
See: **B557** and **B558**

Set for Theatre or Chamber Orchestra [W27]

B566 Blitzstein, Marc. "Premieres and Experiments--1932." *Modern Music* 9, no. 3 (March 1932): 121-127. *See:* **B27a**

Review of "In the Night," one of six works performed at a Pan American Concert in New York, February 16, 1932. Blitzstein considers this Ives composition one of three [the others were Harris's *String Quartet* and Chavez's *Energia*] "interesting or more." Blitzstein writes: "'In the Night' has a lovely texture...recalling the post-Impressionists and particularly Roussel (but considering when it was written, there can be no possibility of imitation or influence). Ives, except in works of this sort, seldom has sufficient craft. I feel a sketched rather than an achieved intention."

B567 Bowen, Meirion. "Concerts; Contemporary." *Music and Musicians* 20, no. 7 (March 1972): 66. *See:* **W27e**

Review of British premiere, November 27, 1971 of Ives's "rollicking" *Set of Pieces for Theatre Orchestra,* performed by the London Sinfonietta. Bowen writes that this work "incorporates hymn tunes, barn dances, and so on, but with a controlled theatrical character that one only appreciates some time after, when recollecting their impact."

**Central Park in the Dark and
The Unanswered Question [W28]**
See also: **B319** and **B547**

B568   Downes, Olin. "Ives Music Played at Columbia Fete." *The New York Times*, May 12, 1946, page 42. *See*: **W28a**

Review of the May 12 premieres of *The Unanswered Question* and *Central Park in the Dark*, Edgar Schenckman conducting students from the Juilliard Graduate School at McMillin Theatre, Columbia University. Since the performance was marred by poor acoustics, "undue preponderance was given to the few instruments which answered the strains from backstage. This work is really an extreme experiment in impressionism, needing a far more sensitive balance and coordination of all elements."

B569   Brant, Henry. "Space as an Essential Aspect of Musical Composition." In *Contemporary Composers on Contemporary Music*, edited by Elliott Schwartz and Barney Childs, pp. 221-242. New York, Chicago, and San Francisco: Holt, Rinehart and Winston, 1967.

Brant opens his essay by remarking that Ives's *The Unanswered Question* constituted one of a handful of his own personal experiences in "spatial effects" before 1951. He later cites this work as the most significant early twentieth-century solution to the problems posed by spatial technique. According to Brant, "this unique, unprecedented little work, written in 1908 [*sic*], presents, with extraordinary economy and concentration, the entire twentieth-century spatial spectrum in music, and offers guidelines for solving all the practical problems involved....The spatial-contrapuntal-polytemporal principles so brilliantly exemplified in this piece are the basis for the more complicated spatial superimpositions present in all my own recent large-scale works."

B570   Jolas, Betsy. "Introduction a la Musique Américaine: Sur 'The Unanswered Question.'" *Musique en Jeu* 1 (November 1970): 13-16.

Programmatic description of *The Unanswered Question* with a brief musical outline and several musical illustrations. Jolas disagrees with Ives's representation of the free human response (the four arguing flutes) to the trumpet's question, and argues that the flute's insufficiently concealed melodic and rhythmic identity "virtually excludes all idea of freedom" ["cette identité exclut pratiquement toute idée de liberté"].

B571 Enke, Heinz. "Charles Ives' 'The Unanswered Question.'" In *Gerhard Schumacher: Zur musikalischen Analyse*, pp. 232-240. (Wege der Forschung. Vol. 257). Darmstadt. Wissenschaftl. Buchgesellschaft, 1974.

Enke discusses selective details concerning the relationship among the three interdependent layers of this work (the string ensemble, the four flutes, and the solitary trumpet). He advocates broad or multiple interpretations, and, in keeping with this approach, instead of accepting Ives's own programmatic outline, instructs his readers not to accept Ives's philosophical guidelines any more seriously than the inscriptions in Debussy's piano preludes.

B572 Larson, Thomas. "Unanswering the Question." *Perspectives of New Music* 20, nos. 1-2 (1982-1983): 363-405.

Larson's purpose in this poetic essay is to convey his "own convergence with the music and writings of Charles Ives and the esthetics and poetry of Charles Olson." In discussing the philosopical ideas of *The Unanswered Question* at length in Part Two, he maintains that it "may be the work which includes the esthetic of inarticulation more so than any other." Not recommended for those whose tastes do not extend beyond traditional expository prose.

B573 Hitchcock, H. Wiley and Noel B. Zahler. "Just What Is Ives's Unanswered Question?" *Notes* 44, no. 3 (March 1988):437-443.

Hitchcock discusses the evolution of the final note of the "question" as intoned by the trumpet (or as Ives wrote, "an oboe if one is being artsy otherwise one of the flutes"). In the "autograph pencil short-score sketch" (1906) Ives concludes the question invariably as a Bb; in the 1930s, he decided to alternate between B and C (a change that can be observed, albeit with several errors in the Peer-Southern edition of 1953). Hitchcock's central question for all Ives's editors is, "Whose taste and judgment are we to respect--those of Ives the composer, or of Ives the reviser, the tinkerer with his own works, the jacker-up of dissonance in them?" Zahler's thoughtful edition offers both versions (or answers) to Ives's questioning trumpet.

Set No. 1, no. 6 [W30]
Calcium Light Night
See: **B557** and **B558**

The Gong on the Hook and Ladder [W31]
See: **B547**

Quarter-Tone Chorale [W34]

B574 Porter, Andrew. "Musical Events: The Sounds of Summer." *The New Yorker* 51, no. 15 (June 2, 1975): 86-89. *See*: **B34a**

Review of a New York premiere performed at "last week's concert" by the Juilliard ensemble, conducted by Richard Dufallo: "At this concert, Charles Ives' 'Chorale for Strings in Quartertones,' a 'lost' work reconstructed by Alan Stout from the third of the 'Quartertone Pieces for Two Pianos,' also had its New York Premiere; defined by two keyboards, the novel harmonies are easier to hear than from a string ensemble."

Tone Roads [W35]

B575 Bales, Richard and Charles Seeger. Tone Roads No. 1, for Chamber Orchestra (performable also as chamber music). New York: Peer International Corp., 1949. *Notes* 7, no. 3 (June 1950): 432-433.

Due to poor communication, *Notes* received two reviews of this publication. The Music Review Editor opted to publish both. Bales criticizes Ives's treatment of repeats which impede the arrival of "his hardy characters safely back home," and for "compounding the difficulties already presented the performers." He is also one of the few writers to point out that the work's duration as listed is more than twice it actual length, a frequent error of other Ives publications and most often left uncorrected. Seeger notes that "for 1911, both tonal and rhythmic dissonance is fantastically predated" and judges the work "an interesting score, but rough and rocky for players and conductor."

B576 Sabin, Robert. "A Charles Ives Work for Chamber Orchestra." *Musical America* 73, no. 1 (1 January 1953): 24.

Enthusiastic review of the first publication of *Tone Roads No. 3* by Southern Music Publishing Corp. Sabin writes that "the bristling rhythmic complexities, the wildly dissonant harmonies, and the wonderful imagination for new sonorities are all characteristic of

Ives." While observing that much of the trio looks "fascinatingly strange and impossible on paper," he expresses his confidence that "such seeming difficulties will work in performance."

Chromâtimelôdtune[W37]
See also: **W57**

B577   Kirkpatrick, John, Chair., with Gunther Schuller, Gerard Schwarz, and Kenneth Singleton. "Three Realizations of *Chromâtimelôdtune*." In *An Ives Celebration: Panels and Papers of the Ives Centennial Festival-Conference,* edited by H. Wiley Hitchcock and Vivian Perlis, pp. 87-109. Urbana: University of Illinois Press, 1977.

Informative and thought-provoking panel transcript in which Schuller, Schwarz, and Singleton discuss their respective realizations of Ives's sketches for *Chromâtimelôdtune* and their varying procedures and objectives when trying to interpret these ambiguous documents. Audience member H. Wiley Hitchcock emphasizes the problems in preparing critical editions for works of Ives that present a mulitiplicity of performance possibilities, and this led to additional audience comments on the difficulties in establishing a performance style for Ives. Chairman Kirkpatrick concluded by describing the contrasts between his and William Masselos's approach to performing Ives and describes "the one time" he heard Ives play the piano. Facsimiles of all four pages, Singleton's transcription of Ives's verbal comments, and excerpts from each realization are included with the panel transcript.

MUSIC FOR BAND
See also: **B549** and **B553**

B578   Brion, Keith, James Sinclair, and Jonathan Elkus. "Ives for Band." *Instrument* 29 (October 1974): 60-62.

"A listing and general description of both published works and those in preparation" of Ives's band music. The annotated entries are arranged in the following categories: Original Band Music, Lost Original Band Music, Band-Influenced Works, and Transcriptions. Includes chronology, publication information, durations, and band grade. Useful source for band leaders.

B579   Elkus, Jonathan. "Charles Ives and the American Band Tradition: A Centennial Tribute." Exeter: American Arts

Documentation Centre, University of Exeter, 1974. *See*: **B203,
B210, B213, B234,** and **B265**

After cutting his way through the morass of imprecise band
taxonomy, e.g., brass band, military band, full military band,
bugle band, cornet band, theater orchestra, Elkus goes on to
describe many subtleties of band traditions and march forms and
Ives's incorporations of them. Also in this informative survey
Elkus explains how "Ives fell right in with Sousa's practice" in his
Intercollegiate March as well as Ives's specific borrowings of formal
and melodic characteristics from Sousa's *The Liberty Bell* in Ives's
second college march, *Omega Lambda Chi.*

MISCELLANEOUS
Ivesiana

B580 Balanchine, George. "Ivesiana." *Center* 1, no. 5 (August-
September 1954). Reprinted as the first part of the "Ivesiana"
entry in *Balanchine's Complete Stories of the Great Ballets*, pp.
341-343 by Balanchine and Francis Mason. Garden City, N.Y.:
Doubleday & Co., Inc., 1977; revised and enlarged from 1954.
[The reprinted version offers a more detailed choreographic
description of the four constant movements and a capsule
summary of the various alterations in the remaining movements
during the 1955 and 1956 seasons].

The choreographer of *Ivesiana* describes his belated interest in
Ives one year prior to this ballet, when he came to view Ives's
music "with increasing respect and admiration." Balanchine is
more "occupied" with Ives's rhythms than his harmonies and
melodies, and in his choreography of six orchestral works, he
"attempted to project" his "new ideas of space in terms of [Ives's]
extensions in rhythms."

B581 Martin, John. "Ballet Presents 'Ivesiana' Suite." *The New York
Times*, September 15, 1954, page 38.

Review of Balanchine's City Center ballet, which premiered on the
previous Tuesday. Unlike Cowell (**B582**), Martin focuses on the
choreography rather than the musical features: "The result will
not please everybody, but it is honestly inspired and wonderfully
wrought....There is no line of continuity whatever, the unity of the
whole depending chiefly upon the marked effect of the composer
upon the choreographer and secondarily upon the latter's instinct
for formal arrangement of the several sections."

B582 Cowell, Henry. "Ivesiana." *The Musical Quarterly* 41, no. 1 (January 1955): 85-89.

Review of Balanchine's City Center ballet which incorporated six short Ives works: *Central Park in the Dark, Over the Pavements, In the Inn, Hallowe'en, The Unanswered Question,* and *In the Night.* Since several of these works were new to New York audiences, Cowell focuses on musical and programmatic features. Of Balanchine's choreography Cowell writes only that "the ballet is original and somewhat daring, even if not always very closely related to the music or to Ives's philosophies."

Variations on America (arr. Schuman)
See also: **W86**

B583 Harrison, Jay S. "The New York Music Scene." *Musical America* 84, no. 6 (July 1964): 35-36.

Review of the world premiere of William Schuman's arrangement of Ives's *Variations on America* for organ (1891), Richard Korn conducting the Orchestra of America. Harrison points out that Schuman heard the original version the previous year at the dedication of the new Philharmonic Hall organ. He considers the work "weak in invention and atmosphere" and concludes that he remains in the dark as to "why it absorbed Mr. Schuman's attention."

CHAMBER MUSIC

General

B584 Morton, Lawrence. "Diminuendo in the West." *Modern Music* 21, no. 4 (May-June 1944): 255-257.

Morton's concert review concludes with the announcement that the concert series, "Evenings on the Roof," would celebrate the seventieth birthdays of Schoenberg and Ives during the coming season. "Of Schönberg we are to hear all the piano works, some songs, and the second, third and fourth quartets. And we are to hear all of the Ives chamber music. Let us hope that other organizations will observe the anniversaries of these two masters whose influence has been so extensive and so beneficial."

B585 Maske, Ulrich. *Charles Ives in seiner Kammermusik für drei bis sechs Instrumente.* Kölner Beiträge zur Musik Forschung, volume 64. Regensburg: Gustav. Bosse, 1971. 164 pp. *See:* **B205**

A survey of Ives's musical style based on a study of twenty-one movements selected from a representative and wide variety of chamber works (1896-1913). The works include: *Largo for Violin, Clarinet, and Piano; Piano Trio; First and Second String Quartets; A Set of 3 Short Pieces; Largo Risoluto I and II; In Re Con Moto Et Al; Hallowe'en;* "Chorale" from *Three Quarter-Tone Pieces for Two Pianos* [**Keyboard, W84**]; *All the Way Around and Back; From the Steeples and the Mountains;* and *Chromâtimelôdtune.* Rather than discussing these works individually, Maske draws on them as needed to illustrate Ives's approach to various musical parameters: melody; harmony; meter, measure, and rhythm [sharply drawn distinctions]; dynamics; form; programmatic elements; and musical conception. Throughout Maske emphasizes Ives's stylistic diversity and the problems in generalizing about Ives's heterogeneous style.

B586 Bader, Yvette. "The Chamber Music of Charles Edward Ives." *The Music Review* 33, no. 4 (November 1972): 292-294.

Brief, cursory, and ultimately disappointing overview of the violin and piano sonatas, string quartets and several other of Ives's chamber works. Bader cites one or more unusual features of each work, two of which, *Tone Roads No. 1* and *Central Park in the Dark,* belong more appropriately with Ives's orchestral compositions. At the outset Bader refers to Ives's "nine-volume series of chamber music works," but does not offer a source (**B2**). She asks why Ives added words to his instrumental melodies and why he chose to "bastardize Italian" with his dynamic markings, but does not present a satisfactory answer to either question.

String Quartets [W41-W43]

B587 Rarig, Howard R., Jr. "The Second String Quartet of Charles Ives." M.M. thesis, Ithaca College, 1952. 123 pp.

Successful early study that focuses on the following musical parameters: melody, rhythm, modality, tonality, harmony, counterpoint, formal structure, and quotations. Using "Nearer, My God, to Thee" as an example, Rarig convincingly demonstrates that "a motivic fragment which has been carefully nurtured and subtly exposed through most of three movements eventually emerges as a principal theme of the quartet." He also shows that Ives's melodic lines follow "dodecaphonic principles" without functioning as twelve-tone rows, that Ives's coherent but unorthodox harmonic language "will prove the most elusive and exasperating to the inflexible analyst," and that Ives used borrowed material as a fundamental part of "a compositional plan." Abundant and substantial musical examples illustrate and support most of Rarig's observations. The list of works in his appendix follows the *International Cyclopedia of Music and Musicians*.

B588 Sapp, Allen. "String Quartet No. 2." *Notes* 12, no. 4 (June 1955): 489-492.

Review of the first publication of the *Second String Quartet* (Peer, 1954). Of the five publications for string quartet reviewed in this article (Jarnach, Lees, Rawsthorne, Denny, and Ives), "the Ives piece alone is problematical" particularly due to its "compulsive four-part counterpoint" which, according to Sapp, fails to establish "the sensitive treatment of the string quartet as a medium," a "favorable" quality shared for the most part by the other works under review. Sapp does acknowledge that "Ives' music is always very carefully made" and that "a common error confuses the rhetorical difficulties mentioned above with careless technique." His final judgment is ambiguous: "In a word the Quartet is Ives at his best and at his most exasperating."

B589 Schonberg, Harold C. Review of the Premiere Performance of Ives's *First String Quartet*, April 24, 1957, Museum of Modern Art, New York City, Kohon String Quartet. *The New York Times*, April

25, 1957, page 35 [excerpt taken from *American Composers Alliance Bulletin* 6, no. 1 (1957): 23]. *See:* **W41a**

"For Ives, this is quite a conservative piece of music. Much of it consists almost of white-key harmony, and the first movement has a Haydnesque simplicity. But ever present is a style that is unmistakably American....Despite some awkward writing, this is a work of pronounced individuality and, in many sections, real beauty."

B590   Trimble, Lester.   Review of the Premiere Performance of Ives's *First String Quartet,* April 24, 1957, Museum of Modern Art, New York City, Kohon String Quartet. *New York Herald Tribune,* April 25, 1957, page 18 [excerpt taken from *American Composers Alliance Bulletin* 6, no. 1 (1957): 23-24]. *See:* **W41a**

"To this listener, the Ives provided the evening's freshest and most intriguing moments. Like many of that composer's works, it was full of little tunes, seemingly half quoted from such songs as 'Bringing in the Sheaves,' surprising harmonic twists, and a general sense of devil-may-care. The second movement, most closely knit of the three, displayed an impressive amount of emotional tension despite its formal vagaries. At no time was the play of fancy less than compelling..."

B591   Ober, William B.   Jacket notes to Ives String Quartets. VOX STDL 501.120 [1964].

Ober in his introductory remarks cites various professional and artistic parallels between Ives and the insurance-executive poet, Wallace Stevens; later he compares Ives's handling of borrowed material in the *Second Quartet* to T. S. Eliot's procedure in *The Waste Land.* These notes, albeit brief, provide a good introduction to the genesis and general formal, tonal, and melodic features of both quartets, and, in the case of the *Second Quartet,* a clear explication of its programmatic content. Nevertheless, Ober attributes several classical references incorrectly to the third movement rather than the second movement of the *Second Quartet.* He also neglects to mention that Ives bases the third movement of the *First Quartet* on "Nettleton" or that Ives proclaims "Westminster Chimes" in the *Second Quartet* finale.

B592   Strongin, Theodore.   "Recordings: How Not to Play Ives." *The New York Times,* November 19, 1967, section 2, page 22.

Review of Juilliard String Quartet recording of Ives's *String Quartets Nos. 1 and 2* **(D38)**. Strongin finds fault with both performances: "The Juilliard treats the first as if it were Haydn at his most mellifluous and the second, Bartók at his most bravura. Neither treatment quite fits...In short, the Juilliard does ample justice to the beauty of Ives's music, but it leaves out his special twang." He is still harsher in his assessment of the 1964 performances by the Kohon String Quartet (reissued in 1967 on Turnabout TV 341-575): "The super-singing style the Kohons adopt dampens both quartets." Despite its poor recording quality, Strongin unreservedly prefers the 1947 Walden Quartet recording of the Ives *Second Quartet* (reissued in 1967) (**D39**), an "almost" beautiful performance that provides the necessary combination of "twang" and "nostalgia."

B593 Daniel, Oliver. "Ives Is A Four-Letter Word." *The Saturday Review* 51, no. 21 (25 May 1968): 59.

Review of all available recordings of the Ives string quartets, two versions of the first (Kohon and Juilliard [**D38**]) and three versions of the second (Kohon, Juilliard [**D38**], and Walden [**D39**]). Daniel favors the "slower...and tonally more rewarding" Juilliard performance of the *First Quartet*, but prefers the "rougher" Kohon interpretation to the Juilliard and the Walden version best of all for the *Second Quartet*. He also makes a good case that Ives chose to delete the opening fugal movement from the *First Quartet*, and that Kirkpatrick was misguided in his successful effort to have it published with the quartet in 1961. Daniel concludes that "if Ives had wanted it there, he would not have removed it and used it as the slow movement of his Fourth Symphony."

B594 Budde, Elmar. "Anmerkungen zum Streichquartett Nr. 2 von Charles E. Ives." In *Bericht über den internationalen musikwissenshaftlichen Kongress Bonn 1970*, edited by Carl Dahlhaus et. al., pp. 303-307. Kassel: Bärenreiter, 1971.

A stylistic overview of the first movement ("Discussions") of Ives's *Second Quartet*. Throughout, Budde emphasizes the lack of connections "im traditionellen Sinne" ("in the traditional sense"), but he nevertheless points out how Ives handles his musical figures with untraditional good sense. He balances general remarks about Ives's stylistic flexibility and need for performance liberties with a detailed examination of the first sixteen measures of the movement.

B595 Schermer, Richard. "The Aesthetics of Charles Ives in Relation to His 'String Quartet No. 2.'" M.A. thesis, California State University, Fullerton, 1980. 166 pp.

Schermer overstates the importance of Transcendentalism as expressed in Ives's *Essays* (**B660**) as "representative of his aesthetic of music in general." As a result, many of his analogies between Transcendentalism and the aesthetic of the *Second Quartet* seem forced. Similarly, Schermer's explanation of how Ives translates his political credo from *The Majority* musically in the quartet fails to convince, and in two long chapters on Ives's musical humor, we really do not learn as much about what is funny in Ives or the *Second Quartet* as we learn in a single paragraph of Ober's jacket notes. *See*: **B591**

Too often Schermer fails to follow through with the kind of explanations that such a study requires. When he writes, for example, that Ives selected Civil War tunes as borrowed material for musical reasons "related to the intervallic, motivic, and rhythmic structure of the work," we never learn how Ives accomplishes this. Despite these limitations, Schermer does offer some interesting observations, such as his remark that Ives "was writing a raison d'être for his own music, using New England transcendentalism as a cornerstone"; his inclusion of complete manuscript facsimiles in an appendix is also a valuable addition.

B596 Cantrick, Susan Birdsall. "Charles Ives's 'String Quartet No. 2': An Analysis and Evaluation." M.M. thesis, Peabody Institute of the Johns Hopkins University, Peabody Conservatory of Music, 1983. 137 pp.

The body of this highly recommended essay consists of an amply-illustrated analysis of the major technical and stylistic issues in each movement. In a following evaluative chapter Cantrick summarizes the analysis and discusses in more detail two central topics, "Stylistic Heterogeneity as an Anomalous Procedure," and "Quotation as a Component of Stylistic Heterogeneity." She succeeds in her objective to discover "the subtler connections between Ives's programmatic conception and his compositional processes," and unlike most studies, Cantrick explores the aesthetic significance of Ives's technical innovations and heterogeneous style thoughtfully and imaginatively.

Appendixes include "A Tentative Comparison of Ives's Autograph Pencil Sketch With the Published Small Score (Peer International Corporation, 1954) by John Kirkpatrick (June 1958)," "Errata Remaining in the 'Corrected' Reprint (Peer 1970) by John

Kirkpatrick (1973)," an "Addenda to John Kirkpatrick's 1973 List
of Errata by Susan Cantrick," and "Sample Pages from the
Library of Congress' Manuscript Photocopy" (**B3**).

MUSIC FOR VARIOUS COMBINATIONS

Largo for Violin,
Clarinet, and Piano [W46]

B597 Persichetti, Vincent. "Largo, for Violin, Clarinet, Piano."
Southern Music Publishing Co., 1953. *Notes* 11, no. 6 (December
1953): 157.

Review of the first publication of this work. Persichetti writes:
"The Ives Largo is one of the composer's better integrated works.
It has musical inevitability and serious intentions. The
unexpected harmonic contrasts and sudden melodic turns
(written in 1901) fall within the musical scope of the average
performer."

Trio for Violin, Cello, and Piano [W49]

B598 Ulrich, Homer. "Trio, for Violin, Cello, Piano." *Notes* 13, no. 3
(June 1956): 527.

Sarcastic review of the Peer score (published in 1955). Ulrich
points out the "faulty" violin and cello parts, which "lack some of
the expressive indications called for in the piano score." Perhaps
for the benefit of those "performers and listeners who subscribe to
the Ives legend, Ulrich concludes his review with the following
jab: "In both parts [violin and cello] the Scherzo's page turn is
quite impossible; it comes in the middle of a movement that
contains scarcely a measure's rest. Perhaps it would do just as
well to play the page twice instead of turning it; I don't believe
that anyone would notice."

B599 Cohn, Arthur. "Decca's Nieuw Amsterdam Trio." *The American
Record Guide* 33, no. 2 (October 1966): 142-143.

Review of "a significant and memorable" Nieuw Amsterdam Trio
recording (Decca DL-10126) of the Ives *Trio*. In contrast to the
Ulrich review (**B598**), Cohn considers this work of Ives "one of his
finest pieces, especially in its outer movements and more
especially the initial division." The "freed tonality" generated by
Ives's "acute independence" of melodic lines prompts Cohn to
describe the first movement as "one that can be more readily

typed Expressionistic than any other movement in the Ives corpus." He comments only briefly on the "magnificently prepared" debut performance.

B600 Harvin, Laurence E. "The Piano Trio from the Performer's Viewpoint with Particular Attention Given to the Ives Trio." D.M.A. dissertation, Florida State University, 1972. 25 pp.

Rudimentary performance suggestions for piano trios in general and the Ives *Trio* in particular. The brevity of this "dissertation" is matched only by its superficiality.

Hallowe'en [W51]

B601 Seeger, Charles. "Hallowe'en, from 'Three Outdoor Scenes,' for 2 violins, viola, cello, piano." Bomart Music Publications, 1949. *Notes* 7, no. 3 (June 1950): 432.

In this single paragraph review Seeger quotes from Ives's preface to *Hallowe'en* and paraphrases Ives's directions for designated combinations of players and their respective dynamic levels on each of the four successive musical repetitions.

Largo Risoluto Nos. 1 and 2 [W52-W53]

B602 T.M.S. "Kohon Group Ends Town Hall Series." *The New York Times*, February 20, 1965, page 16. *See*: **W52a**

Review of the premiere performance of *Largo Risoluto Nos. 1 and 2* and *Scherzo for String Quartet*, performed at Town Hall, February 19, by the Kohon String Quartet. "Both largos really were resolute in Ives's bold way of making a collage with scraps of hymnlike and popular tunes set against independent sustained background elements. The Scherzo was energetic, dissonant and very free in rhythm and in the relationship of voices."

A Set of Three Short Pieces [W55]
No. 2 Scherzo "Holding Your Own," for String Quartet
See: **Largo Risoluto Nos. 1 and 2**

SONATAS FOR VIOLIN AND PIANO [W58-W63]

B603 Tyron, Winthrop. "'Freischutz' at the Metropolitan--Other Music of a New York Week." *Christian Science Monitor*, March 24, 1924, page 10 [designated by the caption heading, "Business Man Who Composes," in **B8**]. *See*: **W60a**

Review of the March 18 premiere of the *Second Violin Sonata* performed by Jerome Goldstein (violin) and Rex Tillson (piano) at Aeolian Hall. Ives defends the right of "a downtown New Yorker" businessman to compose when he writes that he does not know, "Why the pavement is not as much a part of the soil as the pasture, nor why a person should not meditate sonatas as appropriately in a Wall Street office as in a New Hampshire kitchen." Tyron concludes his brief remarks as follows: "The several divisions seemed to me to be built largely out of New England ballad and sacred tune material, some serious, others trivial, and all characteristic of the period under contemplation."

B604 "Concerts for the Month: Jerome Goldstein," *Musical Advance,* April, 1924, pp. [17]-[18]; excerpted in **B215**. *See:* **W60a**

Review of the March 18 premiere of the *Second Violin Sonata.* Ives "has brought back a musical 'History of New England.' In it are pages of revival meetings, Boston Tea Parties, boiled dinners, and those innumerable inrushes of the soul which Emerson received--or said he did."

B605 "Goldstein Completes 'Modernist' Recital At Aeolian Hall." *New York Herald Tribune,* March 19, 1924, page 15. *See:* **W60a**

Review of Ives's *Violin Sonata No. 2* premiere in which "the laurels of the occasion seemed to belong to Pizzetti" [also on the program was the "uneven" *Sonata No. 2* by Milhaud]. The reviewer describes the Ives as "to a considerable extent, program music, of what might be called an advanced French post-romantic type, but with a certain American flavor."

B606 Perkins, Francis D. "Music." *New York Herald Tribune,* January 15, 1940, page 9. *See:* **W63a**

Review of the premiere of the *Fourth Violin Sonata,* January 14, at New York's Museum of Modern Art, Eudice Shapiro (violin) and Irene Jacobi (pianist). "Mr. Ives's work, which takes about eleven minutes to play, does not offer a detailed program to supplement the suggestions of its title, but some general reflection of the atmosphere which this implies can be found in the melodic character of the musical ideas, whose treatment, while not conventional, is consonant with their prevailing vein."

B607 Simon Robert A. "Musical Events: Plenty Going On." *The New Yorker* 18, no. 3 (7 March 1942): 47. *See:* **W63b**

Review of the Carnegie Hall performance of Ives's *Fourth Violin Sonata*, February 25, Joseph Szigeti (violin) and Andor Foldes (piano). "The sonata, with its reminiscences of hymn tunes, has a genial sturdiness and is set forth in terms of fiddling rather than violinism...The people liked the sonata, and they might have raised even more of a rumpus over it if it hadn't had such an abrupt ending."

B608 Morton, Lawrence. "Western Evenings with Ives." *Modern Music* 22, no. 5 (May-June 1945): 186-188. *See:* **W62b**

Review of an "Evenings on the Roof" concert, in which audiences heard Ives's *Third Violin Sonata* "painstakingly deciphered and marvelously played by Sol Babitz (violin) and Ingolf Dahl (piano)." Morton continues: "It is a monumental work, grandly conceived in the full ripeness of the composer's spirit....It is a real tussle for the performers, but joyous and exhilarating."

B609 Flanagan, William. "Two Violin Sonatas." *Musical America* 71, no. 12 (October 1951): 31.

Review of the first publication of the *Second Violin Sonata* (G. Schirmer, 1951) and the *Third* (New Music, 1951), one short paragraph for each. Flanagan writes that "The Revival" finale of the *Second Sonata* "with its hymnodic elements and frenzied, drone-like climax, presents Ives at his most imaginative and evocative," and that the final *Adagio* of the *Third Sonata* is "elegiac in character and reminiscent of the finest pages of the composer's Concord Sonata."

B610 Kohs, Ellis B. "Violin Sonata No. 2." *Notes* 9, no. 2 (March 1952): 329-330.

Review of the first publication of the *Second Sonata* (G. Schirmer, 1951). Kohs writes: "Highly original in form, it has that special blend of the plain, the homespun, and the unexpected, the diatonic hymn tune and chromatically dissonant harmony which are the stamp of this still highly controversial figure...The closing pages of the finale have a color and fervor that are still, after forty years, fresh and tingling."

B611 Keys, Ivor. "Sonata No. 3." *Music & Letters* 33, no. 1 (January 1952): 91-92.

Keys devotes one paragraph of his review of recently published American compositions to Ives's *Third Violin Sonata* (New Music, 1951). Despite "chromatic improvisations which slow down the music and blur its outlines," Keys regards Ives as "an important composer with a big technique," who possesses "a capacity for the memorable and beautiful lyrical phrase," and a composer whose originality is "beyond a doubt." He also mentions the verse and refrain form of the first movement and the jazzy second movement with its instruction to "repeat only if ragged."

B612 Cowell, Henry. "Violin Sonatas Nos. 1 and 3." *The Musical Quarterly* 39, no. 4 (April 1953): 323-325.

Review of the recording of *Sonatas Nos. 1 and 3* with Joan Field (violin) and Leopold Mittman (piano) (Lyrichord LL 17). Cowell writes: "What is perhaps less well known about Ives is that a large portion of his music sounds melodious and understandable to general auditors now, and that they are apt to find it especially moving. To this category belong the present sonatas. They sound unconventional and contain many surprises, but they do not sound 'modernistic.'"

Cowell touches on just a few points for each sonata, the tonality and treatment of quotation in the *First Sonata*, the melodic independence between the violin and piano and the jazz-oriented middle movement in the *Third Sonata*. In a brief evaluation of the performance Cowell praises Fields's "mastery and warmth," and thinks that "the excellent performance is marred only by too much nuance of the sort reserved for late 19th-century European music."

B613 "Violin Sonata No. 1." *Musical Courier* 148, no. 2 (September 1953): 33.

Review of the *First Violin Sonata* (Peer, 1953). "It is a most original composition with a rhapsodic flow of ideas, and rare harmonic effects....There is particularly difficult writing for the pianist, while the violin part is more grateful....It presents a formidable task for the artists, but would be interesting to a contemporary music audience."

B614 Friedheim, Philip. "Violin Sonata No. 1." *Notes* 11, no. 1 (December 1953): 156.

Review of the *First Violin Sonata* (Peer, 1953). "The score makes frequent use of rhythmic devices well ahead of their time, including shifting metrical and rhythmic groupings, as well as intricate cross rhythms....But the unique character of the music arises from the unusual method of handling familiar American melodies. With the exception of the very clear setting of

'Watchman, Tell Us of the Night,' Ives never quotes these themes directly. Instead, his melodic lines are asymmetrical and full of sudden key changes. They seem designed merely to suggest phrases from well-known melodies."

B615 Harrison, Lou. Jacket notes for *Sonatas for Violin and Piano*, by Charles Ives. Mercury MG-50096 [1956]; reissued on Philips World Series Stereo/PHC 2-002 [1966].

In addition to providing brief but insightful program notes for each of the standard four sonatas, Harrison offers his views on the distinctions between folk and popular music, ("folk music always has a system of modes which is the cultural possession of all and the font of musical expression; whereas a popular music is always modeled on the techniques of cultivated music current or just slightly before its time"); and what makes Ives "the National First Composer," ("by means of a technique Ives soundly set up the genre of National Music at a cultivated level").

Harrison also identifies recurring thematic material and formal devices and presents numerous general stylistic observations, such as the importance of "heterophonic polyphony" ("a freeing of melodic lines from any formal prearrangement as to the kind of chords their several junctures should make") in Ives's work.

B616 Schonberg, Harold C. "Records: Ives. The Four Violin Sonatas Played by Drurian." *The New York Times*, July 15, 1956, section 2, page 8.

Review of Drurian/Simms recording of the Violin Sonatas (Mercury MG-50096). Schonberg praises the performances of Drurian, who "approaches the music with the determination not only to outline the notes but also to make them sing" and Simms, "who has the ungrateful task of reproducing some wild keyboard writing." About Ives Schonberg writes that "the more one hears his music the more one realizes that he was one of the originals of composition," and predicts that, because of Ives's formidable performance "hurdles," his music "will probably never be popular or, for that matter, very often played."

B617 Perkins, Laurence. "The Sonatas for Violin and Piano by Charles Ives." M.M. thesis, Eastman School of Music of the University of Rochester, 1961. 174 pp.

A survey with an abundance of descriptive statistical generalities in chapters on form, melody, tonality and harmony, and rhythm (e.g., that out of 3000 tertian chords only 6.7% contain added

harmonic tones). Richly illustrated with 151 musical examples
and an appendix that includes "pre-existent melodies quoted and
other important themes" [unfortuanately Perkins uses
inconvenient arbitrary abbreviations for these themes]. Perkins
notes several errors in the published editions and is convincing in
his contention that Ives quotes "Tell Me the Old Old Story" in the
first movement of the *Fourth Sonata* rather than the similar "Work
for the Night is Coming" designated by Ives [and Henderson] as
the principal melodic source for this movement. Conclusions
stated in the abstract as well as throughout the thesis are
descriptive rather than analytical, but they provide a useful
introduction to this body of work.

B618   Carlson, Paul B. "An Historical Background and Stylistic
       Analysis of Three Twentieth Century Compositions for Violin and
       Piano," pp. 44-68. D.M.A. dissertation, University of Missouri at
       Kansas City, 1964.

       Historical background and stylistic analysis of Stravinsky's *Duo
       Concertant*, Webern's *Four Pieces*, Op. 7, and Ives's *Second Violin
       Sonata*. In the first of two chapters devoted to Ives, Carlson
       presents a biographical sketch, which includes an interesting
       analogy between George Ives's "humanophone" and "the
       pointillistic technique of Anton Webern where a row is distributed
       among various instruments." In his second chapter he provides a
       conventional movement-by-movement descriptive analysis of the
       Second Sonata that is almost exclusively thematic and harmonic.

B619   Rosen, Lee Cyril. "The Violin Sonatas of Charles Ives and the
       Hymn." B.M. paper, University of Illinois, 1965. 97 pp.

       An analytical survey of the four violin sonatas with an emphasis
       on the thematic materials employed in the ten movements (out of
       twelve) derived from hymn tunes. The format is unusual in that
       Rosen treats the thematic materials in the first chapter without
       reference to their hymn roots. Particularly useful are Rosen's
       observations regarding the various degrees of thematic
       interconnectedness between the first and third movements of
       each sonata, and cites evidence favoring a view that these works
       form "some type of tetralogy."

       Rosen concludes that "Ives's use of the hymn goes far beyond
       quotation and motivic reliance," in fact, that "in several instances,
       whole movement organization is based on the hymn." In addition
       to the forty-eight musical illustrations in the main text,
       appendixes are added to show the differences between the

original hymns and Ives's paraphrases of all the sonatas, and the "manipulations" of the central motive of the *Third Sonata* [first movement].

B620 Jacobson, Bernard. "Zukovsky and Kalish Play Ives." *High Fidelity/ Musical America* 16, no. 4 (April 1966): 152. *See:* **W59d**

Review of a Carnegie Hall concert, January 24, in which Paul Zukofsky (violin) and Gilbert Kalish (piano) performed the four violin sonatas. Jacobson praises Ives's "wide expressive range" but criticizes Zukovsky's lack of tonal variety and non-communicative stage presence in his performance of "these rewarding works."

B621 Gratovich, Eugene. "The Sonatas for Violin and Piano by Charles Ives: A Critical Commentary and Concordance of the Printed Editions and the Autographs and Manuscripts of the Yale Ives Collection." D.M.A. dissertation, Boston University School of Fine and Applied Arts, 1968. 354 pp.

Gratovich presents a detailed critical commentary and concordance between the printed editions of the standard four violin sonatas and all extant manuscripts (sketches, patches, copyists copies). His short "introduction to the sources," particularly his description of Ives's calligraphy is an informative summary of Ives's methods and idiosyncracies. For each sonata Gratovich also includes brief but informative sections entitled "discussion and description of sources," and "supplementary considerations."

Appendix A, autograph facsimiles of the *Allegro moderato* from the *Pre-First Sonata* and *Sonatas Nos. 1-3*, and a lithograph facsimile of the *Fourth Sonata* (pages 207-329), are "not microfilmed at the request of the author." Appendixes B-E contain "Extracts from Ives's Opinions on Unusual Chord Spellings," "List of Hymns and Secular Music Quoted in the Violin Sonatas, transcriptions of George Ives's *Fugue No. 4 in Bb,* and Ira Sankey's "There'll Be No Dark Valley," and a transcript of a lecture-demonstration, in which Gratovich summarizes the main content of his dissertation and demonstrates the discrepancies between sources with well-chosen examples. An indispensable source for anyone interested in performing these sonatas.

B622 Walsh, Stephen. "Ives' Violin Sonatas." *Music and Musicians* 16, no. 10 (June 1968): 45. *See:* **W59e**

Review of a March 13 performance of the four violin sonatas "slightly overplayed" by Esther Glazer (violin) and Easley Blackwood (piano). Walsh is unsympathetic to these works and criticizes piano passages, "which meander a great deal," and the generally "stilted and heavy" violin lines, as well as Ives's "dangerous" over-use of hymn tunes, "the despairing gesture of a man who has lost all inspiration of his own."

B623   Echols, Paul. Jacket notes to *Sonatas for Violin and Piano* (Zukofsky and Kalish). Nonesuch HB-73025 [1974] **(D35)**.

Useful background material on the "curious history" and intertwining musical relationship of the four violin sonatas and the *Largo* from the *Pre-First Sonata* (adapted by Ives as the *Largo for Violin, Clarinet, and Piano* and published by Southern Music, 1953). The notes contain liberal quotations from Ives's program notes to *Sonatas Nos. 1, 3, and 4* and other substantial citations from the Ives's *Essays* **(B660)** and *Memos* **(B378)**.

B624   Gratovich, Eugene. "The Violin Sonatas." *Music Educator's Journal* 61, no. 2 (October 1974): 58-63; reprinted almost verbatim in "The Violin Sonatas of Charles E. Ives." *The Strad* 85 (December 1974): 471+.

Gratovich introduces his subject by summarizing the compositional history of the four completed violin sonatas and the three unfinished sonatas, excerpted from the lecture found in Appendix E of his dissertation **(B621)**. The bulk of the article is a movement-by-movement thematic (and occasionally harmonic) description of *Sonatas Nos. 1-4*. The brief comments include a well-integrated listing of borrowed materials and musical illustrations of several motives from *Sonatas Nos. 2 and 4*.

B625   McCandless, William Edgar. "Cantus Firmus Techniques in Selected Instrumental Compositions, 1910-1960," pp. 155-177. Ph.D. dissertation, Indiana University, 1974.

McCandless devotes one chapter to an analysis of Ives's *Violin Sonata No. 4*. He describes how Ives's *cantus firmus* (i.e., borrowed melody) technique departs from selected works by Bartók, Berg, Copland, Hindemith, and Stravinsky but finds a greater parallel between Ives and Debussy with their shared predilection for melodic fragmentation, ostinato accompaniments, and their "thickening of a melodic line into a chord stream." Although the analysis is primarily thematic, McCandless does not neglect to integrate form and harmony. Within a short chapter he offers a number of astute observations on Ives's purposeful handling of borrowed material, such as the following: "Ives always begins the motive [of "Work Song"] on the mediant rather than the dominant," thus foreshadowing "Beautiful River."

B626 Rangell, Andrew Reed. "The Violin-Piano Sonatas of Charles Ives." Ph.D. dissertation, The Juilliard School, 1976. 93 pp.

One might dispute his opening claim that the violin sonatas "incorporate a body of popular musical materials in a density not equalled in Ives' other genres," but Rangell proves faithful to his "foremost concern," i.e., "the nature of this incorporation." Rangell for the most part presents clear descriptive analyses and succeeds in providing an aesthetic framework for each movement, but the Lilliputian bibliography of one item does not allow his work to build on past scholarship.

Considering that the Kirkpatrick *Catalogue* (**B7**) constitutes Rangell's sole excursion into the secondary literature, it is disconcerting that, when discussing the first movement of the *First Sonata*, he contradicts or simply overlooks Kirkpatrick (and others) when he denies any "hymn tune or other popular musical material as its generative and emotional source." *See*: **B125** and **B617-618**.

B627 Mandel, Alan, Chairman, Nancy Mandel, Eugene Gratovich, Regis Benoit, Daniel Stepner, and John Kirkpatrick. "On Performing the Violin Sonatas." Panel discussion on performance problems in Ives's music at the Ives Centennial Conference, 1974. In *An Ives Celebration*, ed., H. Wiley Hitchcock and Vivian Perlis, pp. 127-140. Urbana: University of Illinois Press, 1977.

Enlightening discussion by a panel composed of three violin and piano teams that have performed the Ives violin sonatas. Particularly valuable are the various suggested solutions to difficult performance issues and the discussions (in one case including a facsimile of a problematic passage from the *Second Sonata* autograph) of certain passages where the published editions are inaccurate or misleading. Many of the issues raised, such as whether or not to include the optional auxiliary "piano drumming" in the *Second Sonata* or how to respond to Ives's call for interpretative freedom, are relevant to prospective performers of any Ives genre.

B628 Gabbi, Marianna Paone. "Charles Ives: The Violin Sonatas, A Lecture Recital." D.M.A. dissertation, North Texas State University, 1978. 25 pp.

In this printed lecture portion of a lecture-recital Gabbi presents a superficial account of Ives's violin sonatas. In her discussion of the *Second Sonata*, she fails to grasp the significance of the first movement's title, "Autumn." Less excusably, although hymn sources form a crucial component of each sonata, Gabbi omits all references to this phenomenon.

B629 Gratovich, Eugene. "Ives Second Violin Sonata: Performance Alternatives." *American String Teacher* 29, no. 2 (1979): 46-49.

An introduction to the sources of Ives's *Second Violin Sonata* and a discussion of various errors and inadequacies in the published edition (G. Schirmer, 1951). Gratovich demonstrates that Ives's autograph, which was not consulted in the preparation of the Schirmer edition, can facilitate a richer and more accurate representation of Ives's intentions. Although he includes some descriptive analysis, Gratovich focuses on how the sources clarify the meaning of specific problematic passages. In his concluding remarks he calls for a new approach to Ives editions: "Ideally, a suitable performance edition of this sonata should offer alternate 'ossia' versions containing Ives' directions and all the music so that the performer could arrive at his own version." [Lou Harrison offers a related suggestion in **B254**.]

B630 Bonham, Robert John. "Some Common Aesthetic Tendencies Manifested in Examples of Pioneer American Cabins and Old Harp Music and in Selected Works of H. H. Richardson and Charles E. Ives." Ph.D. dissertation, Ohio University, 1981. 380 pp.

Bonham explores two unique early American cultural developments, log cabins and shape-note hymnody, as possible foundations for the highly sophisticated architecture of Henry Hobson Richardson (1838-1886) and Ives's equally sophisticated use of musical resources "drawn from indigenous materials." In his imaginative treatment of these arts Bonham asks, "Was there something specifically American in the frontier experience which subsequently became an important (though largely unseen) continuing force, playing a role in modifying adopted traditions?" He uses the violin sonatas as a representative genre to determine "whether a significant parallel exists between the features of his work and those of the early vernacular art which can serve as a means of illuminating a common American quality in each."

B631   Freed, Richard. "A Superb New Set of Charles Ives's Violin/Piano Sonatas from Authoritative Performers of His Music." *Stereo Review* 47 (November 1982): 70-71.

Review of the Stepner/Kirkpatrick recording (**D44**) of the four standard violin sonatas and the premiere recording of the *Fifth Sonata*, "which actually consists of violin-and piano versions of three of the four orchestral pieces [excluding *The Fourth of July*] that Ives gathered together as his *Holidays* Symphony." Freed compares these recordings favorably with the Zukovsky/Kalish performances (**D35**): "Throughout the new set the feeling for the music seems a bit freer and folksier, with that engaging spontaneity, as well as cragginess, that most of us tend to identify as 'Ivesian.'" Freed also finds the Stepner/Kirkpatrick performances "slightly more convincing than those on Nonesuch," but recommends that "true Ivesians" acquire both pairings, "precisely because of the differences between them."

B632   Kirkpatrick, John. Jacket notes to Charles Ives's *Five Violin Sonatas*. Music Masters 20056/57 [1982] (**D44**).

Brief but authoritative biographical essay and short descriptions of each sonata accompanied by Ives's program notes. The longest description is appropriately reserved for the premiere item,the *Fifth Violin Sonata* (1909-11?) based on three of the four *New England Holidays*. Kirkpatrick provides informative background on the genesis of this work and explains how *Decoration Day*, "the only complete violin *Holiday*," began as a work for violin and piano before it was arranged for orchestra.

KEYBOARD

Piano Works (General)
See also: **B50** and **B286**

B633 Cowell, Henry. "Current Chronicle." *The Musical Quarterly* 35, no. 3 (July 1949): 458-462.

After a long paragraph on the *First Piano Sonata*, Cowell focuses on the *Three-Page Sonata*. Writing to offset criticisms of Ives's formal weaknesses, Cowell is eager to demonstrate that in this work "Ives's sense of interval development is very keen."

B634 Sykes, James. "Program Notes on the Shorter Piano Pieces of Charles Ives." Jacket notes for "The Short Piano Pieces of Charles Ives," Folkways FM 3348 [1964] (**D53**).

In these notes to a recording that includes the first commercially released performances of *The Anti-Abolitionist Riots*, *Study No. 22*, *Some Southpaw Pitching*, and *The Varied Air with Protests*, Sykes offers brief descriptive comments, and, for the last work cited, an explanation of Ives's "early example of free 'twelve-tone technique.'"

B635 Frankenstein, Alfred. "The Complete Piano Works--Old Friends and Fresh Discoveries." *High Fidelity/Musical America* 18, no. 6 (June 1968): 81.

Review of Mandel's recording of the "complete" piano music (**D48**). Because "Mr. Mandel is the first pianist to have mastered all, or even any considerable amount, of the music of Ives in addition to the sonatas," Frankenstein considers him "the first great Ives keyboard player." Furthermore, Mandel more than compensates for being "the world's worst editor," when he performs the great sonatas and creates order out of Ives's "primeval chaos of notes" in the great sonatas to a "degree unprecedented" in the reviewer's experience.

B636 Salzman, Eric. "The Piano Music of Charles Ives." *HiFi/Stereo Review* 21, no. 2 (August 1968): 72-73.

Review of Mandel's recording of the "complete" piano music, "one of the major bodies of twentieth-century piano music" (**D48**). Salzman briefly praises the high performance level throughout the set and focuses on Mandel's achievement in digging out the numerous smaller works, "among Ives' most imaginative, stirring, and successful pieces," and recording them for the first time. Salzman's only major complaint is reserved for Mandel's vague program notes.

B637 Cohn, Arthur. "Alan Mandel Plays All Twenty-Seven of the Piano Works of Ives." *The American Record Guide* 35, no. 7 (March 1969): 548-549.

In this review of **D48** Cohn praises Mandel's technique and his "sensitivity that perfectly projects the Ivesian spirituality." He also offers strong positive evaluations of the three works that Ives chose to call a sonata. For Cohn the *"Concord" Sonata* "has a scope of concentrated expressiveness that is the equal of the late Beethoven Piano Sonatas." He also joins Salzman (**B636**) in deploring Mandel's confusing program notes, and writes of the "urgent need" for a comprehensive study of Ives's music.

B638 Wuellner, Guy S. "The Smaller Piano Works of Charles Ives." *The American Music Teacher* 22, no. 5 (1973): 14-16.

A summary of formal and stylistic features in five solo piano works that had been published by 1973 (*Three-Page Sonata, Some Southpaw Pitching, The Anti-Abolitionist Riots, Study No. 22,* and *Three Protests*) and *Three Quarter-Tone Pieces* for two pianos. For the majority of pianists who are unable to negotiate the two large piano sonatas, Wuellner suggests these shorter works as an alternative and asserts that they "can be successfully performed by talented piano students of college age."

B639 Burk, James M. "Ives Innovations in Piano Music." *Clavier* 13, no. 7 (1974): 14-16.

An introductory survey of Ives's numerous innovations in the seven piano works then in print. Burk cites briefly unusual harmonic features such as bitonality and tone clusters, Ives's departure from formal, metrical, and melodic norms, and the less-often considered innovations of marginalia, memos, and more substantial philosophical accompaniments. *See:* **B641**

B640 McCrae, Elizabeth. "The Piano Music." *Music Educator's Journal* 61, no. 2 (October 1974): 53-57.

McCrae briefly surveys Ives's utilization of and departure from 19th-century piano figuration, his idiosyncratic treatment of ragtime, his practice of using additional instruments, and his prevalence for motivic development and cyclic form. At the outset

McCrae suggests that the absence of any easy solo piano compositions may make it advisable for aspiring Ives piano enthusiasts to begin by playing the accompaniments to the *114 Songs*. The largest proportion of the article consists of musical illustrations.

B641 Hinson, Maurice. "The Solo Piano Music of Charles Ives (1874-1954)." *The Piano Quarterly* 23, no. 88 (1974-1975): 32-35.

Descriptive summaries of the seven works in print as of 1974, the three sonatas, *The Anti-Abolitionist Riots*, *Some Southpaw Pitching*, *Study No. 22*, and *Three Protests* (i.e., *Varied Air with Variations*). Hinson's summary of this last mentioned work includes excerpts from Ives's marginalia. The comments here, though brief, are far more substantial and informative than those of the author's *Guide to the Pianist's Repertoire*, edited by Irwin Freundlich. Bloomington and London: Indiana University Press, 1973; revised and enlarged, 1987.

B642 Mandel, Alan. "Charles Ives's Music for the Piano." In *Student Musicologists at Minnesota* 6 (1975-1976): 201-217.

The title of this article is misleading, since Mandel focuses almost entirely on the studies, take-offs, and other short piano works rather than the large sonatas. Most of the summary descriptions of these works are taken without alteration from his notes to "The Complete Piano Music" [1968] (**B48**), but Mandel has added clarifying, albeit cursory, introductory and concluding remarks in which he places these compositions within a musicological context.

B643 Garvelmann, Donald. "Immersed in Ives." *The American Record Guide* 40, no. 9 (August 1977): 16-19.

Review of Nina Deutsch's recording of the "Complete Works for Solo Piano" (**D47**), a version that differs from Mandel as much in the degree of its completion as it does interpretatively. Although she records the commercial premiere of the *Four Emerson Transcriptions*, a work omitted from Mandel's "complete" set, Deutsch manages to exclude twenty-one pieces recorded by Mandel. Garvelmann, who liked "only half" of Deutsch's interpretations, including the "control and sensitivity" of her *First Sonata* performance, especially criticizes her humorless playing, and his preference for the Mandel version invariably emerges. Nevertheless, in positive contrast to Mandel, Deutsch's "devotion and enthusiasm are reflected in her informative liner notes."

B644   Wiley, Joan Marie. "A Comparative Analysis of Charles E. Ives'
'First Sonata' and 'Sonata No. 2.'" M.A. thesis, California State
University, Fullerton, 1980. 90 pp.

This study is less a comparative analysis of Ives's two large piano
sonatas than two separate studies, each of which emphasizes
Ives's treatment of musical motives. The longer chapter on the
motivic properties of *"Concord" Sonata* is also the clearer; the
summary of the *First Sonata*, however, shines less brightly and its
thesis is unconvincing. In neither analysis does Wiley consider
previous commentary on the sonatas.

B645   Kolosick, J. Timothy. "A Computer-Assisted, Set-Theoretic
Investigation of Vertical Simultaneities in Selected Piano
Compositions by Charles E. Ives." Ph.D. dissertation, University
of Wisconsin, Madison, 1981. 170 pp.

Using five short published piano works and with the aid of a
computer Kolosick tries "to search for possible recurring patterns
within vertical relationships." Unfortunately, Kolosick, by his
own admission, does not exploit the computer's full potential. His
analysis of *Study No. 22*, for example, is based entirely on its first
measure, arguably too small a sample to accommodate broad
generalizations. In his appropriately modest conclusions,
Kolosick found "no one continuing, guiding principle," and was
forced to accept the fact that "the similarity ratios for adjacent
sets were helpful only to a limited extent." Not surprisingly, the
strongest structural units occurred within the twelve-tone
melodies of *Varied Air and Variations*.

PIANO SONATAS
First Piano Sonata [W64]

B646   Downes, Olin. "Masselos Pleases in Piano Program." *The New
York Times*, March 28, 1949, page 17. *See*: **W64b**

Review of Masselos's March 27 Carnegie Hall performance of
Ives's *First Piano Sonata*. Downes describes the sonata, which he
believes should not have been performed last, as "a work of
immense length, very rich in ideas, rising to passages of a rare
vision! At the same time a score which needs some condensation
and some artistic discipline." He praises Masselos's "musician's
grasp and fire" and virtuosity, but does not believe that the
performance contained the "finish or exactly achieve nuance" that
Masselos achieved in other works on the program.

B647 Glanville-Hicks, Peggy. "William Masselos: Pianist Presents Ives Sonata at Y.M.H.A. Hall." *New York Herald Tribune*, February 18, 1949, page 18. *See:* **W64a**

Review of Masselos's February 17 premiere performance of Ives's *First Piano Sonata.* Glanville-Hicks describes the work as "full of the fabulous Ives talent," a work that "gets close to atonality...seemingly from instinct and sheer momentum rather than by deliberate design or theory." Her evaluation of Masselos is a total rave: "He brings as an artist strength, insight, grace, and an astonishing technical control, both mechanically and of that region where the devices of technique become fused in interpretative exposition."

B648 Roy, Klaus George. "Copland Harvard Talk." *The Christian Science Monitor*, March 20, 1952, page 4. *See:* **W64c**

Review of Copland's final Norton lecture at Harvard. For Roy the "most absorbing and revealing" portions were Copland's discussion of the Ives phenomenon. Following the lecture "the young pianist William Masselos gave a masterful and superbly controlled performance" of Ives's rarely heard *First Piano Sonata.* In reviewing this work Roy notes "an indigenous jazz style in this work which far excels Gershwin in artless sincerity," and that its "originality and lyricism are amazing for music of that time, and valid still for ours."

B649 Harrison, Lou. "On Ives's First Piano Sonata." Preface to 1954 edition of *Charles E. Ives First Sonata For Piano.* New York: Peer International Corporation, 1954; reprinted on page ii of revised edition, 1979.

In this introduction to the first publication of Ives's *First Piano Sonata,* Harrison is the first to identify the motive that links its various movements, a descending minor second followed by a descending minor third. Harrison, the transcriber and editor of "one of the most gripping and eloquent of the works of the turn of the century," minimizes his own invaluable contribution and maximizes that of its first interpreter, William Masselos. He describes the *First Piano Sonata* as "the penultimate romantic sonata, the same composer's *Concord* probably the last," and considers it no less than "one of the most gripping and eloquent of the works of the turn of the century."

B650   Newman, William S. "Charles Ives: First Sonata for Piano." New York: Peer International Corp., 1954. *Notes* 12, no. 2 (March 1955): 331.

Newman praises Harrison's "helpful preface" and judges this "epoch-maker" of a sonata as "generally more coherent and readily intelligible than Ives' better-known *Second* or '*Concord*' *Sonata.*" In a paragraph-length critique Newman manages to admire Ives's rhythms and use of hymns as well as a basic motive, his harmony and form, and to commend Masselos's performance and recording.

B651   Marshall, Dennis. "Charles Ives's Quotations: Manner or Substance?" *Perspectives of New Music* 6, no. 2 (1968): 45-56; reprinted in *Perspectives on American Composers*, edited by Benjamin Boretz and Edward T. Cone, pp. 13-24. New York: W. W. Norton & Co., Inc., 1971.

One of the most important and frequently cited articles in the Ives literature. Earlier writers occasionally had contradicted the widely-held view that Ives used his borrowed materials either arbitrarily or exclusively for programmatic purposes. Nevertheless, Marshall's article, which uses the two scherzo movements from the *First Sonata* as its primary examples, is the first convincing systematic demonstration of the care with which Ives selected his borrowed material for their common melodic and structural properties. The motivic interconnectedness among Ives's pre-selected material is thus "at the very core of his compositional thought." Marshall also briefly discusses how "Ives makes use of a single borrowed tune at the very core of the structure" in *The Fourth of July*.

B652   Klein, Howard. "Ives: A White Heat of Conviction." *The New York Times*, April 16, 1967, section 2, page 26.

Review of Masselos's second recording of Ives's *First Sonata* (RCA LSC-2941). Klein praises Masselos for his skill in negotiating the range of difficulties present in this work and his "massive powerhouse of a performance." Although he emphasizes the importance of Ives's musical utilization of his Protestant heritage, Klein assures us that "you don't have to be Protestant to like Charles Ives." Ives aficianados of many faiths will be gratefully relieved to learn this.

B653 Mumper, Robert Dwight. "The First Piano Sonata of Charles Ives and The Four Piano Sonatas of Edward MacDowell," pp. 1-93. D.M.A. dissertation, Indiana University, 1971.

Musical illustrations dominate the text in this brief survey. In separate chapters Mumper briefly discusses formal features of each movement and presents a wide assortment of musical idioms that follow "the nomenclatures introduced by Riedel and Oudal" **(B130)**. He also offers an uncritical movement-by-movement "Comparison of the Published Edition with the Second Manuscript," concluding that "the absence of substantive alterations, together with the aforementioned evanescent character of Ives's music, would suggest that another edition is unnecessary, even ill-advised." An appendix includes the pre-existent music quoted by Ives in the sonata.

B654 Greenfield, Ruth Wolkowsky. "Charles Edward Ives and the Stylistic Aspects of His First Piano Sonata." D.M.A. dissertation, University of Miami, 1976. 73 pp.

Greenfield's survey, which focuses on Ives's treatment of motives, is superficial, often confusing, and poorly researched. She relies excessively on copious musical illustrations, and many of her unsubstantiated assertions fail to convince. She is on more solid ground when discussing tonality and form (e.g., her view of the finale as a theme and twelve variations), but these ideas too are described rather than developed.

B655 Cameron, Janet. "An Analysis of the First Movement of the First Piano Sonata by Charles Ives." Seminar paper, University of Illinois, 1979. 23 pp.

Cameron follows a general aesthetic background essay with an organic interpretation of the first movement of Ives's *First Piano Sonata*. She argues that "relationships and patterns, though hidden, are introduced in the first measures, exploited throughout, and summarized at the end," and that "each theme or section has something in it which is related to the whole." She also expresses her view that such an organic approach is "typical of the way Ives handled his musical materials in this entire *Sonata* and is the main reason for the musical cohesiveness of this work."

B656 Masselos, William. "Preface" to *Charles E. Ives Sonata No. 1 For Piano*. New York: Peer International Corp., 1979.

The first interpreter of this work reminisces about the months prior to its 1949 premiere when Lou Harrison was transcribing Ives's manuscript photostats that he had received in 1936. Masselos opens and closes his preface by stressing the mystique and labyrinthine nature of the work and the importance of considering it as an "inspired improvisation, with each performance having a character quite its own."

B657   Henck, Herbert. "Versehen-Versehren. 2. Lanze. Zur Neuausgabe von Charles E. Ives' Erster Klaviersonate." *Neuland* 2 (1981-1982): 206-207.

Review of the second edition of the *First Piano Sonata*. Henck's principal criticism is that the mistakes of the first edition are invariably repeated. Henck notes unexplained discrepancies between the the facsimile pages of Ives's manuscripts included in the edition and the printed edition. He also chastizes the edition for neglecting to incorporate Kirkpatrick's important melodic correction (**B378**, p. 57) at the conclusion of movement IVa. Henck completes his attack by citing a large number of additional errors.

B658   Newman, Ron. "Ragtime Influences on the Music of Charles Ives." *Proceedings of NAJE Research* 5 (1985): 110-121.

After summarizing what is known about Ives's exposure to ragtime and quoting Ives's opinions on ragtime from the *Essays* (**B660**) and *Memos* (**B378**), Newman focuses on how Ives transformed this popular style, "one of nature's ways of giving art raw material," to suit his idiosyncratic musical needs in the *First Sonata*. Substantial musical illustrations are included.

B659   Taylor, Paul Franklyn. "Stylistic Heterogeneity: The Analytical Key to Movements IIa and IIb from the First Piano Sonata by Charles Ives." D.M.A. dissertation, University of Wisconsin-Madison, 1986. 127 pp.

Full-scale systematic application of Starr's stylistic analysis (**B770** and **B606**) to two movements of Ives's *First Piano Sonata*. Like Starr, Taylor "attempts to integrate an analysis of the traditional form-making elements in each work with an analysis of its pattern of stylistic change." He preceeds his analysis of the *First Piano Sonata* with a brief examination of *On the Antipodes* from traditional (**B797** and **B812**) to non-traditional approaches such as Burkholder's (**B284**), "which illustrate the essence of Starr's method."

Of the two movements Taylor considers IIa, in which "different types of writing are used to illuminate the formal divisions created essentially by thematicism," within the mainstream of earlier European art music. More "truly *innovative*" according to Taylor is IIa: "Ives has created a movement in which the various 'types' of writing form the principal subject matter and the motives illuminate them (rather than the reverse)." Taylor also discusses the "relevance of stylistic heterogeneity to other works by Ives, especially the "Emerson" movement from *"Concord"* *Sonata*, and presents a strong case that "stylistic heterogeneity is actually a link with earlier musical practice rather than a break with it."

Second Piano Sonata [W65]
["Concord, Mass., 1840-1860"]

B660 Ives, Charles. *Essays Before a Sonata.* New York: Knickerbocker Press, 1920; reprinted in *Essays Before a Sonata, The Majority, and Other Writings by Charles Ives,* selected and edited by Howard Boatwright, pp. xxv-102. New York: W. W. Norton, 1970. [Excerpts in *Piano Sonata No. 2 ("Concord, Mass., 1840-1860").* Second edition, prepared by Ives with the assistance of George F. Roberts. New York: Arrow Music Press, 1947.] *See*: **B93, B96, B102, B104, B124, B128, B132, B164, B323, B662-665, B730**

Ives's explanatory introduction to *"Concord" Sonata* and central essay on aesthetics. He describes his purpose behind the *Essays* and the sonata in an Author's Preface as follows: "An attempt to present (one person's) impression of the spirit of transcendentalism that is associated in the minds of many with Concord, Mass. of over a half century ago. This is undertaken in impressionistic pictures of Emerson and Thoreau, a sketch of the Alcotts, and a *scherzo* supposed to reflect a lighter quality which is often found in the fantastic side of Hawthorne. The first and last movements do not aim to give any programs of the life or of any particular work of either Emerson or Thoreau, but, rather, composite pictures or impressions."

After a "Prologue" in which Ives offers a short and inconclusive personal debate on the nature of program music, he presents separate essays on each of the Concord Transcendentalists followed by an extended "Epilogue." At the conclusion of his philosophical exploration of Emerson Ives explains the extra-musical significance of the four-note message of Beethoven's *Fifth Symphony* that pervades Ives's Transcendental work: "We would place its translation above the relentlessness of fate knocking at the door, above the greater human message of destiny, and strive to bring it towards the spiritual message of Emerson's revelations, even to the 'common heart' of Concord."

In a brief sketch of Hawthorne Ives expands on his "Preface" when he notes his efforts "to suggest some of his wilder, fantastical adventures in the half-childlike, half-fairylike phantasmal realms" rather than Hawthorne's fundamental part, i.e., "the influence of sin upon the conscience." In the equally brief essay devoted to "The Alcotts," Ives does "not attempt to follow the philosophic raptures of Bronson Alcott" but to capture "the memory of that home under the elms--the Scotch songs and the family hymns that were sung at the end of each day." As part of his more extended essay on Thoreau, Ives offers a possible "program" for his "Thoreau" movement, beginning with "Thoreau's thought on an autumn day of Indian summer at Walden" and concluding as "the poet's flute is heard out over the pond."

The "Epilogue" constitutes the longest and most philosophical portion of the *Essays*. Ives considers numerous issues, conveys his strong opinions on many composers (e.g., Rossini, Wagner, Bach, Beethoven, Richard Strauss, Debussy, Mahler, Chopin), and explores several dualisms, including repose and truth, genius and talent, sound and music, all of which are embraced by a central substance-manner dualism. Ives explains and develops at length various ramifications of his idea that "the higher and more important value of this dualism is composed of what may be called reality, quality, spirit, or substance against the lower value of form, quantity, or manner."

B661   Bellamann, Henry. "Reviews: 'Concord, Mass., 1840-1860' (A Piano Sonata by Charles E. Ives)." *Double Dealer* 2 (October 1921): 166-169.

In this first major review of an Ives work since the public performance of *The Celestial Country* in 1902, Bellamann attributes to Ives "a broad, strong and original style with no recognizable derivations from Debussy, Strauss or Strawinsky [*sic*]." Perhaps because Bellamann based his review on a "reading" rather than a performance, he exaggerates the unplayability of the work. Although he discounts organic unity in the work, he writes of "a psychic kind of connection that might in this case reasonably be called a musical logic." His overall assessment of the work, particularly when considering Ives's obscurity in 1921, is strongly positive: "An essay of lofty thought and feeling" with "moments of achievement elevating and greatly beautiful."

B662 Kramer, A. Walter. "A Pseudo-Literary Sonata!!!" *Musical America* 33, no. 23 (April 2, 1921): 36. *See:* **B660**

Sarcastic review of Ives's *"Concord" Sonata* and *Essays.* Kramer quotes Ives's famous dedication, unprinted in subsequent editions: "These prefatory essays were written by the composer for those who can't stand his music--and the music for those who can't stand his essays: to those who can't stand either, the whole is respectfully dedicated." Speaking for *Musical America* Kramer responds in italics that, *"We can't stand either."* He describes the sonata itself as "without any doubt the most startling conglomeration of meaningless notes that we have ever seen engraved on white paper" [including Bartók's *Second String Quartet*], and praises Ives, who in his accompanying note, "Complimentary--copies are not sold," had the insight to realize the "unsalable quality of his music."

B663 Stringham, Edward [rightly Edwin] J. "Ives Puzzles Critics with His Cubistic Sonata and 'Essays.'" *Rocky Mountain News* (Denver), July 31, 1921, page 1+. *See:* **B660**

Review of Ives's *Essays* and *"Concord" Sonata*, which Stringham had recently received from the author and composer. The reviewer acknowledges that he is "at sea" in his comprehension of these two works. He asks his readers therefore to accept his comments as "impressions rather than judgment" and "with a grain of salt." He suggests that while "some of the composer's statements are witty, informative and make unusually fascinating reading," we should not take Ives's satirical jabs at 'cubistic' music seriously. Furthermore, the difficult work is "not worth the trouble involved to master it." If *"Concord" Sonata* has any claim to musical distinction, it is because it manages to exceed the cacophonous level of any recent work. So pervasive is this cacophony according to Stringham's ears that he attributes to "oversights" the rare occasions that he discovered "a few orthodox chords."

B664 Walker, Ernest. Review of *"Concord" Sonata* and *Essays Before a Sonata. Music & Letters* 2, no. 3 (1921): 287-288. *See:* **B660**

Walker credits Ives with a sense of humor and concedes that "some of the few pages that are in any way concerned with music have good sense under their verbiage." He remains caustically skeptical about the worth of the sonata itself, which "may be safely recommended as a tonic to anyone bored with the reactionary conservatism of European extremists." He criticizes the two-fisted tone clusters ("best practised on someone else's instrument"), the strip of board in "Hawthorne," and even the tonal passages in "The Alcotts" "that sound exactly like a beginner's first attempts at harmony exercises."

B665 "Concord Unconquered." *Musical Courier* 82, no. 17 (April 28, 1921): 22. *See:* **B660**

Another sarcastic response to Ives's *"Concord" Sonata* and accompanying *Essays.* The anonymous reviewer concludes his brief but relentless indictment with the uncharitable proposal that Ives, who "aspires to become the Mark Twain of music," create a 'Jumping Frog' theme which "would descend far into the depths of the musical pool, dragging the composer along with it, there to remain cool and silent forever."

B666 "Music Club Hears Lecture Recital On Modern Sonata." *Atlanta Constitution,* January 5, 1922, page 2. *See:* **W65f**

Review of the program presented to the Atlanta Music Club the previous day, in which Dean H. H. Bellamon [*sic*] of Chicora College, South Carolina, presented a lecture on "The Sonata" with musical illustrations by the pianist, Marion Purcell. The correspondent writes that Bellamann "dwelt at special length on the sonata of Charles Ives, which is called "Concord, Mass.-- 1840-60." and in which he brought out the delightful personal eccentricities of the composer as well as the good points of his work."

B667 Bernstein, Leonard. "The Absorption of Race Elements into American Music." Senior thesis, Harvard University, 1939; reprinted in *Findings,* pp. 36-99. New York: Simon and Schuster, 1982.

In the last musical example of this thesis [*Findings,* pp. 92-97] Bernstein tries to explain what musical features complement the literary program of *"Concord" Sonata* and make it American. He points out the New England hymn playing in "The Alcotts," but considers more significant Ives's syncopative rhythms and certain melodic and harmonic inflections that make *"Concord" Sonata* "practically a piece of jazz." Considering the fact that *"Concord" Sonata* had only recently received its premiere performance, this thesis from one of Ives's most influential champions from 1951 to the present is a remarkable historical document.

B668 Carter, Elliott. "The Case of Mr. Ives." [Part of "Forecast and Review."] *Modern Music* 16, no. 3 (March-April 1939): 172-176; reprinted in *Perspectives of New Music* 2, no. 2 (1964): 27-29 and in *The Writings of Elliott Carter*, compiled, edited, and annotated by Else Stone and Kurt Stone, pp. 48-51. Bloomington & London: Indiana University Press, 1977. *See*: **W65a** and **W651**

A review of the January and February premiere performances of *"Concord"* Sonata and the first of a series of reviews, articles, and interviews that reveal Carter's evolving and frequently contradictory views of his former mentor. Carter introduces the review with some personal reminiscences of his encounters with Ives in the 1920s and argues that Ives's innovations are exaggerated because of his practice of adding dissonances and polyrhythms after the alleged completion of a work. Although Carter finds "much good in the sonata," he finds the work "more often original than good," and emphasizes the absence of logic, the naive use of quotation, and especially the formal weaknesses. A review with a far-reaching impact on the future critical assessment of Ives. *See*: **B337-344**

B669 Downes, Olin. "Concert Devoted to Music by Ives." *The New York Times*, February 25, 1939, page 18. *See*: **W651**

Review of the February 24 Town Hall recital with Kirkpatrick and Minna Hager. Downes focuses his review on *"Concord"* Sonata, Kirkpatrick's repeat performance of his Town Hall premiere January 20. He praises Ives's individuality and comments that "the sonata is filled with interesting ideas," but he is unable to comprehend "its structural form" and therefore is unable "to come to a definite conclusion about such music."

B670 Gilman, Lawrence. "Music: A Masterpiece of American Music Heard Here for the First Time." *New York Herald Tribune*, January 21, 1939, page 9. *See*: **W65a**

Review of Kirkpatrick's Town Hall January 20 recital of *"Concord"* Sonata, perhaps the most important and often-quoted review of an Ives performance during Ives's lifetime. Gilman begins by describing Ives as "probably the most original and extraordinary of American composers," and provides some background on Ives and the philosophical and programmatic underpinning of *"Concord"* Sonata.

Gilman assesses the work with unequivocal praise: "This sonata is exceptionally great music--it is, indeed, the greatest music composed by an American, and the most deeply and essentially American in impulse and implication....The Hawthorne movement is a Scherzo of unearthly power and intensity, transcending its subject. In the Thoreau movement, there is music of a poetic fervor and exaltation in which the essence of Thoreau's imagination is magically captured and conveyed. But it is the thought of Emerson that has drawn from Mr. Ives a quality of musical utterance which is altogether extraordinary and unique." Gilman concludes his review by describing Kirkpatrick as "a poet and a master, [and] an unobtrusive minister of genius."

B671   Kolodin, Irving. "Pianist Plays Work By Ives." *New York Sun,* January 21, 1939. *See*: **W65a**

Review of Kirkpatrick's January 20 Town Hall premiere of *"Concord" Sonata.* Kolodin praises "Ives's musicality," his "amazing perception" in anticipating 20th-century techniques, and singles out Ives's "most serious deficiency...a lack of discipline, an inability to distinguish between the gold and the dross that issued from his imagination." He concludes by acclaiming Kirkpatrick's "enthusiasm," "facility," and "complete comprehension."

B672   Rosenfeld, Paul. "Ives's Concord Sonata." [Part of "Forecast and Review."] *Modern Music* 16, no. 2 (January-February 1939): 109-112. *See*: **W65k**

Review of Kirkpatrick's performance of "the first complete public performance" (and first from memory) of *"Concord" Sonata,* Cos Cob, Connecticut, November 28, 1938. This concert preceded the more widely publicized Town Hall premieres in January and February 1939 reviewed by Carter (**B668**), Gilman (**B670**) et. al. [**W65a** and **W65l**]. Rosenfeld writes of a pair of "melodic germs," the opening motto of Beethoven's *Fifth Symphony* and a melody that he identifies as "a tender, wooing, chromatic little subject." He also compares some of the more original musical features with the avant-gardists Cowell and Ornstein and discusses the Transcendental qualities of the work. Rosenfeld parallels Gilman's assessment when he writes that the "Thoreau" finale "seemed music as beautiful at the very least as any composed by an American," and that the work as a whole contained America's "most intense and sensitive musical experience."

B673   Sebastian, John.   "Charles Ives at Last." *New Masses*, February 7, 1939, page 30. [Rossiter points out that John Sebastian was a *nom de plume* for Goddard Lieberson (**B215**)].   *See*: **W65a**

Review of Kirkpatrick's January 20 premiere of *"Concord" Sonata*. Although Sebastian (Lieberson) expresses their gratitude to the pianist "for his splendid performance," he considers this long overdue event "a shameful landmark." He states at the outset that the works of this "virile and inventive" composer, America's Tom Mooney, have been "imprisoned in an obscurity which amounts to criminal neglect." In contrast to most early reviewers he writes of an underlying unity behind Ives's heterogeneity: "He speaks in many languages, in refinements of tone qaulity, overtones, polyrhythms [*sic*], atonality, metrical changes of a surprising nature, and complicated jazz rhythms [*sic*]. These are not mere devices, they are functional to the evolution of a single idea."

B674   Simon, Robert A.   "American Music--Swing Drops In--Recitalists." *The New Yorker* 14, no. 50 (January 28, 1939): 44-45.   *See*: **W65a**

Review of Kirkpatrick's January 20 premiere performance of *"Concord" Sonata*. Simon writes that "Mr. Kirkpatrick handled it with no apparent effort, and lent to it an improvisatory manner that seemed exactly right for this music." He recognizes the originality that "makes it hard to assimilate at a first hearing," and concludes with the presumption that "Mr. Ives' compositions won't appear so strange when one gets to listen to them frequently, and more performances seem to be in order."

B675   "Insurance Man." *Time* 33, no. 5 (30 January 1939): 44-45.

The occasion of Kirkpatrick's premiere performance of *"Concord" Sonata* precipitated a profile which emphasizes Ives's quirky double life, "his horror of publicity," and his self-deprecatory dedicatory preface to his *Essays*. Nevertheless, *Time* also includes the begrudging recognition that Ives is regarded "even by conservative critics as one of the most individual and authentically American of all U.S. composers" and that Gilman assessed the work as "the greatest music composed by an American." *See*: **B670**

B676   Wendt, Rudolph.   "A Study of Charles Ives' Second Pianoforte Sonata, 'Concord, Mass, 1840-60.'" M.A. thesis, Eastman School of Music, 1946.   76 pp.

Of historical interest as the first graduate study devoted to a work by Ives. Wendt's generously illustrated stylistic analysis focuses on Ives's realization of programmatic elements as revealed in the *Essays*, his technical innovations, and his "harmonic audacity and diversity." Although of limited usefulness to modern Ives scholars, Wendt's thesis provides an unprecedentedly competent musical description of this work, and reveals an appreciation for Ives's heterogeneity rare for its time.

B677 Cowell, Henry. "Charles Ives: Second Pianoforte Sonata, "Concord, Mass., 1840-1860." *Notes* 5, no. 3 (June 1948): 412-413.

Review of the second edition of *"Concord" Sonata*, Arrow Music Press, 1947. Cowell writes briefly about the Beethoven *Fifth Symphony* quotation and its significance, and modestly disclaims credit for "discovering" Ives, attributing this honor instead to Bellamann and E. Robert Schmitz. He also expresses his gratitude for this publication and criticizes only the absence of Ives's original "Prose" indication [top of page 1] and "Verse" indications [top of pages 5 and 8].

B678 Slonimsky, Nicholas. "Bringing Ives Alive." *Saturday Review of Literature* 31, no. 35 (28 August 1948): 45+.

Slonimsky rejoices on the occasion of Columbia's recent release of Kirkpatrick's 1945 unissued recording of *"Concord" Sonata* (Columbia MM-749). He focuses on the programmatic content of the work, its Transcendentalism, and its "new type of impressionism, in which ideas and convictions, and even politics, are used as programmatic content."

B679 Taubman, Howard. "Records: Ives Sonata. Columbia Issues 'Concord' Piano Work Played by John Kirkpatrick." *The New York Times*, July 18, 1948, section 2, page 5.

Review of Kirkpatrick's historic recording of *"Concord" Sonata* (Columbia MM-749). Taubman would like to issue certificates of merit to Kirkpatrick as well as to Columbia for their dedication to this music. Of the performance Taubman writes that "Mr. Kirkpatrick takes the technical difficulties in stride and concentrates successfully on the large design and the poetry of the score."

B680 Cohn, Arthur. "Not Once but Twice--the 'Concord' Sonata." *The American Record Guide* 28, no. 10 (June 1962): 802-803.

Review of two recordings of *"Concord" Sonata* by George Pappastavrou (**D56**) and Aloys Kontarsky [Time Records Stereo S/8005]. Cohn writes sparingly of the performances, e.g., Pappastavrou's "poetic demeanor" and Kontarsky's "Teutonic impact." Instead he focuses on the work itself, the greatness of which according to Cohn, "lies in the waywardness of no formal musical agenda." For Cohn also "the Sonata has a dignity that is as acute as late Beethoven."

B681   Frankenstein, Alfred. "Ives's 'Concord' Sonata--A Great Day for American Music." *High Fidelity/ Musical America* 12, no. 4 (April 1962): 62-63; reprinted in *American Composers Alliance Bulletin* 10, no. 2 (1962): 17.

Review of Pappastavrou's recording of *"Concord" Sonata* (**D56**). Like many reviewers Frankenstein concentrates on the work itself rather than a performance, quoting liberally from Ives's *Essays Before a Sonata* (**B660**). He offers high but non-specific praise of this performance of "the greatest of American piano sonatas," when he writes: "The new recording makes me feel that I have really heard the *Concord* Sonata for the first time."

B682   Helm, Everett. "Another Concord Sonata." *Musical America* 82, no. 6 (June 1962): 27-28.

Review of the Pappastavrou (**D56**) and Kontarsky (Time S/8005) recordings of *"Concord" Sonata*. Helm concedes that both pianists have mastered the formidable technical challenges of the work, but "there is no difficulty in choosing between these two recordings of this great work." Despite the greater sonic brilliance of the Kontarsky recording, Pappastavrou "has penetrated more deeply into the meaning of the music" and achieved a "more complete identification with the spirit of Ives."

B683   Salzman, Eric. "Two 'Concords' At Once." *The New York Times*, May 27, 1962, section 2, page 18.

Comparative review of two recently released recordings of *"Concord" Sonata:* Kontarsky (Time S/8005) and Pappastavrou (**D56**). Salzman provides some of the philosophical and aesthetic background for the work, conveys his performance criterion, and explains why he believes the Pappastavrou interpretation to be the more satisfying. Briefly, Pappastavrou "has an over-all sense of motion through line and phrase that is more musical, more sensible and simply more relevant" than Kontarsky, who "does not recognize the coherence of the ideas and their concrete development."

B684   Clarke, Henry Leland. "Reviews of Records. Charles Ives: *Second Pianoforte Sonata--"Concord, Mass., 1840-1860." The Musical Quarterly* 50, no. 1 (January 1964): 114-115.

Review of Kontarsky's recorded performance of *"Concord" Sonata* (Time S/8005). Clarke interprets Ives's combination of Beethoven's *Fifth Symphony* and "local tunes" as indicative of Ives's "passionate love for all things German." Another German touch is the "untied suspension" in "Emerson," which Clarke considers "akin to Schumann's use of it" in his *Album for the Young* (No. 30). Not surprisingly, Kontarsky's Teutonic approach makes his interpretation "the best now available."

B685   Clark, Sondra Rae. "The Transcendental Philosophy of Charles E. Ives as Expressed in *The Second Sonata for Pianoforte*, 'Concord, Mass., 1840-1860.'" M.A. thesis, San Jose State College, 1966. 77 pp.

Clark supports her central thesis "that Charles Ives's transcendental philosophy played a major part in his musical expression," and she successfully examines "the composer's expressed intentions and their fulfillment in the character and mood of the music" in *"Concord" Sonata*, Ives's principal Transcendental work. Although she devotes more emphasis to "Emerson" and "The Alcotts," her programmatic interpretation of "Hawthorne" and "Thoreau" are especially imaginative and believable.

B686   Kirkpatrick, John. Jacket notes for "The *'Concord' Sonata*, by Charles Ives." Columbia MS 7192 [1968].

Authoritative notes by the pianist who premiered this work in 1938 and 1939 and arguably the leading Ives authority since the composer's death in 1954. The notes include a valuable summary of the origins and compositional genesis for each movement and a precise identification and explanation of Kirkpatrick's departures from the second published edition [1947].

B687   Moore, David W. "John Kirkpatrick: 'Concord' Revisited." *The American Record Guide* 35, no. 7 (December 1968): 546-547.

Review of Kirkpatrick's second commercially released recording of *"Concord" Sonata* (Col. MS 7192). Moore surveys Kirkpatrick's sparse but important recording output of neglected and "misjudged creative figures," summarizes the principal points that this Ives pioneer makes in his jacket notes (**B686**), and compares Kirkpatrick's recording favorably to all other versions. He especially praises Kirkpatrick's "rubati pared down to the minimum necessary to get all his points across," and his "amazing clarity and feeling in any tempo." For this reviewer, Kirkpatrick's recording "offers the last word on this knotty and challenging piece."

B688   Sahr, Hadassah Gallup. "Performance and Analytic Study of Selected Piano Music by American Composers," pp. 1-48. Ed.D. dissertation, Columbia University, 1969.

Along with works by Gottschalk, Griffes, Copland, and Thomson, Sahr chose to analyze "Thoreau" from Ives's *"Concord" Sonata*. Unfortunately, she does not attain her stated purpose, i.e., to use analysis to achieve "more effective performance and teaching of the music." Unfortunately, Sahr's descriptive analysis lacks a broad interpretative vision, and her ideas for performance are sparser and less helpful than her stated purpose suggests.

B689   Schonberg, Harold C. "Don't Try to Please the Ladies, Rollo." *The New York Times*, March 30, 1969, section 2, page 19; reprinted as "Ives: Compulsiveness, Complexity, Dissonance and Power" in *Facing the Music*, pp. 147-151. New York: Summit Books, 1981.

Schonberg discusses and quotes from Ives's handwritten marginalia discovered in a copy of *"Concord" Sonata* that the *New York Times* critic had received as a gift. In Appendix 7 of *Memos* Kirkpatrick acknowledges Schonberg's sharing of these important "scribblings" and reproduces them in full. *See:* **B378**

B690   Clark, Sondra Rae. "The Evolving *Concord Sonata*: A Study of Choices and Variants in the Music of Charles Ives." Ph.D. dissertation, Stanford University, 1972. 375 pp.

This dissertation with its thesis "that Ives did not intend the 'Concord Sonata' to be limited to either of the printed editions," provides an important contribution to Ives scholarship. Exhibiting an impressive command of the sources, Clark clarifies the intricate pre-publication history of this work, explains and illustrates through musical examples hundreds of variant possibilities that Ives entered in fourteen copies of the first edition, and discusses Ives's extensive unpublished performance notes. An indispensable resource for any further source study of this work.

B691 Goudie, Andrea. "Exploring the Broad Margins: Charles Ives's Interpretation of Thoreau." *The Midwest Quarterly* 13, no. 3 (April 1972): 309-317.

Goudie considers a musical composition, especially the "Thoreau" movement of Ives's *"Concord" Sonata* "an equally valuable source of interpretive insight" as scholarly and critical studies of this author. For Goudie "Ives's intellectual interpretation of Thoreau's thinking (the essay) and his aesthetic interpretation of the moods which give rise to this thinking (the music) possess a subtle but...real correlation." She also argues somewhat tenuously that Ives's detailed program "is an interesting companion piece to his music, but his music transcends by far his program for it."

B692 McCalla, James W. "Structural and Harmonic Innovations in the Music of Schoenberg, Stravinsky and Ives Prior to 1915," pp. 59-83. M.M. thesis, New England Conservatory of Music, 1973.

McCalla uses *"Concord" Sonata* as his paradigm for exploring Ives's form and harmony. He also considers the relationship between pure music and an extra-musical program. In comparing Ives to Schoenberg he concludes that "Ives's music is less directly tied to specific words but more closely related to a general philosophy."

B693 Albert, Thomas Russel. "The Harmonic Language of Charles Ives' *Concord Sonata.*" D.M.A. dissertation, University of Illinois, 1974. 67 pp.

Albert begins with the premise that "an examination of the philosophical intent of the *Concord Sonata* offers a foundation for an understanding of the musical inconsistencies found in the work as an aural experience." He goes on to explore how Ives's harmonic language can be explained as a direct response to his philosophical intent. Although Albert does not explore these relationships at great length, he offers some thoughtful generalizations, both philosophical and harmonic, and shows a fine sense for selective harmonic detail.

B694 Clark, Sondra Rae. "The Elements of Choice in Ives's *Concord Sonata.*" *The Musical Quarterly* 60, no. 2 (April 1974): 167-186.

A capsulation of Clark's dissertation (**B690**). Again Clark argues that scholars and performers contradict Ives's musical philosophy when they "ignore or quickly dismiss Ives's suggestions to play the *Concord Sonata* in various ways." She focuses on the evidence in Ives's unpublished Performance Notes and his extensive revisions in fourteen copies of the first edition between 1919 and 1947 that Ives considered many versions equally appropriate in a performance of this work. According to Clark, the various sources reveal "an evolution toward an increasing diversity of inspiration rather than an ultimate resolution."

B695 ____. "Ives and the Assistant Soloist." *Clavier* 13, no. 7 (1974): 17-20.

Although many of the variant versions that Ives entered before and after the 1919 edition appeared in 1947, the composer's suggestions in his Performance Notes and manuscripts for an assistant soloist were not indicated in this second edition. Clark explains the scope of Ives's call for help and argues that although he recognized that pianists would not want to share their glory by adding a third hand, "Ives not only suggested but preferred a second player on the bench." *See*: **B690**

B696 Babcock, Michael J. "Ives's 'Thoreau': A Point of Order." *American Society of University Composers Proceedings* 9 and 10 (1974-1975): 89-102.

Babcock attempts to discredit the view "that Ives invariably abhorred the use of system" by revealing "systematic use of structural models" in the "Thoreau" movement from *"Concord"* *Sonata*. He fills the article with numerous cycle-of-fifth wheels that emphasize "symmetric deployment," but his graphics do not always compensate for an obscure prose style. Babcock concludes his essay with the musical realization of programmatic elements in the movement, especially Ives's references to Thoreau's Aeolian harp.

B697 Fisher, Fred. "Ives's Concord Sonata." *Piano Quarterly* 92 (1975-1976): 23-27.

Fisher praises this work for "its careful attention to structural detail on the one hand and its titanic, spontaneous outbursts on the other." He explains some of Ives's motivic linkages that can be clarified in a good performance and traces the organic growth of one such motive, "a scale-wise segment of three notes followed by a downward leap of a fifth." According to Fisher, Ives intentionally borrowed this motive from Brahms's *Second Piano Sonata*, Op. 2. For Fisher also, "the ideal interpretation is a romantic one" with appropriate rubato and a balanced "juxtaposition of the scholarly and the impetuous." *See*: **B706**

B698   Hall, David. "The Quintessence of Ives." *Stereo Review* 39, no. 2 (August 1977): 124.

Review of Kalish's recording of *"Concord" Sonata* (**D54**). Hall considers this "fabulous masterpiece" the "quintessence of Ives' musical thought" and Kalish "one of the most intelligent and sensitive of Ives interpreters." He stresses the "poetic dimension" that Kalish adds to the "magnificently architectural reading" of Kirkpatrick (Col. MS 7192) and the "demonic Kontarsky version" (Time S/8005) and offers thoughtful and specific praise for each movement.

B699   Kalish, Gilbert. Jacket notes for "Charles Ives Piano Sonata No. 2." Nonesuch H-71337 [1977] (**D54**).

Kalish's notes emphasize the challenge of Ives's "unorthodox demands," especially the "ephemeral quality of the printed text" and the composer's instruction that each performer use Ives's notes as a flexible foundation "to make his own speeches on." Following useful background information the notes present excerpts from Ives's *Essays* relevant to each movement. *See*: **B660**

B700   Starr, Lawrence. "Charles Ives: The Next Hundred Years-- Towards a Method of Analyzing the Music." *The Music Review* 38, no. 2 (May 1977): 101-111.

An important article in which Starr espouses an original thesis that Ives "embraced stylistic heterogeneity as a *basic principle* of musical composition and deliberately set about writing music that would reveal the artistic viability of this principle." Particularly effective are Starr's well-articulated generalizations about Ives's historical and aesthetic significance and his explanation of how Ives uses detail and stylistic heterogeneity in "The Alcotts" to create "an internally coherent, carefully structured piece."

B701   Briner, Andres. "Ein amerikanischer Denkstil in der Concord-Sonata. Zu einem Aspekt des Transzendentalisten Charles E. Ives." In *Zwischen den Grenzen. Zum Aspekt des Nationalen in der Neuen Musik*, edited by Dieter Rexroth, pp. 54-61. Frankfurter Studien 3, B. Schott's Söhne, Mainz 1979.

Briner discusses Ives's Transcendental aesthetic as revealed in *"Concord" Sonata.* He emphasizes the historical importance of Ives's "offenene Form" ("open form") in *"Concord" Sonata,* attributing this idea to Ives's desire to capture the spirit of the American pioneer. Briner does not attribute a direct scientific correlation between *"Concord" Sonata* and nineteenth-century Transcendentalism, but he does allow that this work expresses specifically American qualities.

B702 Chmaj, Betty E. "Sonata for American Studies: Perspectives on Charles Ives." *Prospects: An Annual of American Culture Studies,* edited by Jack Salzman, 4 (1979): 1-58.

The largest part of this essay is devoted to a study of *"Concord" Sonata* "from the point of view of American Studies rather than from a narrowly technical musical standpoint." In the substantial opening portion of the essay, Chmaj surveys the evolution of critical assessments towards Ives (the notes include "A Little Anthology of Opinions, 1924-75"), defends the view that "substance *determines* manner" in Ives's music, and demonstrates parallels between Ives's prose style in his *Essays* **(B660)** and his Transcendentalism. Of particular interest are Chmaj's comparisons between Ives and Frank Lloyd Wright and Ives and Whitman. She also offers a perceptive observation when she notes the ubiquitous "*lack* of recognition, except by Ives himself, of the role of his wife" in the Ives literature. *See:* **B710**

B703 Conen, Hermann. "'All the Wrong Notes are Right.' Zu Charles Ives' 2. Klaviersonate 'Concord, Mass., 1840-60.'" *Neuland* 1 (1980): 28-42.

An important non-English survey of *"Concord" Sonata.* Conen demonstrates a sure grasp of the secondary literature and his summary of the work's genesis includes several details omitted in Clark's dissertation **(B690)**. He devotes the largest portion of his essay to a general analysis of "Emerson" and "Thoreau," but does not neglect to touch on the principal philosophical and aesthetic issues of the work as whole, especially its relationship to Ives's *Essays Before a Sonata* **(B660)**.

B704 Ghander, Ann. "Charles Ives: Organisation in *Emerson.*" *Musicology: The Journal of the Musicological Society of Australia* 6 (1980): 111-127.

At the outset of this article Ghander cites several commentaries on *"Concord" Sonata* from Bellamann **(B661)** to Clark **(B690)** and discusses "the development of critical opinion towards Ives" as illustrated by Bellamann (**B326**), Carter (**B668**), and Mellers (**B41** and **B53**). She agrees with Cowell that two themes dominate the "Emerson" movement of this work (**B354**) and then considers the intervallic and rhythmic development of four additional themes. After presenting a brief structural outline of "Emerson," Ghander examines its tonality, which she concludes is less important than Ives's "rarely equalled" organization of "specific intervals and pitches."

B705   Schubert, Giselher. "Die Concord-Sonata von Charles Ives. Anmerkungen zur Werkstruktur und Interpretation." In *Aspeckte der musikalischen Interpretation. Festschrift z. 70 Geburtstag von Sava Savoff*, edited by Hermann Danuser, pp. 121-138. Hamburg: K. D. Wagner, 1980.

A summary of the origins of *"Concord" Sonata* and its relationship to works that grew out of the sonata, such as the *Emerson Transcriptions* and *The Celestial Railroad*. Schubert compares the two editions of *"Concord" Sonata* (1920 and 1947), but inexplicably neglects Clark's comprehensive study of the variants between these editions and Ives's compositional additions to fourteen copies of the first edition (**B690**). The article also includes a discussion of the work's structure and its aesthetic foundation.

B706   Fisher, Fred. *Ives' Concord Sonata.* Denton, TX: C/G Productions, 1981.

Fisher asks his readers at the outset "whether or not this unorthodox approach can accomplish what academic or textbook methodologies have thus far failed to do." Assuming one can even locate this book [the Yale Collection copy can be found in the vicinity of the *Cabalas*], most readers will find many of the bones that Fisher tosses rather far-fetched. Others will be fascinated by his imaginative, almost mystical approach.

Fisher devotes his main effort to supporting his view (first espoused in **B697**) that in addition to the well-known motive from Beethoven's *Fifth Symphony*, Ives inserted in this work conscious connections with Bach (*Es ist genug*, the musical signature BACH, and the key scheme of the partitas), and the principal motives from Beethoven's *"Hammerklavier" Sonata* and Brahms's *Second Piano Sonata*. In the process of presenting these and other often highly conjectural but occasionally plausible theories,

Fisher offers a number of reasonable as well as original motivic connections within the *"Concord" Sonata* itself.

B707 Kramer, Lawrence. "A Completely New Set of Objects." In *Music and Poetry: The Nineteenth Century and After*, pp. 171-202. Berkeley and Los Angeles: University of California Press, 1984.

Kramer uses Ives's *"Concord" Sonata* as his central example to reveal connections and parallels between Ives and his poetic counterpart, Wallace Stevens. For Kramer, both "Stevens and Ives confront the need to treat place transcendentally as a metaphysical burden, not a rhetorical challenge....The burden itself can be defined as the task of creating what Stevens calls 'a completely new set of objects,': works of art in which the local and absolute, the contingent and the transcendent, fuse into a single form."

B708 Crutchfield, Will. "The 'Concord' Sonata: An American Masterpiece." *Opus* 1, no. 4 (June 1985): 21-22+.

Review of McDonald's Musical Heritage recording of *"Concord" Sonata* (Musical Heritage 4907). Crutchfield reveals a comprehensive knowledge of Ives's variant versions, and in addition to a review of the present performance, offers a broad and detailed comparison of earlier recordings of the work, especially "the best and differentest *Concords*," Kirkpatrick's (1968) and Kalish's (1977) **(D54)**. His comments on Ives's own recording of selected portions of the work are also thoughtful and instructive.

B709 Fruehwald, Robert Douglas. "Part 2. Motivic Transformation in the 'Thoreau' Movement of Charles Ives' *Concord Sonata*." Ph.D. dissertation, Washington University, 1985. 91 pp.

Profusely illustrated and charted essay on the motivic interconnections in "Thoreau." Fruehwald concludes that "the musical materials of the work do contribute to the definition of the piece's formal boundaries," and that "underneath the diversity of 'Thoreau' lies a thread of motivic unity." Perhaps most imaginative is Fruehwald's analysis of the musical pun by which Ives relates *Bethany* to *Massa's in the Cold, Cold, Ground*, the latter's identity in turn "clouded by the fact that it is also related to the other material of the piece." Unfortunately, for the most part Fruehwald lets his musical examples speak for him and rarely attempts to go beyond his detailed motivic descriptions.

B710   Chmaj, Betty E.   "Charles Ives and the *Concord Sonata*." In
Papers of the European Association of American Studies, edited by
Roland Hagenbuchle. Germany: EAAS, 1987.

Movement-by-movement discussion of *"Concord" Sonata*, a work
which Chmaj interprets as Ives's attempt "to impose the Unity of
the Oversoul on the chaos of experience, to demonstrate an
underlying Transcendental unity beneath all manner of variety."
Chmaj considers Ives's programmatic descriptions of "Hawthorne"
and "Thoreau" in the *Essays* (**B660**) "perfectly clear" and "easy to
follow" (respectively). She also emphasizes the importance and
ubiquity of the "double consciousness," i.e., "a bedeviling division
between two polar attitudes--one static and serene, the other
dynamic and rugged," in this and other Ives works.

OTHER MUSIC FOR PIANO SOLO

General

B711   Magee, Noel. "The Short Piano Works of Charles Ives." M.M.
thesis, Indiana University, 1966. 143 pp.

Analysis and manuscript description of the short piano works
contained in the photostat volume that Ives sent to Kirkpatrick in
1938: *Three-Page Sonata, Rough and Ready, The Seen and
Unseen, Waltz-Rondo, Song Without (Good) Words, Scene-Episode,
Bad Resolutions, Three Protests or Varied Air & Variations*, and the
Studies Nos. 2, 5-9, 15, 20-23, and 27. Magee appends his
insightful commentary with transcriptions of all of the above
works with the exception of the previously published *Three-Page
Sonata*, the *Three Protests* and *Studies Nos. 9 and 22.* The most
valuable secondary source on these important but largely
unknown works.

B712   Davis, Peter G. "Mandel Offers Ives Premieres." *The New York
Times*, March 24, 1968, page 92. *See*: **W77a** and **W78b**

Review of a Town Hall recital, March 23, in which pianist Alan
Mandel premiered Ives's *Five Take-offs* and eight piano studies.
Davis describes the *Take-offs* as "written in Ives's most engaging
tongue-in-cheek style"; he attributes "more substance" to the
studies and comments on selected features of *Studies Nos. 5, 6, 7,
and 20*, concluding that, "these fascinating miniatures, in fact,
illustrate the entire Ives vocabulary in microcosm." Davis also
bestows much praise on Mandel, who "coped brilliantly with the
music's ferocious difficulties."

B713 Henck, Herbert. "'Waltz-Rondo' und andere Klavierstuecke von Charles Ives." *Neuland* 1 (1980): 44-46.

Henck follows analytical remarks on the *Waltz-Rondo* with a critical review of Ives editions in general and Kirkpatrick's edition of this work in particular. Henck describes the complexities in editing Ives, and is particularly sensitive to the performance problems that conflicting manuscripts present.

Three-Page Sonata [W76]
See also: **B50**, **B330**, **B633**, and **B711**

B714 Taubman, Howard. "New Works Given by Music Society." *The New York Times*, April 26, 1949, page 29. Reprinted in **B717** along with the April 25 program. *See*: **W76a**

Taubman writes that the *Three-Page Sonata* "is slight, but has some pleasantly syncopated pages."

B715 Joyce, Mary Ann. "The *Three-Page Sonata* of Charles Ives: An Analysis and a Corrected Version." Ph.D. dissertation (Part II), Washington University, 1970. 45 pp., not including Cowell's edition.

A brief but valuable source. In contrast to Cowell's description of this work as a "sonata movement" (**B633**), Joyce makes a good case for considering it a "three-movement sonata." Although she does not mention the significant B-A-C-H theme, Joyce provides a good short movement-by-movement introduction to various musical parameters. Of special usefulness, however, are the twenty-eight musical illustrations that clearly show errors in Cowell's 1949 edition when compared on a parallel column with Ives's manuscript version.

The errors are simply but accurately described (e.g., "pitch error" [10 total], "accent omitted," [4 total], "rhythm error," "tie omitted," and "repeat sign omitted." [3 each]). Joyce follows this list of corrections with a transcription and a facsimile of Ives's three-page manuscript which inspired its well-known title.

B716 Toncitch, Voya. "Charles Ives: Three-Sonata [*sic*] Pour Piano." *Revue Musical de Suisse Romande* 22, no. 3 (1969): 3+; translated into German and reprinted as "'Three Page Sonata' by Charles Ives." *Melos: Zeitschrift für neue Musik* 39, no. 5 (August-September 1972): 277-279.

Toncitch offers a section-by-section descriptive overview of this work and a general defense of Ives's historical importance and compositional competence.

B717   Shelton, Gregory Allard. "An Analysis of Charles Ives's 'Three-Page Sonata for Piano.'" M.A. thesis, The American University, 1985. 214 pp.

Shelton's thesis is most useful for its discussion of the *Three-Page Sonata* sources and for its thorough comparison between the 1949 Cowell edition and the 1975 Kirkpatrick edition, the latter closely approximating Joyce's unpublished transcription (**B715**). Shelton also makes several valuable stylistic comments on Ives's serial procedures and quotation in this work.

Take-offs [W77]
See: **B113** and **B711-712**

Studies [W78]
See: **B50, B113,** and **B711-712**

B718   Thomson, Virgil. "Music: Select and Impressive." *New York Herald Tribune* April 4, 1950, page 19. *See*: **W78a**

Review of the League of Composers April 3 recital in Carl Fischer Hall, in which Jack Cox performed Ives's *Anti-Abolitionist Riots* and the premiere of *Some Southpaw Pitching*. Thomson described both of these short works as "good fun and good music" and singles out for comment the latter work, which "contains not only some vigorous left-hand exercise but also a real fine corny hymn tune."

B719   Bruderer, Conrad. "The Studies of Charles Ives." Ph.D. dissertation, Indiana University, 1968. 95 pp.

Transcription and commentary on Ives's eleven extant studies for piano solo. The transcriptions of *Studies 9* and *22* were made by Bruderer; the remaining transcriptions are reprinted here from Magee's thesis (**B711**) with the authors's permission. Bruderer offers brief but useful insights on the transcription and performance difficulties of each study.

B720   Dumm, Robert. "Performer's Analysis of an Ives Piano Piece." *Clavier* 13, no. 7 (1974): 21-25.

The piano piece under scrutiny in this article is *Study No. 22*. In addition to a thematic analysis of this twenty-eight measure work, Dumm offers analytical reasons why Kirkpatrick was correct to include the present measure 27 ["a penciled patch at the bottom of Ives' manuscript"]. Dumm also provides numerous specific performance suggestions.

B721   Swift, Richard. "Charles Ives: Study No. 22 for Piano, edited by John Kirkpatrick." *Notes* 31, no. 1 (September 1974): 158-159.

Brief review of this second and "scrupulously edited" publication of *Study No. 22*. Swift's approval of Kirkpatrick's "excellent text, pruned of egregious errors, and handsomely printed" is followed by a short description of the piece and a call for similar critical editions of the unpublished studies.

B722   Henck, Herbert. "Aus Zweiter Hand: Charles E. Ives' 'Study Nr. 20.'" *Neuland* 3 (1982-1983): 242-243.

Henck reviews the first publication of this work edited by Kirkpatrick (Merion, 1981). Throughout his review Henck challenges the editorial principle in which the editor attempts "to balance the advantages" of the pencil sketch and the ink copy according to his personal editorial judgment rather than to produce a true "textkritische Ausgabe," i.e., "a critical edition of the text."

B723   Ward, Keith C. "Musical Idealism: A Study of the Aesthetics of Arnold Schoenberg and Charles Ives." D.M.A. dissertation, Northwestern University, 1985. 228 pp. *See*: **Ives and His Contemporaries** (Schoenberg)

Ward's analyses of two Ives piano works, *Anti-Abolitionist Riots in Boston in the 1850's (Study No. 9) [pp. 127-135] and Some Southpaw Pitching (Study No. 21)* [pp. 135-147], appears within the context of the largest comparative study of Ives and Schoenberg. For *Study No. 9* he offers useful historical background and identifies programmatic connections; for *Study No. 21* he focuses on various musical parameters such as form ("a modified sonata"), texture, melody, rhythm and meter. In an appendix Ward includes his 1981 edition of the *Anti-Abolitionist Riots* [forthcoming from Peer]. As a counterpart to Ives, Ward presents a generous analysis of Schoenberg's *Three Piano Pieces*, Op. 11.

Ward devotes the majority of his dissertation to a survey of the aesthetics of Ives and Schoenberg, including the cultural and musical roots of Schoenberg's "expressive need" and the Transcendental underpinning that supports Ives's "musical honesty." In his conclusion Ward contrasts Schoenberg's search for system and organic unity with Ives's "diametrically opposed" musical philosophy." He also notes numerous and significant similarities, especially their view that "the idea remained the root of art," and explores several manifestations of this shared idealism.

Waltz-Rondo [W79]
See: **B711** and **B713**

Varied Air and Variations [W81]
See: **B711**

The Celestial Railroad [W82]

B724 "Rovinsky to Premiere Ives Work." *Musical Courier* 143, no. 4 (February 15, 1951): 67.

Announcement of the radio premiere of *The Celestial Railroad* by the pianist, Rovinsky, who had earlier presented the live premiere of the work at Town Hall. The announcement describes the composition as "a resetting of an older work" by Ives (without identifying this older work as the "Hawthorne" movement from *"Concord" Sonata*) and gives a synopsis of the Hawthorne story upon which the piano work takes its name and program.

PIANO DUETS

Three Quarter-Tone Pieces [W84]

B725 Downes, Olin. "Franco-American Musical Society." *The New York Times*, February 15, 1925, page 26. *See*: **W84b**

Review of the premiere of Ives's "Chorale" and "Allegro" from *Three Quarter-Tone Pieces*, performed by Hans Barth and Sigmund Klein at Aeolian Hall the previous evening. Downes writes: "The music heard last night impressed us in all three cases as having been thought in the customary tonal and semi-tonal medium. The result was simply that the music sounded a good deal out of tune. At a first hearing it had little interest."

B726 Henderson, William J. [from a clipping in the *New York Sun* (dated 16 February 1925) in *Miscellaneous Scrapbook*, page 1, in the Sibley Music Library, Eastman Conservatory, Rochester, NY]. *See*: **W84b**

Review of the premiere performance of "Chorale" and "Allegro" from Ives's *Three Quarter-Tone Pieces*. The reviewer writes: "It required two pianos for the delivery of a Chorale and an Allegro by Charles E. Ives....The naked exhibition of quarter-tone effects did not come until the second number and this attracted many of the listeners to laughter, but calmer consideration will, perhaps, bring to some of them a realization of the truly estimable character of the melodic sequences."

B727 Ives, Charles E. "Some 'Quarter-Tone' Impressions." *Franco-American Musical Society Quarterly Bulletin* (March 1925): 24-33; reprinted in *Essays Before a Sonata, The Majority and Other Writings by Charles Ives*, selected and edited by Howard Boatwright, pp. 105-119. New York: W. W. Norton, 1970. *See:* **B660**

Ives explores the theoretical foundation and expressive potential of quarter-tones. He voices his conviction that quarter-tones can be assimilated with tonal systems, measures their "contribution...to rhythm in their ability to relieve the monotony of literal repetition," considers their "purely sensuous side," and concludes that "quarter-tones or no quarter-tones, why tonality as such should be thrown out for good, I can't see." He also offers brief prefatory notes for the quarter-tone exercises that would eventually become known as *Three Quarter-Tone Pieces for Two Pianos*.

B728 Boatwright, Howard. "Ives' Quarter-Tone Impressions." *Perspectives of New Music* 3, no. 2 (Spring-Summer 1965): 22-31; reprinted in *Perspectives on American Composers*, edited by Benjamin Boretz and Edward T. Cone, pp. 3-12. New York: W. W. Norton & Co., Inc., 1971.

Thoughtful historical and analytical overview of Ives's *Three Quarter-Tone Pieces*. Boatwright writes insightfully on the quarter-tone experiments of Ives's father, the genesis of the work, and its aesthetic and theoretical premises as expressed by Ives in his essay, "Some 'Quarter-Tone' Impressions" *See:* **B727** (edited by Boatwright)

B729 Cohn, Arthur. "New Music from Odyssey--Splitting Semitones." *American Record Guide* 34, no. 12 (August 1968): 1086-1088.

Cohn discusses the "three principal impediments against microtonal music" and the solutions offered by Hába and others in this valuable introductory guide to the appreciation of quarter-tone music. He devotes only a short portion of the article, however, to Ives's *Three Quarter-Tone Pieces.*

B730 Souster, Tim. Review of *Essays Before a Sonata and Other Writings,* by Charles Ives, edited by Howard Boatwright. *Tempo* 89 (Summer 1969): 34. *See:* **B660**

Souster focuses exclusively on one of the "other writings" referred to in the title, namely "Some Quartertone Impressions." He asserts hyperbolically at the outset that Ives's essay "must contain some of the most perspicacious and prophetic writing on music of this century," and continues by praising the essay's pragmatism and "the fact that its speculations are preceded by aural experience."

B731 Pappastavrou, George. "Ives' Quarter-Tone Pieces." *Clavier* 13, no. 7 (1974): 31-32.

After their premiere in 1925 these pieces remained unperformed until Pappastavrou re-introduced them in 1963. [One year earlier Pappastavrou had the distinction of making the first recording of *"Concord" Sonata* (**D56**) since Kirkpatrick's recorded premiere was issued in 1948]. In this article Pappastavrou explains the impossible physical problems of tuning a grand piano up a quarter-tone as Ives suggests and offers the practical and aesthetically sound solution of tuning one piano a quarter-tone down. He also singles out special passages that intrigue him and discusses a few ensemble problems.

B732 Perison, Harry. "The Quarter-tone System of Charles Ives." *Current Musicology* 18 (1974): 96-104.

A summary and explication of Ives's quarter-tone theories as expressed in the composer's 1925 essay, "Some Quarter-Tone Impressions." Perison also provides examples of how Ives applied his theories to the *Three Quarter-Tone Pieces* that received their premiere the year of the essay. Although he acknowledges the historical importance of these three pieces in which "Ives contrived a reasonably developed quarter-tone system," Perison concludes that Ives "considered the system tentative at best."

ORGAN MUSIC

B733 Noss, Luther. "Charles Ives: Variations on 'America' (1891); 'Adeste Fideles' in an Organ Prelude (1897)." New York: Music Press, Inc., 1949. *Notes* 7, no. 3 (June 1950): 446.

Review of the first and to date only publication of Ives's organ works. [A new edition was commissioned by Presser in 1988]. The *Variations*, despite the "glimpse of things to come" in the polytonal interludes is considered mainly as a work of old-fashioned musical fun ("at best an amusing novelty for recital programs"); he describes *Adeste Fideles* as an "extraordinary fragment" with "a convincing ethereal haze" of dissonance.

B734 Birkby, Arthur. "Ives, the Organist." *Clavier* 13, no. 7 (1974): 29-30.

Unaware that the largest number of organ compositions disappeared as a result of Ives's abandoning them at the Central Presbyterian Church in New York when he resigned his organ position in 1902, Birkby speculates that Ives avoided the organ in response to the "unfavorable atmosphere" towards this instrument during the middle and late 19th century. Birkby is unsympathetic to the two works known to him. He assesses *Adeste Fideles* as a "completely arbitrary bit of nonsense" and the *Variations on America* as "not important, but lots of fun!"

B735 "Unpublished Organ Works of Charles Ives Premiered." *The Diapason* 65, no. 10 (September 1974): 3. *See:* **W85a**

Announcement of five premieres of unpublished Ives organ works, April 21, 1974, as part of the Ives Centennial Festival sponsored by and held at the University of Minnesota: *Variations on Jerusalem the Golden; Organ Fugue for Prof. H. W. Parker; Four Interludes for Hymns*; and *Fugue in C Minor.* The announcement credits Jeffrey Wasson, who presented an introductory lecture prior to Kim Kasling's performance, with editing these works from Ives manuscripts. The concert also included performances of the two published organ works, *Adeste Fidelis* and *Variations on America.*

B736 Wasson, Jeffrey. "The Organ Works of Charles Ives: A Research Summary." In *Student Musicologists at Minnesota* 6 (1975-1976): 280-289.

A useful annotated summary of all known Ives organ works conveniently arranged by categories according to their state of completion or availability. For each work Wasson imparts pertinent chronological and manuscript information, and he offers thoughtful suggestions regarding reconstruction possibilities for the incomplete and even the lost compositions.

B737 Schuneman, Robert. "Kim Kasling in Chicago--A Review." *The Diapason* 67, no. 2 (January 1976): 9+.

Review of two organ concerts in which Ives works were performed in newly-edited versions by Wasson: *Variations on Jerusalem the Golden* and *Canzonetta*. The editor preceded Kasling's second concert, entirely devoted to Ives, with a lecture. Also at this second concert Kasling premiered Wasson's arrangement of "The Alcotts" from *"Concord" Sonata*, described by the reviewer as "a surprisingly substantive and idiomatic organ piece, displaying far more depth of expression than all the other works."

General

B738 Thomson, Virgil. "Music--Crude but Careful." *New York Herald Tribune*, March 4, 1948, page 17. *See:* **W90a**

Review of performances of Ives's *Psalm 67* and the first New York performance of his *Three Harvest Home Chorales*, March 3 at Carnegie Hall, Robert Shaw conducting the Collegiate Chorale. Thomson dismisses *Psalm 67* as "a dissonant diatonic piece that never quite comes off," and gives more (and largely favorable) attention to the less familiar *Chorales*: "All are polytonal and of intrinsic harmonic interest. Whether they are musically interesting all through and genuinely expressive or merely supreme examples of Yankee ingenuity I am not sure, though they were performed twice." He concludes with genuine praise for the Ives "storehouse of many good things" and his pleasure to hear any Ives work that is "carefully performed."

B739 Sabin, Robert. "Twentieth-Century Americans." In *Choral Music: A Symposium*, edited by Arthur Jacobs, pp. 371-372. Baltimore: Penguin Books, 1963; reprinted 1978.

In this survey of twentieth-century American choral music, Sabin glances at *Psalm 67*, with its bitonality which he views as "very mild for Ives," [musical illustration of the B section included] and the *Harvest Home Chorales*, of which he writes that "their fantastic dissonances and harmonic combinations, are like all of Ives's music--so powerfully expressive that one forgets their idiosyncrasies."

B740 Malloch, William. "More Stravinsky by Stravinsky--And Ivesian Explorations." *High Fidelity* 10, no. 8 (August 1966): 12, 15, and 18.

In the Ives portion of this article Malloch discusses how the producer of Columbia records, John McClure, in addition to his commitment to recording all the works of Stravinsky with the composer conducting, "has declared his intention of documenting on discs every note of Charles Ives that can be put into performable shape." Malloch then discusses the forthcoming series of Ives choral music in new performance editions and often in premiere performances by Gregg Smith and his chorale.

B741 Miller, Philip L. "Music for Chorus." *The American Record Guide* 33, no. 5 (January 1967): 410+.

Review of Ives's *Music for Chorus* performed by the Gregg Smith Singers (Columbia MS-6921). Miller notes the historical significance of this recording that contains numerous first releases, contrasts the choral-orchestral versions with their song versions, "marvels" at Ives's "courage in offering such things to the choirs of the nineties," and cites for special distinction the "haunting and infinitely peaceful setting" of *Psalm 90*. He also praises the performers for their "splendid account of all this exciting music."

B742 Hall, David. "The Choral Music of Charles Ives." *HiFi/Stereo Review* 18, no. 1 (January 1967): 74-75.

Review of Ives's *Music for Chorus* (Columbia MS-6921), conducted by Gregg Smith. Although Hall prefers the recording and performance quality of Shaw's version of the *Harvest Home Chorales* (RCA Victor LSC/LM 2676), "this by no means diminishes the enormous importance of this Columbia album either in terms of interpretative merit, musical substance, or spacious and highly effective stereo sonics." Of the other works on the Columbia album, most of which are premiere recordings, Hall ranks *Psalm 90*, "a major Ives masterpiece," a work of "unerring declamatory power and stunning textural tone-painting....the finest and most moving work in the album." Completing the album are *General William Booth, Serenity, The Circus Band, December, The New River*, and *Psalms 24, 67, 100, and 150*.

B743 Kumlien, Wendell Clarke. "The Sacred Choral Music of Charles Ives: A Study in Style Development." D.M.A. dissertation, University of Illinois, 1969. 564 pp. [An abstract, not included in the dissertation, was published in *The Choral Journal* 16, no. 2 (1975): 21].

"A detailed examination of twenty-three sacred choral compositions." Kumlien examines the sources (Chapter I), discusses Ives's "choice of sacred texts" and his religious upbringing and church related experiences (Chapter II), and surveys"twelve choral works from 1885 to 1898" (Chapter III), and "eleven works from 1894 to 1902" (Part IV). For each work in

Chapters III and IV Kumlien provides source information and editorial suggestions, a discussion of the text and its treatment, and a structural analysis. In Part V, "summary and conclusions," Kumlien points out the more salient features of each work, those elements which are pertinent to the development of Ives's style." [Quotations excerpted from the 1975 abstract.] The dissertation concludes with two useful appendixes: Appendix I, "Unpublished Editions and Reconstructions" (18 works); and Appendix II, "Photostat Copies of Original Manuscripts Used for Reconstructions by the Author" (6 works).

Early sacred works analyzed: *Psalm 42; Benedictus; I Think of Thee; Turn Ye, Turn Ye; Communion Service; Crossing the Bar; Search Me; O Lord, God of My Life; Easter Carol; Lord God, Thy Sea Is Mighty; The Light That Is Felt; All-Forgiving.*
Experimental and mature works analyzed: *Psalms 67, 150, 54, 25, 24, 100, 14, 135,* and *90; Processional: Let There Be Light; Three Harvest Home Chorales.*

B744 Frankenstein, Alfred. "New Ivesian Discoveries." *High Fidelity* 20, no. 3 (March 1970): 92.

Review of the second volume of Ives's choral music, conducted by Gregg Smith (Columbia MS 7321 [1969]). Among the sacred choral works on Side 1 Frankenstein considers *Psalm 25* "the most important" and *Psalm 135* "also a major work." *Psalms 14* and *54* are "more admirable for their ingenuities than their expressiveness." Frankenstein also praises the secular choral music on side 2, especially the exceedingly brief *Duty* and *Vita* and the nine wide-ranging solo songs that round out the disc: *Let There Be Light; Walt Whitman; On the Antipodes; The Last Reader; Luck and Work; Like a Sick Eagle; Tolerance; Incantation; The Pond; At Sea; The Children's Hour;* and *The Rainbow.*

B745 Miller, Philip L. "Review of Ives Choral Music." *The American Record Guide* 36, no. 9 (May 1970): 674.

Review of the second volume of Ives's choral music, conducted by Gregg Smith, Columbia MS 7321 [1969]. Miller quotes Smith's assertion that "this recording completes the cycle of Psalms except for No. 23, which has been lost"; in fact, Smith has overlooked the immature *Psalm 42*, composed when Ives was eleven, which is also extant. Miller looks at the issue of whether an "operatic" or "commercial" vocal style is more appropriate to Ives [the present song performances lean towards the commercial but "lovers of good vocalism should not be scared off"], and concludes that "it is a testimony to the solidity of Ives's music that two such different approaches are acceptable."

B746 Tipton, Julius R. "Some Observations on the Choral Style of Charles Ives." *American Choral Review* 12 (1970): 99-105.

Tipton confines his observations to two Ives choral works, *Psalm 24* and the *Three Harvest Home Chorales*. The illustrated remarks are sometimes erroneous (e.g., the accepted completion date for the *Chorales* is 1901, but Tipton gives 1912 without citing a reason for his departure), and too often superficial or simply unclear. Among his more helpful observations Tipton notes Ives's practice of featuring a particular interval within a musical section and his surprising textual associations, dissonance for God and consonance for man, in *Psalm 24*.

B747 Kumlien, Wendell C. "The Music for Chorus." *Music Educator's Journal* 61, no. 2 (October 1974): 48-52.

An overview of Ives's sacred and secular choral works. Although Kumlien does not provide a grand total of Ives's choral output [about seventy works], he prefaces his survey with the information that "about thirty of his choral scores probably can never be completed, since entire sections or organ parts are missing or were not written down," and that "twenty-two of his original choral scores were retranscribed for voice and piano for inclusion in several published song collections." Kumlien mentions the three adolescent choral works that Ives composed between 1885 and 1888 and the larger group of works composed between 1888 and 1893 that "are of more historical interest because they show more originality in the development of Ives's style."

The largest section in Kumlien's article consists of brief but useful musical descriptions of the Psalm settings and other "astonishing sacred choral works" that Ives composed between 1894 and 1902 [at least two Psalms, *25* and *100*, which he lists as "in manuscript" since have been published]. Finally, Kumlien surveys the songs for unison choir and orchestra (1909-1920), most of which Ives transcribed for solo voice and piano and placed in his *114 Songs*. *See*: **B743**

B748 Lamb, Gordon H. "Charles Ives 1874-1954." *The Choral Journal* 15, no. 2 (1974): 12-13.

Introductory remarks and paragraph evaluations of several published Ives choral works: *Psalms 67, 90*, and *150*; *Three*

Harvest Home Chorales; Charlie Rutlage; Walking; Evening; Circus Band; The Celestial Country; and *General Booth Enters into Heaven.* Lamb focuses on the performance possibilities for each work before concluding with an itemized discography of Ives's choral music available in 1974.

B749   Smith, Gregg. "Charles Ives: The Man and His Music; Charles Ives and His Music for Chorus." *The Choral Journal* 15, no. 3 (1974): 17-20.

In his introductory remarks Smith, an ardent champion of Ives choral music as editor and conductor, conveys his unexpurgated enthusiam for Ives's genius. He places the choral works in historical perspective, points out that Ives's abrupt change from sacred to secular choral music after 1902 paralleled his decision to focus his professional life exclusively on business, and surveys Ives's choral work as a whole. He then categorizes Ives's published choral music "by forces involved," e.g., "large chorus and large orchestra," "chorus and chamber orchestra," "chorus and piano(s)," and "other choral music," and catalogs all of the published Ives choral music in helpful annotated lists arranged by Ives's three choral publishers, Presser-Mercury, Peer-International, and Associated Music.

B750   Sole, Kenneth Gale. "A Study and Performance of Five Psalms Settings and The Celestial Country by Charles Edward Ives." D.M.A. dissertation, University of Southern California, 1976. 211 pp.

The five psalms Sole has selected to analyze are *Psalms 14, 67, 90, 100,* and *150.* For each he provides source information (and calligraphically stunning performance editions *of Psalms 14, 100,* and *139* in an appendix), a discussion of musical features such as harmony and form, and a proportionally generous amount of commentary on the meaning of the texts and Ives's accommodation to this meaning. Sole's lack of sympathy with *The Celestial Country* leads to rather perfunctory, albeit useful, analytical remarks and outlines for each movement of this work. He considers it merely a "student exercise," in which Ives exhibits "a lack of concern over many musical considerations, the treatment of the text being but one" and posits the untenable hypothesis that Ives presented this inferior student work knowing that he would be resigning from Central Presbyterian Church. Finally, Sole discusses performance issues and offers practical rehearsal solutions for each work, concluding that *Psalm 14* and parts of *Psalm 90* pose by far the greatest difficulties.

B751   Groh, Jack Curran. "A Conductor's Analysis of and Preparation
and Approach to Polyrhythms: With Particular Attention to
Polyrhythms in Certain of the Choral Works of Charles E. Ives."
D.M.A. dissertation, University of Missouri, Kansas City, 1978.
83 pp. [Abstract published in *Missouri Journal of Research in
Music Education* 4, no. 3 (1979): 92-93].

A useful thesis for any conductor interested in a method to
rehearse Ives's polyrhythms. Although he discusses polyrhthmic
problems in *Psalm 54* and the applicability of his thesis to other
Ives works (e.g., *Psalm 135*), Groh's primary focus is on the
second *Harvest Home Chorale*. He selected this work because it
presents a "high degree of polyrhythmic activity...where on several
occasions there exits the rhythmic ratio of 9:8:6."

After establishing that the work is worthy of rehearsal time and
deserves a rhythmically precise performance, he then proposes a
methodical approach that can reduce rehearsal time to ten hours.
Among his rehearsal techniques Groh proposes rhythmic drills,
the use of a Billotti Trinome (a machine that can simultaneously
produce three different tempos), walking and chanting, videotape,
and sixty hours of private practice by the conductor. Those who
follow Groh's precepts can expect "an increased facility in left
hand cueing and conducting."

The Celestial Country [W89]

B752   "A New Cantata." *The New York Times*, April 20, 1902, page 12.
[The complete review is reprinted in **B750**]. *See:* **W89a**

Review of the April 18 performance of Ives's *The Celestial Country*,
performed at the Central Presbyterian Church. After describing
the work and Alford's "not particularly felicitous English version,"
the reviewer voiced his view that the performance suffered
irreparably from insufficient performing forces--an octet when a
full chorus was needed. The reviewer described the work as
"scholarly and well made...spirited and melodious, and, with a
full chorus, should be as effective in the whole as it was on this
occasion in some of the details." Three numbers were cited as the
"most successful": *Naught That Country Needeth, Seek the Things
Before Us,* and the *Intermezzo.*

B753   "Charles E. Ives' Concert and New Cantata, 'The Celestial
Country.'" *Musical Courier* 44, no. 17 (23 April 1902): 34. [Most
of the review is reprinted in **B750**]. *See:* **W89a**

Review of the April 18 performance of Ives's *The Celestial Country*, performed at the Central Presbyterian Church. Ives, introduced as a student of Parker, is praised for producing a work marked by "homogeneity, coming from the interweaving of appropriate themes." The reviewer also describes the Intermezzo as "full of unusual harmonies and pleasing throughout," the finale as exhibiting "some original ideas, many complex rhythms and effective part writing," and "a triumphant close."

That Ives was impervious to all of this praise is evident from a cursory examination of his personal copy of this review, across which he wrote "damn rot and worse," and within a few days of this concert Ives resigned permanently from his position as organist of Central Presbyterian. There would be few professional concerts (and no reviews) of Ives's music forthcoming until 1921. *See*: **Appendix 2**

B754 Yellin, Victor Fell. "Review of the First Recording of *The Celestial Country*, by Charles E. Ives." *The Musical Quarterly* 60, no. 3 (July 1974): 500-508.

The release of Farberman's recording of *The Celestial Country* **(D59)** prompted a consideration of the work. According to Yellin, this work "provides us with the link, until now missing, that finally joins Ives to the march of American music history and enables us to make objective, rather than invidious, comparisons between Ives and his music master of four years, Parker." In fact, Yellin considers Ives's "lack of discipline and impatience for success" a "tragedy" that could have been avoided had Ives "allowed himself to learn more from Parker, thereby developing greater self-critical faculties and a surer technique of composition."

Yellin goes on to examine "the myth of Ives's independence from Parker," and dispels this myth persuasively when noting the textual and stylistic parallels between Parker's *Hora Novissima* and Ives's *The Celestial Country* that reveal Ives's unmistakable indebtedness to his teacher. Yellin also asks whether the lukewarm reviews for his most ambitious work might be "one of the main reasons why Ives forsook music as a profession."

B755 Balshaw, Paul A. "The Celestial Country: An Introduction." *The Choral Journal* 15, no. 7 (1975): 16-20.

After providing background based on Yellin's historical overview and the parallels between Ives and Parker **(B755)**, Balshaw presents an illustrated musical overview of the structure, texture, harmony, and rhythm in Ives's *The Celestial Country*. In the process Balshaw offers strong negative criticisms, such as Ives's "simplistic" and "unoriginal" reuse of musical material (structure), the "unidiomatic" writing for keyboards and strings (texture), Ives's decision to be harmonically 'safe' and traditional, and his failure to use repetitive rhythms "judiciously." Balshaw considers *The Celestial Country* musically inferior but of great historical usefulness for those wishing to trace Ives's stylistic evolution.

B756   Koch, Gerhard R. "'Das himmlische Land' von Ives." *Musica* 29, no. 3 (1975): 230-233. *See*: **W89b**

Review of the Hessian Radio Orchestra Frankfurt performance of Ives's *The Celestial Country*, the first European performance of the work. Koch stresses the uncharacteristically traditional style of the work, even when considering the relatively early composition date, and contrasts this style with Ives's better known avant-garde writing from the same period.

B757   Harris, Roger. Review of *The Celestial Country*. *Music and Musicians* 27, no. 10 (June 1979): 64+. *See*: **W89c**

Review of an April 21 performance of Ives's *The Celestial Country*, Queen Elizabeth Hall, with Andrew Parrott conducting the Taverner Choir. Harris writes that "this performance gave us the rare opportunity of making an acquaintance with a little-known but equally worth-while composer--Ives the traditionalist," that "Ives manages to use the traditional materials in a remarkably fresh and imaginative way," and that the work "deserves further hearings."

Psalms [W113-116, 119-122]

B758   Siebert, Mark. "Psalm XXIV." *Notes* 14, no. 4 (September 1957): 618-619.

In this short review of the first publication of *Psalm 24* (Mercury, 1955) Siebert focuses on the "formidable" performance difficulties, e.g., "the line of any given part is completely impossible." He hesitates to call Ives's "vertical tonal blocks" chords and criticizes "the excessive use of dotted rhythms," but writes that Ives's "expression" is "fresh and quite appropriate to the text."

B759   Vinquist, Mary Ann. "The Psalm Settings of Charles Ives." M.A. thesis, Indiana University, 1965. 102 pp.

In this survey of Ives's choral psalms Vinquist explores the psalm tradition in New England and the "decline of congregational Psalm singing" before Ives was born. She also discusses the textual departures between Ives's settings and his sources, especially the King James version. Vinquist's musical observations are arranged by musical parameter (melody, harmony, rhythm, and form) rather than by individual psalms. The text contains useful contemporary samples of Orders of Worship from the two churches where Ives served as organist from 1898 and 1902, the First Presbyterian Church in Bloomfield, New Jersey, and the Central Presbyterian Church in New York City, and the appendix includes complete facsimiles of *Search me, O Lord* and *Psalm 90* and portions of *Psalms 14, 23, 24,* and *54.*

B760 Christiansen, Larry A. "Charles E. Ives and the Sixty-Seventh Psalm." *Music/The AGO-RCCO Magazine* 3, no. 2 (February 1969): 20-21.

Christiansen clearly discusses the relationship between the textual and musical form and briefly describes important formal, harmonic, and rhythmic features of *Psalm 67.* Among his illustrated observations Christiansen notes how Ives used "sharp" (minor 2nd/major 7th) dissonances to prepare for resolving "mild" (major 2nd/minor 7th) dissonances, a practice "functionally comparable to the relationship of dissonance and consonance in the context of monotonal tertian structures."

B761 Wells, William B. "Sacred Choral Octavos" and "Psalm 150." *Notes* 30, no. 3 (1974): 634-640.

Brief comments on several choral works of Ives and Schoenberg, including the recently published *Celestial Country* and *Psalm 90,* and a review of the publication of Ives's *Psalm 150* (Merion, 1972). Like most writers in Ives's centennial year, Wells focuses on such matters as the precocious bitonality of *Psalm 67,* the "canonic 12-tone" *Psalm 25* ("fifteen or so years before Schoenberg had evolved his 12-tone theories"), the "sytematic plan" of *Psalm 24,* and the "rhythmic complexity" of *Psalm 135.* Wells also reiterates the frequently voiced contrasts between Schoenberg, the "utter professional," with Ives, who "approached music as an avocation." Wells's central point is that "while many of the psalm settings fail to convince as complete works, they are interesting for their audacious musical experiments."

B762 Engen, David P. "The Choral Psalms of Charles Ives: A Performer's Analysis of Psalm 90." *Church Music (St. Louis)* 1 (1976): 20-27.

Engen follows preliminary remarks, based in large part on Cowell's biography (**B354**) with a musical analysis of *Psalm 90*, in which he focuses on the work's harmonic unity. He gives special attention to a description of the five opening chords that Ives labelled and used throughout the work as unifying elements against the unwavering C major ostinato in the bass, and presents a useful outline that indicates where these chords appear in each of the seventeen verses. Other features of the article include suggestions for organ registrations in each verse and a list of 80 church and organ compositions by Ives. *See also*: **B763-764**

B763 Grantham, Donald. "A Harmonic 'Leitmotif' System in Ives's Psalm 90." *In Theory Only* 5, no. 2 (May-June 1979): 3-14.

Grantham, like Engen (**B762**), describes Ives's five labelled chords, but Grantham, in addition to providing a table also provides numerous illustrated examples to show where these "leitmotifs" occur throughout the work. His central thesis is that "whenever a psalm verse suggests one of the religious concepts defined in the introduction, the leitmotif associated with that concept is used in the musical representation of the verse." He also explains those passages in which the great-minded Ives avoids Emerson's "foolish consistency" to this thesis. *See also*: **B764**

B764 Alwes, Chester L. "Formal Structure as a Guide to Rehearsal Strategy in Psalm 90 by Charles Ives." *The Choral Journal* 25, no. 8 (1985): 21-25.

Alwes adds to Engen (**B762**) and Grantham (**B763**) by discussing the three extant sources for *Psalm 90*, "all of which date from 1923-24." Although Alwes's emphasis is on rehearsal techniques that will facilitate the performance of the work rather than an analysis of the work itself, he does show by musical example how Ives uses a "wrath" leitmotif throughout the work. He also discusses two techniques that are prominent in Psalm 90 and other choral works, "whole-tone motion away from and back to a unison and the use of palindrome structures."

B765 Hitchcock, H. Wiley. "Ivesiana. The Gottschalk Connection." *Newsletter of the Institute for Studies in American Music* 15, no. 1 (November 1985): 5.

Hitchcock shares his discovery (in slightly less than a column) that in Ives's *Psalm 90*, "the second half-verse [of Verse 6] quotes baldly from Louis Moreau Gottschalk's celebrated piano piece *The Last Hope*." The author offers several possibilities to explain the meaning of this particular quotation, but concludes that "Ives's intention" is "puzzling indeed."

Miscellaneous

Three Harvest Home Chorales [W90]
See also: **B50**

B766 Sabin, Robert. "Choral and Piano Works by Charles Ives Issued." *Musical America* 69, no. 8 (June 1949): 28.

Review of the publication of the *Three Harvest Home Chorales* (Mercury, 1949). Sabin describes Ives "as one of those prophetic artists who rise completely above the fashions and foibles of their time" and bestows unequivocal praise for the human as well as esthetic value in "this outwardly forbidding music." After a brief comment on each chorale, Sabin concludes that "choral directors with courage and imagination should welcome the publication of these pieces, for they will richly reward the labor expended on them."

Johnny Poe [W101]

B767 Kerner, Leighton. "Lilacs in Bloom" *The Village Voice* 26 (28 January 1981): 66. See: **W101b**

Review of the New York premiere of *Johnny Poe*, January 12, in Carnegie Hall, performed by the Brooklyn Philharmonia. Kerner describes the work, one of Ives's last (1925), as "a male-chorus-and-orchestra song about a popular Princeton man killed in World War I." The work is filled with dissonant "jabs" and "bites." "And there's a stunning middle section of *Sprechstimme* that the men of the Brooklyn Philharmonia Chorus and C. W. Post College Chorus barked out proudly." Kerner concludes that the work (published in Kirkpatrick's edition by Peer, 1978) "should be in every male-chorus library."

Lincoln, the Great Commoner [W92]

B768 Kammerer, Rafael. "Orchestras of America Offers Lincoln Program." *Musical America* 80, no. 3 (March 1960): 24.

Review of the premiere of *Lincoln, the Great Commoner*, February 10, Carnegie Hall, with Richard Korn conducting the Orchestra of America. The program also included three other works based on Lincoln and two "Negro Rhapsodies." Of Ives's "significant piece of Americana" Kammerer writes: "This score of Ives is as stunning a *tour de force* of planned chaos as can be found in all music."

Processional: Let There Be Light [W123]

B769 Woodward, Henry. "Processional: Let There Be Light." *Notes* 13, no. 2 (March 1956): 349.

In this brief review of the first publication of Ives's *Processional* (Peer, 1955) Woodward writes that "the music is harsh and vigorous, and, while I am not altogether convinced of it on paper, I suspect it comes off brilliantly in performance."

They Are There! [W99b]

B770 Siebert, Mark. "They Are There: A War Song March, 1917." *Notes* 20, no. 4 (1963): 565-566.

Review of the first publication of Ives's *They Are There! A War Song March, 1917* (Peer, 1961). Siebert notes the "curious" but "typical" state of affairs that such a work, "written in the mood of spirited indignation characteristic of America in 1917, should finally turn up in print in 1961." He describes the main formal and tonal features briefly, cites Ives's many quotations, and offers the following judgment: "A more wonderfully extravagant and appropriate 'war march song' can hardly be imagined than the present work, in which Ives fully reflected the spirit of the time in his own inimitable manner."

SONGS

General

B771 Ives, Charles. "'Postface' to 114 Songs." Redding Conn.: By the author, 1922; reprinted in *Essays Before a Sonata, The Majority, and Other Writings by Charles Ives*, selected and edited by Howard Boatwright, pp. 120-131. New York: W. W. Norton, 1970. *See*: **B660**

Ives explains that like "every normal man" he has "creative insight (an unpopular) and an interest, desire and ability to express it (another unpopular statement)." Thus he offers his extraordinary collection of *114 Songs* to the world. In adapting a passage from James Bailey's *Life in Danbury* Ives explains that he has "not 'written a book at all,'" but "merely cleaned house." Apparently Ives shares the view of the 'Danbury News Man' "who became convinced that a man never knows his vices and virtues until that great and solemn event, that first sunny day in spring when he wants to go fishing, but stays home and *helps* his wife clean house."

Ives does not share his often-quoted comments on the songs until his final paragraph. He wants songs to have "a *few* rights, the same as other ordinary citizens." Should songs not be allowed to remain 'in the leaf' [i.e., unsung] or to "be free at times from the dominion of the thorax, the diaphragm, the ear, and other points of interest?"

B772 _____. "Letter to the Sun." *New York Evening Sun*, September 10, 1922; reprinted in *Essays Before a Sonata, The Majority, and Other Writings by Charles Ives*, selected and edited by Howard Boatwright, pp. 132-133. New York: W. W. Norton, 1970. *See*: **B660**

Ives informs the *New York Sun* that his "offer to send complimentary copies [of *114 Songs*] to anyone was made in an inconspicuous place at the back of the book," and laments the "public demand" that the *Sun* created by publicizing it and making it ostentatiously conspicuous. Writes Ives: "If I'd intended to play the role of public-benefactor to your readers, I'd offer to distribute Schubert's songs--not mine."

B773 Patterson, Frank. "The Perfect Modernist--A Little Primer of Basic Principles (Twelfth Installment)." *Musical Courier* 85, no. 12 (21 September 1922): 20.

Review of the printed but unpublished *114 Songs* which Ives had recently sent to the *Musical Courier*. Patterson notes with relief that this volume "has swept away the clouds of misapprehension" formed the previous year when they received Ives's *"Concord" Sonata.* Now the *Musical Courier* knows that Ives, "the American Satie, not only deserves ridicule, but that he *intends* his music to be a joke." Patterson focuses on Ives's accompanying "facetious comments," and writes of the music only that "few people, scarcely any amateurs, possess sufficient piano technic to play these compositions."

B774 Meyer, Alfred H. "Yaddo--A May Festival." *Modern Music* 9, no. 4 (May-June 1932): 172-176. *See:* **W133a**

Review of the first Festival of Contemporary American Music concerts that took place on April 30 and May 1 at Yaddo, Saratoga Springs, New York. Meyer devotes one paragraph of his review to the seven Ives songs performed on this historic occasion [published in *Seven Songs*], and within this short space manages to praise four: "The melody is strikingly unconventional and economical, with marvelously apt certainty of expressive touch. The accompaniments often contain shrewdly chosen bits of realistic suggestion." He considers the "religioso" finale of *Charlie Rutlage* the finest "example of purely musical humor," and he is genuinely moved by the touching sincerity and gentlest accompaniments...of the genuinely religious" song, *Serenity.*

B775 Rosenfeld, Paul. "Two Native Groups." *The New Republic* 75 (5 July 1933): 209-210. *See:* **W133a**

Rosenfeld expresses his hope that the recent performances of Ives songs at the Yaddo Festival and the second Pan-American concert "prognosticates the reimpression of the volume in which the 'old master' of modern American music originally collected the entire hundred and fourteen of his lyrics [*sic*]." After discussing the Americanisn of Ives's volume, Rosenfeld concludes that it is a "worthy confession and consequence of the old national belief that all things possessing breath of their own, no matter how dissimilar, are ultimately compatible."

B776 Berger, Arthur. "The Songs of Charles Ives." *Musical Mercury* 1 (October-November 1934): 97-98.

Although he grants Ives the title, "father of indigenous music,"
Berger severely reprimands Ives for composing "crude and
redundant" and often "confused" music which, despite "*outre*"
technical devices, is fundamentally derivative. He does, however,
exempt *Charlie Rutlage* from these criticisms. Berger also
acknowledges the apparent contradiction of his concluding
endorsement of "a product of which so much has been said in
deprecation." In his defense Berger admits "that despite their
many flaws the significant works of Charles Ives have had a
unique appeal" to himself "and many others."

B777 Copland, Aaron. "One Hundred and Fourteen Songs." *Modern
Music* 11, no. 2 (January-February 1934): 59-64; reprinted as
"The Ives Case" in *Our New Music*, pp. 149-161. New York:
McGraw Hill, 1941; reprinted with additional comments in *The
New Music*, pp. 109-117. New York: W. W. Norton, 1968.

An important early assessment of Ives and his songs. Copland
begins by noting the apologetic tone in Ives's "Postface" (**B771**),
which accompanied the publication of his *114 Songs* in 1922,
recalls his "first impression" of "confusion" and adds fifteen to
Ives's list of eight songs of "little or no value." He praises four
songs from the "first songs of importance...around 1900," and
considers *Where the Eagle* "remarkable for its depth of feeling, its
concision, its originality." Copland is less favorably disposed to
the "comparatively undistinguished" songs from 1908-1910, the
adaptations from orchestral and chamber music, and the songs
Ives labelled "war songs" and "street songs."

In his evaluation of Ives's most important songs (1919-1921)
Copland writes that "taken as a whole, and despite many and
serious shortcomings, these songs are a unique and memorable
contribution to the art of song-writing in America." He attributes
"weaknesses" as a consequence of Ives's "lack of that kind of self-
criticism which only actual performance and public reaction can
bring." In an addendum dated 1967 and published in *The New
Music* (1968), Copland gives himself a "pat on the back" for his
perspicacity in 1934, but pleads guilty to an overly severe
judgment of Ives's ability to "organize his material, particularly in
his larger works."

B778 Downes, Olin. "American Music Sung by Thomas." *The New York
Times*, March 25, 1940, page 10. *See*: **W150a**

Review of a Town Hall recital sung by John Charles Thomas, in
which *Pigeons in the Grass, Alas* from *Four Saints in Three Acts*

"brought down the house." In reviewing the two Ives songs performed in this program Downes characterized *The Greatest Man* as "wholly unconventional in metrical structure and poetic idiom...a song which could be placed in no category of song written thus far known" and *The White Gulls* as a "far more subtle and exceedingly different mood picture."

B779   Ruff, Erwin. "A Study of Five Songs of Charles Ives." M.A. thesis, Eastman School of Music of the University of Rochester, 1942. 44 pp.

Historically important as the first dissertation devoted solely to Ives. The five songs discussed, chosen in part to contradict the myth that Ives was impossibly difficult to perform, are *Two Little Flowers, Serenity, The Greatest Man, Evening,* and *Ann Street.* Ruff does not substantiate his interpretations (e.g., "melody converted rhythmically to portray the 'amorous' feeling") and his assertion that a figure suggests the "Gershwinian manner" cannot withstand chronological scrutiny, but he demonstrates a sympathy, rare in 1942, for Ives's "amazing facility in organizing many styles and idioms into a unified whole." Most original are several examples of "rhythmic, melodic, and chordal tone painting."

B780   Schaefer, Theodore. "1. Chanson de Florian. 2. It Strikes Me That... 3. The Light That Is Felt." *Notes* 7, no. 4 (September 1950): 636-637.

Review of the publication of three Ives songs (Mercury, 1950). Schaefer describes the *Chanson de Florian* as "engaging, piquant Ives," *It Strikes Me That* as "bombastic, ranting Ives," and *The Light That Is Felt* as "tender and appealing Ives."

B781   Sear, H. G. "Charles Ives, Song Writer." *Monthly Musical Record* 81 (1951): 34-42.

A survey of Ives's song output. According to Sear, "we have assimilated the [German] *Lieder* for themselves," but "to understand the songs of Ives we need to know something of the man himself." Our knowledge of Ives's desire to express his individuality, for example, "explains and even excuses...many things that appear in the songs, and for that matter, in the whole of his output." Although Sear considers quotation in music "never a desirable habit," he acknowledges Ives's "ability to digest in his own music the tunes of other men and other times." He concludes by suggesting that "a group of them would add salt to many a recital."

B782 "Ten Songs by Charles Ives." *Musical Courier* 148, no. 6 (15 November 1953): 26.

Brief description of Ives's *Ten Songs* (Peer, 1953). "The settings, highly unconventional, include some of the more easily performed of his creations. Particularly memorable are *Omens and Oracles*, and *Forward into Light*, the latter from a cantata, *The Celestial Country*."

B783 Hume, Paul. "Ten Songs." *Notes* 11, no. 3 (June 1954): 449-450.

Review of the publication of Ives's *Ten Songs* (Peer, 1953). Despite the "fine possibilities" in *The Circus Band* and *Memories*, Hume writes that "in general the songs lack the power and appositeness to text that make the later Ives songs unique in their strength."

B784 Sabin, Robert. "Ten Songs." *Musical America* 74, no. 13 (1 November 1954): 26.

Review of Ives's *Ten Songs* (Peer, 1953). Sabin briefly places the collection in chronological perspective (1888-1902) and mentions the author of each text. In reviewing the songs Sabin writes that "there is not one that does not bear the stamp of Ives's emotional sincerity and amazing creative daring." He concludes that "none of these ten songs measures up to Ives's best, but all of them possess strong historical interest, and several might well find a place on recital programs."

B785 Miller, Philip L. "Ives Songs." *The American Record Guide* 21, no. 11 (July 1955).

Review of Boatwright and Kirkpatrick recording of twenty-three Ives songs (Overtone OVER 7). Miller notes Ives's "curious mixture of old and new," and that his "music needs just the mixture of humility and assurance the present interpreters bring to bear upon it." His concluding remarks go as far as to praise this recording unequivocally "as the finest contribution to the literature of recorded American song any artist has made to date."

B786 Lowens, Irving. "Twelve Songs and Fourteen Songs." *Notes* 13, no. 2 (March 1956): 354-355.

Review of two Ives song publications, *Twelve Songs* (Peer, 1954) and *Fourteen Songs* (Peer, 1955). Lowens has "no intention of getting caught in the middle of the current Ives war" and takes a middle ground between those who consider Ives a "genius" and those who cry "fraud." He calls attention to Ives's own sense of spoofing in three songs and cites the "utterly fantastic yet strangely moving lengthy quotation from the *Marseillaise* in *In Flanders Fields*, the "creepy harmonization" of Mason's hymn in *Watchman*, and several "indubitably serious, dreadfully difficult songs" in these "essential acquisitions."

B787 Nathan, Hans. "The Modern Period--United States of America." In *A History of Song*, edited by Denis Stevens, pp. 431-437. New York: W. W. Norton, 1960.

In this brief survey of Ives song writing style Nathan maintains that in Ives's "basic method" of creating individualized musical images for each literary image, the composer creates "an additive song structure--a decisive departure from the practice of the nineteenth century." Although he acknowledges Ives's originality, Nathan writes that the songs "often convince not so much in toto (by way of large-scale musical relationships and contrasts) as through an accumulation of bold details."

B788 Gooding, David. "A Study of the Quotation Process in the Songs for Voice and Piano of Charles Edward Ives." M.A. thesis, Western Reserve University, 1963. 94 pp.

Following Kirkpatrick's *Catalogue* (**B7**) Gooding lists the Ives songs that contain quotations ("non-original material"), distinguishes six categories of usage, and provides numerous musical examples in each category. He also speculates on additional unidentified melodic material that suggests "non-original" sources. Although Gooding's contribution to scholarship is relatively inconspicuous, his various tables and appendixes and bracketed quotations in the thirty-six musical illustrations are arranged for maximum usefulness.

B789 Layton, Bentley. "An Introduction to the 114 Songs." B.A. thesis, Harvard University, 1963. 135 pp.

In his thoughtful overview of Ives's philosophy Layton fulfills his stated purpose of providing "an aesthetic introduction" to Ives's *114 Songs*. He explores "Ives's concept of music," and discusses the *114 Songs* in relationship to this concept, and concludes that Ives composed "as a philosopher as well as an artist." Not only does Layton contribute to an understanding of Ives's interpretation of Emerson, he presents what may be the only serious discussion of the influence of Henry Sturt, an article of whom Ives cites in his *Essays* (**B660**). Layton also discusses how Ives uses analogy and text to achieve formal unity and the "versatility" and "potential subtlety" of Ives's controversial practice of quotation. In addition to the insightful treatment of the *114 Songs*, Layton's thesis is a worthwhile study of Ives's aesthetic thought.

B790   Newman, Philip Edward. "The Songs of Charles Ives." Ph.D. dissertation, University of Iowa, 1967. 3 volumes. [Vol. 1, 289 pages; Vol. 2, 441 pages; Vol. 3, published songs. "Not microfilmed at request of school. Available for consultation at University of Iowa Library"].

In Volume 1 Newman provides a chronological overview of Ives's 153 extant songs (out of his grand total of 205 songs) divided into seven periods, emphasizing those songs in each period which display unusual technical and stylistic features. Another chapter (Chapter 3) devoted to "those musical characteristics difficult to survey adequately in a chronological presentation" includes discussions of the following topics: "Experimental or Schematic Songs," "Dodecaphonic Premonitions," "Songs to Non-English Texts," "Songs Rearranged from Earlier Music," "Use of Musical Quotations," and "Final Cadences." In Chapter 4 Newman considers "Ives's Choice of Texts," and in Chapter 5 he discusses "Manuscript Marginalia, Footnotes, and Notes Under Titles."

Newman introduces Volume 2 with an itemized outline of Ives song collections, published and unpublished, including the little-known song collections (from two to twenty-seven songs) that Ives bound between 1898 and 1919. Newman then discusses individually all of Ives's known songs, arranged chronologically according to the period classification of Volume 1. For each song Newman includes texts and text variants, dates, derivations, location in published and unpublished sources, later version, publication errors and variants between published versions, notes under titles, footnotes to published versions, marginalia on manuscripts, range, special markings, length, lists of musical quotations, an outline of song forms, and finally, "an impression of the song's mood, musical characteristics, and to some extent, performance difficulties."

The appendixes in Volume 1 are especially useful: "Songs in Numerical Order," "Published Songs," "Unpublished Songs,"

"Songs To Be Published," "Settings of Non-english Texts or English Translations," "Authors of Poems Set by Ives," "Musical Quotations Appearing in the Songs," "Standard Song Texts and Hymn Texts Used by Ives," and "Publishers of Ives's Songs." The bibliography includes a large number of reviews of Ives works in every genre.

B791   Kirkpatrick, John. ed. "Preface" to *Eleven Songs and Two Harmonizations*. New York: Associated Music, 1968.

Kirkpatrick ponders why Ives decided to exclude the songs and harmonizations of this important edition. He describes Ives's "understandably reticent" attitude about his early church solos (*Rock of Ages* and *Far From My Heav'nly Home*), his distaste for "romanticizing" about death (*There is a Certain Garden* and *No More*), his growing discomfort with his early heartsongs (*A Scotch Lullaby* and *God Bless and Keep Thee*) and songs of courtship (*Pictures*). Among other still less tangible causes for omission Kirkpatrick posits Ives's "lack of confidence" in his later work (*A Sea Dirge*), a possible insecurity with French (*The One Way*), the privacy of his allusion to Debussy's style (*Yellow Leaves*), the "tenuousness" of *Peaks*, and his unwillingness to claim as his own "a modest accompaniment for practical performance" (*Christmas Carol* and *In the Mornin'*).

B792   Miller, Philip L. "Songs by Charles Ives and Others." *The American Record Guide* 35, no. 4 (December 1968): 305.

Review of the Marni Nixon recording of thirteen Ives songs (Nonesuch H-71209). Miller compares Nixon's renditions with the songs which overlap with other recordings and places her interpretations an easy winner over Puffer (**D66**) but less "melting" than Boatwright [he also mentions Nixon's "one novelty," *Soliloquy*]. Miller also rates Ives's songs highly: "I wonder if any other composer has contributed so much to the permanent literature of American song."

B793   Sly, Caroline Ware. "The Language of Ives's Solo Songs." M.A. thesis, Smith College, 1970. 157 pp.

Following introductory chapters on Ives's life and aesthetics, Sly offers a thoughtful chronological survey of Ives's songs. She traces Ives's evolving attitude towards quotation and his increasingly sophisticated musical treatment of his borrowed material [only one song according to Sly, *Slow March*, incorporates this technique prior to 1911]. As a result of her analysis Sly concludes that "the musical idea that usually is the generating impulse in an Ives song is a sonority." Songs treated at some length include (in chronological order): *The Circus Band*; *In Summer Fields*; *The Children's Hour* ["the first song to show us any of the promise that Ives later fulfills"]; *Rough Wind*; *Harpalus*; *Walking*; *The Cage*; *A Farewell to Land*; *Requiem* [the first important song that includes a quotation]; *Lincoln, the Great Commoner*; *General William Booth*; *The Swimmers*; *Tom Sails Away*; *Evening*; *Hymn* ["the most interesting musical treatment of a piece of quote material"]; *Walt Whitman*; and *Majority*.

B794 Hurst, Rolland Wood. "A Study, Analysis, and Performance of Selected Songs by Charles Ives." Ed.D. dissertation, 1971. 158 pp.

An overview of Ives's songs and an analysis of thirty-one selected for performance. Hurst borrows Kirkpatrick's seven chronological categories ("Pre Yale" to "Final Songs"), and adds seven stylistic categories (e.g., "conventional idiom," "experimental harmony") and seven textual groupings (e.g, "descriptive and narrative songs" and "biographical songs"). The strength of this dissertation is Hurst's analysis of the thirty-one songs, particularly his imaginative (if not always persuasive) performance suggestions.

B795 Miller, Philip L. "House of Many Mansions: The Songs of Charles Ives and the American Experience." *The American Record Guide* 37, no. 9 (May 1971): 563+.

Review of twenty-three songs recorded by Evelyn Lear and Thomas Stewart on Columbia M-30229 (1971). Miller briefly notes special features of each song and points out several "firsts" (e.g., *There Is A Lane* and the solo song version of *Duty*). He praises "the two singers and their strong and vital pianist" [Alan Mandel] and concludes with his endorsement that "in every way this release is a major addition to the Ives discography."

B796 Boatwright, Howard. "The Songs." *Music Educator's Journal* 61, no. 2 (October 1974): 42-47.

In his overview of Ives's songs Boatwright touches on numerous topics. He surveys Ives's choice of texts from popular poets and newspapers to Ives's own texts, which comprise "nearly a third" of the total, and he quotes liberally from Ives's "Postface" (**B771**). He also includes a brief publication history of Ives's songs, about which Boatwright raises a disturbing thought: "Considering how slowly his music gained acceptance, one may wonder what would have become of it if Ives had had no financial resources to assure the existence and circulation (though limited) of printed copies." He concludes with the assessment that Ives's songs "stand at the center of American song just as those of Schubert are at the center of the German lied."

B797   Schoffman, Nachum. "The Songs of Charles Ives." Ph.D. dissertation, Hebrew University, 1975. 377 pp.

Schoffman devotes the largest portion of his dissertation to separate anaylses of twenty songs, "not chosen by any criterion of excellence or special significance, but simply to cover the entire field of inquiry with as little duplication as possible." The songs chosen include: *When Stars Are in the Quiet Skies*; *In Summer Fields*; *Romanzo di Central Park*; *The Cage*; *Like a Sick Eagle*; *Soliloquy*; *The Innate*; *A Farewell to Land*; *At Sea*; *Old Home Day*; *Majority*; *The Swimmers*; *August, September, December*; *Grantchester*; *West London*; *Evening*; *Aeschylus and Sophocles*; and *On the Antipodes*. He begins each analysis with a discussion of the song's genesis (e.g., works in other genres that used the same material, Ives's adaptation of the original text), and he never fails to discuss Ives's revisions in subsequent publications, whenever applicable. Schoffman presents a broad range of parameters and demonstrates an impressive command of Ives's technical procedures.

Schoffman's stated purpose in Part II is to present "general conclusions about Ives's methods of composition...classified by stylistic elements." He continues to emphasize songs, while citing examples from other genres. The subject areas discussed include: Texts; Manner of Declamation; Notation; Intervals; Chords; Complexes; Textures; Compound Polyphony; Quotations; Time; Seriality; Working Out; Convergence, Summation, Emergence; Forms; Indeterminacy; and Programmaticism. "Part III contains a summation of Part II, in the form of a concise restatement of the components of the style, and an attempt to place the phenomenon of Ives in its correct historical perspective." Appendixes include an alphabetical list of songs and publications and an alphabetical list of "those songs which are derived or adapted from previously composed works."

B798   "Can You Play Over 100 Songs by Ives on One Program? (100th Birthday Salute--Marathon Concert at Unity Christ Church, St. Louis)." *Triangle* 69, no. 4 (1975): 9

Review of an unusual Ives Centennial Birthday Concert (October 20, 1974) in St. Louis, in which 141 Ives songs were performed. Jay Willoughby (voice) and Evelyn Sillars (pianist) contributed 112 of this grand total. The songs were presented to a rotating audience (ranging between 200 and 400) in chronological order within a seven hour period--including an hour recess for birthday cake.

B799 Barr, Raymond A. "The Art Songs of Charles Ives." In *South Florida's Historic Ives Festival, 1974-1976*, edited by F. Warren O'Reilly, pp. 53-56.

Summary of Ives's "Postface" (**B771**) followed by brief comments on the relationship between music and text in the following representative songs: *The Greatest Man*; *Two Little Flowers*; *An Election*; *Majority*; and *General William Booth.*

B800 Freed, Richard. "Songs of Charles Ives: A Listening Experience One Is as Eager to Share as to Repeat." *Stereo Review* 37, no. 3 (September 1976): 86.

Unconditionally positive review of the seventeen songs recorded by Jan DeGaetani (mezzo-soprano) and Gilbert Kalish (piano) (**D63**). Freed describes these performances as a "staggering display of virtuosity" and a "genuine inspiration." Nevertheless, he is still more impressed with "the richness and variety of the songs themselves."

B801 Morgan, Robert P. "DeGaetani Is Ives: Up to All Expectations." *High Fidelity/Musical America* 26, no. 8 (August 1976): 84.

Review of DeGaetani's recording of seventeen Ives songs accompanined by Kalish (**D63**). Morgan considers this disc a "milestone, not only for those interested in Ives, but for anyone concerned with the development of 'art' song" and cites specific examples in support of his assertion that DeGaetani (with a significant contribution from Kalish) is unsurpassed as an interpreter of this literature.

B802 Bloomingdale, Wayne. "Must a Song Always Be a Song?" *American Music Teacher* 26, no. 5 (1977): 14.

A brief essay designed for singers unfamiliar with Ives's songs. Bloomingdale introduces the uninitiated to the notion that "The Idea is more important than the actual sound" in an Ives song. He also groups the songs into four "specific areas of thought and experience" and briefly describes the nature of each.

B803 Hitchcock, H. Wiley. "Charles Ives's Book of 114 Songs." In *A Musical Offering: Essays in Honor of Martin Bernstein*, edited by Edward H. Clinksdale and Claire Brook, pp. 127-135. New York: Pendragon Press, 1977.

Excellent introduction to Ives's major song publication, the *114 Songs*. For Hitchcock, "the most striking thing about Ives, outside of his radical and experimental turn of mind, is his embracing without reservation both the cultivated and vernacular traditions of American music." Hitchcock also views Ives as "a man of his time, not ahead of it," a man who retained his spiritual identity to the late nineteenth century in America and who never relinquished his ties to the "'household' song of sentiment, a genre piece giving voice to some emotion of affection, nostalgia, or yearning."

B804 Miller, Philip L. "Ives: 19 Song Recording." *The American Record Guide* 40, no. 3 (February 1977): 36-37.

Review of the Fischer-Dieskau recording of nineteen Ives songs (accompanied by Ponti) on DG 2530 696 [1976]. Miller is severe with Fischer-Dieskau and judges the non-American singer unable to "speak freely" except in the three German songs. He also surveys briefly other renditions of Ives songs and among these ranks the Boatwright/Kirkpatrick 1955 recordings at the top of his list with the Nixon/McCabe team "runnersup," and the DeGaetani/Kalish pairing (**D63**) a surprisingly distant third. In keeping with his decision "to look with a little reverence" at this body of literature, Miller views Ives's setting of *Ich grolle nicht* as decidedly less distinguished than Schumann's.

B805 Elson, James. "The Songs of Charles Ives (1874-1954)." *National Association of Teachers of Singing Bulletin* 35, no. 1 (1978): 9-11.

Conventional biographical survey followed by a brief glimpse at Ives's *114 Songs*. In considering Ives's choice of texts Elson states that "many of Ives' best efforts were inspired by verses of little literary merit, but which commented on America's heritage, history, or political events." After providing terse remarks on several individual songs, he confidently asserts that "singers and accompanists at almost all levels of vocal and musical ability are sure to find at least a few of them suitable for study or recital use."

B806 Friedberg, Ruth C. "Charles Ives." In *American Art Song and American Poetry Vol. 1. America Comes of Age*, pp. 43-89. Metuchen N.J. and London: The Scarecrow Press, Inc., 1981.

Friedberg has selected twelve songs in order to explore "the relationships between Ives and those leading American poets of the nineteenth and early twentieth centuries": *The Children's Hour* (Longfellow); *The Light That Is Felt* and *Serenity* (Whittier); *The Last Reader* (Holmes); *The Indians* (Sprague); *Duty* (Emerson); *Walt Whitman* (Whitman); *General William Booth Enters into Heaven* (Lindsay); *Thoreau* (Thoreau); *The Swimmers* (Untermeyer); *Afterglow* (Cooper, Jr.); and *Maple Leaves* (Aldrich). She points out the consistency of Ives's "nonobservance of poetic integrity, which includes using fragments of larger poems, word repetition and omission, changes in word order or in the words themselves, and occasional retitling of the original poem" as well as Ives's "careful and effective attention to the details of word setting that is in the finest tradition of art song compositions and belies any suspicion of randomness that might arise from the poetic fragmentation."

Friedberg includes some brief but useful information on each poet, discusses Ives's specific departures from the original poems, suggests possible motivations (e.g., Ives's tendency to omit pessimistic poetic passages), and describes how Ives conveys general moods as well as individual word painting for each text. Liberal musical illustrations accompany the text.

B807 Velten, Klaus. "Ein Komponist zwischen den Zeiten; traditioneller Geist und fortschritiche Gestaltungsweise in Klavier liedern von Charles Ives." *Musik und Bildung* (December 1983): 11-15.

General analysis of *In Summer Fields* (*Feldeinsamkeit*) [complete score from *114 Songs* included], *Mists*, and *The White Gulls*. Of special interest is Velten's analogy between the piano accompaninent in *Mists* (i.e., the three-chord repetitions on a pedal point) and the "disposition" of whole-tone scale material in Debussy's piano prelude *Voiles*. As he does in his analysis of *Evening* (**B810**), Velten stresses Ives's expression of the "symbolic rebuke between nature and mankind in the organization of the tonal materials" ("das symbolische Verweisen zwischen Natur und Mensch in der Organisation des Tonmaterials").

Individual Songs
[arranged alphabetically]

B808 [*Ann Street*, **W156**] Starr, Lawrence. "Style and Substance: 'Ann Street' by Charles Ives." *Perspectives of New Music* 15, no. 2 (Spring-Summer 1977): 23-33.

An important and provocative analysis of an Ives work. After providing a convincing demonstration "that *Ann Street* is in fact a unified and coherent piece in a very traditional sense," Starr explains that he considers analysis "inadequate, simply because it would fail to illuminate the most basic auditory phenomenon of the piece: the frequent and sometimes violent changes of character every few bars." Starr then dissects the song's nineteen measures into nine "sectional divisions...based on changes in musical idiom," and concludes that the resulting "stylistic pattern...a basic source of unity and coherence" is independent of traditional concepts of unity or "programmatic text painting." *See also*: **B700**

B809 [*The Cage*, **W195**] Euteneuer-Rohrer, Ursula Henrietta. "Charles E. Ives: 'The Cage.'" *Neuland* 1 (1980): 47-51.

Brief formal, melodic, rhythmic, and harmonic analysis of *The Cage*. Other areas of focus include the relationship between music and text and especially the significant lack of coincidence between the vocal line and the piano accompaniment (synchronized only on the word "wonder"). Includes a reprinting of the score from *114 Songs*.

B810 [*Evening*, **W133**] Velten, Klaus. "Der Kuenstler und die Natur-- ein Interpretation--beitrag zum Liedshaffen vor Charles." *Musik und Bildung* 13 (September 1981): 544-546.

Analysis of *Evening* with an emphasis on programmatic elements. Velten suggests that Ives in his setting of Milton, bases his formal musical structure on the voice of nature. The essay includes a score of the complete song.

B811 ['*In the Mornin*' (arr. of *Give Me Jesus*)] Hitchcock, H. Wiley. "Charles Ives and the Spiritual 'In the Morning'/*Give Me Jesus*." Publication forthcoming in a *Festschrift* honoring Eileen Southern of Harvard University.

Hitchcock relates how the Negro spiritual, *Give Me Jesus*, was sung to Ives by a family friend, Miss Evelyn Stiles, and compares the Stiles/Ives version with other versions unknown to Ives published between 1867 and 1925 [Ives's version apparently dates from 1929]. Hitchcock supports his judgment that "the Stiles/Ives melody transcends in shapeliness any of the other versions" and demonstrates Ives's "respect and affection for oral-tradition music reflected in transcriptions of breathtaking accuracy: Béla Bartók." Similarly Hitchcock explains how Ives's accompaniment "transcends in richness of detail, and artfulness in general" the other published accompaniments and "supports, matches, and in subtle ways enlarges upon the rhythmic nuances of the melody 'as Miss Stiles must have sung it.'"

B812 [*On the Antipodes*, **W279**] Argento, Dominick. "A Digest Analysis of Ives' 'On the Antipodes.'" In *Student Musicologists at Minnesota* 6 (1975-1976): 192-200.

The term "digest analysis" in the title refers to the fact that only an outline of Mr. Argento's lecture (taken by an unidentified student) has been published. Nevertheless, the student took good notes and the digest is a detailed one. Argento provides numerous examples that demonstrate Ives's sensitivity to textual nuances revolving around the central textual idea of antipodal contrasts. His analysis of tempo, meter, rhythm, counterpoint, and form reinforce this sensitivity but also conveys that, "at every level, Ives breaks up what almost becomes a mechanical procedure."

B813 [*Serenity*, **W173**] Green, Douglass M. "*Exempli gratia*: A Chord Motive in Ives's *Serenity*." *In Theory Only* 4, no. 5 (October 1978): 20-21.

Green argues that Ives's *Serenity* "can be understood as a case of a chord progression generating the overall structure of a piece." One might arrive at the opposite conclusion [in response to Green's assertion that "metrical placement of the voice and accompaniment make it clear that the C# ø7 is a neighbor chord which serves to prolong the main harmony B ø9-7,"], about *which* harmony Ives's metrical placement confirms as "main," but Green's analysis, including his brief comments on the relationship between text and music, is otherwise convincing.

B814 [*Sunrise*, **W285**] Kirkpatrick, John. "*Sunrise*: Charles Ives' Last Composition." *Peters Notes* 1, no. 2 (1978): 7.

Kirkpatrick focuses on Ives compositional work, "the tentative sketch of the poem" [the complete final text is included] and the much revised musical sketch, which "shows uncertainty in medium." He suggests that "violin is the best all-round choice for the '2nd *voice*,'" and advocates an arrangement of "the whole accompaniment for violin and piano as freely as would be advantageous to the musical statement, while remaining faithful to Ives's concept and texture."

B815 [*The Things Our Fathers Loved,* **W174**] Coleman, Judy Bounds. "Charles Ives: The Man and His Songs." *The Midwest Quarterly* 1, no. 4 (July 1960): 295-320.

After a biographical overview and general remarks about Ives's songs Coleman analyzes *The Things Our Fathers Loved.* She discusses the programmatic significance of Ives's borrowed material and tries to show how Ives used rhythm, harmony, and melody to illustrate a text that "seems to emanate from the subconscious." The complete song is included in the text.

B816 [*The Things Our Fathers Loved,* **W174**] Feder, Stuart. "The Nostalgia of Charles Ives: An Essay in Affects and Music." *The Annual of Psychonalysis* 10 (1982): 301-332.

Feder considers "the possibility that psychoanalysis might be informed by music rather than the opposite; that a study of how affect achieves auditory representation might say something about the nature of the affect itself in mental life." After reviewing the literature on nostalgia, Feder examines in some detail Ives's song, *The Things Our Fathers Loved,* "a concentrated work of art" that "both represents and communicates nostalgia."

B817 [*Vote for Names,* **W277**] Schoffman, Nachum. "Charles Ives's Song 'Vote for Names.'" *Current Musicology* 23 (1977): 56-68.

Schoffman argues at the outset that the published realization of this unfinished song (Peer, 1968) "is an inadequate expression of the material that *does* appear in the manuscript." He then discusses Ives's verbal notations in order "to understand the historical background, and the ideas embodied in the song," and explains in detail what prompted the difficult editorial decisions he needed to make. Unfortunately, the faintness of the facsimile makes it difficult to confirm Schoffman's notational accuracy, but his realization (included) is clearly reasoned as well as imaginative.

Appendix 1
Alphabetical
List of Compositions

Numbers following each title, e.g., W247, refer to the **Works and Performances** section of this volume.

Abide with Me, W247
Adeste Fideles, W88 *See*: *Prelude on Adeste Fideles*
Aeschylus and Sophocles, W280
Afterglow, W170
Allegro, W226:3
All-Enduring, W259
All-forgiving, Look on Me, W118
All the Way Around and Back, W54
America Variations See: *Variations on America*
Amphion See: *From "Amphion"*
Ann Street, W156
Anti-Abolitionist Riots, The See: Studies, W78:9
At Parting, W246
At Sea, W135
At the River, W176
August, W166
Autumn, W191
Autumn Landscapes from Pine Mountains, W24
Because of You, W267
Because Thou Art, W270
Bells of Yale, or Chapel Chimes, The, W130
Benedictus in E, W104
Berceuse, W224:2
Boys in Blue, The, W127
Bread of the World, W108
Browning Overture See: *Robert Browning Overture*
Cage, The, W195
Camp Meeting, The, W178
Canon, W242:1 & 2
[Canzonetta], F, W87
Cartoons (Take-offs), W29
Celestial Railroad, The, W82
Celestial Country, The, W89
Central Park in the Dark, W28:2

Chanson de Florian, W209
Charlie Rutlage, W141
Children's Hour, The, W205
Christmas Carol, A, W231
Chromâtimelôdtune, small orchestra, W37
Chromâtimelôdtune, brass quartet, piano, W57
Circus Band, The, W187
Collection, The, W169
Communion Service, W107
"Concord" Sonata See: Piano Sonatas, W65
Country Band March, W23
Cradle Song, W164
Crossing the Bar, W106
December, W93 and W168
Decoration Day See: Symphonies, W4:2
Decoration Day, violin and piano *See*: Violin Sonatas, W61
Disclosure, W138
Down East, W186
Dreams, W216
Duty See: *Two Slants [Christian and Pagan]*, no. 1
Easter Carol, W111
Ein Ton See: *From Night of Frost in May*
Election, An See: *"Nov. 2, 1920"*
Elégie, W208
Emerson Overture/Concerto, W14
Ending Year, The, W193:2 and W266:2
Evening, W133
Evidence, W189:2
Farewell to Land, A, W275
Far from My Heav'nly Home, W248
Fède, La, W165
Feldeinsamkeit See: *In Summer Fields*
Flag Song, W269
Four Transcriptions from Emerson, W80
Fourth of July, The See: Symphonies, W4:3
Forward into Light, W230
For You and Me!, W128
[Friendship], W254
From "Amphion," W237
From Night of Frost in May, W215:2
From "Paracelsus," W161
From the Steeples and the Mountains, W45
From "The Swimmers," W158
Frühlingslied See: *I Travelled among Unknown Men*
Fugue in 4 keys, on The Shining Shore, W20

"1,2,3," W172
One Way, The, W281
On Judges Walk See: Rough Wind
On the Antipodes, W279
On the Counter, W159
Orchestral Set No. 1 See: Symphonies, W5
Orchestral Set No. 2 See: Symphonies, W6
Orchestral Set No. 3 See: Symphonies, W8
Over the Pavements, W25
Overture and March "1776," W22
Overture in g, W11
Paracelsus See: From "Paracelsus"
Peaks, W282
Perfect Day, A, W252
Piano Sonatas:
>   *First Piano Sonata,* W64
>   *Second Piano Sonata "Concord, Mass., 1840-60,"* W65
Piano Trio See: Trio for Piano, Violin, and Cello
Pictures, W272
Pond, The, W143 *See: Remembrance*
Postlude in F, W10
Prelude, trombone, 2 violins, organ, W44
Prelude on Adeste Fideles, W88
Premonitions, W155
Processional, W123
Psalms:
>   *Psalm 14,* W120
>   *Psalm 24,* W116
>   *Psalm 25,* W121
>   *Psalm 42,* W102
>   *Psalm 54,* W115
>   *Psalm 67,* W114
>   *Psalm 90,* W124
>   *Psalm 100,* W119
>   *Psalm 135,* W122
>   *Psalm 150,* W113
Quarter-tone Chorale, strings, W34
Qu'il m'irait bien, W207
Ragtime Dances Nos. 1-4, small orchestra, W21
Ragtime Dances, piano, W75
Rainbow, The (So May It Be!), W33 and W139
Religion, W147
Remembrance [The Pond], W143 *See: The Pond*
Resolution, W144
Requiem, W276

Robert Browning Overture, W15
Rock of Ages, W249
[Romanzo di Central Park], W227
Rosamunde, W210:1 & 2
Rosenzweig, W226:2
Rough Wind, W200:2
Runaway Horse on Main Street, W40 and W274
Scherzo (Over the Pavements) See: Over the Pavements
Scotch Lullaby, A, W261
Sea Dirge, A, W284
Sea of Sleep, The See: Those Evening Bells
Search Me O Lord, W109
See'r, The, W160
Sehnsucht See: Allegro
September, W167
Serenade, W126
Serenity, W173
[Set of Five Take-Offs], W77
Set of 3 Short Pieces, A, W55
Set No. 1, small orchestra, W30
Set No. 2, small orchestra, W32
Set No. 3, small orchestra, W36
Set for Theatre or Chamber Orchestra, W27
Side Show, The, W163
Slow March, W245
Slugging a Vampire, W203:2
Some Southpaw Pitching See: Studies, W78:21
Sneak Thief, W97
Soliloquy or a Study in 7th and Other Things, W273
Song, W257
Song for Anything, A, W220:3
Song for Harvest Season, W256
Song of Mary's, A, W129
Song of the Dead, The See: The Ending Year and *The Waiting Soul*
Songs My Mother Taught Me, W239
Son of a Gambolier, A, W185
South Wind, The, W228:2
Spring Song, W196
String Quartets:
> *First String Quartet*, W41
> *Pre-Second String Quartet*, W42
> *Second String Quartet*, W43
Studies Nos. 1-23, piano, W78
Sunrise, W285
Swimmers, The See: From "The Swimmers"

Symphonies:
> *First Symphony,* W1
> *Second Symphony,* W2
> *Third Symphony,* W3
> *A Symphony: New England Holidays,* W4
> *First Orchestral Set (A New England Symphony; Three Places in New England),* W5
> *Second Orchestral Set,* W6
> *Fourth Symphony,* W7
> *Third Orchestral Set,* W8
> *Universe Symphony,* W9

Take-off No. 3 "Rube trying to walk 2 to 3!!!," W50
(Take-offs), small orchestra *See: Cartoons*
Take-offs, piano *See:* [Set of Five Take-Offs]
Tarrant Moss, W203:1
Thanksgiving and/or Forefather's Day See: Symphonies, W4:4
There Is a Certain Garden, W255
There Is a Lane, W202:2
They Are There!, W99:2 and W181:2
Things Our Father's Loved, The, W174
This Year's at the Spring, W125
Thoreau, W179
Those Evening Bells, W194:2
Three Harvest Home Chorales, W90
Three Improvisations, W83
Three-Page Sonata, W76
Three Places in New England See: Symphonies, W5
Three Protests See: Varied Air and Variations
Three Quarter-Tone Pieces, W84
Through Night and Day, W253
To Edith, W243
Tolerance, W190
Tom Sails Away, W182
Tone Roads et al, W35
Trio for Violin, Cello, and Piano, W49
Turn Ye, Turn Ye, W105
Two Little Flowers, W235
Two Slants (Christian and Pagan), W94 and W140
Unanswered Question, The, W28:1
Universe Symphony See: Symphonies, W9
Variations on America, W86
Variations on Jerusalem the Golden, W85
Varied Air and Variations [with *Three Protests*], W81
Violin Sonatas:
> *Pre-First Violin Sonata,* W58

Appendix 2
Premieres, Publications, and Recordings (1887 - 1954)

Premieres

1887? *Psalm* 42; Danbury, CT; Methodist Church [*W102a*]

1888 (January 16) *Holiday Quickstep*: Danbury, CT; Taylor's Opera House; George Ives's Theater Orchestra; George Ives, conductor [*W17a*]

1888-1889? *Benedictus in E*: Danbury, CT; Baptist Church [*W104a*]

1889 (February 21) *I Think of Thee, My God*: Brewster, NY [*W103a*]

1889-1890 (April 14, 1889 or April 13, 1890) *Turn Ye, Turn Ye*: Danbury, CT; Baptist Church [*W105a*]

1890 (May 25) *Abide with Me*: Danbury, CT; Baptist Church; William Oakley (voice) [*W247a*]

    ? (November) *Communion Service*: Danbury, CT; St. James Episcopal Church [*W107a*]

1890-1891 (May 24, 1890 and/or Mary 25, 1891) *Crossing the Bar*: Danbury, CT; Baptist Church [*W106a*]

1891 (July 4) *Variations on America*: Brewster, NY; Ives [*W86a*]

1892 (April 17) *Easter Carol*: Danbury, CT; Baptist Church [*W111a*]

    (October) *March "Intercollegiate"*: Danbury, CT; Danbury Fairground; Danbury Band [*W38a*]

    (December 11) *I Come to Thee*: Danbury, CT; Baptist Church [*W110a*]

1895 (June 4) *The Light That Is Felt*: New Haven; Center Church; John Griggs (bass) [*W117a*]

1896 or 1897 (June 14) *Psalm 150*: New Haven; Center Church; John
Griggs, director [*W113a*]

1897   *The Bells of Yale, or Chapel Chimes*: New Haven; Yale Glee Club
[*W130a*]

1897-1898 ? *Psalms 24 and 100*: New Haven, Center Church; Newark,
NJ, Newark Presbyterian; Bloomfield, NJ, Bloomfield Presbyterian
[*W116a* and *W119a*]

1902   (April 18) *The Celestial Country*: New York; Central Presbyterian
Church; Annie Wilson (soprano); Emma Williams (contralto); E.
Ellsworth Giles (tenor); George A. Fleming (baritone); The
Kaltenborn String Quartet; Ives (organ) [*W89a*]

1904   (May 21) *Ragtime Dances Nos. 1 and 2*: New Haven; Hyperion
Theater; Frank A. Fichtl, conductor [*W21a*]

1917   (on or about April 15) *In Flanders Fields*: New York; Waldorf-
Astoria; McCall Lanham (vioice); William Lewis (piano) [*W180a*]

(April 22) *Third Violin Sonata*: New York; Carnegie Chamber Music
Hall; David Talmadge (violin); Stuart Ross (piano) [*W62a*]

1924   (March 18) *Second Violin Sonata*: New York; Aeolian Hall; Jerome
Goldstein (violin); Rex Tillson (piano) [*W60a*]. (February 8) *Three
Quarter-Tone Pieces*; Mew York; Chickering Hall; Hans Barth and
Sigmund Klein [lecture by E. Robert Schmitz] [No.3] *[W84a]*.

1925   (February 14) *Three Quarter-Tone Pieces*: New York; Aeolian Hall;
Hans Barth and Sigmund Klein (piano) [Nos. 2 and 3] [*W84b*]

1927   (January 29) *Fourth Symphony* (first and second movements):
New York; Town Hall; New York Philharmonic; Euguene Goosens,
conductor [*W7a*]

1931   (January 10) *First Orchestral Set* (chamber version): New York;
Town Hall; Boston Chamber Orchestra; Nicholas Slonimsky,
conductor [*W5a*]

(September 3) *Washington's Birthday*: San Francisco; New Music
Society Orchestra; Nicholas Slonimsky, conductor [*W4b*]

(December 27) *Decoration Day*: Havana; Havana Philharmonic;
Amadeo Roldan; conductor [*W4c*; see also *W4a*]

1932   (February 16) *Set for Theatre or Chamber Orchestra*: New York; New School for Social Research; Pan American Chamber Orchestra; Adolph Weiss, conductor [*W27a*]

(February 21) *The Fourth of July*: Paris; Paris Symphony Orchestra; Nicholas Slonimsky, conductor [*W4d*]

(May 1) *Evening, Charlie Rutlage, The Indians, Maple Leaves, The See'r, Serenity*, and *Walking*: Saratoga Springs, NY; Hubert Linscott (baritone); Aaron Copland (piano) [*W133a*]

(December 8) *The New River* (song): Hamburg, Germany; Musikhall, Kleiner Saal; Mary Bell (soprano); Henry Cowell (piano) [*W133b*]

1934   (April 15) *The New River* and *December* (choral versions): New York; Town Hall; Nicholas Slonimsky, conductor [*W91a* and *W93a*]

(May 28) *Hallowe'en*: Stringart String Quartet [*W51a*]

1937   (May 6) *Psalm 67*: New York; WPA's Theatre of Music; Madrigal Singers; Lehman Engel, director [*W114a*]

1939   (January 20): *Second Piano Sonata*: New York; Town Hall; John Kirkpatrick [*W65a*]

(February 24) *The Greatest Man, Ann Street, The Side Show, The Things Our Fathers Loved, At the River, Down East, Autumn, Berceuse*, and *General William Booth Enters into Heaven*: February 24, 1939; New York; Town Hall; Mina Hager (mezzo-soprano); John Kirkpatrick (piano) [*W133c*]

1940   (January 14) *Fourth Violin Sonata*: Eudice Shapiro (violin); Irene Jacobi (piano) [*W63a*]

(March 24) *The White Gulls*: Town Hall; John Charles Thomas (baritone) [*W150a*]

1942   (April 13) *Fourth Symphony* (third movement): New York; Columbia Concert Orchestra; Bernard Herrmann, conductor (WABC radio broadcast) [*W7c*]

(November 2) *The Last Reader, From "The Swimmers," Rough Wind*, and *The Children's Hour*: New York; Town Hall; Doris Doe (mezzo-soprano); Hellmut Baerwald (piano) [*W134a*]

1946   (March 31) *First Violin Sonata*: New York; Joan Field (violin); Ray
       Lev (piano) [*W59a*].

       (April 5) *Third Symphony*: New York; Carnegie Chamber Music
       Hall; New York Little Symphony Orchestra; Lou Harrison,
       conductor [*W3a*]

       (May 11) *The Unanswered Question* and *Central Park in the Dark*:
       New York; McMillan Theatre; Juilliard Graduate School; Edgar
       Schenckman, on stage conductor; assistant, Theodore Bloomfield
       [*W28a*]

       (September 15) *Second String Quartet*: Saratoga Springs, NY;
       Walden String Quartet [*W43a*]

1948   (March 2) *Three Harvest Home Chorales*: New York; Collegiate
       Chorale [*W90a*]

       (March 12) *Four Transcriptions from Emerson*: New York; W.
       Aitken [*W80a*]

       (May 24) *Trio for Violin, Cello, and Piano*: Berea, OH; Baldwin-
       Wallace College Faculty Trio [*W49a*]

1949   (February 17) *First Piano Sonata*: New York; Town Hall; William
       Masselos [*W64a*]

       (April 25) *Three-Page Sonata* (for piano): New York; Museum of
       Modern Art; William Masselos [*W76a*]

1950   (April 30) *Studies Nos. 9 and 21*: New York; Jerrold Cox [*W78a*]

1951   (February 22) *Second Symphony*: New York; Carnegie Hall; New
       York Philharmonic; Leonard Bernstein, conductor [*W2a*]

1953   (April 26) *First Symphony*: Washington, DC; National Gallery of
       Art; National Gallery Orchestra; Richard Bales, conductor [*W1a*]

1954   (April 9) *A Symphony: "New England Holidays"* (*Thanksgiving* and
       complete four-movement cycle): Minneapolis; Northrop Memorial
       Auditorium; Minneapolis Symphony Orchestra; Antal Dorati,
       conductor [*W4e*]

Publications

1896   *For You and Me!*, for TTBB men's chorus. Molineux' Collection of
       Part Songs and Choruses for Male Voices, No. 966. New York:
       Geo. Molineux, 1896. [*W128*]

March (Two-Step)--Intercollegiate March. Philadelphia: Pepper & Co., 1896. [*W38*]

A Scotch Lullaby, for voice and piano. Text by Charles Edmund Merrill, Jr. *Yale Courant* 33 (December Third Week, 1896): 125-127. [*W261*]

William Will: A Republican Campaign Song. Text by Susan Benedict Hill. New York: Willis Woodward & Co., 1896. [*W260*]

1897   *A Song of Mory's,* for voice and piano. Text by Charles Edmund Merrill, Jr. *Yale Courant* 33 (February Fourth Week, 1897): 280-281. [*W129*]

1920   *Second Pianoforte Sonata ("Concord, Mass., 1840-60").* Redding, Conn.: By the Author, 1920. [*W65*]

1922   *114 Songs.* Redding, Conn.: By the Author, 1922.

1923   *50 Songs.* Redding, Conn.: By the Author, 1923.

1929   *The Fourth Symphony, for large orchestra, by Charles E. Ives. New Music* 2, no. 2 (1929). [second movement] [*W7:2*]

1932   *Lincoln, the Great Commoner,* for voices and orchestra. From the poem by Edwin Markham., San Francisco: New Music, 1932; reprint edition Bryn Mawr: Merion Music, n.d.; reprint edition n.p.: Edwin F. Kalmus, n.d. [*W92*]

A Set of Pieces for Theatre Orchestra. New Music Quarterly 5, no. 2 (January 1932); reprint edition, New York: New Music Edition, n.d.; reprint edition, n.p.: Edwin F. Kalmus, n.d. [*W27*]

Seven Songs. Cos Cob Press, 1932; reprint editions, Arrow Music Press, 1939, and Associated Music Publishers, 1947.

1933   *Four Songs.* New York: Mercury Music, 1933; reprint edition, 1950.

Thirty-four Songs. New Music 7, no. 1 (1933); reprint edition, Bryn Mawr: Merion Music, n.d.

1935   *Nineteen Songs. New Music* 9, no. 1 (1935); reprint edition, Bryn Mawr: Merion Music, n.d.

1939   *Sixty-seventh Psalm,* for SATB chorus. New York and London: Associated Music Publishers, 1939. [*W114*]

1942   *Serenity*, for voice or unison voices and piano. Text by John
        Greenleaf Whittier. New York: Associated Music Publishers, [ca.
        1942]. [*W173*]

        *Sonata No. 4 for Violin and Piano ("Children's Day at the Camp
        Meeting")*. New York: Arrow Music Press, 1942; reprint edtition,
        New York and London: Associated Music Publishers, n.d. [*W63*]

1947   *Piano Sonata No. 2 ("Concord, Mass., 1840-1860")*. Second edtion,
        prepared by Ives with the assistance of George F. Roberts. New
        York Arrow Music Press, 1947; reprint edtion by Associated
        Music Publishers, n.d. [*W65*]

        Study No. 22 for piano. *New Music* 21, no. 1 (October 1947): 8-9.
        [*W78:22*]

        Symphony No. 3: "The Camp Meeting." [Edited by Lou Harrison]
        [New York]: Arrow Music Press, [1947]. [*W3*]

        Three Protests [From *Varied Air and Variations*.] *New Music* 21,
        no. 1 (October 1947). [*W81*]

1949   *The Anti-Abolitionist Riots in the 1830's and 1840's* (Study No. 9),
        for piano solo. Edited by Henry Cowell. New York: Mercury
        Music, [1949]; reprint edition with corrected preface, Bryn Mawr:
        Mercury Music, n.d. [*W78:9*]

        Hallowe'en, for piano and string quartet. Hillsdale, New York:
        Boelke-Bomart, 1949. [*W51*]

        Some Southpaw Pitching (Study No. 21), for piano solo. Edited by
        Henry Cowell. New York: Mercury Music, 1949. [*W78:21*]

        Three Harvest Home Chorales, for SATB chorus with organ or
        piano. New York: Mercury Music, 1949; reprinted edition, Bryn
        Mawr: Mercury Music, n.d. [*W90*]

        Tone Roads No. 1, for chamber orchestra. New York: Peer
        International, 1949. [*W35:1*]

        Three-Page Sonata, for piano solo. [Edited by Henry Cowell.] New
        York: Mercury Music, 1949. [*W76*]

        *Variations on "America" for organ [and] Adeste fidelis in an organ
        prelude*. New York: Music Press, 1949; reprint edition, Bryn
        Mawr: Merion Music, n.d. [*W86* and *W88*]

1950   *Chanson de Florian*, for voice and piano. New York: Mercury
        Music, [1950]. [*W209*]

The Light That Is Felt, for voice and piano. New York: Mercury Music, 1950. [*W197*]

1951   *Second Sonata*, for violin and piano. New York and London: G. Schirmer, 1951. [*W60*]

Sonata No. 3 for Violin and Piano. Edited by Sol Babitz and Ingolf Dahl. Bryn Mawr: Merion Music, 1951. [*W62*]

Symphony No. 2. New York: Southern Music Publishing Company, 1951. [*W2*]

1952   *Ilmenau* ("Over all the tree tops"), for voice and piano. Text by Goethe. New York: Peer International, 1952. [*W199*]

A Night Song, for voice and piano. New York: Peer International, 1952. [*W219*]

Tone Roads No. 3, for chamber orchestra. New York: Peer International, 1952. [*W35:3*]

1953   *Largo*, for violin, clarinet, and piano. New York: Southern Music Publishing Company, 1953. [*W46*]

First Sonata, for violin and piano. New York: Peer International, 1953. [*W59*]

Ten Songs. New York: Peer International, 1953.

The Unanswered Question, for chamber orchestra. [New York]: Southern Music Publishing Company, 1953. [*W28:1*]

1954   *First Sonata for Piano*. Edited by Lou Harrison and William Masselos. New York: Peer International, 1954. [*W64*]

Scherzo: (Over the Pavements), for chamber orchestra. New York: Peer International, 1954. [*W25*]

String Quartet No. 2. New York: Peer International, 1954. [*W43*]

Twelve Songs. New York: Peer International, 1954.

Commercial Recordings Issued in Ives's Lifetime

1934   *A Symphony: "New England Holidays"* ("Barn Dance" from "*Washington's Birthday*"); *Set for Theatre Orchestra* ("*In the Night*"). The Pan American Chamber Orchestra; Nicolas Slonimsky, conductor. New Music Quarterly Recordings Vol I, No. 5, (1934); reissued on Orion ORD-7150 (1971). [*D16*]

1935   *General William Booth Enters Into Heaven.* Radiana Pazmor
(soprano); Genevieve Pitot (piano). New Music Quarterly
Recordings Vol. II, No.4 (1935); reissued on Composer
Recordings, Inc., CRI S-390E. [*D45*]

1938   *Ann Street; Charlie Rutlage; Evening; The Greatest Man;
Resolution; Two Little Flowers.* Mordecai Bauman (baritone);
Albert Hirsh (piano). New Music Recordings 1412 (1938);
reissued on Composer Recordings, Inc., CRI S-390E. [*D45*]

1939   *Psalm 67.* The Madrigal Singers; Lehman Engel, conductor.
Columbia 17 139-D.

1940   *Hymn; The Last Reader.* Ethel Luening (soprano); Lionel Nowak
(piano). Yaddo I.2.

1942   *Fourth Sonata for Violin and Piano ("Children's Day at the Camp
Meeting").* Joseph Szigeti (violin); Andor Foldes, (piano). New
Music Recordings NMR no. 1612 (1942); reissued on Composer
Recordings, Inc., CRI S-390E. [*D45*]

1947   *Second String Quartet.* The Walden String Quartet. Disc set 775
(ca. 1947); reissued on Period SPLP-501 (1950) and Folkways FM-
3369 (1967). [*D39*]

   Third Sonata for Violin and Piano [second and third movements].
Sol Babitz (violin) Ingolf Dahl (piano). Alco set AR-101 (ca. 1947).

1948   *At the River; The Cage; The Children's Hour; The Circus Band;
Cradle Song; Harpalus; Mists; The New River; A Night Song;
"1,2,3"; Rough Wind; The Side Show; Thoreau; Two Little Flowers;
Two Slants (Vita).* Ernest McChesney (tenor); Otto Herz (piano).
Concert Hall Series C Album 7.

   First Piano Sonata ["*In the Inn*" only]. John Kirkpatrick, piano.
Columbia 72535-D in set MM-749.

   Psalm 67. Hamline Choir; Robert Holiday, conductor. Hamline A
Capella Choir H.U.5 (ca. 1948); reissued on New Records Inc.
NRLP-305 (1951).

   Second Piano Sonata ("Concord, Mass., 1840-60"). John
Kirkpatrick, piano. Columbia MM-749 (1948); reissued on
Columbia ML-4250 (1950).

1949   *Three Places in New England* ["*The Housatonic at Stockbridge*"
only]. Janssen Symphony of Los Angeles; Werner Janssen,

conductor. Artist 100 (1949); reissued on Everest SDBR-3118 (1964).

1950   *Third Symphony ("The Camp Meeting").* National Gallery Orchestra; Richard Bales, conductor. WCFM LP-1.

1951   *Central Park in the Dark; Hallowe'en; Scherzo: Over the Pavements; The Unanswered Question.* The Polymusic Chamber Orchestra; Vladimir Cherniavsky (i.e., Will Lorin), conductor. Polymusic PRLP-1001.

    Charlie Rutlage. Randolph Symonette (bass-baritone); Leslie Harnley (piano). Colosseum CLPS-1008.

    Largo, for clarinet, violin and piano; *Second Sonata for Violin and Piano.* David Weber (clarinet); Elliot Magaziner (violin); Frank Glazer (piano). Polymusic PRLP-1001.

    First Sonata for Violin and Piano; Third Sonata for Violin and Piano. Joan Field (violin); Leopold Mittman (piano). Lyrichord LL-17.

    Second Sonata for Violin and Piano. Patricia Travers (violin); Otto Herz (piano). Columbia ML-2169.

1953   *At Parting; At Sea; At the River; A Christmas Carol; Feldeinsamkeit* (in English)*; Ich grolle nicht* (in English)*; Mists; A Night Thought; Tolerance; Walt Whitman; When Stars Are in the Quiet Skies.* Jacqueline Greissle (soprano); Josef Wolman (piano). SPA Records SPA-9.

    First Piano Sonata. William Masselos, piano. Columbia ML-4490. [D52]

    Set for Theatre Orchestra. Stell Anderson, piano; Vienna State Opera Orchestra; Jonathan Sternberg, conductor. Oceanic OCS-31.

1954   *Second Symphony.* Vienna Philharmonia Orchestra; F. Charles Adler, conductor. SPA Records SPA-39.

    Three Places in New England. American Recording Society Orchestra (i.e., Vienna Symphony Orchestra); Walter Hendl, conductor. American Recording Society ARS-116 (ca. 1954); reissued on Desto DST-6403E (1964). [D25]

Appendix 3
Ives's Writings

See: **B9**

Music and Aesthetics

Essays Before a Sonata. New York: Knickerbocker Press, 1920; reprinted
in *Essays Before a Sonata, The Majority, and Other Writings by
Charles Ives*, selected and edited by Howard Boatwright, pp. xxv-
102. New York: W. W. Norton, 1970. Excerpts in *Piano Sonata
No. 2 ("Concord, Mass., 1840-1860")*. Second edition, prepared by
Ives with the assistance of George F. Roberts. New York: Arrow
Music Press, 1947. See: **B660**

"'Postface' to *114 Songs*." Redding, Conn.: By the author, 1922;
reprinted in *Essays Before a Sonata, The Majority, and Other
Writings by Charles Ives*, selected and edited by Howard
Boatwright, pp. 120-131. New York: W. W. Norton, 1970. See:
B771

"Letter to the *Sun*." *New York Evening Sun*, September 10, 1922;
reprinted in *Essays Before a Sonata, The Majority, and Other
Writings by Charles Ives*, selected and edited by Howard
Boatwright, pp. 132-133. New York: W. W. Norton, 1970. See:
B772

"Some 'Quarter-Tone' Impressions," *Franco-American Musical Society
Quarterly Bulletin* (March 1925): 24-33; reprinted in *Essays
Before a Sonata, The Majority, and Other Writings by Charles Ives*,
selected and edited by Howard Boatwright, pp. 105-119. New
York: W. W. Norton, 1970. See: **B726**

"The Fourth Symphony for Large Orchestra," *New Music* 2, no. 2
(January 1929) [Conductor's Note for the Second Movement];
reprinted in *Symphony No. 4*. Performance score edited by
Theodore A. Seder, Romulus Franceschini, and Nicholas Falcone,
pp. 12-14. Preface by John Kirkpatrick. New York: Associated
Music Publishers, 1965. Excerpts reprinted as "Music and Its
Future" in *American Composers on American Music: A Symposium*,
edited by Henry Cowell, pp. 191-198. Stanford: Stanford

University Press, 1933. Reprint. New York: Frederick Ungar, 1962. *See:* **B379**

Memos [1931-1932; corections, revisions, and additions 1933-1934]. *Charles E. Ives Memos,* edited by John Kirkpatrick. New York: W. W. Norton, 1972. *See:* **B378**

"Notes for a Set of Pieces for Theater or Chamber Orchestra." *New Music* 5 (January 1932): 24. *See:* **W27**

[Program Note]. *"Three Places in New England": An Orchestral Set."* Boston: C. C. Birchard & Co., c.1935. *See:* **W5**

"'Children's Day at the Camp Meeting.' A Program Note for the Fourth Violin Sonata." *Modern Music* 19, no. 2 (January-February 1942): 115-117. Reprint. New York: Associated Music Publishers, c.1942, p. 21. *See:* **W63**

[Program Note]. *The Anti-Abolitionist Riots in the 1830's and 1840's,* for piano solo. Edited by Henry Cowell. New York: Mercury Music, [1949]; reprinted with corrected preface. Bryn Mawr: Mercury Music, n.d. *See:* **W78:9**

"Notes on the Symphony." *Symphony No. 2.* New York: Southern Music Publishing, 1951. *See:* **W2**

"Forward." *The Unanswered Question.* New York: Southern Music Publishing, 1953, p. 2. *See:* **W28:1**

[Program Note]. *Central Park in the Dark.* Edited by Jacques-Louis Monod, with notes by John Kirkpatrick. Hillsdale, N.Y.: Boelke-Bomart, 1973. *See:* **W28:2**

Politics and Society

"Stand by the President and the People" [1917]; published in *Essays Before a Sonata, The Majority, and Other Writings by Charles Ives,* selected and edited by Howard Boatwright, pp. 134-138. New York: W. W. Norton, 1970. *See:* **B371**

"A People's World Nation" [1918; additions in early 1940's]. In *Essays Before a Sonata, The Majority, and Other Writings by Charles Ives,* selected and edited by Howard Boatwright, pp. 225-231. New York: W. W. Norton, 1970. *See:* **B372**

"The Majority" [1919-1920]; published in *Essays Before a Sonata, The Majority, and Other Writings by Charles Ives*, selected and edited by Howard Boatwright, pp. 139-199. New York: W. W. Norton, 1970. See also *George's Adventure*, Appendix 9 of *Charles E. Ives: Memos*, edited by John Kirkpatrick, pp. 205-228. New York: W. W. Norton, 1972. *See:* **B373**

"Concerning a Twentieth Amendment" [1920]. "A Suggestion for a Twentieth Amendment," "Correspondence with William H. Taft," and "Letter to Editors." In *Essays Before a Sonata, The Majority, and Other Writings by Charles Ives*, selected and edited by Howard Boatwright, pp. 200-214. New York: W. W. Norton, 1970. *See:* **B374**

"College Athletics." [Letter to the Editor from Another Yale Graduate]. *The New York Times*, May 14, 1922, section 8, page 8. *See:* **B376**

"Letter to Franklin D. Roosevelt" [January 6, 1938] and "Memoranda" [1935-1938]. In *Essays Before a Sonata, The Majority, and Other Writings by Charles Ives*, selected and edited by Howard Boatwright, pp. 215-224. New York: W. W. Norton, 1970. *See:* **B380**

Insurance
See: **B12**

"The Minimum and the Maximum" [1916]. Eleven page booklet published by Ives and Myrick.

"Writing Big Policies of Life Insurance." *The Eastern Underwriter*, September 26, 1919 (*Life Insurance Salesmanship Edition*).

"The Amount to Carry--Measuring the Prospect." *Eastern Underwriter*, September 17, 1920, part 2 (Life Insurance Salesmanship Edition), pp. 35-38; issued by Ives & Myrick, printed c. 1921-1923; reprinted with "Correspondence with Darby A. Day," February 7, 1920, in *Essays Before a Sonata, The Majority, and Other Writings by Charles Ives*, selected and edited by Howard Boatwright, pp. 232-242. New York: W. W. Norton, 1970. *See:* **B375**

"How to Read the Rate Book" [1920]. Nineteen page booklet published by Ives & Myrick.

"Memorandum to President Peabody" [1920]. Fifteen page typescript.

Untitled. *The Eastern Underwriter*, August 18, 1922 (*Life Insurance Salesmanship Edition*).

"Broadway." Ives & Myrick, Managers The Mutual Life Insurance Co. of New York, 46 Cedar Street, New York. Printed, by request, from Agency Bulletins July-September 1922. Reprinted in Appendix 10 of *Charles E. Ives: Memos*, edited by John Kirkpatrick, pp. 229-235. New York: W. W. Norton, 1972. *See*: **B377**

"Digest of a Selling Presentation" [1923]. Three-page typewritten mimeograph.

"The Program--Its Use and Possibilities." *The Eastern Underwriter*, September 18, 1925 (*Life Insurance Salesmanship Edition*).

"National Bank Officers Should Carry Insurance." *The Eastern Underwriter*, March 5, 1926.

"Agents Training" [1929]. Five-page typewritten memorandum.

"General Suggestions" [n.d.]. Seven-page typewritten mimeograph.

"The Relation Which the Cost of Adequate Life Insurance..." [n.d.]. Two-page brochure.

Correspondence and Diaries
See: **B9**

Ives's personal letters prior to 1924 were typed by John Kirkpatrick and remain in his personal collection. They are arranged in the following packets:

"Ives Family Letters etc. 1880-1897"

"Ives Family Letters etc. 1903-1908"

"Additional Letters, mostly 1907-1908." Compiled July 1964.

"Ives Family Letters etc. 1910-1923."

Microfilm copy. New Haven. Yale University, John Herrick Jackson Music Library, Ives Collection.

Most of the Ives correspondence beginning in 1924 is located in the Yale University Music Library Archival Collection Mss 14. For an itemized and dated list of contents arranged alphabetically by correspondents see Perlis (**B9**), pp. 22-158.

A. General, Personal and Music Series III, Boxes 27-33

B. Business and Institutional Series III, Boxes 34-36

C. Miscellaneous (tax records, documents, incomplete, other)Series III, Boxes 37-39

Additional collections of Ives correspondence:

New York Public Library, John Becker Collection

University of Mississippi Library

Lincoln Center for the Performing Arts Library, Henry Cowell Collection

John Kirkpatrick private collection

Herman Langinger private collection

Ives's Diaries and Notebooks are located in the Yale University Music Library Archival Collection, Mss 14, Series V, Box 45. For a full description of their contents see the "Preface" to the Kirkpatrick *Catalogue* (**B7**).

Appendix 4
Books and Collections
of Essays on Ives

Books

[See the **Bibliography** for a listing of reviews.]

Bernlef, J. and Reinbert de Leeuw. *Charles Ives.* Amsterdam: DeBezige Bij, 1969. *See also*: Collections *(Student Musicologists at Minnesota).* *See*: **B121**

Burkholder, J. Peter. *Charles Ives: The Ideas Behind the Music.* New Haven and London: Yale University Press, 1985. *See*: **B296**

Cowell, Henry, and Sidney Cowell. *Charles Ives and His Music.* New York: Oxford University Press, 1955; 2nd edition enlarged and reprinted 1969; unabridged reprint of the 2nd edition. New York: Da Capo Press, 1983. *See*: **B354**

De Lerma, Dominique-René. *Charles Ives, 1874-1954: A Bibliography of His Music.* Kent, Ohio: Kent State University Press, 1970. *See*: **B5**

Echols, Paul C. [Catalogue of Charles Ives's Music.] Yale Univeristy Press, forthcoming. *See*: **B6**

Elkus, Jonathan. "Charles Ives and the American Band Tradition: A Centennial Tribute." Exeter: American Arts Documentation Centre, University of Exeter, 1974. *See*: **B579**

Hitchcock, H. Wiley, ed. *Charles Ives Centennial Festival-Conference.* Program Booklet. New York: G. Schirmer and Associated Music Publishers, 1974. *See*: **B171**

_____. *Ives.* London: Oxford University Press, 1977. *See*: **B252**

and Vivian Perlis, ed. *An Ives Celebration: Papers and Panels on the Charles Ives Centennial Festival-Conference*, edited by H. Wiley Hitchcock and Vivian Perlis. Urbana: University of Illinois Press, 1977. For an itemized list of contents see Collections *(An Ives Celebration).* *See*: **B253**

Ives, Charles. *Essays Before a Sonata, The Majority, and Other Writings by Charles Ives*, selected and edited by Howard Boatwright. New York: W. W. Norton, 1970. *See*: **B660**.

_____. *Charles E. Ives: Memos* [*See*: Kirkpatrick]

Kirkpatrick, John. *A Temporary Mimeographed Catalogue of the Music Manuscripts and Related Materials of Charles Edward Ives 1874-1954*. New Haven: Library of the Yale School of Music, 1960; reprint, 1973. *See*: **B7**

_____. ed. *Charles E. Ives: Memos*. New York: W. W. Norton, 1972. *See*: **B378**

Maske, Ulrich. *Charles Ives in seiner Kammermusik für drei bis sechs Instrumente*. Ph.D. dissertation, Köln Universität, 1971; published as Volume 64 of the Kölner Beiträge zur Musik Forschung. (Regensburg: Gustav. Bosse, 1971). *See*: **B585**

Perlis, Vivian. *Charles Ives Papers*. New Haven: Yale University Music Library, 1983. *See*: **B9**

_____. *Charles Ives Remembered: An Oral History*. New Haven and London: Yale University Press, 1974. *See*: **B318**

Perry, Rosalie Sandra. *Charles Ives and the American Mind*. Kent, OH: Kent State University Press, 1974; revised version of "Charles Ives and American Culture." Ph.D. dissertation, University of Texas at Austin, 1972. *See*: **B179**

Reed, Joseph W. *Three American Originals: John Ford, William Faulkner, and Charles Ives*. Middletown, CT: Wesleyan University Press, 1984. *See*: **B361**

Riedel, Johannes, ed. *Student Musicologists at Minnesota*. [*See*: Collections (*Student Musicologists at Minnesota*)]

Rossiter, Frank R. *Charles Ives and His America*. New York: Liveright, 1975; revised and expanded version of "Charles Ives and American Culture: The Process of Development, 1874-1921." Ph.D. dissertation, Princeton University (Department of History), 1970. *See*: **B215**

Sive, Helen R. *Music's Connecticut Yankee: An Introduction to the Life and Music of Charles Ives*. New York: Atheneum, 1977. *See*: **B260**

Vinay, Gianfranco. *L'america musicale di Charles Ives.* Torino [Turin]: Giulio Einaudi, 1974. *See:* **B187**

Warren, Richard. *Charles E. Ives: Discography.* New Haven: Historical Sound Recordings. Yale University Library, 1972 [distributed by Greenwood Press, Westport CT]; updated edition in preparation. *See:* **B17**

Wooldridge, David. *From the Steeples and Mountains: A Study of Charles Ives.* New York: Alfred A. Knopf, 1974. *See:* **B192**

Collections of Essays on Charles Ives

Clavier. 13, no. 7 (October 1974). **B639, B695, B720, B731,** and **B734**

Current Musicology, 18 (1974): 41-45, 96-119. **B172, B185, B190,** and **B732**

> Other essays on Ives appeared in the next two issues of *Current Musicology: See:* **B201, B217,** and **B222**

An Ives Celebration: Papers and Panels on the Charles Ives Centennial Festival-Conference, edited by H. Wiley Hitchcock and Vivian Perlis. **B245-247, B249, B251, B254-257, B577,** and **B627**

Neuland 1 (1980): 3-58. **B11, B276-277, B545, B703, B713,** and **B809**

> Other essays on Ives appeared in the next two issues of *Neuland: See:* **B657** and **B722**

Parnassus: Poetry in Review 3, no. 2 (Spring-Summer 1975): 295-396. **B197, B221, B223, B225, B343, B367,** and **B370**

Soundings: Ives, Ruggles, Varèse. Soundings: Spring, 1974. **B108, B147, B160,** and **B364**

South Florida's Historic Ives Festival, 1974-1976, F. Warren O'Reilly, ed. 64 pages. **B224, B240-241, B243, B386, B398, B427,** and **B799**

Student Musicologists at Minnesota. Johannes Riedel, editor. 6 (1975-1976): 1-302. **B12, B121, B235-236, B320, B325, B328, B491, B642, B736, B812**

> A two-part essay on Ives appeared in preceding issues of *Student Musicologists at Minnesota. See:* **B345**

Appendix 5
Dissertations, Theses, and Senior Essays

1939   Bernstein, Leonard. "The Absorption of Race Elements into American Music." Senior thesis, Harvard University, 1939; reprinted in *Findings*, pp. 36-99. New York: Simon and Schuster, 1982. *See*: **B667**

1942   Ruff, Erwin, "A Study of Five Songs of Charles Ives." M.A. thesis, Eastman School of Music, 1942. *See*: **B779**

1943   Logan, Adeline Marie. "American National Music in the Compositions of Charles Ives." M.M. thesis, University of Washington, 1943. *See*: **B40**

1946   Wendt, Rudolph. "A Study of Charles Ives' Second Pianoforte Sonata, 'Concord, Mass., 1840-60.'" M.A. thesis, Eastman School of Music, 1946. *See*: **B676**

1951   Myers, Betty Dustin. "The Orchestral Music of Charles Ives." Ph.D. dissertation, Indiana University, 1951. *See*: **B411**

1952   Rarig, Howard R., Jr. "The Second String Quartet of Charles Ives." M.M. thesis, Ithaca College, 1952. *See*: **B587**

1954   Moore, Ralph Joseph, Jr. "The Background and the Symbol: Charles E. Ives: A Case Study in the History of American Cultural Expression." Senior essay, American Studies Department, Yale College, 1954. *See*: **B65**

1955   Plinkiewisch, Helen E. "A Contribution to the Understanding of the Music of Charles Ives, Roy Harris, and Aaron Copland." Ph.D. dissertation, Columbia University, 1955. *See*: **B77**

1959   Gerschefski, Peter. "A Critical Analytical Study of Two Works of Charles Ives." M.M. thesis, University of Southern California, 1959. *See*: **B412**

1960   Frantz, Donald Howe, Jr. "Search for Significant Form, 1905-1915: An Evaluation of the Symbols of Tradition and Revolt in

American Literature, Painting, and Music." Ph.D. dissertation, Religion, University of Southern California, 1960. *See:* **B319**

1961 Buhrman, Laurel Chenault. "An Analysis of the Music of Charles Ives." M.A. thesis, University of Oklahoma, 1961. *See:* **B87**

Gerald, Patricia E. "An American Meets Europe: Charles Edward Ives." Bachelor thesis, Radcliffe College, 1961.

Mays, Kenneth Robert. "The Use of Hymn Tunes in the Works of Charles Ives." M.M. thesis, Indiana University, 1961. *See:* **B90**

Perkins, Laurence. "The Sonatas for Violin and Piano by Charles Ives." M.A. thesis, Eastman School of Music, University of Rochester, 1961. *See:* **B617**

1963 Gooding, David. "A Study of the Quotation Process in the Songs for Voice and Piano of Charles Edward Ives." M.A. thesis, Western Reserve University, 1963. *See:* **B788**

Hanks, Sarah Elizabeth. "Charles Ives: The Creative Process of the Composer Especially in the Second Pianoforte Sonata, Concord, Mass., 1840-1860." M.A. thesis, Smith College, 1963.

Layton, Bentley. "An Introduction to the 114 Songs." B.A. thesis, Harvard University, 1963. *See:* **B789**

1964 Carlson, Paul B. "An Historical Background and Stylistic Analysis of Three Twentieth Century Compositions for Violin and Piano." D.M.A. dissertation, University of Missouri at Kansas City, 1964. *See:* **B618**

1965 Rosen, Lee Cyril. "The Violin Sonatas of Charles Ives." B.M. paper, University of Illinois, 1965. *See:* **B619**

Vinquist, Mary Ann. "The Psalm Settings of Charles Ives." M.A. thesis, Indiana University, 1965. *See:* **B759**

Wilson, Donald Malcolm. "Metric Modulation in the Music of Charles Ives," pp. 86-133. Part two of a B.A. thesis, Cornell University, 1965. *See:* **B105**

1966 Bryant, Sister Emily Marie. "Avant-Garde Character of Charles Ives' Music Exemplified in Various Works." M.A. thesis, Mount St. Mary's College, Los Angeles, 1966. *See:* **B107**

Clark, Sondra Rae. "The Transcendental Philosophy of Charles E. Ives as Expressed in *The Second Sonata for Pianoforte*, 'Concord,

Mass., 1840-1860.'" M.A. thesis, San Jose State College, 1966. *See:* **B685**

Magee, Noel. "The Short Piano Works of Charles Ives." M.M. thesis, Indiana University, 1966. *See:* **B711**

Sullivan, Timothy. "An Approach to Analysis of the Second Movement of Symphony No. 4 by Charles E. Ives and An Essay on Compositions Based on Observations on the Same Work." Senior thesis, Yale School of Music, 1966. *See:* **B522**

1967   Montague, Stephen R. "The Simple and Complex in Selected Works by Charles Ives." M.M. thesis, Florida State University, 1967.

Newman, Philip Edward. "The Songs of Charles Ives." Ph.D. dissertation, University of Iowa, 1967. *See:* **B790**

1968   Bruderer, Conrad. "The Studies of Charles Ives." D.M.A. dissertation, Indiana University, 1968. *See:* **B719**

Gratovich, Eugene. "The Sonatas for Violin and Piano by Charles Ives: A Critical Commentary and Concordance of the Printed Editions and the Autographs and Manuscripts of the Yale Ives Collection." D.M.A. dissertation, Boston University School of Fine and Applied Arts, 1968. *See:* **B621**

Frank, Alan Robert. "The Music of Charles Ives: For Presentation in the Listening Program of the Secondary School." Ed.D., Teacher's College, Columbia University, 1969. *See:* **B123**

Henderson, Clayton Wilson. "Quotation as a Style Element in the Music of Charles Ives." Ph.D. dissertation, Washington University, 1969. *See:* **B125**

Kumlien, Wendell Clarke. "The Sacred Choral Music of Charles Ives: A Study in Style Development." D.M.A. dissertation, University of Illinois, 1969. *See:* **B743**

Sahr, Hadassah Gallup. "Performance and Analytic Study of Selected Piano Music by American Composers." Ed.D. dissertation, Columbia University, 1969. *See:* **B688**

Ward, Charles. "The Use of Hymn Tunes as an Expression of 'Substance' and 'Manner' in the Music of Charles E. Ives, 1874-1954." M.A. thesis, University of Texas at Austin, 1969. *See:* **B131**

1970   Hutchinson, Mary Ann. "Unrelated Simultaneity as an Historical Index to the Music of Charles Ives." M.M. thesis, Florida State University, Tallahassee, 1970. *See*: **B136**

Joyce, Mary Ann. "The *Three-Page Sonata* of Charles Ives: An Analysis and a Corrected Version." Ph.D. dissertation, Washington University, 1970. *See*: **B715**

Rinehart, John McLain. "Ives' Compositional Idioms: An Investigation of Selected Short Compositions as Microcosms of His Musical Language." Ph.D. dissertation, Ohio State University, 1970. *See*: **B140**

Rossiter, Frank R. "Charles Ives and American Culture: The Process of Development, 1874-1921." Ph.D. dissertation, Princeton University (Department of History), 1970; revised and expanded as *Charles Ives and His America*. New York: Liveright, 1975. *See*: **B215**

Sly, Caroline Ware. "The Language of Ives's Solo Songs." M.A. thesis, Smith College, 1970. *See*: **B793**

1971   Call, William Anson. "A Study of the Transcendental Aesthetic Theories of John S. Dwight and Charles E. Ives and the Relationship of These Theories to Their Respective Work as Music Critic and Composer." D.M.A. dissertation, University of Illinois, 1971. *See*: **B524**

Hurst, Rolland Wood. "A Study, Analysis, and Performance of Selected Songs by Charles Ives." Ed.D. dissertation, Columbia University, 1971. *See*: **B794**

Maske, Ulrich. "Charles Ives in seiner Kammermusik für drei bis sechs Instrumente." Ph.D., dissertation, Köln Universität, 1971; published as Volume 64 of the *Kölner Beiträge zur Musikforschung* (Regensburg: Gustav Bosse Verlag, 1971). *See*: **B585**

Mumper, Robert. "The First Piano Sonata of Charles Ives." Ph.D. dissertation, Indiana University, 1971. *See*: **B653**

1972   Clark, Sondra Rae. "The Evolving *Concord Sonata*: A Study of Choices and Variants in the Music of Charles Ives." Ph.D. dissertation, Stanford University, 1972. *See*: **B690**

Eiseman, David. "Charles Ives and the European Symphonic Tradition: A Historical Reappraisal." Ph.D. dissertation, University of Illinois, 1972. *See*: **B420**

Harvin, Laurence E. "The Piano Trio from the Performer's Viewpoint with Particular Attention Given to the Ives Trio." D.M.A. dissertation, Florida State University, 1972. *See:* **B600**

Perry, Rosalie Sandra. "Charles Ives and American Culture." Ph.D. dissertation, University of Texas at Austin, 1972; reprinted as *Charles Ives and the American Mind.* Kent, OH: Kent State University Press, 1974. *See:* **B179**

1973   Wallach, Laurence, "The New England Education of Charles Ives." Ph.D. dissertation, Columbia University, 1973. *See:* **B156**

1974   Albert, Thomas Russel. "The Harmonic Language of Charles Ives' *Concord Sonata.*" D.M.A. dissertation, University of Illinois, 1974. *See:* **B693**

Booth, Earl Walter. "New England Quartet: E. A. Robinson, Robert Frost, Charles Ives and Carl Ruggles." Ph.D. dissertation, University of Utah, 1974. *See:* **B362**

McCandless, William Edgar. "Cantus Firmus Techniques in Selected Instrumental Compositions, 1910-1960." Ph.D. dissertation, Indiana University, 1974. *See:* **B625**

Ward, Charles. "Charles Ives: The Relationship Between Aesthetic Theories and Compositional Processes." Ph.D. dissertation, University of Texas at Austin, 1974. *See:* **B189**

1975   Magers, Roy Vernon. "Aspects of Form in the Symphonies of Charles E. Ives." Ph.D. dissertation, Indiana University, 1975. *See:* **B425**

Schoffman, Nachum. "The Songs of Charles Ives." Ph.D. dissertation, Hebrew University, 1975. *See:* **B797**

Stein, Alan. "The Musical Language of Charles Ives' Three Places in New England." D.M.A. dissertation, University of Illinois, 1975. *See:* **B490**

1976   Brooks, William Fordyce. "Sources and Errata List for Charles Ives' Symphony No. 4, Movement II." D.M.A. dissertation, University of Illinois, 1976. *See:* **B531**

Cordes, Joan Kunselman. "A New American Development in Music: Some Characteristic Features Extending from the Legacy of Charles Ives." Ph.D. dissertation, Louisiana State University, 1976. *See:* **B232**

Greenfield, Ruth Wolkowsky. "Charles Edward Ives and the Stylistic Aspects of His First Piano Sonata." D.M.A. dissertation, University of Miami, 1976. *See*: **B654**

Quackenbush, Margret Diane. "Form and Texture in the Works for Mixed Chamber Ensemble by Charles Ives." M.A. thesis, University of Oregon, 1976. *See*: **B239**

Rangell, Andrew Reed. "The Violin-Piano Sonatas of Charles Ives." Ph.D. dissertation, The Juilliard School, 1976. *See*: **B626**

Sole, Kenneth Gale. "A Study and Performance of Five *Psalm* Settings and *The Celestial Country* by Charles Edward Ives." D.M.A. dissertation, University of Southern California, 1976. *See*: **B750**

Walker, Gwyneth. "Tradition and the Breaking of Tradition in the String Quartets of Ives and Schoenberg." D.M.A. dissertation, University of Hartford, 1976.

1978 Badolato, James Vincent. "The Four Symphonies of Charles Ives; A Critical, Analytical Study of the Musical Style of Charles Ives." Ph.D. dissertation, Catholic Univeristy of America, 1978. *See*: **B430**

Gabbi, Marianna Paone. "Charles Ives: The Violin Sonatas, A Lecture Recital." D.M.A. dissertation, North Texas State University, 1978. *See*: **B628**

Groh, Jack Curran. "A Conductor's Analysis of and Preparation and Approach to Polyrhythms: With Particular Attention to Polyrhythms in Certain of the Choral Works of Charles E. Ives." D.M.A. dissertation, University of Missouri, Kansas City, 1978. *See*: **B753**

Kavanaugh, James Vincent. "Music and American Transcendentalism: A Study of Transcendental Pythagoreanism in the Works of Henry David Thoreau, Nathaniel Hawthorne, and Charles Ives." Ph.D. dissertation, Yale University, 1978. *See*: **B431**

Lorenz, Christof. "Das Liedschaffen Charles Ives." Dissertation, Cologne, 1978.

Milligan, Terry Gilbert. "Charles Ives: A Study of the Works for Chamber Ensemble Written Between 1898 and 1908 Which Utilize Wind Instruments." D.M.A. dissertation, University of Texas at Austin, 1978. *See*: **B555**

1979   Cameron, Janet. "Analysis of the First Movement of the First Piano Sonata by Charles Ives. Seminar paper, University of Illinois, 1979. *See*: **B655**

Ward, Keith C. "Charles Edward Ives: An Autobiography in Sound." M.A. thesis, Northwestern University, 1979.

1980   Schermer, Richard. "The Aesthetics of Charles Ives in Relations to His 'String Quartet No. 2.'" M.A. thesis, California State University, Fullerton, 1980. *See*: **B595**

Wiley, Joan Marie. "A Comparative Anaylsis of Charles E. Ives' 'First Sonata' and 'Sonata No. 2.'" M.A. thesis, California State University, Fullerton, 1980. *See*: **B644**

1981   Bonham, Robert John. "Some Common Aesthetic Tendencies Manifested in Examples of Pioneer American Cabins and Old Harp Music and in Selected Works of H. H. Richardson and Charles E. Ives." Ph.D. dissertation, Ohio University, 1981. *See*: **B630**

Kolosick, J. Timothy. "A Computer-Assisted, Set-Theoretic Investigation of Vertical Simultaneities in Selected Piano Compositions by Charles E. Ives." Ph.D. dissertation, University of Wisconsin, Madison, 1981. *See*: **B645**

1982   Coakley, John Pius. "The Artistic Process as Religious Enterprise: The Vocal Texts of Charles Ives and the Poetry of E. E. Cummings." Ph.D., dissertation, American Civilization, Brown University, 1982. *See*: **B359**

Daugherty, Michael Kevin. "Goethe and Emerson, the Link between Aesthetic Theories and Compositional Process of Gustav Mahler and Charles Ives." M.A. thesis, Yale University, 1982. *See*: **B385**

1983   Burkholder, J. Peter. "The Evolution of Charles Ives's Music: Aesthetics, Quotation, Technique." Ph.D. dissertation, Universtiy of Chicago, 1983: Chapters 1-4 reprinted as *Charles Ives: The Ideas Behind the Music*. New Haven and London: Yale University Press, 1985; Chapter 5 reprinted as "Quotation and Emulation: Charles Ives's Uses of His Models." *The Musical Quarterly* 71, no. 1 (1985): 1-26. A revised version of Chapters 6-9 will appear in a forthcoming volume, *The Evolution of Charles Ives's Music*, by Yale University Press. *See*: **B284**

Cantrick, Susan Birdsall. "Charles Ives's 'String Quartet No. 2':
An Analysis and Evaluation." M.M. thesis, Peabody Institute of
the Johns Hopkins University, Peabody Conservatory of Music,
1983. *See*: **B596**

Gingerich, Lora Louise. "Processes of Motivic Transformation in
the Keyboard and Chamber Music of Charles E. Ives." Ph.D.
dissertation, Yale University, 1983. *See*: **B286**

Harvey, Mark Sumner. "Charles Ives: Prophet of American Civil
Religion." Ph.D. dissertation, Boston University Graduate School
of the History of Religion, 1983. *See*: **B288**

Hilliard, John Stanley. "Part II: Charles Ives' Robert Browning
Overture: Style and Structure." D.M.A. dissertation, Cornell
University, 1983. *See*: **B546**

1984　Lipkis, Laurence Alan. "Aspects of Temporality in Debussy's
'Jeux' and Ives' 'Symphony No. 4' Fourth Movement." Ph.D.
dissertation, University of California at Santa Barbara, 1984.
See: **B536**

1985　Fruehwald, Robert Douglas. "II. Motivic Transformation in the
'Thoreau' Movement of Charles Ives' Concord Sonata." Ph.D.,
dissertation, Washington University, 1985. *See*: **B709**

Gibbens, John Jeffrey. "Debussy's Impact on Ives: An
Assessment." D.M.A. dissertation, University of Illinois, 1985.
See: **B360**

Shelton, Gregory Allard. "An Analysis of Charles Ives's 'Three-
Page Sonata for Piano.'" M.A. thesis, The American University,
1985. *See*: **B717**

Ward, Keith Charles. "Musical Idealism: A Study of the
Aesthetics of Arnold Schoenberg and Charles Ives." D.M.A.
dissertation, Northwestern University, 1985. *See*: **B723**

1986　Taylor, Paul Franklin. "Stylistic Heterogeneity: The Analytical Key
to Movements IIa and IIb from the First Piano Sonata by Charles
Ives." D.M.A. dissertation, University of Wisconsin-Madison,
1986. *See*: **B659**

Winters, Thomas Dyer. "Additive and Repetitive Techniques in
the Experimental Works of Charles Ives." Ph.D. dissertation,
University of Pennsylvania, 1986. *See*: **B307**

Appendix 6
Documentary Broadcasts, Films, and Videocassettes on Ives

See the Warren discography (**B17**, pp. 111-113) for a more detailed list of contents for Nos. 1-5 and 7.

1. *Charles Ives: American Original*, from "The World of Music Program No. 17; National Educational Television; 1/2 hour; original broadcast taped by WNDT, Newark, New Jersey, 1965 (film).

2. *In Search of Charles Ives;* Canadian Broadcasting Corporation; 2 hours; Toronto, Canada; original broadcast ca. April 26, 1965.

3. *Musical Experimenters*, from "Music in the Twenties"; National Educational Television; 1/2 hour; original broadcast taped in or near Boston, Massachusetts; first broadcast June 6, 1965.

4. *Charles Ives: The Fourth Symphony*; National Educational Television; 1 hour; original broadcast taped in New York City; first broadcast December 17, 1965 (film)

5. *Signalement van Charles Ives*; Vara-Televisiedienst, Hilversum, the Netherlands; 3/4 hour; broadcast February 6, 1969.

6. *Charles E. Ives--Versicherungsagent und Komponist"* and *Charles E. Ives--Werk, Interpretation, Rezeption."* Köln, Baden-Baden, WDR/SWF, 1970-71. See also the television documentary, *Ives at Minnesota, April 7-May 17, 1970*," a report on the Charles Ives Festival at the University of Minnesota in Minneapolis. Köln, WDR, 1970-71. All three related films are produced by Hans G. Helms. *See*: **B235**, note 18

7. *Modern Music and the Debt to Charles Ives*, from "Yale Reports"; 2 parts, each 1/2 hour; originally broadcast by WTIC, Hartford, Connecticut: Part 1 on December 27, 1970; Part 2 on January 3, 1971.

8. *Charles Ives: Holidays--Washington's Birthday and The Fourth of July.* Filmstrip. 1972. 100 frames color. 35 mm. LC 72-736382

9. *Three Places in New England--Ives.* Filmstrip. 1973. 160 frames color. 35 mm. LC 73-734911

10. *A Good Dissonance Like a Man;* 59 minutes; film biography of Charles Ives produced by Theodor Timreck; originally broadcast on television over the Public Broadcast Service on October 11, 1976. Motion picture. 1977. 2 reels, color. 16 mm. LC 77-700367. Available on videocassette from Films Inc., Home Vision, 5547 N. Ravenswood, Chicago, IL 60640. [For additional information, including lists of awards, see "Charles Ives Film Biography," *National Association of Teachers of Singing Bulletin* 34, no. 3 (1978): 54.]

11. "Are My Ears On Wrong?--A Profile of Charles Ives." Open University Educational Enterprises Ltd. color. 25 min. (1980). Videorecording. 1982. 1 videocassette. LC 82-706856. Contents: Interviews with Aaron Copland and Elliott Carter; performances by the Chilingirian String Quartet and the BBC Symphony Orchestra; "dramatized sequences of Ives's childhood"; excerpts from *Concord Sonata* performed by John Kirkpatrick. According to the Open University Catalogue, the profile was "filmed in Ives' own studio at the piano on whicn it was composed.

    Note: The Open University Catalogue also describes a book by I. Bonighton and R. Middleton, *Ives and Varèse* (1979) [108 pages] that was discovered after it could be incorporated into the numbered bibliographic references. The Catalogue promises that this book "introduces the music of Ives and Varèse and puts it into the context of other American music of the time and of contemporary European music.

12. *Music in Time. Land of Our Fathers.* Videorecording. 1982. 1 videocassette (U-matic) 60 min. LC 85-066558.

Author Index

General Index

Abbott, Jacob, B96
Abide with Me, W247
Adams, Henry, B319-320
Adams, John, B478
Academy of St. Martin-in-the-
    Fields, D23
"Adagio cantabile *The Innate*" *See*:
    A Set of 3 Short Pieces, no.
    3
"Adagio sostenuto *At Sea*" *See*:
    Set No. 3, no. 1
Adam, Claus, D38
*Adeste Fideles See: Prelude on
    Adeste fideles*
Aeolian Hall *See*: New York
Aeschylus and Sophocles, W280,
    B2, B797
Afterglow, W170, D64, D66, B806
Aitken, W., W80a
Alard Quartet, D41
Albert, Thomas Russel, B693
Albright, William H., B232
Album for the Young See:
    Schumann, Robert
Alcott, Bronson, B96, B660
Alcotts (family), B96, B219, B660
"Alcotts, The" *See*: Piano Sonatas,
    (Second); [no. 3]
Aldrich, Thomas Bailey, W154,
    B806
Alexander, Michael J., B302
Alexander, Roberta, D62
Alford, Henry, W89, W90:3, W229-
    230, B752
Allegro, W226:3,
All-Enduring, W259
All-forgiving, Look on Me, W118,
    B3, B743
All Love, B156
Allmers, Hermann, W213
All the Way Around and Back,
    W54, B2-3, B239, B307,
    B549-550, B585

"Allegretto sombreoso (From
    Incantation)" *See: Set No.
    1*, no. 6
Alwes, Chester L., B764
American Brass Quintet, D31
American Music Festival, W1a,
    B435
American Recording Society
    Orchestra, B486
American Scholar See: Emerson,
    Ralph Waldo
American Symphony Orchestra, p.
    10, W7d, W12a, W13a,
    W15b, D7, D13, D17,
    B507, B512-513, B516
American Woods Overture, B314
America Variations See:
    Variations on America
Amphion See: From "Amphion"
"Andante *The Last Reader*" *See*:
    Set No. 2, no. 3
Ann Street, W156, D11, D45, D63,
    D66, B550, B553
Anderson, William, B195
Andriessen, Louis, B246
Anti-Abolitionist Riots, The See:
    Study no. 9
Appalachian Spring See: Copland,
    Aaron
Argento, Domenick, B812
"Arguments" *See*: String Quartets,
    Second [no. 2]
Ariosto, Ludovico, W165
Arnold, Matthew, W236, B139
Arrow Music Press, W3, W63,
    B466, B677
Art of Fugue See: Bach, Johann
    Sebastian
Arts and Industries Building *See*:
    Washington, DC
Associated Music Publishers, Inc.
    (AMP), W3, W4:1 & 3, W7,
    W10, W12-13, W30, W32,
    W36, W39, W58, W63,
    W65, W67, W79-80, W82-

About the Author

GEOFFREY BLOCK is an Associate Professor of Music History at the University of Puget Sound. He has published articles and reviews on Mozart, Beethoven, and jazz, and is currently writing a book on American musical theater.